OXFORD READINGS IN PHILOSOPHY

THE PHILOSOPHY OF ACTION

Published in this series

The Problem of Evil, edited by Marilyn McCord Adams and
Robert Merrihew Adams
The Philosophy of Artificial Intelligence, edited by Margaret A. Boden
The Philosophy of Artificial Life, edited by Margaret A. Boden
Self-Knowledge, edited by Quassim Cassam
The Philosophy of Law, edited by R. M. Dworkin
Environmental Ethics, edited by Robert Elliot
Theories of Ethics, edited by Philippa Foot
The Philosophy of Mind, edited by Jonathan Glover
Scientific Revolutions, edited by Ian Hacking
The Philosophy of Mathematics, edited by W. D. Hart
Conditionals, edited by Frank Jackson
The Philosophy of Time, edited by Robin Le Poidevin and
Murray MacBeath
The Philosophy of Action, edited by Alfred R. Mele
The Philosophy of Religion, edited by Basil Mitchell
Meaning and Reference, edited by A. W. Moore
A Priori Knowledge, edited by Paul K. Moser
The Philosophy of Science, edited by David Papineau
Political Philosophy, edited by Anthony Quinton
Explanation, edited by David-Hillel Ruben
The Philosophy of Social Explanation, edited by Alan Ryan
Propositions and Attitudes, edited by Nathan Salmon and Scott Soames
Consequentialism and its Critics, edited by Samuel Scheffler
Applied Ethics, edited by Peter Singer
Causation, edited by Ernest Sosa and Michael Tooley
Theories of Rights, edited by Jeremy Waldron
Free Will, edited by Gary Watson
Demonstratives, edited by Palle Yourgrau

Other volumes are in preparation

THE PHILOSOPHY
OF ACTION

edited by

ALFRED R. MELE

OXFORD UNIVERSITY PRESS
1997

Oxford University Press, Great Clarendon Street, Oxford OX2 6DP

Oxford New York
Athens Auckland Bangkok Bogota Bombay
Buenos Aires Calcutta Cape Town Dar es Salaam
Delhi Florence Hong Kong Istanbul Karachi
Kuala Lumpur Madras Madrid Melbourne
Mexico City Nairobi Paris Singapore
Taipei Tokyo Toronto
and associated companies in
Berlin Ibadan

Oxford is a trade mark of Oxford University Press

Published in the United States by
Oxford University Press Inc., New York

British Library Cataloguing in Publication Data
Data available

Library of Congress Cataloging in Publication Data
The philosophy of action / edited by Alfred R. Mele.
—(Oxford readings in philosophy)
Includes bibliographical references and index.
Contents: Actions, reasons, and causes / Donald Davidson—The problem of action / Harry G.
Frankfurt—Trying (as the mental 'pineal gland') / Brian O'Shaughnessy—Acting for reasons / Robert
Audi—Reasons explanation of action / Carl Ginet—A causal theory of intending / Wayne A. Davis—
Practical reasoning / Gilbert Harman—Two faces of intention / Michael Bratman—Settled objectives
and rational constraints / Hugh J. McCann—Intentional action / Alfred R. Mele and Paul K. Moser—
Mechanism, purpose, and explanatory exclusion / Jaegwon Kim—Agency and causal explanation /
Jennifer Hornsby.
1. Act (Philosophy) I. Mele, Alfred R., 1951– . II. Series.
B105.A35P49 1997 128'.4–dc20 96–8682
ISBN 0–19–875174–5.—ISBN 0–19–875175–3 (pbk.)

ISBN 0–19–875174–5
ISBN 0–19–875175–3(Pbk)

1 3 5 7 9 10 8 6 4 2

Typeset by Best-set Typesetter Ltd., Hong Kong
Printed in Great Britain by
Biddles Ltd, Guildford and King's Lynn

CONTENTS

INTRODUCTION

ALFRED R. MELE

A pair of questions are central to the philosophy of action. (1) What are actions? (2) How are actions to be explained? The questions call, respectively, for a theory of the nature of action and a theory of the explanation of actions. In short, philosophers of action want to know both what it is that explanations of actions explain and how actions are properly explained. One hopes that a full-blown philosophy of action will solve part of the mind–body problem and illuminate the issues of free will, moral responsibility, and practical rationality. But action is well worth understanding in its own right, as well.

Ordinary explanations of human actions draw upon a rich psychological vocabulary. In attempting to explain such actions, we appeal to agents' beliefs, desires, reasons (construed as psychological states by some), intentions, decisions, plans, and the like, and sometimes to deliberation or more modest forms of practical reasoning. Occasionally, we advert as well to finely distinguished traits of character and emotions. Traditionally, philosophers have refined and exploited this vocabulary in an effort to produce theories of the explanation of intentional human behaviour. An underlying presupposition is that common-sense explanations framed in these terms have enjoyed a considerable measure of success. We understand the behaviour of others and ourselves well enough to co-ordinate and sustain the wealth of complicated, co-operative activities integral to normal human life; and the understanding we have achieved is expressed largely in our common-sense psychological vocabulary. Even if the acceptability of this general approach to the explanation of action were taken for granted, however, we would face a variety of important questions about action and action-explanation. For example, inquiring minds still would want to know what actions are, what it is to act intentionally, what constitutes acting for a reason, whether proper explanations of actions are causal explanations or explanations of some other kind, and how the psychological or mental items (states, events, and processes) that are supposed to be explanatory of action are to be understood. These issues and the viability of the general approach just described constitute the primary focus of the essays reprinted here and of this introduction.

1. INDIVIDUATING ACTIONS

Question (1) 'What are actions?' suggests two others. How are actions different from non-actions? How are actions different from one another? I start with the latter, the question of *action-individuation*.

By the end of the 1970s, a lively debate over action-individuation had produced a collection of relatively precise alternatives: a fine-grained view, a coarse-grained view, and componential views. The first treats *A* and *B* as different actions if, in performing them, the agent exemplifies different act-properties. Thus, if I start my car by turning a key, my starting the car and my turning the key are two different actions, since the act-properties at issue are distinct. The second counts my turning the key and my starting the car as the same action under two different descriptions. Views of the third sort regard my starting the car as an action having various components, including my moving my hand, my turning the key, and the car's starting. Where proponents of the other two theories find, alternatively, a single action under different descriptions or a collection of related actions, advocates of the various componential views locate a 'larger' action having 'smaller' actions among its parts.

Interest in action-individuation has waned, owing partly to the development of a precise, detailed map of the conceptual terrain. Toward the end of an excellent chapter on the topic Carl Ginet remarks, 'the issue over the individuation of action, though sufficiently interesting in its own right, is not one on which much else depends'.[1] I am inclined to agree, and in this essay I proceed in a way that is neutral regarding the leading contending theories of individuation.

2. A CAUSAL APPROACH: OBJECTIONS, REPLIES, AND ALTERNATIVES

A popular approach to understanding both the nature of action and the explanation of actions emphasizes causation. Causal theories of action hold that an event's being an action depends upon how it was caused.

---

[1] Carl Ginet (1990), *On Action* (Cambridge: Cambridge University Press), 97.

These theories feature as causes such psychological or mental items as beliefs, desires, intentions, and related events (e.g. acquiring an intention to *A now*). If causal theories of action are on the right track, they provide a metaphysical underpinning for a popular causal view of the explanation of actions—the view that actions are to be explained, causally, partly in terms of items of the kind just mentioned. The conjunction of these two ideas—one about what actions are and the other about how actions are to be explained—may be termed *causalism*.[2]

Causalism typically is embraced as part of a naturalistic stand on agency according to which mental items that play causal/explanatory roles in action are in some way dependent upon or realized in physical states and events. A range of options are open in this connection: indeed, any viable solution to the mind–body problem that supports the idea that 'the mental' has a significant causal/explanatory role in action would, in principle, be welcomed by causalists. Causalism also is non-restrictive on the free-will issue. Although some causalists have endorsed compatibilism (i.e. the thesis that free will is compatible with determinism), compatibilism certainly is not entailed by causalism.[3] Provided that causation is not essentially deterministic, causalists can embrace libertarianism, the conjunction of incompatibilism, and the thesis that free will exists.[4] Some non-causalists are incompatibilists, but there is no entailment here either. Harry Frankfurt, a compatibilist,[5] rejects causalism in Chapter 2.

On an attractive causal theory of action, actions are like money in a noteworthy respect. The piece of paper with which I just purchased a Coke is a genuine US dollar bill partly in virtue of its having been produced (in the right way) by the US Treasury Department. A duplicate bill produced with plates and paper stolen from the Treasury Department is a counterfeit dollar bill, not a genuine one. Similarly, in typical causal theories, a certain event occurring at *t* is my raising my right hand at *t*—an action—partly in virtue of its having been produced 'in the right way' by certain mental items. An event someone else secretly produces by remote control—one including a visually indistinguishable rising of my right hand—is

---

[2] I borrow the term 'causalism' from G. Wilson (1989), *The Intentionality of Human Action* (Stanford, Calif.: Stanford University Press). (Wilson is a non-causalist.)

[3] Determinism may be succinctly defined as 'the thesis that there is at any instant exactly one physically possible future' (P. van Inwagen (1983), *An Essay on Free Will* (Oxford: Clarendon Press), 3). Some readers will wish to insert 'after the Big Bang' between 'instant' and 'exactly'.

[4] In A. Mele (1995), *Autonomous Agents* (New York: Oxford University Press) I develop three positions on free will, each of which relies on causalism: a libertarian position, a compatibilist position, and a position that is agnostic about compatibilism while advocating the existence of free will.

[5] Harry Frankfurt (1988), *The Importance of What We Care About* (Cambridge: Cambridge University Press), chs. 1–2.

not a raising of my right hand by me, even if it feels to me as though I am raising my hand. Notice that the view under consideration does not identify actions with *non-actional* events caused in the right way.[6] That would be analogous to identifying genuine US dollar bills with pieces of printed paper that (1) are not genuine US dollar bills, and (2) are produced in the right way by the US Treasury Department. And, of course, so identifying genuine US dollar bills would be absurd.

The idea that actions are to be explained, causally, in terms of mental states or events is at least as old as Aristotle: 'the origin of action—its efficient, not its final cause—is choice, and that of choice is desire and reasoning with a view to an end' (*Nicomachean Ethics* 1139ª31–2). And it has enjoyed a considerable following. Owing partly to the influence of Wittgenstein and Ryle, this idea fell into philosophical disfavour for a time. The first major source of its revival was Donald Davidson's 'Actions, Reasons, and Causes' (Ch. 1 this volume).

There Davidson rebuts a collection of arguments against the causal approach. Some are still being advanced in various forms. I will take up two of these arguments and then turn to some further alleged problems for causalism.

(A) *The logical connection argument*

The most celebrated argument at the time hinged on the premiss that cause and effect must be 'logically distinct'. Because there is a logical or conceptual connection between an agent's wanting (intending, having a reason) to *A* and her *A*-ing, the latter cannot be an effect of the former; or so it was claimed.

Davidson's reply is incisive: causation is a relation between events, no matter how we describe them; the logical connections at issue are connections between event-*descriptions*. If *x*, the striking of the bell, caused *y*, the bell's tolling, our describing *x* as 'the cause of the bell's tolling' (as in, 'the cause of the bell's tolling caused the bell's tolling') plainly cannot change the fact that *x* caused *y*—the 'logical' connection between subject and predicate notwithstanding.

(B) *An argument from reasons-explanations*

The argument is straightforward. Causal explanations are lawlike; reasons-explanations are not; so reasons-explanations are not causal explanations,

<hr>

[6] Cf. M. Brand (1984), *Intending and Acting* (Cambridge, Mass.: MIT Press), ch. 1.

and when we explain actions in terms of reasons, we are not explaining them in terms of causes.

Davidson agrees that A causes B only if 'some law covering the events at hand exists' (Ch. 1: 41). But he argues that the law need not be framed in terms of A-s and B-s; and he suggests that the causal transactions required for the production of action are lawlike, even though there are no (strict or suitably rigorous) psychophysical or psychological laws.[7] The idea evolves into 'anomalous monism' in later papers of his (1980, chs. 11–14; 1993[8]), a view characterized by the following three theses: (1) 'at least some mental events interact causally with physical events' (*Principle of Causal Interaction*); (2) 'when events are related as cause and effect, then there exists a closed and deterministic system of laws into which these events, when appropriately described, fit' (*Principle of the Nomological Character of Causality*); (3) 'there are no precise psychophysical laws' (*Anomalism of the Mental*).[9] The three principles jointly imply 'monism', Davidson argues: 'If psychological events are causally related to physical events, there must, by [2], be laws that cover them. By [3], the laws are not psychophysical, so they must be purely physical laws. This means that psychological events are describable, taken one by one, in physical terms, that is, they are physical events'.[10]

This raises some interesting and important questions. If as Davidson claims, the only (strict) laws are physical laws, why should we think that the *mental* features of physical events and states are causally relevant to the production of action? Are psychological or psychophysical laws required, after all, by typical causal theories of action or action-explanation? If there are no such laws, are we saddled with epiphenomenalism (the thesis that mental events and states are caused by, but do not cause, physical events and states) or worse?

Jaegwon Kim (Ch. 11) defends a principle—'the explanatory exclusion principle'—that, he contends, explains why neuroscience and 'vernacular psychology', including causal explanations of actions in terms of reasons, cannot peacefully coexist. The principle, in its metaphysical form, asserts that two distinct explanations of the same event 'can both be correct

---

[7] A psychophysical law links mental events or states (e.g. intentions) with physical events or states (e.g. bodily motions).

[8] Donald Davidson (1980), *Essays on Actions and Events* (Oxford: Clarendon Press); and id. (1993), 'Thinking Causes', in J. Heil and A. Mele (eds.), *Mental Causation* (Oxford: Clarendon Press).

[9] Principle 1 is quoted from Davidson (1980), *Essays on Actions and Events*, 208, as are the names of the principles. Principles 2 and 3 are quoted from p. 231. Incidentally, the intended root of 'anomalous' and 'anomalism' in the Davidsonian expressions reproduced here is the alpha privative prefixed to *nomos* in classical Greek, 'absence of law'.

[10] Davidson (1980), *Essays on Actions and Events*, 231.

explanations only if either at least one of the two is incomplete or one is dependent on the other' (p. 275). He writes: 'Vernacular psychology and neuroscience each claim to provide explanations for the same domain of phenomena, and because of the failure of reduction in either direction, the purported explanations must be considered independent. Hence, by the exclusion principle, one of them has to go' (p. 281). Kim suggests that it is vernacular psychology that has to go, but only as a theory having the function of generating 'law-based causal explanations and predictions'—it may survive as a normative enterprise (n. 46).

Jennifer Hornsby (Ch. 12) advances a strikingly different view of things. She maintains that actions are events and that the explanation of action is causal explanation, and she argues that actions are not 'accessible' from the 'impersonal' (or neuroscientific) point of view. Actions, owing to their ineliminable connections with belief, desire, intention, and the like, and to the irreducibility that Kim mentions, disappear in a purely impersonal view of things. If there are actions, there are beliefs, desires, and intentions; and, Hornsby argues, the point of view from which actions are present is the only point of view from which they can be explained.

(C) *Arguments from causal deviance*

Instances of deviant causal chains raise difficulties for causal analyses of action, as Harry Frankfurt observes in Ch. 2. (This issue is not addressed in Chapter 1.) The alleged problem about *intentional* action in particular, as Paul Moser and I put it in Chapter 10, is that 'whatever psychological causes are deemed both necessary and sufficient for a resultant action's being intentional, cases can be described where, owing to a deviant causal connection between the favoured psychological antecedents and a pertinent resultant action, that action is not intentional' (cf. Frankfurt, Ch. 2).

The most common examples of deviance divide into two types. Cases of *primary deviance* raise a problem about a relatively direct connection between mental antecedents and resultant bodily motion. Cases of *secondary deviance* focus on behavioural consequences of intentional actions and on the connection between these actions and their consequences. The following are, respectively, representative instances of the two types of case:

A climber might want to rid himself of the weight and danger of holding another man on a rope, and he might know that by loosening his hold on the rope he could rid himself of the weight and danger. This belief and want might so unnerve him as to cause him to loosen his hold [unintentionally].[11]

A man may try to kill someone by shooting at him. Suppose the killer misses his victim by a mile, but the shot stampedes a herd of wild pigs that trample the intended victim to death.[12]

Instructive attempts to resolve the problems such cases pose highlight four points (see Audi, Ch. 4; Brand 1984[13]; Harman, Ch. 7; Mele and Moser, Ch. 10; Searle 1983[14]; Thalberg 1984[15]). (1) A necessary condition of an A-ing's being an intentional action is that it be an action, and in many cases of deviance the pertinent event seems not to be an action. For example, the climber's 'loosening his hold' is more aptly described as the rope's slipping from his trembling fingers. (2) An analysis of action may preclude there being a gap between the agent's action and its pertinent psychological causes, thus eliminating the possibility of primary deviance. If, for example, every intentional action has the acquisition of a 'proximal' intention (an intention to do something *straightaway*) as a *proximate* cause, there is no room between cause and action for primary deviance.[16] (3) Intention (or one's preferred psychological item) should be given a *guiding* function in the development of intentional action. (4) An action's being intentional depends upon its fitting the agent's conception or representation of the manner in which it will be performed—a condition violated in the shooting case, standardly interpreted. For development of these ideas, see Chapters 4, 7, and 10.

Some attempts to come to grips with causal deviance invoke the thesis that all intentions are self-referring. Gilbert Harman puts the view succinctly: 'the intention to do A is the intention that, because of that very intention, one will do A' (Ch. 7). The basic idea is that intentions specify how they will lead to action, and that if they do not lead to action in (roughly) that way—as in many cases of deviance—they have not issued in intentional action. I have argued in response that incorporating non-intention-referring plans into intentions is no less successful in blocking deviance and avoids problematic commitments of the thesis that every intention refers to itself (Mele 1992a[17]). For a critical reply, see Harman 1993.[18]

---

[11] Ibid. 79.   [12] Ibid. 78.

[13] Brand (1984), *Intending and Acting*, ch. 1.

[14] J. Searle (1983), *Intentionality* (Cambridge: Cambridge University Press).

[15] I. Thalberg (1984), 'Do Our Intentions Cause Our Intentional Actions', *American Philosophical Quarterly* 21: 249–60.

[16] '*Proximate* cause' may be defined as follows: x is a proximate cause of y if and only if x is a cause of y and there is nothing z such that x is a cause of z and z is a cause of y.

[17] A. Mele (1992a), *Springs of Action* (New York: Oxford University Press), ch. 11.

[18] G. Harman (1993), 'Desired Desires', in R. Frey and C. Morris (eds.), *Value, Welfare, and Morality* (Cambridge: Cambridge University Press).

A third variety of deviance ('tertiary deviance', Mele 1987b[19]) merits attention. It was originally brought to bear against Myles Brand's claim that 'S's A-ing during t is an intentional action [if] (i) S's A-ing during t is an action; and (ii) ... S has an action plan P to A during t such that his A-ing is included in P and he follows P in A-ing'.[20] Here is an example:

Fred is taking a machine-readable multiple choice test. His strategy is to circle on the question-sheet the identifying letters next to the answers that he feels certain are correct and then, after all such circling is completed, to fill in the corresponding spaces on his answer-sheet. ...

An hour has elapsed, and Fred is reading the forty-fifth question. He is confident that the answer is 'bee', which word appears next to the letter 'a' on his question sheet. However, as a result of an understandable momentary confusion, he circles the letter 'b'. As luck would have it, 'b' is the correct answer. Later, when filling in the answer sheet, Fred looks at the circled 'b' under question 45 and fills in the space under 'b' on his answer-sheet—intending thereby to provide the right answer.[21]

Fred provides the correct answer to question 45 by filling in the space under 'b' on the answer-sheet. But his providing the correct answer, in light of the deviant history of his intention, seems too accidental to be intentional. Still, Fred did what he intended *at the time* to do then— namely, to provide the correct answer by filling in the space under 'b' on the answer-sheet. Further, his so doing was initiated and guided by his intention to do so, an intention incorporating a plan that he followed. (Notice that the causal deviance occurs *prior* to Fred's forming the pertinent intention and therefore is neither primary nor secondary deviance.) In Chapter 10, Paul Moser and I develop a causal analysis of intentional action designed to be immune to all three sorts of deviance.

(D) *Frankfurt's argument*

In Chapter 2, Harry Frankfurt advances an argument against causalism from what might be termed 'passive action'. He writes:

A driver whose automobile is coasting downhill in virtue of gravitational forces alone may be entirely satisfied with its speed and direction, and so he may never intervene to adjust its movement in any way. This would not show that the movement of the automobile did not occur under his guidance. What counts is that he was prepared to intervene if necessary, and that he was in a position to do so more or less effectively. Similarly, the causal mechanisms which stand ready to affect the course of a bodily movement may never have occasion to do so; for no negative feedback

---

[19] A. Mele (1987b), 'Intentional Action and Wayward Causal Chains: The Problem of Tertiary Waywardness', *Philosophical Studies* 51: 55–60.

[20] Brand (1984), *Intending and Acting*, 28.

[21] Mele (1987b), 'Intentional Action and Wayward Causal Chains', 56.

of the sort that would trigger their compensatory activity may occur. The behaviour is purposive not because it results from causes of a certain kind, but because it would be affected by certain causes if the accomplishment of its course were to be jeopardized. (Ch. 2: 48)

In the absence of a desire or intention regarding 'the movement of the automobile', there would be no basis for the driver's being 'satisfied' with the speed and direction of his car. So we may safely attribute a pertinent desire or intention to the driver, whom I shall call Al. What stands in the way of our holding that Al's acquiring a desire or intention to coast down hill is a cause of his action of coasting, and that some such cause is required for the purposiveness of the 'coasting'? Even if Al passed out momentarily at the wheel and then, upon regaining consciousness, noticed that his car was moving smoothly down hill, his allowing this to continue to happen, owing to his *satisfaction* with the car's speed and direction, depends (conceptually) on his having some relevant desire or intention regarding the car's motion; and prior to his allowing the continuation he is not purposively or intentionally coasting down hill—he is merely being carried down hill. We are left with the same question.

Perhaps, unbeknownst to Al, the brakes, accelerator pedal, and steering-wheel are no longer working: his car would continue moving as it is even if he were to lack the desire or intention in question. But then Al is not performing an action of coasting down hill—he is merely being carried along by a vehicle over which he has no control. And if he is performing no such action, he is not purposively or intentionally coasting, even if he thinks he is. (Notice that the claim that Al *is* purposively coasting in this case is at odds with Frankfurt's own position on purposive behaviour; for it is false that Al would have corrected the car's course if he had deemed it unsatisfactory.)

So suppose that the car is in normal working order and that Al knows how to operate it, is not paralysed, and so on. Then it is natural to say that Al is coasting in his car (or allowing the car to continue to coast, in the scenario in which he wakes up in a moving car) *because* he wants to, or intends to, or has decided to—for an identifiable reason (e.g. to conserve petrol). And the 'because' here is naturally given a causal interpretation. In a normal case, if Al had not desired, or intended, or decided to coast, he would not have coasted; and it is no accident that, desiring, or intending, or deciding to coast, he coasts. So, setting aside general worries about mental causation, it looks as though Al's coasting does have a mental cause.[22]

---

[22] Consider a scenario that differs from the preceding one only in the following respect and in ways entailed by the change. If Al had not decided to coast, he would have been utterly indifferent about the motion of his car—in which case he would have done nothing to alter the

Frankfurt might reply that even if Al's coasting has a suitable mental cause, his coasting is purposive 'not because it results from causes of a certain kind, but because it would be affected by certain causes if the accomplishment of its course were to be jeopardized'. The idea is that what accounts for the purposiveness of the coasting is not any feature of how it is caused but rather that Al 'was prepared to intervene if necessary, and that he was in a position to do so more or less effectively'.

This reply is problematic. Imagine that, throughout the episode, Al was satisfied with how things went and did not intervene. He decided to coast and the coasting was purposive. Imagine further that although Al intended to intervene if necessary, an irresistible mind-reading demon would not have allowed him to intervene. If Al had abandoned his intention to coast or had decided to intervene, the demon would have paralysed Al until his car ran its course. The coasting is purposive even though Al was *not* 'in a position to [intervene] more or less effectively'. And this suggests that what accounts for the purposiveness of Al's coasting in the original case does not include his being in a position to intervene effectively. There are, moreover, versions of the case in which Al's coasting is purposive even though he is not prepared to intervene. Suppose Al is a reckless fellow and he decides that, no matter what happens, he will continue coasting. He has no conditional intention to intervene. Even then, other things being equal, his coasting is intentional and purposive.

Regarding causal theories of action, Frankfurt writes: 'it is beyond their scope to stipulate that a person must be in some particular relation to the movements of his body *during* the period of time in which he is presumed to be performing an action. The only conditions they insist upon as distinctively constitutive of action may cease to obtain, for all the causal accounts demand, at precisely the moment when the agent commences to act' (Ch. 2, 43). However, some causalists have argued that the causal role of the mental items on which they focus (intentions, or beliefs and desires) includes a sustaining and guiding function (see, e.g. Audi, Ch. 4; Brand 1984; Mele 1992a; Mele and Moser, Ch. 10). And they may hold that Al performs the action of coasting down hill in his car partly in virtue of his car's motion's being causally sustained by an intention or desire of his to coast.[23]

---

car's course and the car would have continued coasting. In this scenario, it is false that if Al had not decided to coast, the car would not have continued coasting. Even so, Al's deciding to coast is plausibly regarded as a cause of the continued coasting. Compare: X dialled Y's phone number at t, but if X had not done so, Z would have done so (at t). X's dialling is a cause of Y's phone's ringing at $t1$, even though the phone would have rung at $t1$ if X's dialling had not occurred.

[23] Is this suggestion threatened by the scenario that features a non-interfering demon? In that case, Al's car would have continued to coast even if Al had not continued to intend to coast.

(The other sort of behaviour to which Frankfurt alludes in the quoted passage is subject to a similar causalist treatment.)

(E) Ginet's alternative to causalism

Non-causalists tend to agree with causalists that actions are to be explained in terms of reasons, intentions, and the like. But they disagree with causalists about the nature of the explanations offered. For non-causalists, desires and intentions may be loci of agents' purposes in doing what they do intentionally, but they make no causal contribution to intentional action. Obviously, some non-causalists are moved by considerations of the sort discussed in subsections A–D. Some are moved as well, or instead, by considerations of free will and self-knowledge, by the thought that actions should not depend for their status as actions on anything external to them (including their causal history), and by a general scepticism about causation. In the preceding subsection, I commented briefly on Frankfurt's non-causalist position. Here I will consider Carl Ginet's (Ch. 5 and 1990).

In Chapter 1, Davidson issues the following challenge to non-causalists: given that when we act intentionally we act for reasons, provide an account of the reasons *for which* we act that does not treat (our having) those reasons as figuring in the causation of the relevant behaviour! The challenge is particularly acute when an agent has more than one reason for *A*-ing but *A*-s only for some subset of those reasons. For example, Al has a pair of reasons for mowing his lawn this morning. First, he wants to mow it this week and he believes that this morning is the most convenient time. Second, Al has an urge to repay his neighbour for the rude awakening he suffered recently when she turned on her mower at the crack of dawn and he believes that his mowing his lawn this morning would constitute suitable repayment. As it happens, Al mows his lawn this morning only for one of these reasons. In virtue of what is it true that he mowed it for this reason, and not for the other, if not that this reason (or his having it), and not the other, played a suitable causal role in his mowing?

In Chapter 5, Ginet develops an interesting response to the challenge in rebutting a pair of arguments against his position on free action.[24] Consider

---

Even so, his continuing so to intend was a causal sustainer of his actual continued coasting. That continued coasting was a willing coasting and an action. The counterfactual coasting sustained by paralysis is neither a willing coasting nor an action; it is not the same event as the continued coasting at the actual world. The continued coasting at the actual world is *motivated*—a causal notion—by Al's persisting intention to coast. If Al were to abandon the intention, *that* coasting would cease.

[24] For a related answer, see Wilson (1989), *Intentionality of Human Action*.

a 'reasons explanation' of the form 'S V-ed in order (thereby) to U' (p. 118). 'The only thing *required* for the truth of a reasons explanation of this sort', Ginet writes, 'besides the occurrence of the explained action, is that the action have been *accompanied* by an intention with the right sort of content' (p. 119). In particular, it is not required that the intention figure in the causation of V or any part of V. 'Given that S did V', Ginet contends, it is sufficient 'for the truth of "S V-ed in order to U"' that 'concurrently with her action of V-ing, S intended by *that* action to U (S intended *of* that action that by it she would U).' He adds: 'If from its inception S intended of her action of opening the window that by performing it she would let in fresh air . . . , then *ipso facto* it was her purpose in that action to let in fresh air, she did it in order to let in fresh air.' Further, 'The content of the intention is . . . the proposition "By *this* V-ing (of which I am now aware) I shall U". It is owing to this direct reference that the intention is about, and thus explanatory of, *that particular* action' (p. 120).

Ginet's position is problematic.[25] Imagine that S had the following two *de re* intentions while opening the window, and that both were present at the time of the completion of that action: the intention, N, of her opening the window, 'that by it she would' let in some fresh air, and the intention, O, of her opening the window, that by it she would gain a better view of the street. Suppose that a neuroscientist, without altering the neural realization of N itself, renders that realization incapable of having any effect on S's bodily movements (and any effect on what else S intends) while allowing the neural realization of O to figure normally in the production of movements involved in S's opening the window. Here, one might plausibly argue, O helps to explain S's opening the window and N does not. And if that is right, Ginet is wrong. For, on his view, the *mere presence* in the agent of an intention about her V-ing (where V-ing is an action) is sufficient for that intention's being explanatory of her action.

Ginet argues elsewhere that agents sometimes act in the absence of any relevant desire or intention whatever. He claims that some volitions (volitions being actions) are cases in point, as are some 'exertions' of the body. For example, 'a voluntary exertion could occur [owing to an associated volition] quite spontaneously, without being preceded or accompanied by any distinct state of desiring or intending even to try . . . to exert, and it would still be an action, a purely spontaneous one'.[26] In the case of a *voluntary* exertion of the body, Ginet says, 'a causal connection between

---

[25] The following criticism of Ginet's view derives from Mele (1992a), *Springs of Action*, ch. 13.
[26] Ginet (1990), *On Action*, 9.

the willing and the body's exertion is required',[27] but the volition itself, for Ginet, need not be caused (even in part) by, or concurrent with, any desire or intention.

So suppose that in S, standing within arm's reach of a window, a steady stream of volitions spontaneously springs up (volitions being momentary actions[28]), as a result of which S's body moves in such a way as to come into contact with the window and smoothly open it in a conventional way. Suppose further that all this happens in the absence of any relevant intention or desire. Since the volitions produce the bodily movements that in turn cause the window to open, we have the makings of a causal explanation of all but the volitional element in S's opening the window. (The first and spontaneous volition in the stream is the 'initial part or stage' of the voluntary exertion and the action.[29]) And the volitional element, on Ginet's view, needs no explanation at all.

Augment the case with an intention. Imagine that S intends of her opening the window 'that by it she' will let in some fresh air, but that her intention, N, is incapable of playing a causal role in producing the bodily movements or members of the volitional stream, owing again to the machinations of our neuroscientist. I do not see how N can have any more explanatory significance in the present case than it apparently had in the earlier *two*-intention case—that is, none at all. One might be tempted to think that the intention is explanatory of the action, on the grounds that, in the absence of *any* relevant intention or desire, S's opening the window— that action—would be incomprehensible. But if Ginet is right, such an action requires no intention or desire at all for its occurrence: a spontaneous stream of volitions can do the work. Moreover, for readers who think it bizarre that, in the absence of any relevant intention, a steady stream of 'volitions' of a kind suitable for window-opening bodily movements would occur in an agent, and who therefore want to bring some intention into the explanatory picture, the best candidate would seem to be an intention that is *causally explanatory* of the supposed occurrence of the causally effective volitions.

I should add that, in my opinion, Ginet is entirely correct in rejecting the thesis that 'reasons explanation' requires the truth of determinism. But notice that causal explanation does not entail determinism, unless causation is essentially deterministic. Audi's position on reasons-explanation in Chapter 4 is in the causalist camp, but the essay displays no commitment to determinism.

---

[27] Ibid. 39.   [28] Ibid. 32–3.   [29] Ibid. 30.

(F) *Agent causation*

A theory of action that would merit significant attention in a volume on free will, but is not represented in this volume, is the 'agent causation' theory. Although I cannot do it justice here, a brief description is in order. Some theorists have viewed free will or free action as incompatible with *caused* willing or acting, on any standard construal of causation. However, if freedom of these kinds requires agential control, and if control is, as it seems to be, a causal phenomenon, these theorists face a significant problem. Roderick Chisholm, Richard Taylor, and others have appealed to 'agent causation' in this connection. As Taylor describes it, it is 'causation of events by beings or substances that are not events'.[30] Chisholm claims, similarly, that we have agent causation only when 'there is some event, or set of events, that is caused, *not* by other events or states of affairs, but by the man himself, by the agent'.[31] 'On this view', Taylor writes, 'it is a man himself, and not merely some part of him or something within him'—for example, 'desires, choices, acts of will, and so on' (p. 49)—'that is the cause of his own activity' (p. 51). The view supposedly has the dual advantage for libertarians of circumventing the control problem, 'by conceding that human behaviour is caused', and blocking determinism, by placing agents at the beginning of causal chains issuing in actions: 'Some . . . causal chains, on this view, have beginnings, and they begin with agents themselves' (Taylor 1963: 52; cf. Chisholm 1966, Clarke 1993,[32] Taylor 1966,[33] and Thorp 1980[34]) For instructive criticism of agent causation by a libertarian, see Kane 1989.[35]

(G) *Volitions and trying*

Some philosophers have argued that volitions, or acts of willing, are essential to intentional action (e.g. Ginet 1990; McCann 1974;[36] O'Shaughnessy,

[30] R. Taylor (1963), *Metaphysics* (Englewood Cliffs, NJ: Prentice-Hall), 52.

[31] R. Chisholm (1966), 'Freedom and Action', in Keith Lehrer (ed.), *Freedom and Determinism* (New York: Random House), 17.

[32] R. Clarke (1993) 'Towards a Credible Agent–Causal Account of Free Will', *Noûs* 27: 191–203.

[33] R. Taylor (1966), *Action and Purpose* (Englewood Cliffs, NJ: Prentice-Hall).

[34] J. Thorp (1980), *Free Will: A Defence Against Neurophysiological Determinism* (London: Routledge & Kegan Paul). J. Bishop (1983) in 'Agent Causation', *Mind* 92: 61–79, defends a related brand of agent-causation, motivated largely by problems that causal deviance poses for the project of providing an 'event-causal' analysis of intentional action. For such an analysis of intentional action that accommodates causal deviance, see Chapter 10.

[35] R. Kane (1989), 'Two Kinds of Incompatibilism', *Philosophy and Phenomenological Research* 50: 219–54.

[36] H. McCann (1974), 'Volition and Basic Action', *Philosophical Review* 83: 451–73.

Chapter 3). In itself, this idea is neutral on the question whether causalism is correct. Volitionists may seek to supplement non-volitionist causal theories of action with volitions, or they may defend an alternative to causal theories.

Brian O'Shaughnessy, in Chapter 3, identifies willing (or volition) with *trying* (p. 54). Trying, for O'Shaughnessy, is an 'inner' or 'mental' event. When one successfully tries to raise one's right arm, 'trying to raise the arm causes the act-neutral event of arm rising' (p. 62). 'The act of raising the arm is a complex event, constituted out of a causally linked pair of events, the trying and the arm rising' (p. 70). If an event's counting as a trying depends upon how it is caused, O'Shaughnessy's analysis of physical action is consistent with causalism about action.

Trying, O'Shaughnessy argues, serves a 'crucial bridge function between mind and body, not unlike that allotted by Descartes to the pineal gland' (p. 65). Trying 'is like a psychic promontory that all but juts into the physical world'. It is a 'mental event' that is '*standardly* a cause of physical change' (p. 66). Imagine (if you can) that an agent who is unknowingly paralysed tries to raise her right arm and there is no bodily motion at all. Then, we can say, her trying is a purely mental event, an act of will. Suppose that she subsequently recovers and again tries—this time successfully—to raise the arm. Should we say that her trying in this case, too, is a purely mental event, something that falls short of jutting into the physical world?

I doubt it (and O'Shaughnessy himself retracts the idea in *The Will*, ii. 100–11). Recently, I tried to raise my right arm in a contest of strength, while Kent, a large and powerful fellow, was trying to hold it down. I tried so long and so hard that I broke out in a sweat and strained a muscle. Would a purely mental trying have affected me so? Trying to *A* may be understood as making an effort to *A*, however modest that effort may be. (When, e.g. I intentionally turn my computer on, I am trying to do that, even if I encounter no special resistance and need to make no special effort.) The trying continues as long as the effort does. My effort to raise my arm included considerable muscular exertion. If my trying to raise my arm was my making that effort, my trying included this muscular exertion.

My trying was not *limited* to my muscular exertion, however. To see this, consider another attempted arm-raising. Although an injury has deprived Ben of all sensation in his right arm, he has retained the ability to move it. During an experiment, a physician blindfolds Ben, administers a dose of curare, and asks Ben to raise his right arm over his head and hold it there until he receives further instructions. Ben proximally intends to do so. The drug takes effect after signals from Ben's brain have started down the efferent pathway to his right arm, but paralysis sets in before the muscles can contract. Moments later, Ben believes that he has raised his arm and that he is now holding it over his head. When the blindfold is removed, he is surprised to see his right arm at his side. Ben sincerely reports that he tried to raise it and that he felt certain that he raised it.[37]

Ben's surprise is nicely explained on the hypothesis that he tried to raise his arm. While trying, Ben would receive a kind of feedback, 'efferent copy', registering that motor signals were sent. Receipt of this feedback, a product of Ben's trying, would explain his experience of trying. Since that experience is not accompanied by evidence of failure, Ben predictably would believe that he raised his arm.[38]

If Ben tried to raise his arm, his trying involved no muscular motion. In what did the trying consist? Frederick Adams and I have argued that it consists in a certain neurophysiological event with a certain causal history.[39] As we see it, Ben began trying to raise his arm when his proximal intention to raise it began to play its functional role. Certain neurophysiological effects of the acquisition of that intention—effects appropriate to his raising his arm—realize his trying to raise his arm partly in virtue of their causal history. Ben's attempt was both initiated by the acquisition of his proximal intention and motivationally sustained by the intention's continued presence. On this view, my own attempt to raise my arm in the contest with Kent encompassed neurophysiological events of the sort that occur in Ben's case and muscle contractions, as well.

3. INTENTION AND GENERAL PROBLEMS FOR ANALYSES OF INTENTIONAL ACTION

Intentional action is of primary importance in the philosophy of action. If there were no intentional actions, actions would be of little interest at best, and perhaps there would be no actions at all. (Davidson has argued that every action is intentional under some description,[40] a thesis Hornsby endorses in Chapter 12.) In discussions of freedom of action, intentional action occupies centre stage: we are much less concerned with conditions for the freedom of non-intentional actions. And although we are morally

---

[37] This case, a version of which appears in F. Adams and A. Mele (1992), 'The Intention/ Volition Debate', *Canadian Journal of Philosophy* 22: 323–38, is inspired by the description of Landry's patient quoted in W. James (1981), *The Principles of Psychology*, ii (Cambridge, Mass.: Harvard University Press), 1101–3.

[38] For further discussion, and references to some relevant empirical literature, see Adams and Mele (1992), 'The Intention/Volition Debate'.

[39] Ibid.   [40] Davidson (1980), *Essays on Actions and Events*, ch. 3.

accountable for some unintentional actions, as in cases of negligence, moral assessment of actions is focused primarily upon intentional actions.

Presumably, there is some interesting connection between intentional actions and intentions. But what are intentions? And what is the connection? In this section, I discuss two competing approaches to characterizing intention and then turn to some general problems for the project of analysing intentional action.[41]

There is, predictably, considerable agreement that intentions are closely linked to desires and beliefs. It is generally recognized that intention has a motivational dimension, and 'desire' (like 'want') is often used in the literature as an umbrella term for motivation. Further, intention is widely, if not universally, regarded as involving a 'confidence' condition of some sort, a condition naturally explicated in terms of belief. Few people are inclined to maintain that a person who believes that her chances of winning today's lottery are about one in a million *intends* to win the lottery, no matter how strongly motivated she is to win. However, philosophers are divided on how close the connection is between intentions, on the one hand, and desires and beliefs, on the other. Some—attracted, perhaps, by the popular idea that desire and belief are the most fundamental representational states of mind[42]—hold that intentions are reducible to combinations of desires and beliefs.[43] Others have argued that attempts at such reduction are doomed to failure.[44]

In Chapter 6, Wayne Davis offers a reductive belief/desire analysis of intention:

S intends that p iff [i.e. if and only if] S believes that p because he desires that p and believes his desire will motivate him to act in such a way that p. (p. 147)

Believing p, as Davis conceives it, 'is equivalent to being more certain of p than of not-p' (p. 133), and 'desiring p is equivalent to preferring p rather than not-p' (p. 135). (Davis's conception of desiring is at odds with a

---

[41] See Wilson (1989), *The Intentionality of Human Action* for a third approach, according to which intentions are not attitudes.

[42] For resistance to this idea, see Brand (1984), *Intending and Acting*, and J. Searle (1983), *Intentionality*.

[43] See, e.g. R. Audi (1973), 'Intending', *Journal of Philosophy* 70: 387–402, and id. 'Intending, Intentional Action, and Desire', in J. Marks (1986) (ed.), *The Ways of Desire* (Chicago: Precedent); M. C. Beardsley, 'Intending', in A. Goldman and J. Kim (1978) (eds.) *Values and Morals* (Dordrecht, Neth.: Reidel); W. Davis, Ch. 6.

[44] See, e.g. Brand (1984), *Intending and Acting*; M. Bratman (1987), *Intention, Plans, and Practical Reason* (Cambridge, Mass.: Harvard University Press), and id. Ch. 8; Davidson (1980), *Essays on Actions and Events*, ch. 5; G. Harman, Ch. 7; H. McCann (1986a), 'Rationality and the Range of Intention', *Midwest Studies in Philosophy* 10: 191–211; Mele (1992a), *Springs of Action*; and Searle (1983), *Intentionality*.

common conception according to which the same person can simultaneously desire to A and desire not to A: e.g. watching her son struggle with
his homework, Ann may desire to help him with it; but she may also, at the
same time, desire not to help him with it, thinking that he would benefit
most if he were to complete his assignment on his own. Obviously, Ann
cannot simultaneously prefer each of the options identified to the other.)

Although Davis's is the most promising belief/desire analysis of intention that I have seen, it is problematic.[45] Since, for Davis, desiring is preferring, two different senses of 'preference' merit attention. In one sense—an
evaluative one—preferring A to B is giving A a higher evaluative rating
than B. In another sense—a *motivational* one—preferring A to B is being
more strongly motivated to A than to B.[46] Suppose that Ann satisfies
the belief/desire conditions specified in Davis's analysis, on a reading of
'desire' as evaluative preference. Watching her son, Ann believes that she
will refrain from helping him because she desires (= prefers in the evaluative sense) this and believes that her desire will motivate her to refrain
from helping. Ann knows that, ordinarily, she acts on the basis of her
evaluative preferences, and she deems it likely that she will do so in this
case too: she is 'more certain' of this than of the contrary. Even so, given
how pathetic her son looks, Ann is sorely tempted to help him, and she
is unsettled about what to do. She is considering giving in to temptation. This seems coherent. If it is, Davis's analysis fails, on the current
reading; for if Ann is unsettled about what to do and is considering helping
her son, she does not—not yet, anyway—*intend* to refrain from helping
him.

Essentially the same problem arises on the motivational reading. Suppose that although Ann believes that it would be best not to help her son,
she is more strongly motivated to start helping him soon than to refrain
from doing so. Suppose, further, that she knows she usually succumbs to
temptation in cases of this kind and, accordingly, is 'more certain' that her
desire to help will motivate her to help than that it will not so motivate her.
However, Ann still is unsettled about whether to help. She is considering
making an effort to resist temptation for the child's good. Given Ann's
unsettledness, it is false that she intends to help her son—even though she
satisfies Davis's conditions, on the current reading of 'desire'.[47]

---

[45] For an objection like the one to be advanced, see H. McCann (1986*b*), 'Intrinsic Intentionality', *Theory and Decision* 20: 251–2.

[46] For roughly this distinction, see G. Watson (1977), 'Skepticism about Weakness of Will',
Philosophical Review 86: 320–1 and A. Mele (1987*a*), *Irrationality* (New York: Oxford University Press).

[47] Compare this case with Davis's case of Alan (p. 147). For detailed discussion of cases of this
kind, see Mele (1992*a*), *Springs of Action*, ch. 9 and id. (1995), *Autonomous Agents*, ch. 3.

The points just made about settledness point toward an alternative view of intention as an attitude that is irreducible to belief/desire complexes. Functions plausibly attributed to intentions include initiating and sustaining intentional actions, guiding intentional behaviour, helping to coordinate agents' behaviour over time and their interaction with other agents, and prompting and appropriately terminating practical reasoning. Some philosophers have advanced non-reductive accounts of intention designed to accommodate these functions (see n. 44). According to a representative account of this kind,[48] intentions are executive attitudes toward plans. Plans—which range from simple representations of 'basic' actions to complex strategies for achieving remote goals—constitute the representational contents of intentions.[49] What distinguishes intentions from other practical attitudes—e.g. desires—is their distinctive practical nature. Although one can harbour a desire to do something without being at all settled upon doing it, to intend to do something is, in part, to be settled upon doing it (but not necessarily irrevocably). Such settledness upon a course of action constitutes a psychological commitment to executing the pertinent plan of action, a commitment of a kind arguably constituted exclusively by intentions.[50]

As I mentioned, it is natural to suppose that intention and intentional action are importantly related. It is noteworthy in this connection that Robert Audi's account of acting for a reason in Chapter 4 makes no mention of intention; for acting for a reason is often *identified* with acting intentionally.[51] However, Audi, like Davis, attempts to analyse intentions as complexes of beliefs and desires,[52] and he regards the reasons for which we act as, in part, states of affairs that express something we desire and are connected to action through belief (Ch. 4: 76). If intentions can be reduced to belief/desire complexes, an analysis of acting for a reason might *implicitly* accord intentions a major role in intentional action.

---

[48] Mele (1992a), *Springs of Action*.

[49] Roughly speaking, *basic* actions differ from non-basic actions in not being performed by way of the agent's performing another action.

[50] The commitment aspect of intention receives detailed treatment in Bratman (1987), *Intentions, Plans, and Practical Reason*. Also see R. Audi (1991), 'Intention, Cognitive Commitment, and Planning', *Synthese* 86: 361–78. Incidentally, I take decisions (when construed as states of mind) to be actively produced intentions. In deciding, one forms an intention; the intention formed may be termed a 'decision' (Mele (1992a), *Springs of Action*, ch. 9). But not all intentions are actively produced (Mele (1992a), 141).

[51] Taking off from Gregory Kavka's (1983) toxin puzzle ('The Toxin Puzzle', *Analysis* 43: 33–6), I have argued both that counterexamples to this alleged identification are provided by some bizarre scenarios and that the bizarreness required to generate a telling counterexample is itself revealing (A. Mele (1992c), 'Intentions, Reasons, and Beliefs: Morals of the Toxin Puzzle', *Philosophical Studies* 68: 171–94).

[52] Audi (1973), 'Intending', and id. (1986) 'Intending, Intentional Action, and Desire'.

For expository purposes, it will be useful to have before us a pair of proto-analyses of doing something intentionally, one framed in terms of intentions and the other in terms of reasons. With the stipulation that '*A*' is an action variable, the following will do:

(A1) *S* intentionally *A*-ed if and only if *S* *A*-ed in the way that *S* intended to *A*.

(A2) *S* intentionally *A*-ed if and only if *S* *A*-ed for a reason.

Both proto-analyses enjoy intuitive support. Again, there is, presumably, some important, substantial connection between what we intend to do and what we do intentionally. Similarly, it seems, intentional action is a species of behaviour intimately bound up with agents' desires and beliefs; and desires, perhaps typically in conjunction with beliefs linking desired goals to prospective instrumental behaviour, arguably constitute *reasons* for action. I will consider four problems for the proto-analyses. Both the problems and the proto-analyses are neutral on issues that divide causalists and noncausalists about intentional action.

(A) *Side effects*

Consider an example of Gilbert Harman's (Ch. 7: 151). 'In firing his gun', a sniper who is trying to kill a soldier, 'knowingly alerts the enemy to his presence'. Harman claims that although the sniper 'does not intend to alert the enemy to his presence', he nevertheless *intentionally* alerts the enemy, 'thinking that the gain is worth the possible cost'. If Harman is right, *A1* and *A2* are both false. Not only does the sniper not intend to alert the enemy, he does not alert them *for a reason* either (even if his alerting them is part of some 'larger' action that is done for a reason). Michael Bratman makes the same general claim, illustrated by a scenario featuring a runner who reluctantly wears down some heirloom shoes (Ch. 8: 199–203).

Harman's sniper and Bratman's runner do not unknowingly, inadvertently, or accidentally perform the actions at issue. For that reason, many will deny that the sniper *unintentionally* alerted the enemy and that the runner *unintentionally* wore down his shoes. But that denial does not, in any *obvious* way, commit one to insisting that the actions in question are *intentional*. Perhaps there is a middle ground between intentional and unintentional action. Arguably, actions that an agent in no way aims at performing but that are not performed unknowingly, inadvertently, or accidentally are properly located on that middle ground. They might be *non*-intentional, as opposed to *un*intentional (cf. Ch. 10: 230–31).

(B) *Belief-constraints*

Anticipated side effects are not the only alleged problem for the thesis—dubbed by Bratman the 'Simple View'—that intentionally *A*-ing entails intending to *A*. Some putative belief-constraints on intentions, or *rational* intentions, also pose problems. Bratman argues that intention has a normative side that includes, among other things, demands that an agent's intentions be internally consistent (individually and collectively), consistent with the agent's beliefs, and means-end coherent (Ch. 8; cf. Harman, Ch. 7). *Rational* intentions, he maintains, meet those demands. Concerning beliefs in particular, he contends that *S* *rationally* intends to *A* only if, 'other things being equal', *S* does 'not have beliefs inconsistent with the belief that [he] will *A*' (p. 186).

The normative demands figure significantly in a much-discussed argument of Bratman's against the Simple View (Ch. 8). The argument turns on an example featuring a pair of video games and an ambidextrous player whom I shall call Bart. Bart's task is to hit video targets with video missiles. In the main case, he is simultaneously playing two games, each with its own target and firing mechanism, and he knows that the machines are 'so linked that it is impossible to hit both targets' (p. 184). (He knows that hitting a target ends both games, and that 'if both targets are about to be hit simultaneously', both machines shut down before the targets can be hit.) Bart simultaneously tries to hit the target on machine 1 and tries to hit the target on machine 2. He succeeds in hitting the former—'in just the way that [he] was trying to hit it, and in a way which depends heavily on [his] considerable skills' (p. 184)—but, of course, he misses the latter.

Supposing that Bart hits target 1 *intentionally*, proponents of the Simple View must say that he intended to hit it. Since Bart's attitude toward hitting that target is not relevantly different from his attitude toward hitting target 2, they apparently must hold as well that he intended to hit target 2. Bratman claims that having *both* intentions, given what Bart knows (namely, that he cannot hit both targets), would be irrational. Yet, it seems perfectly rational of Bart to have proceeded as he did. So given the point about the symmetry of Bart's attitudes toward the targets, Bratman concludes that he did not have either intention. And if Bart hit target 1 intentionally in the absence of an intention to hit it, the Simple View is false.

If trying to *A* requires intending to *A*, Bratman's video games argument fails. For then, trying to hit each target, Bart would intend to hit each. Hugh McCann has argued that trying to *A* and intending to try to *A* are each sufficient for intending to A.[53] And I have argued that his arguments are unsuccessful.[54] Here, I set the details of that dispute aside and take up a portion of McCann's defence of the Simple View in Chapter 9.

Some critics of the Simple View are also critical of the idea that intentions are reducible to complexes of beliefs and desires (e.g. Bratman, Harman, and Mele), and McCann argues that they are in danger of having to settle for an unwanted reductive analysis of intention (Ch. 9). Bratman, who suggests that a 'guiding desire'—e.g. to hit target 1—can play the role of an intention,[55] receives the brunt of the attack. McCann observes that once it is conceded that desires can stand in for intentions, reductionists will justifiably ask what functional need there is for a notion of intention that is irreducible to desire and belief. However, opponents of the Simple View need not follow Bratman in appealing to guiding desires. On my own view, for example, intentions to *try* to A can stand in for intentions to A, but intentions to try to A are *intentions*.[56] The agent's attitude toward A-ing is not one of intending *to* A, but neither is it merely one of desiring to A. It is, rather, an intending-to-try attitude toward A-ing, and intending to try is a species of intending. (My view is a version of Bratman's 'Single Phenomenon View' (Ch. 8: 194–203).)

Normally, at least, one who intends to try to A has A-ing as a goal, purpose, or objective. McCann contends that 'there is no ordinary sense in which terms like 'goal' or 'purpose' signify objectives that guide deliberation and behaviour, but fall short of being intentions' and that an intention to A is 'implicit in' an intention to try to A (Ch. 9: 221). I disagree. Poor Lydia, who has only one dollar, would love to have a million. There are no lotteries in her state, but there is a weekly million-dollar contest for amateur golfers. Contestants pay a dollar for the privilege of taking one shot at making a hole in one from a distance of 180 yards. Lydia has never hit a golf ball, but desperately wanting to become a millionaire and thinking that there is a remote chance that she will make a hole in one, she enters the contest. She has seen golf on television, and she estimates her chances of holing her shot at about one in a million. As Lydia eyes the ball, she deliberates about how she might achieve the *goal* or *objective* of making a hole in one, giving special attention to what club to use. She selects a three wood, lines up the shot, and then swings hard, with the goal or objective of

[53] H. McCann (1986a), 'Rationality and the Range of Intention'; and id. (1989), 'Intending and Planning: A Reply to Mele', *Philosophical Studies* 55: 107–10; cf. Ch. 9 and F. Adams (1986), 'Intention and Intentional Action: The Simple View', *Mind and Language* 1: 281–301.
[54] A. Mele (1989), 'She Intends to Try', *Philosophical Studies* 54: 101–6; and id. (1992a), *Springs of Action*, 132–5.
[55] Bratman (1987), *Intention, Plans, and Practical Reason*, 137; cf. Ch. 8.
[56] Mele (1992a), *Springs of Action*, ch. 8.

making a hole in one. Lydia does not hit the ball just for the sake of hitting it. Nor is her objective in hitting it limited to something less than hitting a hole in one. Her goal is to hit a hole in one, thereby winning a million dollars.

This little story evidently is coherent and completely in line with ordinary usage of such terms as 'goal' and 'objective'. So McCann must hold that, despite her awareness of the astronomical odds against her holing the shot, Lydia *intends* to hole it, whereas others would contend that, instead, she fervently hopes or strongly desires to hole it, or intends to try to hole it. Since, as McCann says, ordinary senses of terms are at issue and not philosophers' technical uses, the assertion that Lydia intends to hit a hole in one seems seriously mistaken (cf. Davis, Ch. 6: 133, and Harman, Ch. 7: 151 on winning lotteries). (Put yourself in Lydia's shoes as she approaches the ball. Given your belief that your chances of holing the ball are about one in a million, would it be true that you intend to hole it, or would it rather be the case that you intend to try to hole it?) Further, it is utterly plausible that Lydia intends to *try* to hit a hole in one. Thus, it is plausible that she has an *intention* regarding her goal of hitting a hole in one, even though that intention is not an intention *to hit a hole in one*.

The objection just advanced is directed at an important element in McCann's attempted refutation of some criticisms of the Simple View. It is not an objection to the Simple View itself. Ultimately, I think, the fate of the Simple View rests on whether its truth is required for the *explanation* of intentional actions. I have argued elsewhere that the truth of the Simple View is not required for this purpose.[57] But I have argued as well that the belief-constraints to which McCann objects are not required for this purpose either.[58]

(C) *Intrinsically motivated actions*

I turn now to reasons and to *A2*. On a popular account, the reasons for which we act—*effective reasons*—are complexes of beliefs and desires or pro-attitudes (Davidson, Ch. 1). Thus, the reason for which I crossed the road might be constituted by a desire to get to the other side and a belief that doing so requires a crossing. This account of effective reasons seems not to do justice to what Audi (Ch. 4) terms 'intrinsically motivated actions'—actions done for their own sakes, from 'intrinsic' desires. When

---

[57] Ibid.

[58] My strategy (Mele (1992a), *Springs of Action*, ch. 8) was to catalogue various functions of intentions and to argue that intention's having these functions does not depend upon the truth of various alleged belief-constraints.

something, *A*, is done for its own sake *alone*, it is *not* done from a desire for something further, *F*, and a belief that identifies *A*-ing as suitably related to *F*. However, if the reasons for which we *A* are sometimes constituted wholly by intrinsic desires to *A*, such cases can easily be handled.[59] Intrinsically motivated actions arguably are a problem, not for *A2* itself, but for a particular conception of effective reasons.

Rosalind Hursthouse (1991)[60] appeals to a species of intrinsically motivated action, 'arational action', in an attempt to undermine *A2*. Examples of arational actions include striking an inanimate object in anger and gouging out the eyes in a photograph of a hated person. She also adduces, but in another category, 'actions prompted by odd physical cravings'—e.g. licking something furry when 'seized by a sudden desire' to do so (pp. 62–3). Such actions, as Hursthouse observes, often are not done for the sake of some further goal, and they typically seem unreasonable. But it would be a mistake to infer from this that they are done for no reason at all. If our reasons can be every bit as bizarre as our actions, proponents of *A2* have no special cause for worry. A man with an irrational urge to drink a can of paint (Davidson, Ch. 1) and the knowledge that drinking the paint requires removing the lid might *pry off the lid* for a reason, and I have not encountered compelling grounds for thinking that he cannot *drink the paint* for a reason, too—a reason constituted by an intrinsic desire to drink it.

(D) *Luck*

A more interesting problem for *A2* has attracted little attention (as a problem for *that* thesis). In Chapter 4, Audi claims that all actions done for a reason are intentional (p. 104). This popular thesis is challenged by some cases of extraordinary luck. Connie, who has never fired a gun, is offered a large cash prize for hitting the bull's-eye on a distant target that even experts normally miss. She carefully aims and fires, hitting the target dead centre in just the (direct) way she hoped she would. Many readers, I think, would happily (but perhaps mistakenly) say that Connie's hitting the bull's-eye—that action—was done for a reason.[61] After all, she wanted the money and believed that to get it she must hit the bull's-eye, and this helps to explain her carefully aiming and firing at the target. (That Connie hit the

---

[59] Ibid. ch. 6.

[60] R. Hursthouse (1991), 'Arational Actions', *Journal of Philosophy* 88: 57–68.

[61] For resistance, see A. Mele (1992b), 'Acting for Reasons and Acting Intentionally', *Pacific Philosophical Quarterly* 73: 355–74. Incidentally, intuitions tend to shift when the agent succeeds in a way that diverges significantly from her plan, or from her (perhaps tacit) assumptions about what a successful *A*-ing would involve. If the bullet had ricocheted off several rocks into the bull's-eye, would Connie's hitting the bull's-eye have been done for a reason?

bull's-eye for a reason is compatible with Audi's account of acting for reasons, but see Chapter 4: 89 for an indication that he might reject this assessment of Connie's action.) But was Connie's hitting the bull's-eye an *intentional* action? To simplify matters, suppose that Connie has no natural talent for marksmanship: she tries equally hard to win even larger prizes for duplicating the feat, fires five hundred rounds at the target, and does not even come close.

Here intuitions differ. According to Christopher Peacocke, an agent who makes a successful attempt 'to hit a croquet ball through a distant hoop' *intentionally* hits the ball through the hoop.[62] But Brian O'Shaughnessy maintains that a novice who similarly succeeds in hitting the bull's-eye on a dartboard does not intentionally hit the bull's-eye.[63]

Luck is also a problem for *A1*, of course. Just suppose that Connie, who mistakenly thinks that modern weaponry makes target shooting easy, *intends* to hit the bull's-eye by aiming and firing at it. She hits it in just the way intended, but was her hitting it an intentional action? Readers inclined to answer affirmatively should consider a similarly benighted person who intends to disarm a doomsday device. She thinks that all she need do to disarm it is to punch in any ten-digit code, whereas, in fact, only one ten-digit code will work; and wanting to disarm the machine, she intends to disarm it by entering ten digits. If she luckily punches in the right code, thereby disarming the machine, does she disarm it intentionally? (Does she disarm it *for a reason*—perhaps one constituted by a desire to save the world and a belief that she can ensure her doing that by disarming the machine?) The problems that luck poses for a proper understanding of intentional action are examined in Chapter 10.[64]

4. CLOSING COMMENTS

My aim in the essay was to introduce readers both to central issues and debates in the philosophy of action and to the twelve essays that follow. The objections I have voiced are intended primarily to promote reflection on the following essays, not to settle issues. A comprehensive philosophy of action will include a stand on each of the main issues discussed here: the nature of action, trying, action-explanation, reasons for action, intention,

---

[62] C. Peacocke (1985), 'Intention and *Akrasia*', in B. Vermazen and M. Hintikka (eds.), *Essays on Davidson* (Oxford: Clarendon Press).

[63] B. O'Shaughnessy (1980), *The Will*, ii (Cambridge: Cambridge University Press), 325; cf. Harman, Ch. 7, 151.

[64] Other apparent problems are posed by sudden and impulsive actions and by subsidiary actions. For a response, see Chapter 10.

and intentional action. However, it should not be thought that a particular stand on one topic will commit one to a position on all the others. For example, causalists and non-causalists alike can accept or reject the idea that intentions (or effective reasons for action) are identical with belief/ desire complexes, the thesis that trying is always a strictly mental action, and the Simple View of the connection between intention and intentional action. Students are encouraged, therefore, to investigate each issue raised in the following essays on its own terms.

My aim in selecting articles for this volume was to provide students with first-rate, accessible essays on traditional issues in the philosophy of action that have become dominant issues in the area. Thus, traditional issues in which interest has waned (e.g. action-individuation and basic action) receive only incidental attention in this volume, and less traditional topics in which interest is growing (e.g. group action and group intentions) are not represented here. Owing to reasonable constraints on space, much excellent work could not be included, but my Further Reading section provides some guidance.

Parts of this introduction derive from my (1992d) 'Recent Work on Intentional Action', *American Philosophical Quarterly* 29: 199–217. I am grateful to the executive editor for permission to use material from that article, to Michael Bratman and Peter Momtchiloff for helpful written comments on a draft of this introduction, and to Robert Audi, Michael Bratman, Peter Momtchiloff, and Paul Moser for advice about the selection of essays.

1

ACTIONS, REASONS, AND CAUSES

DONALD DAVIDSON

What is the relation between a reason and an action when the reason
explains the action by giving the agent's reason for doing what he did?
We may call such explanations *rationalizations*, and say that the reason
rationalizes the action.

In this paper I want to defend the ancient—and common-sense—
position that rationalization is a species of ordinary causal explanation.
The defence no doubt requires some redeployment, but not more or less
complete abandonment of the position, as urged by many recent writers.[1]

I

A reason rationalizes an action only if it leads us to see something the
agent saw, or thought he saw, in his action—some feature, consequence, or
aspect of the action the agent wanted, desired, prized, held dear, thought
dutiful, beneficial, obligatory, or agreeable. We cannot explain why someone did what he did simply by saying the particular action appealed to him;
we must indicate what it was about the action that appealed. Whenever
someone does something for a reason, therefore, he can be characterized
as (*a*) having some sort of pro attitude toward actions of a certain kind, and
(*b*) believing (or knowing, perceiving, noticing, remembering) that his
action is of that kind. Under (*a*) are to be included desires, wantings, urges,
promptings, and a great variety of moral views, aesthetic principles,

Donald Davidson, 'Actions, Reasons, and Causes', *Journal of Philosophy* 60 (1963), 685–700.
© 1963 Donald Davidson. Reprinted by permission of the author.

[1] Some examples: G. E. M. Anscombe (1959), *Intention* (Oxford); Stuart Hampshire (1959),
Thought and Action (London); H. L. A. Hart and A. M. Honoré (1959), *Causation in the Law*
(Oxford); William Dray (1957), *Laws and Explanation in History* (Oxford); and most of the
books in the series edited by R. F. Holland, *Studies in Philosophical Psychology*, including
Anthony Kenny (1963), *Action, Emotion and Will* (London), and A. I. Melden (1961), *Free
Action* (London). Page references in parentheses will all be to these works.

economic prejudices, social conventions, and public and private goals and values in so far as these can be interpreted as attitudes of an agent directed toward actions of a certain kind. The word 'attitude' does yeoman service here, for it must cover not only permanent character traits that show themselves in a lifetime of behaviour, like love of children or a taste for loud company, but also the most passing fancy that prompts a unique action, like a sudden desire to touch a woman's elbow. In general, pro attitudes must not be taken for convictions, however temporary, that every action of a certain kind ought to be performed, is worth performing, or is, all things considered, desirable. On the contrary, a man may all his life have a yen, say, to drink a can of paint, without ever, even at the moment he yields, believing it would be worth doing.

Giving the reason why an agent did something is often a matter of naming the pro attitude (*a*) or the related belief (*b*) or both; let me call this pair the *primary reason* why the agent performed the action. Now it is possible to reformulate the claim that rationalizations are causal explanations, and give structure to the argument as well, by stating two theses about primary reasons:

1. For us to understand how a reason of any kind rationalizes an action it is necessary and sufficient that we see, at least in essential outline, how to construct a primary reason.

2. The primary reason for an action is its cause.

I shall argue for these points in turn.

II

I flip the switch, turn on the light, and illuminate the room. Unbeknownst to me I also alert a prowler to the fact that I am home. Here I do not do four things, but only one, of which four descriptions have been given.[2] I

---

[2] We would not call my unintentional alerting of the prowler an action, but it should not be inferred from this that alerting the prowler is therefore something different from flipping the switch, say just its consequence. Actions, performances, and events not involving intention are alike in that they are often referred to or defined partly in terms of some terminal stage, outcome, or consequence.

The word 'action' does not very often occur in ordinary speech, and when it does it is usually reserved for fairly portentous occasions. I follow a useful philosophical practice in calling anything an agent does intentionally an action, including intentional omissions. What is really needed is some suitably generic term to bridge the following gap: suppose '*A*' is a description of an action, '*B*' is a description of something done voluntarily, though not intentionally, and '*C*' is a description of something done involuntarily and unintentionally; finally, suppose $A = B = C$. Then A, B, and C are the same—what? 'Action', 'event', 'thing done', each have, at least in some

flipped the switch because I wanted to turn on the light, and by saying I wanted to turn on the light I explain (give my reason for, rationalize) the flipping. But I do not, by giving this reason, rationalize my alerting of the prowler nor my illuminating of the room. Since reasons may rationalize what someone does when it is described in one way and not when it is described in another, we cannot treat what was done simply as a term in sentences like 'My reason for flipping the switch was that I wanted to turn on the light'; otherwise we would be forced to conclude, from the fact that flipping the switch was identical with alerting the prowler, that my reason for alerting the prowler was that I wanted to turn on the light. Let us mark this quasi-intensional[3] character of action descriptions in rationalizations by stating a bit more precisely a necessary condition for primary reasons:

C1. *R* is a primary reason why an agent performed the action *A* under the description *d* only if *R* consists of a pro attitude of the agent toward actions with a certain property, and a belief of the agent that *A*, under the description *d*, has that property.

How can my wanting to turn on the light be (part of) a primary reason, since it appears to lack the required element of generality? We may be taken in by the verbal parallel between 'I turned on the light' and 'I wanted to turn on the light'. The first clearly refers to a particular event, so we conclude that the second has this same event as its object. Of course it is obvious that the event of my turning on the light can't be referred to in the same way by both sentences, since the existence of the event is required by the truth of 'I turned on the light' but not by the truth of 'I wanted to turn on the light'. If the reference were the same in both cases, the second sentence would entail the first; but in fact the sentences are logically independent. What is less obvious, at least until we attend to it, is that the event whose occurrence makes 'I turned on the light' true cannot be called the object, however intensional, of 'I wanted to turn on the light'. If I turned on the light, then I must have done it at a precise moment, in a particular way—every detail is fixed. But it makes no sense to demand that my want be directed at an action performed at any one moment or done in some unique manner. Any one of an indefinitely large number of actions

contexts, a strange ring when coupled with the wrong sort of description. Only the question 'Why did you (he) do *A*?' has the true generality required. Obviously, the problem is greatly aggravated if we assume, as Melden does (*Free Action*, p. 85), that an action ('raising one's arm') can be identical with a bodily movement ('one's arm going up').

[3] 'Quasi-intentional' because, besides its intensional aspect, the description of the action must also refer in rationalizations; otherwise it could be true that an action was done for a certain reason and yet the action not have been performed. Compare 'the author of *Waverley*' in 'George IV knew that author of *Waverley* wrote *Waverley*'.

would satisfy the want, and can be considered equally eligible as its object. Wants and desires often are trained on physical objects. However, 'I want that gold watch in the window' is not a primary reason, and explains why I went into the store only because it suggests a primary reason—for example, that I wanted to buy the watch.

Because 'I wanted to turn on the light' and 'I turned on the light' are logically independent, the first can be used to give a reason why the second is true. Such a reason gives minimal information: it implies that the action was intentional, and wanting tends to exclude some other pro attitudes, such as a sense of duty or obligation. But the exclusion depends very much on the action and the context of explanation. Wanting seems pallid beside lusting, but it would be odd to deny that someone who lusted after a woman or a cup of coffee wanted her or it. It is not unnatural, in fact, to treat wanting as a genus including all pro attitudes as species. When we do this and when we know some action is intentional, it is empty to add that the agent wanted to do it. In such cases, it is easy to answer the question 'Why did you do it?' with 'For no reason', meaning not that there is no reason but that there is no *further* reason, no reason that cannot be inferred from the fact that the action was done intentionally; no reason, in other words, besides wanting to do it. This last point is not essential to the present argument, but it is of interest because it defends the possibility of defining an intentional action as one done for a reason.

A primary reason consists of a belief and an attitude, but it is generally otiose to mention both. If you tell me you are easing the jib because you think that will stop the main from backing, I don't need to be told that you want to stop the main from backing; and if you say you are biting your thumb at me because you want to insult me, there is no point in adding that you think that by biting your thumb at me you will insult me. Similarly, many explanations of actions in terms of reasons that are not primary do not require mention of the primary reason to complete the story. If I say I am pulling weeds because I want a beautiful lawn, it would be fatuous to eke out the account with 'And so I see something desirable in any action that does, or has a good chance of, making the lawn beautiful'. Why insist that there is any *step*, logical or psychological, in the transfer of desire from an end that is not an action to the actions one conceives as means? It serves the argument as well that the desired end explains the action only if what are believed by the agent to be means are desired.

Fortunately, it is not necessary to classify and analyse the many varieties of emotions, sentiments, moods, motives, passions, and hungers whose mention may answer the question 'Why did you do it?' in order to see how, when such mention rationalizes the action, a primary reason is involved.

Claustrophobia gives a man's reason for leaving a cocktail party because we know people want to avoid, escape from, be safe from, put distance between themselves and, what they fear. Jealousy is the motive in a poisoning because, among other things, the poisoner believes his action will harm his rival, remove the cause of his agony, or redress an injustice, and these are the sorts of things a jealous man wants to do. When we learn a man cheated his son out of greed, we do not necessarily know what the primary reason was, but we know there was one, and its general nature. Ryle analyses 'he boasted from vanity' into 'he boasted on meeting the stranger and his doing so satisfies the lawlike proposition that whenever he finds a chance of securing the admiration and envy of others, he does whatever he thinks will produce this admiration and envy'.[4] This analysis is often, and perhaps justly, criticized on the ground that a man may boast from vanity just once. But if Ryle's boaster did what he did from vanity, then something entailed by Ryle's analysis is true: the boaster wanted to secure the admiration and envy of others, and he believed that his action would produce this admiration and envy; true or false, Ryle's analysis does not dispense with primary reasons, but depends upon them.

To know a primary reason why someone acted as he did is to know an intention with which the action was done. If I turn left at the fork because I want to get to Katmandu, my intention in turning left is to get to Katmandu. But to know the intention is not necessarily to know the primary reason in full detail. If James goes to church with the intention of pleasing his mother, then he must have some pro attitude toward pleasing his mother, but it needs more information to tell whether his reason is that he enjoys pleasing his mother, or thinks it right, his duty, or an obligation. The expression 'the intention with which James went to church' has the outward form of a description, but in fact it is syncategorematic and cannot be taken to refer to an entity, state, disposition, or event. Its function in context is to generate new descriptions of actions in terms of their reasons; thus 'James went to church with the intention of pleasing his mother' yields a new, and fuller, description of the action described in 'James went to church'. Essentially the same process goes on when I answer the question 'Why are you bobbing around that way?' with 'I'm knitting, weaving, exercising, sculling, cuddling, training fleas'.

Straight description of an intended result often explains an action better than stating that the result was intended or desired. 'It will soothe your nerves' explains why I pour you a shot as efficiently as 'I want to do something to soothe your nerves', since the first in the context of

---

[4] Gilbert Ryle (1949), *The Concept of Mind* (London), 89.

explanation implies the second; but the first does better, because, if it is true, the facts will justify my choice of action. Because justifying and explaining an action so often go hand in hand, we frequently indicate the primary reason for an action by making a claim which, if true, would also verify, vindicate, or support the relevant belief or attitude of the agent. 'I knew I ought to return it', 'The paper said it was going to snow', 'You stepped on *my* toes', all, in appropriate reason-giving contexts, perform this familiar dual function.

The justifying role of a reason, given this interpretation, depends upon the explanatory role, but the converse does not hold. Your stepping on my toes neither explains nor justifies my stepping on your toes unless I believe you stepped on my toes, but the belief alone, true or false, explains my action.

III

In the light of a primary reason, an action is revealed as coherent with certain traits, long- or short-termed, characteristic or not, of the agent, and the agent is shown in his role of Rational Animal. Corresponding to the belief and attitude of a primary reason for an action, we can always construct (with a little ingenuity) the premisses of a syllogism from which it follows that the action has some (as Miss Anscombe calls it) 'desirability characteristic'.[5] Thus there is a certain irreducible—though somewhat anaemic—sense in which every rationalization justifies: from the agent's point of view there was, when he acted, something to be said for the action.

Noting that non-teleological causal explanations do not display the element of justification provided by reasons, some philosophers have concluded that the concept of cause that applies elsewhere cannot apply to the relation between reasons and actions, and that the pattern of justification provides, in the case of reasons, the required explanation. But suppose we grant that reasons alone justify in explaining actions; it does not follow that the explanation is not also—and necessarily—causal. Indeed our first condition for primary reasons (C1) is designed to help set rationalizations apart from other sorts of explanation. If rationalization is, as I want to

---

[5] Miss Anscombe denies that the practical syllogism is deductive. This she does partly because she thinks of the practical syllogism, as Aristotle does, as corresponding to a piece of practical reasoning (whereas for me it is only part of the analysis of the concept of a reason with which someone acted), and therefore she is bound, again following Aristotle, to think of the conclusion of a practical syllogism as corresponding to a judgement, not merely that the action has a desirable characteristic, but that the action is desirable (reasonable, worth doing, etc.).

argue, a species of causal explanation, then justification, in the sense given by C1, is at least one differentiating property. How about the other claim: that justifying is a kind of explaining, so that the ordinary notion of cause need not be brought in? Here it is necessary to decide what is being included under justification. Perhaps it means only what is given by C1: that the agent has certain beliefs and attitudes in the light of which the action is reasonable. But then something essential has certainly been left out, for a person can have a reason for an action, and perform the action, and yet this reason not be the reason why he did it. Central to the relation between a reason and an action it explains is the idea that the agent performed the action *because* he had the reason. Of course, we can include this idea too in justification; but then the notion of justification becomes as dark as the notion of reason until we can account for the force of that 'because'.

When we ask why someone acted as he did, we want to be provided with an interpretation. His behaviour seems strange, alien, outré, pointless, out of character, disconnected; or perhaps we cannot even recognize an action in it. When we learn his reason, we have an interpretation, a new description of what he did which fits it into a familiar picture. The picture certainly includes some of the agent's beliefs and attitudes; perhaps also goals, ends, principles, general character traits, virtues or vices. Beyond this, the redescription of an action afforded by a reason may place the action in a wider social, economic, linguistic, or evaluative context. To learn, through learning the reason, that the agent conceived his action as a lie, a repayment of a debt, an insult, the fulfilment of an avuncular obligation, or a knight's gambit is to grasp the point of the action in its setting of rules, practices, conventions, and expectations.

Remarks like these, inspired by the later Wittgenstein, have been elaborated with subtlety and insight by a number of philosophers. And there is no denying that this is true: when we explain an action, by giving the reason, we do redescribe the action; redescribing the action gives the action a place in a pattern, and in this way the action is explained. Here it is tempting to draw two conclusions that do not follow. First, we can't infer, from the fact that giving reasons merely redescribes the action and that causes are separate from effects, that therefore reasons are not causes. Reasons, being beliefs and attitudes, are certainly not identical with actions; but, more important, events are often redescribed in terms of their causes. (Suppose someone was burned. We could redescribe this event 'in terms of a cause' by saying he was burned.) Second, it is an error to think that, because placing the action in a larger pattern explains it, therefore we now understand the sort of explanation involved. Talk of patterns and contexts does not answer the question of how reasons explain actions, since the relevant pattern or context contains both reason and action. One way we can explain an event is by placing it in the context of its cause; cause and effect form the sort of pattern that explains the effect, in a sense of 'explain' that we understand as well as any. If reason and action illustrate a different pattern of explanation, that pattern must be identified.

Let me urge the point in connection with an example of Melden's. A man driving an automobile raises his arm in order to signal. His intention, to signal, explains his action, raising his arm, by redescribing it as signalling. What is the pattern that explains the action? Is it the familiar pattern of an action done for a reason? Then it does indeed explain the action, but only because it assumes the relation of reason and action that we want to analyse. Or is the pattern rather this: the man is driving, he is approaching a turn; he knows he ought to signal; he knows how to signal, by raising his arm. And now, in this context, he raises his arm. Perhaps, as Melden suggests, if all this happens, he does signal. And the explanation would then be this: if, under these conditions, a man raises his arm, then he signals. The difficulty is, of course, that this explanation does not touch the question of why he raised his arm. He had a reason to raise his arm, but this has not been shown to be the reason why he did it. If the description 'signalling' explains his action by giving his reason, then the signalling must be intentional; but, on the account just given, it may not be.

If, as Melden claims, causal explanations are 'wholly irrelevant to the understanding we seek' of human actions (p. 184) then we are without an analysis of the 'because' in 'He did it because . . .', where we go on to name a reason. Hampshire remarks, of the relation between reasons and action, 'In philosophy one ought surely to find this . . . connection altogether mysterious' (p. 166). Hampshire rejects Aristotle's attempt to solve the mystery by introducing the concept of wanting as a causal factor, on the grounds that the resulting theory is too clear and definite to fit all cases and that 'There is still no compelling ground for insisting that the word "want" *must* enter into every full statement of reasons for acting' (p. 168). I agree that the concept of wanting is too narrow, but I have argued that, at least in a vast number of typical cases, some pro attitude must be assumed to be present if a statement of an agent's reasons in acting is to be intelligible. Hampshire does not see how Aristotle's scheme can be appraised as true or false, 'for it is not clear what could be the basis of assessment, or what kind of evidence could be decisive' (p. 167). Failing a satisfactory alternative, the best argument for a scheme like Aristotle's is that it alone promises to give an account of the 'mysterious connection' between reasons and actions.

IV

In order to turn the first 'and' to 'because' in 'He exercised *and* he wanted to reduce and thought exercise would do it', wc must, as the basic move,[6] augment condition C1 with:

C2. A primary reason for an action is its cause.

The considerations in favour of C2 are by now, I hope, obvious; in the remainder of this paper I wish to defend C2 against various lines of attack and, in the process, to clarify the notion of causal explanation involved.

(A) The first line of attack is this. Primary reasons consist of attitudes and beliefs, which are states or dispositions, not events; therefore they cannot be causes.

It is easy to reply that states, dispositions, and conditions are frequently named as the causes of events: the bridge collapsed because of a structural defect; the plane crashed on take-off because the air temperature was abnormally high; the plate broke because it had a crack. This reply does not, however, meet a closely related point. Mention of a causal condition for an event gives a cause only on the assumption that there was also a preceding event. But what is the preceding event that causes an action?

In many cases it is not difficult at all to find events very closely associated with the primary reason. States and dispositions are not events, but the onslaught of a state or disposition is. A desire to hurt your feelings may spring up at the moment you anger me; I may start wanting to eat a melon just when I see one; and beliefs may begin at the moment we notice, perceive, learn, or remember something. Those who have argued that there are no mental events to qualify as causes of actions have often missed the obvious because they have insisted that a mental event be observed or noticed (rather than an observing or a noticing) or that it be like a stab, a qualm, a prick or a quiver, a mysterious prod of conscience or act of the will. Melden, in discussing the driver who signals a turn by raising his arm, challenges those who want to explain actions causally to identify 'an event which is common and peculiar to all such cases' (p. 87), perhaps a motive or an intention, anyway 'some particular feeling or experience' (p. 95). But of course there is a mental event; at some moment the driver noticed (or thought he noticed) his turn coming up, and that is the moment he signalled. During any continuing activity, like driving, or elaborate

---

[6] I say 'as the basic move' to cancel the suggestion that C1 and C2 are jointly *sufficient* to define the relation of reasons to the actions they explain. I believe C2 can be strengthened to make C1 and C2 sufficient as well as necessary conditions, but here I am concerned only with the claim that both are, as they stand, necessary.

performance, like swimming the Hellespont, there are more or less fixed purposes, standards, desires, and habits that give direction and form to the entire enterprise, and there is the continuing input of information about what we are doing, about changes in the environment, in terms of which we regulate and adjust our actions. To dignify a driver's awareness that his turn has come by calling it an experience, much less a feeling, is no doubt exaggerated, but whether it deserves a name or not, it had better be the reason why he raises his arm. In this case, and typically, there may not be anything we would call a motive, but if we mention such a general purpose as wanting to get to one's destination safely, it is clear that the motive is not an event. The intention with which the driver raises his arm is also not an event, for it is no thing at all, neither event, attitude, disposition, nor object. Finally, Melden asks the causal theorist to find an event that is common and peculiar to all cases where a man intentionally raises his arm, and this, it must be admitted, cannot be produced. But then neither can a common and unique cause of bridge failures, plane crashes, or plate breakings be produced.

The signalling driver can answer the question 'Why did you raise your arm when you did?', and from the answer we learn the event that caused the action. But can an actor always answer such a question? Sometimes the answer will mention a mental event that does not give a reason: 'Finally I made up my mind'. However, there also seem to be cases of intentional action where we cannot explain at all why we acted when we did. In such cases, explanation in terms of primary reasons parallels the explanation of the collapse of the bridge from a structural defect: we are ignorant of the event or sequence of events that led up to (caused) the collapse, but we are sure there was such an event or sequence of events.

(B) According to Melden, a cause must be 'logically distinct from the alleged effect' (p. 52); but a reason for an action is not logically distinct from the action; therefore, reasons are not causes of actions.[7]

One possible form of this argument has already been suggested. Since a reason makes an action intelligible by redescribing it, we do not have two events, but only one under different descriptions. Causal relations, however, demand distinct events.

Someone might be tempted into the mistake of thinking that my flipping of the switch caused my turning on of the light (in fact it caused the light to go on). But it does not follow that it is a mistake to take 'My reason for

---

[7] This argument can be found, in one or more versions, in Kenny, Hampshire, and Melden, as well as in P. Winch (1958), *The Idea of a Social Science* (London), and R. S. Peters (1958), *The Concept of Motivation* (London). In one of its forms, the argument was of course inspired by Ryle's treatment of motives in *The Concept of Mind*.

flipping the switch was that I wanted to turn on the light' as entailing, in part, 'I flipped the switch, and this action is further describable as having been caused by my wanting to turn on the light'. To describe an event in terms of its cause is not to identify the event with its cause, nor does explanation by redescription exclude causal explanation.

The example serves also to refute the claim that we cannot describe the action without using words that link it to the alleged cause. Here the action is to be explained under the description: 'my flipping the switch', and the alleged cause is 'my wanting to turn on the light'. What possible logical relation is supposed to hold between these phrases? It seems more plausible to urge a logical link between 'my turning on the light' and 'my wanting to turn on the light', but even here the link turned out, on inspection, to be grammatical rather than logical.

In any case there is something very odd in the idea that causal relations are empirical rather than logical. What can this mean? Surely not that every true causal statement is empirical. For suppose 'A caused B' is true. Then the cause of $B = A$; so, substituting, we have 'The cause of B caused B', which is analytic. The truth of a causal statement depends on *what* events are described; its status as analytic or synthetic depends on *how* the events are described. Still, it may be maintained that a reason rationalizes an action only when the descriptions are appropriately fixed, and the appropriate descriptions are not logically independent.

Suppose that to say a man wanted to turn on the light *meant* that he would perform any action he believed would accomplish his end. Then the statement of his primary reason for flipping the switch would entail that he flipped the switch—'straightway he acts', as Aristotle says. In this case there would certainly be a logical connection between reason and action, the same sort of connection as that between 'It's water-soluble and was placed in water' and 'It dissolved'. Since the implication runs from description of cause to description of effect but not conversely, naming the cause still gives information. And, though the point is often overlooked, 'Placing it in water caused it to dissolve' does not entail 'It's water-soluble'; so the latter has additional explanatory force. Nevertheless, the explanation would be far more interesting if, in place of solubility, with its obvious definitional connection with the event to be explained, we could refer to some property, say a particular crystalline structure, whose connection with dissolution in water was known only through experiment. Now it is clear why primary reasons like desires and wants do not explain actions in the relatively trivial way solubility explains dissolvings. Solubility, we are assuming, is a pure disposition property: it is defined in terms of a single test. But desires cannot be defined in terms of the actions they may rationalize, even though the relation between desire and action is not simply empirical; there are other, equally essential criteria for desires— their expression in feelings and in actions that they do not rationalize, for example. The person who has a desire (or want or belief) does not normally need criteria at all—he generally knows, even in the absence of any clues available to others, what he wants, desires, and believes. These logical features of primary reasons show that it is not just lack of ingenuity that keeps us from defining them as dispositions to act for these reasons.

(C) According to Hume, 'we may define a cause to be an object, followed by another, and where all the objects similar to the first are followed by objects similar to the second.' But, Hart and Honoré claim, 'The statement that one person did something because, for example, another threatened him, carries no implication or covert assertion that if the circumstances were repeated the same action would follow' (p. 52). Hart and Honoré allow that Hume is right in saying that ordinary singular causal statements imply generalizations, but wrong for this very reason in supposing that motives and desires are ordinary causes of actions. In brief, laws are involved essentially in ordinary causal explanations, but not in rationalizations.

It is common to try to meet this argument by suggesting that we do have rough laws connecting reasons and actions, and these can, in theory, be improved. True, threatened people do not always respond in the same way; but we may distinguish between threats and also between agents, in terms of their beliefs and attitudes.

The suggestion is delusive, however, because generalizations connecting reasons and actions are not—and cannot be sharpened into—the kind of law on the basis of which accurate predictions can reliably be made. If we reflect on the way in which reasons determine choice, decision, and behaviour, it is easy to see why this is so. What emerges, in the *ex post facto* atmosphere of explanation and justification, as *the* reason frequently was, to the agent at the time of action, one consideration among many, *a* reason. Any serious theory for predicting action on the basis of reasons must find a way of evaluating the relative force of various desires and beliefs in the matrix of decision; it cannot take as its starting point the refinement of what is to be expected from a single desire. The practical syllogism exhausts its role in displaying an action as falling under one reason; so it cannot be subtilized into a reconstruction of practical reasoning, which involves the weighing of competing reasons. The practical syllogism provides a model neither for a predictive science of action nor for a normative account of evaluative reasoning.

Ignorance of competent predictive laws does not inhibit valid causal explanation, or few causal explanations could be made. I am certain the window broke because it was struck by a rock—I saw it all happen; but I am not (is anyone?) in command of laws on the basis of which I can predict what blows will break which windows. A generalization like "Windows are fragile, and fragile things tend to break when struck hard enough, other conditions being right' is not a predictive law in the rough—the predictive law, if we had it, would be quantitative and would use very different concepts. The generalization, like our generalizations about behaviour, serves a different function: it provides evidence for the existence of a causal law covering the case at hand.

We are usually far more certain of a singular causal connection than we are of any causal law governing the case; does this show that Hume was wrong in claiming that singular causal statements entail laws? Not necessarily, for Hume's claim, as quoted above, is ambiguous. It may mean that 'A caused B' entails some particular law involving the predicates used in the descriptions 'A' and 'B', or it may mean that 'A caused B' entails that there exists a causal law instantiated by some true descriptions of A and B.[8] Obviously, both versions of Hume's doctrine give a sense to the claim that singular causal statements entail laws, and both sustain the view that causal explanations 'involve laws'. But the second version is far weaker, in that no particular law is entailed by a singular causal claim, and a singular causal claim can be defended, if it needs defence, without defending any law. Only the second version of Hume's doctrine can be made to fit with most causal explanations; it suits rationalizations equally well.

The most primitive explanation of an event gives its cause; more elaborate explanations may tell more of the story, or defend the singular causal claim by producing a relevant law or by giving reasons for believing such exists. But it is an error to think no explanation has been given until a law has been produced. Linked with these errors is the idea that singular causal statements necessarily indicate, by the concepts they employ, the concepts that will occur in the entailed law. Suppose a hurricane, which is reported on page 5 of Tuesday's *Times*, causes a catastrophe, which is reported on page 13 of Wednesday's *Tribune*. Then the event reported on page 5 of Tuesday's *Times* caused the event reported on page 13 of Wednesday's

---

[8] We could roughly characterize the analysis of singular causal statements hinted at here as follows: 'A caused B' is true if and only if there are descriptions of A and B such that the sentence obtained by putting these descriptions for 'A' and 'B' in 'A caused B' follows from a true causal law. This analysis is saved from triviality by the fact that not all true generalizations are causal laws; causal laws are distinguished (though of course this is no analysis) by the fact that they are inductively confirmed by their instances and by the fact that they support counterfactual and subjunctive singular causal statements.

Tribune. Should we look for a law relating events of these *kinds*? It is only slightly less ridiculous to look for a law relating hurricanes and catastrophes. The laws needed to predict the catastrophe with precision would, of course, have no use for concepts like hurricane and catastrophe. The trouble with predicting the weather is that the descriptions under which events interest us—'a cool, cloudy day with rain in the afternoon'—have only remote connections with the concepts employed by the more precise known laws.

The laws whose existence is required if reasons are causes of actions do not, we may be sure, deal in the concepts in which rationalizations must deal. If the causes of a class of events (actions) fall in a certain class (reasons) and there is a law to back each singular causal statement, it does not follow that there is any law connecting events classified as reasons with events classified as actions—the classifications may even be neurological, chemical, or physical.

(D) It is said that the kind of knowledge one has of one's own reasons in acting is not compatible with the existence of a causal relation between reasons and actions: a person knows his own intentions in acting infallibly, without induction or observation, and no ordinary causal relation can be known in this way. No doubt our knowledge of our own intentions in acting will show many of the oddities peculiar to first-person knowledge of one's own pains, beliefs, desires, and so on; the only question is whether these oddities prove that reasons do not cause, in any ordinary sense at least, the actions that they rationalize.

You may easily be wrong about the truth of a statement of the form 'I am poisoning Charles because I want to save him pain', because you may be wrong about whether you are poisoning Charles—you may yourself be drinking the poisoned cup by mistake. But it also seems that you may err about your reasons, particularly when you have two reasons for an action, one of which pleases you and one which does not. For example, you do want to save Charles pain; you also want him out of the way. You may be wrong about which motive made you do it.

The fact that you may be wrong does not show that in general it makes sense to ask you how you know what your reasons were or to ask for your evidence. Though you may, on rare occasions, accept public or private evidence as showing you are wrong about your reasons, you usually have no evidence and make no observations. Then your knowledge of your own reasons for your actions is not generally inductive, for where there is induction, there is evidence. Does this show the knowledge is not causal? I cannot see that it does.

Causal laws differ from true but non-lawlike generalizations in that their instances confirm them; induction is, therefore, certainly a good way to learn the truth of a law. It does not follow that it is the only way to learn the truth of a law. In any case, in order to know that a singular causal statement is true, it is not necessary to know the truth of a law; it is necessary only to know that some law covering the events at hand exists. And it is far from evident that induction, and induction alone, yields the knowledge that a causal law satisfying certain conditions exists. Or, to put it differently, one case is often enough, as Hume admitted, to persuade us that a law exists, and this amounts to saying that we are persuaded, without direct inductive evidence, that a causal relation exists.[9]

(E) Finally I should like to say something about a certain uneasiness some philosophers feel in speaking of causes of actions at all. Melden, for example, says that actions are often identical with bodily movements, and that bodily movements have causes; yet he denies that the causes are causes of the actions. This is, I think, a contradiction. He is led to it by the following sort of consideration: 'It is futile to attempt to explain conduct through the causal efficacy of desire—all *that* can explain is further happenings, not actions performed by agents. The agent confronting the causal nexus in which such happenings occur is a helpless victim of all that occurs in and to him' (pp. 128, 129). Unless I am mistaken, this argument, if it were valid, would show that actions cannot have causes at all. I shall not point out the obvious difficulties in removing actions from the realm of causality entirely. But perhaps it is worth trying to uncover the source of the trouble. Why on earth should a cause turn an action into a mere happening and a person into a helpless victim? Is it because we tend to assume, at least in the arena of action, that a cause demands a causer, agency an agent? So we press the question; if my action is caused, what caused it? If I did, then there is the absurdity of infinite regress; if I did not, I am a victim. But of course the alternatives are not exhaustive. Some causes have no agents. Primary among these are those states and changes of state in persons which, because they are reasons as well as causes, make persons voluntary agents.

[9] My thinking on the subject of this section, as on most of the topics discussed in this paper, has been greatly influenced by years of talk with Professor Daniel Bennett, now of Brandeis University.

2

THE PROBLEM OF ACTION

HARRY G. FRANKFURT

I

The problem of action is to explicate the contrast between what an agent does and what merely happens to him, or between the bodily movements that he makes and those that occur without his making them. According to causal theories of the nature of action, which currently represent the most widely followed approach to the understanding of this contrast, the essential difference between events of the two types is to be found in their prior causal histories: a bodily movement is an action if and only if it results from antecedents of a certain kind. Different versions of the causal approach may provide differing accounts of the sorts of events or states which must figure causally in the production of actions. The tenet they characteristically share is that it is both necessary and sufficient, in order to determine whether an event is an action, to consider how it was brought about.

Despite its popularity, I believe that the causal approach is inherently implausible and that it cannot provide a satisfactory analysis of the nature of action. I do not mean to suggest that actions have no causes; they are as likely to have causes, I suppose, as other events are. My claim is rather that it is no part of the nature of an action to have a prior causal history of any particular kind. From the fact that an event is an action, in my view, it does not follow even that it has a cause or causes at all, much less that it has causal antecedents of any specific type.

In asserting that the essential difference between actions and mere happenings lies in their prior causal histories, causal theories imply that actions and mere happenings do not differ essentially in themselves at all. These theories hold that the causal sequences producing actions are

Harry G. Frankfurt, 'The Problem of Action', *American Philosophical Quarterly* 15 (1978), 157–62. Reprinted by permission of *American Philosophical Quarterly*.

necessarily of a different type than those producing mere happenings, but that the effects produced by sequences of the two types are inherently indistinguishable. They are therefore committed to supposing that a person who knows he is in the midst of performing an action cannot have derived this knowledge from any awareness of what is currently happening, but that he must have derived it instead from his understanding of how what is happening was caused to happen by certain earlier conditions. It is integral to the causal approach to regard actions and mere happenings as being differentiated by nothing that exists or that is going on at the time those events occur, but by something quite extrinsic to them—a difference at an earlier time among another set of events entirely.

This is what makes causal theories implausible. They direct attention exclusively away from the events whose natures are at issue, and away from the times at which they occur. The result is that it is beyond their scope to stipulate that a person must be in some particular relation to the movements of his body *during* the period of time in which he is presumed to be performing an action. The only conditions they insist upon as distinctively constitutive of action may cease to obtain, for all the causal accounts demand, at precisely the moment when the agent commences to act. They require nothing of an agent, once the specified causal antecedents of his performing an action have occurred, except that his body move as their effect.

It is no wonder that such theories characteristically run up against counterexamples of a well-known type. For example: a man at a party intends to spill what is in his glass because he wants to signal his confederates to begin a robbery and he believes, in virtue of their prearrangements, that spilling what is in his glass will accomplish that; but all this leads the man to be very anxious, his anxiety makes his hand tremble, and so his glass spills. No matter what kinds of causal antecedents are designated as necessary and sufficient for the occurrence of an action, it is easy to show that causal antecedents of that kind may have as their effect an event that is manifestly not an action but a mere bodily movement. The spilling in the example given has among its causes a desire and a belief, which rationalize the man's spilling what is in his glass, but the spilling as it occurs is not an action. That example makes trouble particularly for a causal theory in which actions are construed as essentially movements whose causes are desires and beliefs by which they are rationalized. Similar counterexamples can readily be generated to make similar trouble for other variants of the causal approach.

I shall not examine the various manœuvres by means of which causal theorists have attempted to cope with these counterexamples.[1] In my judgement causal theories are unavoidably vulnerable to such counter-examples, because they locate the distinctively essential features of action exclusively in states of affairs which may be past by the time the action is supposed to occur. This makes it impossible for them to give any account whatever of the most salient differentiating characteristic of action: during the time a person is performing an action he is necessarily in touch with the movements of his body in a certain way, whereas he is necessarily not in touch with them in that way when movements of his body are occurring without his making them. A theory that is limited to describing causes prior to the occurrences of actions and of mere bodily movements cannot possibly include an analysis of these two ways in which a person may be related to the movements of his body. It must inevitably leave open the possibility that a person, whatever his involvement in the events from which his action arises, loses all connection with the movements of his body at the moment when his action begins.

II

In order to develop a more promising way of thinking about action, let us consider the notion that actions and mere happenings are indistinguishable in themselves. This notion is an important element in the motivation for causal theories. If it were thought that actions and mere happenings differ inherently, then it would be obvious that the way to explicate how they differ would be by identifying this inherent difference between them. It is because causal theorists think that there is no other way to differentiate between actions and mere happenings that they seek a differentiating difference among the events that precede them.

David Pears, who believes that desires play an essential causal role in the production of actions, makes this explicit:

---

[1] For discussion of the problem by adherents to the causal approach, cf. Alvin Goldman (1970), *A Theory of Human Action* (Princeton) 61–3; Donald Davidson (1973), 'Freedom to Act', in T. Honderich (ed.), *Essays on Freedom of Action* (London) 153–4; Richard Foley (1977), 'Deliberate Action', *Philosophical Review*, 86: 58–69. Goldman and Davidson evidently believe that the problem of avoiding the counterexamples is an empirical one, which is appropriately to be passed on to scientists. Foley's 'solution' renounces the obligation to provide suitable analysis in another way: he specifies conditions for acting and, when he recognizes that they may be met by spasms and twitches, he simply declares that such movements are none the less actions if they satisfy his conditions.

We simply do not possess the general ability to distinguish between those bodily movements which are actions and those which are mere bodily movements without using as a criterion the presence or absence of the relevant desire.... It is true that there are various intrinsic characteristics of bodily movements which do give some indication of their classification. For example, a very complicated movement was probably produced by a desire. But ... the simplicity of a movement does not even make it probable that it was not produced by a desire.

Because we cannot find any inherent characteristic of action which permits us to distinguish it reliably from mere bodily movement, we must therefore, in Pears' view, 'classify some bodily movements as actions solely by virtue of their origins'.[2]

Pears observes correctly that the movements of a person's body do not definitively reveal whether he is performing an action: the very same movements may occur when an action is being performed or when a mere happening is occurring. It does not follow from this, however, that the only way to discover whether or not a person is acting is by considering what was going on *before* his movements began—that is, by considering the causes from which they originated. In fact, the state of affairs *while* the movements are occurring is far more pertinent. What is not merely pertinent but decisive, indeed, is to consider whether or not the movements as they occur are *under the person's guidance*. It is this that determines whether he is performing an action. Moreover, the question of whether or not movements occur under a person's guidance is not a matter of their antecedents. Events are caused to occur by preceding states of affairs, but an event cannot be guided through the course of its occurrence at a temporal distance.

It is worth noticing that Pears is mistaken when he concedes that very complicated movements, though they may possibly be mere happenings, are probably to be classified as actions. The complicated movements of a pianist's hands and fingers do, to be sure, compellingly suggest that they are not mere happenings. Sometimes, however, complexity may quite as compellingly suggest the likelihood of mere bodily movement. The thrashings about of a person's body during an epileptic seizure, for example, are very complicated movements. But their complexity is of a kind which makes it appear unlikely to us that the person is performing an action.

When does complexity of movement suggest action, and when does it suggest its absence? This depends, roughly speaking, upon whether the movements in question cohere in creating a pattern which strikes us as

[2] David Pears (1971), 'Two Problems about Reasons for Actions', in R. Binkley, R. Bronaugh, A. Marras (eds.), *Agent, Action, and Reason* (Oxford), 136–7, 139.

meaningful. When they do, as in the case of the pianist, we find it difficult to imagine that the movements would have occurred, in just those complicated ways required by the meaningful pattern they have created, unless the pianist had been guiding his hands and fingers as they moved. In the epileptic's case, on the other hand, we find it unlikely that a person would have created such an incoherently complicated pattern if he had been guiding his body through its movements. A person's simple movements, as Pears notes, generally suggest neither an action nor a mere happening. This is because their patterns do not ordinarily strike us as being in themselves either meaningful or incoherent. They do not present us on their faces with any indication of whether or not they are being guided by the person as they occur.

Complexity of body movement suggests action only when it leads us to think that the body, during the course of its movement, is under the agent's guidance. The performance of an action is accordingly a complex event, which is comprised by a bodily movement and by whatever state of affairs or activity constitutes the agent's guidance of it. Given a bodily movement which occurs under a person's guidance, the person is performing an action regardless of what features of his prior causal history account for the fact that this is occurring. He is performing an action even if its occurrence is due to chance. And he is not performing an action if the movements are not under his guidance as they proceed, even if he himself provided the antecedent causes—in the form of beliefs, desires, intentions, decisions, volitions, or whatever—from which the movement has resulted.

III

When we act, our movements are purposive. This is merely another way of saying that their course is guided. Many instances of purposive movement are not, of course, instances of action. The dilation of the pupils of a person's eyes when the light fades, for example, is a purposive movement; there are mechanisms which guide its course. But the occurrence of this movement does not mark the performance of an action by the person; his pupils dilate, but he does not dilate them. This is because the course of the movement is not under *his* guidance. The guidance in this case is attributable only to the operation of some mechanism with which he cannot be identified.

Let us employ the term 'intentional' for referring to instances of purposive movement in which the guidance is provided by the agent. We may say, then, that action is intentional movement. The notion of intentional movement must not be confused with that of intentional action. The term 'intentional action' may be used, or rather misused, simply to convey that an action is necessarily a movement whose course is under an agent's guidance. When it is used in this way, the term is pleonastic. In a more appropriate usage, it refers to actions which are undertaken more or less deliberately or self-consciously—that is, to actions which the agent intends to perform. In this sense, actions are not necessarily intentional.

When a person intends to perform an action, what he intends is that certain intentional movements of his body should occur. When these movements do occur, the person is performing an intentional action. It might be said that he is then guiding the movements of his body in a certain way (thus, he is acting), and that in doing so he is guided by and fulfilling his intention to do just that (thus, he is acting intentionally). There appears to be nothing in the notion of an intentional movement which implies that its occurrence must be intended by the agent, either by way of forethought or by way of self-conscious assent. If this is correct, then actions (i.e. intentional movements) may be performed either intentionally or not.

Since action is intentional movement, or behaviour whose course is under the guidance of an agent, an explication of the nature of action must deal with two distinct problems. One is to explain the notion of guided behaviour. The other is to specify when the guidance of behaviour is attributable to an agent and not simply, as when a person's pupils dilate because the light fades, to some local process going on within the agent's body. The first problem concerns the conditions under which behaviour is purposive, while the second concerns the conditions under which purposive behaviour is intentional.

The driver of an automobile guides the movement of his vehicle by acting: he turns the steering wheel, he depresses the accelerator, he applies the brakes, and so on. Our guidance of our movements, while we are acting, does not similarly require that we perform various actions. We are not at the controls of our bodies in the way a driver is at the controls of his automobile. Otherwise action could not be conceived, upon pain of generating an infinite regress, as a matter of the occurrence of movements which are under an agent's guidance. The fact that our movements when we are acting are purposive is not the effect of something we do. It is a characteristic of the operation at that time of the systems we are.

Behaviour is purposive when its course is subject to adjustments which compensate for the effects of forces which would otherwise interfere with the course of the behaviour, and when the occurrence of these adjustments is not explainable by what explains the state of affairs that elicits them. The behaviour is in that case under the guidance of an independent causal mechanism, whose readiness to bring about compensatory adjustments tends to ensure that the behaviour is accomplished.[3] The activity of such a mechanism is normally not, of course, guided by us. Rather it *is*, when we are performing an action, our guidance of our behaviour. Our sense of our own agency when we act is nothing more than the way it feels to us when we are somehow in touch with the operation of mechanisms of this kind, by which our movements are guided and their course guaranteed.

Explaining purposive behaviour in terms of causal mechanisms is not tantamount to propounding a causal theory of action. For one thing, the pertinent activity of these mechanisms is not prior to but concurrent with the movements they guide. But in any case it is not essential to the purposiveness of a movement that it actually be causally affected by the mechanism under whose guidance the movement proceeds. A driver whose automobile is coasting downhill in virtue of gravitational forces alone may be entirely satisfied with its speed and direction, and so he may never intervene to adjust its movement in any way. This would not show that the movement of the automobile did not occur under his guidance. What counts is that he was prepared to intervene if necessary, and that he was in a position to do so more or less effectively. Similarly, the causal mechanisms which stand ready to affect the course of a bodily movement may never have occasion to do so; for no negative feedback of the sort that would trigger their compensatory activity may occur. The behaviour is purposive not because it results from causes of a certain kind, but because it would be affected by certain causes if the accomplishment of its course were to be jeopardized.

IV

Since the fact that certain causes originate an action is distinct from the considerations in virtue of which it is an action, there is no reason in principle why a person may not be caused in a variety of different ways to perform the same action. This is important in the analysis of freedom. It is widely accepted that a person acts freely only if he could have acted otherwise. Apparent counterexamples to this principle—'the principle of

---

[3] A useful discussion of this way of understanding purposive behaviour is provided by Ernest Nagel (1977), 'Goal-directed Processes in Biology', *Journal of Philosophy*, 74: 271ff. The details of the mechanisms in virtue of which some item of behaviour is purposive can be discovered, of course, only by empirical investigation. But specifying the conditions which any such mechanism must meet is a philosophical problem, belonging to the analysis of the notion of purposive behaviour.

alternate possibilities'—are provided, however, by cases that involve a certain kind of overdetermination. In these cases a person performs an action entirely for his own reasons, which inclines us to regard him as having performed it freely; but he would otherwise have been caused to perform it by forces alien to his will, so that he cannot actually avoid acting as he does.[4]

Thus, suppose a man takes heroin because he enjoys its effects and considers them to be beneficial. But suppose further that he is unknowingly addicted to the drug, and hence that he will be driven to take it in any event, even if he is not led to do so by his own beliefs and attitudes. Then it seems that he takes the drug freely, that he could not have done otherwise than to take it, and that the principle of alternate possibilities is therefore false.

Donald Davidson argues to the contrary that whereas a person does intentionally what he does for his own reasons, he does not do intentionally what alien forces cause him to do. While the movements of his body may be the same in both cases, Davidson maintains that the person is not performing an action when the movements occur apart from pertinent attitudes and beliefs. Someone who has acted freely might have done the same thing even if he had not been moved on his own to do it, but only in the sense that his body might have made the same movements: 'he would not have acted intentionally had the attitudinal conditions been absent.' Even in the 'overdetermined' cases, then, something rests with the agent: 'not . . . what he does (when described in a way that leaves open whether it was intentional), but whether he does it intentionally'.[5]

The issue here is not, as Davidson suggests at one point, whether a person's *action* can be intentional when alien forces rather than his own attitudes account for what he does. It is whether his *behaviour* can be intentional in those circumstances. Now the behaviour of the unknowing addict is plainly as intentional when he is caused to take the drug by the compulsive force of his addiction, as it is when he takes it as a matter of free choice. His movements are not mere happenings, when he takes the drug because he cannot help himself. He is then performing the very same action that he would have performed had he taken the drug freely and with the illusion that he might have done otherwise.

This example is not designed to show that Davidson is mistaken in insisting that there can be no action without intentionality, or in the

---

absence of pertinent attitudinal conditions. Even when the addict is driven to do what he does, after all, his behaviour is presumably affected both by his craving for the drug and by his belief that the procedure he follows in taking it will bring him relief. His movements, as he sticks the syringe into his arm and pushes the plunger, are certainly intentional. However, the relevant problem is not whether an action can occur apart from attitudinal conditions. It is whether it is possible that an action should be caused by alien forces alone.

This will seem to be impossible only if it is thought than an action must have attitudinal conditions among its causes. But it is not essential to an action that it have an antecedent causal history of any particular kind. Even if there can be no action in the absence of certain attitudinal conditions, therefore, it is not as prior causes that these conditions are essential. The example bears upon the point that is actually at issue, by illustrating how an action (including, of course, any requisite attitudinal constituents) may have no causes other than non-attitudinal or alien ones. Thus it confirms the falsity of the principle of alternate possibilities, by showing that a person may be caused by alien forces alone to perform an action which he might also perform on his own.

The example also suggests, by the way, that the attitudinal conditions of a person's action may themselves be alien to him. There is no reason to assume that an addict who succumbs unwillingly to his craving finally adopts as his own the desire he has tried to resist. He may in the end merely submit to it with resignation, like a man who knows he is beaten and who therefore despairingly accepts the consequences defeat must bring him, rather than like someone who decides to join with or to incorporate forces which he had formerly opposed. There are also obsessional and delusional beliefs—e.g. 'If I step on a crack it will break my mother's back'—which a person may know to be false but whose influence he cannot escape. So even if it were true (which it is not) that every action necessarily has attitudinal conditions among its antecedent causes, it might none the less be alien forces alone which bring it about that a person performs an action.

The assertion that someone has performed an action entails that his movements occurred under his guidance, but not that he was able to keep himself from guiding his movements as he did. There are occasions when we act against or independently of our wills. On other occasions, the guiding principle of our movements is one to which we are not merely resigned; rather, we have embraced it as our own. In such cases, we will ordinarily have a reason for embracing it. Perhaps, as certain philosophers would claim, our having a reason for acting may sometimes cause it to be the case that movements of our bodies are guided by us in a manner which reflects that reason. It is indisputable that a person's beliefs and attitudes often have an important bearing upon how what he is doing is to be interpreted and understood; and it may be that they also figure at times in the causal explanations of his actions. The facts that we are rational and self-conscious substantially affect the character of our behaviour and the ways in which our actions are integrated into our lives.

V

The significance to *our* actions of states and events which depend upon the exercise of our higher capacities should not lead us, however, to exaggerate the peculiarity of what human beings do. We are far from being unique either in the purposiveness of our behaviour or in its intentionality. There is a tendency among philosophers to discuss the nature of action as though agency presupposes characteristics which cannot plausibly be attributed to members of species other than our own. But in fact the contrast between actions and mere happenings can readily be discerned elsewhere than in the lives of people. There are numerous agents besides ourselves, who may be active as well as passive with respect to the movements of their bodies.

Consider the difference between what goes on when a spider moves its legs in making its way along the ground, and what goes on when its legs move in similar patterns and with similar effect because they are manipulated by a boy who has managed to tie strings to them. In the first case the movements are not simply purposive, as the spider's digestive processes doubtless are. They are also attributable to the spider, who makes them. In the second case the same movements occur but they are not made by the spider, to whom they merely happen.

This contrast between two sorts of events in the lives of spiders, which can be observed in the histories of creatures even more benighted, parallels the more familiar contrast between the sort of event that occurs when a person raises his arm and the sort that occurs when his arm goes up without his raising it. Indeed, the two contrasts are the same. The differences they respectively distinguish are alike; and they have, as it were, the same point. Each contrasts instances in which purposive behaviour is attributable to a creature as agent and instances in which this is not the case.

This generic contrast cannot be explicated in terms of any of the distinctive higher faculties which characteristically come into play when a person acts. The conditions for attributing the guidance of bodily movements to a

whole creature, rather than only to some local mechanism within a creature, evidently obtain outside of human life. Hence they cannot be satisfac-
torily understood by relying upon concepts which are inapplicable to
spiders and their ilk. This does not mean that it must be illegitimate for an
analysis of human agency to invoke concepts of more limited scope. While
the general conditions of agency are unclear, it may well be that the
satisfaction of these conditions by human beings depends upon the occurrence of events or states which do not occur in the histories of other
creatures. But we must be careful that the ways in which we construe
agency and define its nature do not conceal a parochial bias, which causes
us to neglect the extent to which the concept of human action is no more
than a special case of another concept whose range is much wider.

3

TRYING (AS THE MENTAL 'PINEAL GLAND')

BRIAN O'SHAUGHNESSY

Does a man who intentionally performs an action, try to perform that action? The oddity of *saying* 'He tried to walk across the road', of a normal able-bodied man in a setting of rural peace, may merely be the oddity of saying 'The president is sober this morning' (to use John Searle's[1] example). While it might be absurd to say this to certain people, it would be natural to say it to a man insisting that the president was blind drunk at his breakfast; and presumably, therefore, it can be true even though absurd to speak about in normal circumstances. Analogously, though we speak of trying only when success is in doubt, that doubt could dwell in someone *other than* agent or speaker; so it seems that we misunderstand this linguistic rule if we suppose it unconditionally to forbid mention of trying when one is in no doubt. It follows that sentences attributing trying to an agent must be perfectly intelligible, and capable of truth or falsity, in humdrum circumstances of this kind. Indeed, from a distance such sentences look likely to be true. For we are concerned with situations in which success is not in doubt; and after all, when success is not in doubt, it none the less truly obtains; and wherever there is succeeding, must there not also be trying? This leads me to suppose that trying is an essential constituent of intentional action as such.

1. INTRODUCTION

There is a perfectly genuine sense, suppressed by philosophers of commonsensical orientation, in which *no* event, including intended act-

Brian O'Shaughnessy, 'Trying (as the Mental "Pineal Gland")', *Journal of Philosophy* 70 (1973), 365–86. Reprinted by permission of the Editors of the *Journal of Philosophy* and the author.

[1] 'Assertions and Aberrations' (1966), in Bernard Williams and Alan Montefiore (eds.), *British Analytical Philosophy* (New York: Humanities).

events, can be foretold as an *absolute* certainty. That sense is this: the world is known to have harboured freak happenings; this is a permanent potential of the world, and of no situation can it be said: 'This situation bears a charmed life, it is guaranteed not to harbour such a freak'. Therefore it might. For one thing, we simply do not have 'tabs' on all empirically relevant regions: the depths of the brain and the nervous system, the centre of the earth, the heart of the fundamental particles, not to mention the farthest recesses of outer space—are all completely opaque and might conceivably harbour a disturbing agency. Therefore *the totally aberrant* can never be guaranteed not to happen.

Now it is precisely this refusal of empirical reality ideally to match our mental representations, it is this special brand of uncertainty hanging like a question mark over everything, that gives trying a permanent foothold in intentional action. For as the time of an intended act arrives, the die being cast and the will on the move, that special uncertainty continues to pervade the act. Even if I act with the utmost conviction, say, under the simple heading of moving my arm, I must simultaneously recognize that that arm may fail to budge; and the same holds of the intention as I act, for until completing the act I can always and always might change my mind. Therefore that peculiar uncertainty has two sources: my own mind, and all else; and the first allows for the possibility of freedom, whereas the second gives trying a foothold in all action. Because of this last, 'my will is about to move, but my body may not' retains its intelligibility in *all* situations, in the teeth of commonsensicality. Now this means that a willing that is distinct from bodily phenomena must obtain even in the most favoured epistemological settings. And this willing and trying are one and the same phenomenon.

The so-called indifference to existence, a mark of consciousness, makes one special demand of the world: namely, that it be such that consciousness is *always* potentially at variance with the outer world. Then there must be that in intentional action which is no exception in this respect. If action were simply identical with whatever happened to our limbs, so that the doing of people was as the mere doing of leaves fleeing before the wind, then, no doubt, trying would lose that foothold; but then will, and with it consciousness itself, would prove to be mythical. And yet if all action is intentional under some description,[2] there must at least exist a general

---

[2] Which is not quite true, *pace* Donald Davidson, because of the existence of *senseless action* such as the mere making of idle bodily movements, e.g. occasionally moving one's toes as one sits reading a book. Does nothing lie between being a corpse-like graven image and a vehicle for reason? *How else* but as action is one to characterize the making of these movements, and to what but *the person* is one to attribute them? One can hardly telescope them into mere spasms on the part of the toes. And does one not suddenly become aware of doing them? Yet it is not

intelligible matching of simultaneous intent and bodily phenomena; and the existence of this match is the other mark of the reality of the will. Therefore action marries an absence of *absolute* (i.e. unqualifiable) certainty with a general conformity of simultaneous intent and bodily phenomena. From the first feature comes the internal constituent of action, which is trying or (what we might as well call) willing. From the second feature we derive the causal efficacy in the physical world of that inner event of trying, and this is made possible through the coexistence of a psycho-psycho law connecting intending and trying and a psychophysical law connecting trying and bodily phenomena. Thus, an inner phenomenon with such causal efficacy is a permanent constituent of physical action. Now if intent and bodily phenomena were essentially given by each other, so that their conformity was mutual and essential, then trying would fade from the scene, but it would take will and consciousness with it. In what follows, we shall attempt to substantiate these claims.

2. INSTRUMENTAL TRYING

(A) *The omnipresence of trying in instrumental action*

Suppose a man sets out to start a car by pressing its starter button. Though he may have doubts about the success of his enterprise, it will be allowed that he can none the less 'have a try'. But trying entails the presumption on the agent's part that success is at least a remote possibility. Then let us suppose that, having tried, he succeeds. In that case he will have started the car as a result of trying, and here the trying-act causes the event, engine starting, that confers its name upon the act that he succeeds in performing.

If he was certain he would start the car, whereas we were dubious, then whereas he would have described himself as 'starting the car', we would have said that he was 'merely trying to start it'. Yet there is truth or falsity on this matter; for if the evidence showed it highly unlikely that it would

---

as if they were intentionally senseless, as it were the 'small talk' of bodily movement, for they are not chosen. But if Davidson's claim fails in the letter, it succeeds none the less in the spirit, for these trifling actions can express nothing more distinctive or more mental in our inner life than vague unease; and anyhow they are an afterthought in the scheme of things. They relate to standard examples of action somewhat as do objects that are *mere* lumps of stuff, say rough diamonds, to objects that are both lumps of stuff *and more*, e.g. artefacts, natural kinds. (But whereas all matter might have been in the form of mere chunks, these could not be the only examples of action in the universe.) Such senseless 'raw' acts are not amenable to interpretation, not even the interpretation of having no interpretation, and that is why they are not intentional under any description. Excluding them from the class of all actions would be roughly akin to excluding gold nuggets from the class of material objects.

start, and it failed to start, then it was true that he was merely trying. And this does not derive simply from his failure. For had it been known to all that he would have succeeded, he could have engaged in the activity of *starting the car* even though he might have been interrupted before he had completed the task. That is, *either* he was starting the car without having yet started it *or* he was merely trying to start it without yet starting it; and not both. That is, we oppose starting and only trying.

Now there is an argument designed to show that, even when the agent is and knows he is starting the car, still he *is* trying to start the car. This argument utilizes the possible existence of *divergent cognitive attitudes* toward the intended act. Thus, suppose a third person witnesses the spectacle; and suppose he knows the putative car-starter to be a fantastic pathological liar and this car to be a grossly unreliable instrument; and, to complete the picture, let us suppose him to know that the car starter has a *truly urgent* reason for making a quick getaway. The pathological liar gives vent in an absurdly complacent voice—as it happens on a sound factual basis, having just had the car completely overhauled and tuned—to the announcement that he is 'now about to drive off'. The sceptical onlooker has excellent reasons for doubting the truth of this evident boast. But, because he knows of the urgent reason for making a quick getaway, he does, I suggest, *know* one thing: namely, that the pathological liar is at least going to try and start the car. It follows that it is *true* that he is. Therefore, the car-starter is trying, even as he is more than trying, i.e. even as he is engaged in starting the car. (For he *is* starting it.)

Thus, the presence of scepticism in the onlooker has the effect of blotting out a fact from his view, viz. that the activity of the pathological liar is a starting of the car; but, in doing so, it lays bare a second fact. It seems that the sceptical but rational standpoint of this onlooker has uncovered a trying that must be present *whenever* anyone performs an instrumental task. Such onlookers act unwittingly as separator agencies, rather like magnets that one draws through a fine mixture of iron and copper filings. They draw to themselves an item normally concealed from view. Now all that remains is to extend this account to non-instrumental simple physical actions like raising an arm, and to offer a formula for trying itself. We will begin with the latter, though it is the less important enterprise of the two.

(B) *The definition of trying*

Trying consists in doing, intentionally and with just that purpose, whatever one takes to be needed if, the rest of the world suitably co-operating, one is to perform the action. This formula, rather than the claim that trying is doing what causes the event that gives its name to the action, is what I would tentatively propose.

It meets the difficulties posed by noninstrumental directed activities like walking from A to B. For here trying cannot consist in performing an act that causes an event that gives its name to the act; for the name of this act does not come from an *act-neutral event*. Whereas we name the act of starting the car through the event of car starting, we do not name the walk-act from A to B through any such act-neutral event. Yet this difference will be shown to be little more than a trifle. For what does trying to walk from A to B consist in?

I will mention three equally correct, perfectly compatible, and as yet unproved answers: (1) it consists in walking along such terrain as one thinks will get one from A to B; (2) it is trying to walk, and along such terrain as one thinks will get one from A to B; (3) it is trying to make movements, and of such a kind (etc.) as one thinks will get one from A to B. Of course, such characterizations are used *only in special circumstances*. The first would be natural with a person uncertain of the terrain, 2 with a person both uncertain of the terrain and very drunk, 3 with a person who is recovering from damage to his limbs *and* is very drunk *and* uncertain of the terrain. Happily, this last is no kind of norm; but still 1, 2, and 3 apply in the normal situation.

We discover what trying to walk from A to B consists in, by adopting the standpoint of the rational but sceptical onlooker who knows that the would-be agent has a powerful incentive for walking from A to B and whose scepticism here happens to mislead him. That is, we insert maximum rational scepticism into the situation as a separator agency (with Descartes as our inspiration) and see what it extricates (for that will be trying). Then in this case we discover that the would-be agent is, after all, trying to bring about an act-neutral event; and this holds of *all* physical action. Thus, all physical action involves a willing or bringing about of act-neutral bodily events; and the only difference between the act-neutral events in walking from A to B and in starting the car is that the latter but not the former gives its name to the act.

That act-neutral event is put on display in the following description of the walker's occupation. He is continuously trying to bring about some kind (or other, he need not exactly know what) of scissors motion of legs and arms that possesses the property of propelling his body along; and trying to do this so as thereby to get from A to B. These physical events are indeed act-neutral, for there is no difficulty in supposing them brought about by a machine that completely takes over his body. Though this is not the heading under which a normal agent acts—for this man acts under the heading, walking from A to B—the separator agency shows none the less that such a trying to make movement (etc.) is taking place. Agreed, this makes him sound like the Frankenstein monster venturing forth into the world; but a few laughs are neither here nor there. Anyway, it looks that way only because we illicitly insert the feature: acting under that heading. But of course I have yet to demonstrate that whenever one moves one's limbs one tries to move them.

(C) *The inner–outer dialectic*

Therefore I suggest that trying consists in doing, intentionally and with just that purpose, whatever one takes to be needed if, the rest of the world suitably co-operating, one is to perform that action. For one is always at the mercy of the world, which may at any moment, in the sense already specified, let one down. Indeed, it is a kind of rebuff that consciousness experiences at the hands of the world which, in casting us off from itself, throws us back into ourselves. Because omnipotence is the self-determination that would self-guarantee its own success, trying must be the internalization of the failure of omnipotence. This duality in action: that in the inner world *we* contribute what *we* contribute, while the outer world contributes whatever *it* contributes; this schism or lacuna, the uncertainty of realization, is the reason for *the omnipresence of trying* in all physical action. As T. S. Eliot said: 'between the motion and the act, falls the shadow.'[3] The presence of this shadow, and the omnipresence of trying, are merely concealed by the general reliability of the world. That is, by the absence of *essentially* unintelligible phenomena, such as the discovery of a mathematical formula that generates by substitution an endless number of great melodies; or of *absolutely* unintelligible phenomena, such as the sudden but persisting apparent mythicality of the Atlantic Ocean; or *relatively* unintelligible phenomena, such as the mutation today of a man into an ape. (Such things just do not happen.) Now, that trying is omnipresent beneath this physical reliability is revealed by the separator agency as, so to speak, he scrapes off the barnacles. Indeed, it is only through the general reliability or intelligibility of the world that willing can be a reality. Consciousness itself depends upon that reliability.

Schopenhauer says: 'I cannot really imagine this will without this body.'[4] If this wonderful remark is right, and I am convinced it is, the internal phenomena that occur when one engages in physical action must depend

---

[3] T. S. Eliot (1952), 'The Hollow Men', in e.g. *Collected Poems and Plays* (New York: Harcourt).

[4] A. Schopenhauer (1819), *The World as Will and Idea*, bk. 2, sect. 18.

upon the supposed reality of the body. More, we shall later see that those inner phenomena depend in general constitutively upon the *actual existence* of the body. Therefore, ours is not a Cartesian position, however insightful Cartesian accounts of the mind–body relation are in general, even though we insist that trying is an inner event that is omnipresent in all physical action. And so there seems to occur a kind of dialectic in our account of the will: one that swings from inner to outer, and back again to inner, and back again to outer: that is, from Cartesianism to logical behaviourism, and back again to the omnipresence of the inner event of trying, and on the rebound back again to a discovery of the essential mutual interdependence of trying and of the body upon one another. I suggest that this is a true dialectical synthesizing, rather than a hopelessly swinging pendulum that demonstrates the futility of philosophical argument. Part III of this paper is dedicated to establishing the interior wing of this dialectic, and part IV to the construction of what is at once a corrective in the opposite exterior direction *and* a synthesis of all that precedes it.

3. SIMPLE PHYSICAL ACTION

(A) *Abnormal examples of simple physical action*

Let us now consider the mere moving of a limb. There exist actions that consist in that *and no more*, e.g. crossing one's legs. Alternatively, actions that consist in that *and something else*, e.g. giving a wave. Then consider the case of a man who believes but is not quite certain that his arm is paralysed; suppose him asked at a signal to try and raise his arm. At the given signal he tries, and to his surprise the arm moves; but a moment later he tries again and thinks he has succeeded, only to discover on looking down that he has failed.

Now let us note that, until he looked, it seemed to him that the identical events had happened on both occasions. Three questions arise out of this. (1) Was trying an event on both occasions? (2) Was it an action on both occasions? (3) If it was an event, was it the same kind of event on each occasion? Consider these in turn.

(1) Was trying an event? Certainly, it was true or false that he tried when he saw the signal. Since it was true, there had to be that in the world, located at that time, which made his utterance 'I tried' true; and it was uniquely located at that time. Also, his trying had effects, like the travelling of message phenomena down his nerves or such as an attack of anxiety on his part or rage on the part of a doctor. And it had causes, whether they be

the desire to impress or the decision or intention to try at the time of the signal. Thus, we have here that which is a real individual constituent of the world, unrepeatably located at a point in space and time, with both causes and effects. And this establishes it as an event.

(2) Was trying an action on those occasions? If it is an action, it possesses the peculiar property of being an action that one cannot try to perform. But so what? It is an *internal action*, and internal action is an entirely special domain of the will, raising problems all its own (which I hope to elucidate in a later paper). After all, 'he tried to remember her name' unquestionably reports an action, yet probably it is not possible for him to 'try to try to remember her name', for all genuine attemptings seem to coalesce into being tryings to remember her name. Therefore there exist internal actions that we cannot try to perform. So why not trying itself?

Now the following features are reasons for classifying that trying to raise the arm as an action. It was *an event*, whose occurrence came as *no surprise* to the subject, that he knew of *in no way*, that happened because *he chose* that it should, that he *intended* should happen, whose origin lay in his *reasoned desires*, and that came into existence through the use of *no device*. Thus, it displays almost all the salient features of uncontentious examples of action. And one additional consideration exists in favour of judging it to be an action. Namely, when techniques are employed in trying, say in trying to start a car, trying consists in performing an action to which one stands in a certain relation, viz. that of taking it to be such that, all going well, one thereby performs the attempted action. I conclude that the event of trying that happened as the subject saw the signal was an action, albeit a unique example of the species; but to placate those whose minds shy at that description, I will sometimes refer to it merely as a 'chosen event'.

(3) Was the trying-act that occurred on each occasion the same in kind? On both occasions the man tried to raise his arm, and on each occasion it was an event and action. But was it the same kind of event-action? Now *the best possible description* of that chosen event was: 'trying to raise his arm'. Indeed, that is *all* the agent can say of that mysterious occurrence: it is *the ultimate psychological description*. Then on each occasion that description has application, and the agent knows so independently of knowing whether his arm moved. Thus, he knows he tried to raise his arm each time, irrespective of knowing the truth concerning bodily phenomena, and on each occasion the best possible or ultimate first-person description of that trying-act is the same. I cannot see how to avoid the conclusion that the same kind of trying-act-event occurred on both occasions. In sum: on either occasion a freely chosen event occurred, trying to raise the arm, and

it was the same kind of event both on the occasion of success and on the occasion of failure.

The same act-event occurred, both when the arm rose and when it did not. Therefore, trying and arm rising must be *two* events and two *distinct* events. But now trying must rate as a psychological event; for it is an event whose origin is psychological, whose occurrence is known of in no way, an event that he can know to have happened without knowing whether arm rising occurred, that is not immediately given as located at any specific point in the body (in contrast with toothache or arm-rising), and so on. Therefore, when this man succeeded in raising his arm, a psychological event, freely chosen and intended, occurred side by side with another event, a distinct event, a merely physical and act-neutral event, the event of arm rising.

(B) *Normal examples of simple physical action*

Now let us call once more onto the stage our music-hall team of two: the fantastic and pathological liar, who happens for once to be right, together with his mirror opposite, the sceptical third-person onlooker, who happens for once to be wrong. And let us see whether we can generalize this account to *all* cases of simple physical action. The situation, easy enough to anticipate, is that the liar-agent has a recuperating arm which has made a sudden dramatic recovery; meanwhile the sceptic has had the bad luck to be talking to an ignorant, impressive-looking, and fatuous doctor, working in the ward in which the patient is situated, who assures him it is very unlikely the patient will manage to move his arm until weeks have elapsed; but the liar has had the good fortune to be talking to an eminent specialist who assures him his arm has recovered, and that he will be able to move it the moment the bandages are removed. Finally, the bandages at last having been removed, we suppose the patient to have a powerful incentive to move his arm at a given signal. This is the scene that confronts the sceptic, who views it wryly. At last the signal is given, and the lying patient extravagantly announces that he will now raise his arm for all to see. The sceptic, in a perfectly rational frame of mind, dryly comments, having set eyes upon the most desirable incentive, 'Well, I am sure that he will at least have a try.' And this is something that he *knows*, for he knows the psychological context; and therefore it is something that is *true*; and so this person who knows he has a normal arm tries to raise it when he raises it. *Therefore, when anyone who is aware that he can raise his arm, proceeds then intentionally to raise that arm, he also tries to do what he actually did and knew he could and would do.*

Thus, in normally raising an arm, two distinct events simultaneously happen: one active and psychological, a trying event; the other a merely physical event of a kind that might instead have been caused by no more than a shove, an arm-rising event. Then how do these events relate to each other? Let me briefly return to the man whose arm rose when he was asked to try and raise it. *Why* did his arm rise? Of course, it rose because the muscle had healed; but that merely gives the causally necessary state conditions for the act-event of arm rising to occur. The event explanation is that *he tried* to raise his arm. Provided trying is an event that explains arm rising, that is how things must stand. The event, his trying to raise his arm, explains the distinct simultaneous act-neutral physical event, arm rising. These two distinct events are linked by an explanatory connection. Given a body in a normal state in a world that at that moment permits arm rising—and, because of hysterical phenomena, we add, given a mind in a moderately healthy state—trying to raise the arm is a sufficient condition for the occurrence of the act-neutral bodily event of arm rising. Indeed, a law-like generalization exists, going from left to right, linking trying to raise the arm and arm rising. And let us not suppose, because of the odd qualification of 'given a mind in a moderately healthy state', that these standard conditions for the application of the law are *outré* and exceptional; on the contrary, that precisely characterizes their absence. Therefore, trying both explains and is a sufficient condition of arm rising, in normal physicopsychological circumstances. Therefore the event, trying to raise the arm, normally *causes* the event, arm rising. And this also is very far from exceptional, and happens in *all* cases in which one intentionally raises an arm. A psychological event, doubtless one that is low-grade in the hierarchy of the mental, causes a simple bodily event that might instead have resulted immediately from a mere shove. Therefore, the logically necessary requirements of an intentional act of arm rising are: a causally linked pair of events, trying and arm rising.

We require the occurrence of two events, one mental and the other physical; and the existence of a causal relation between the two. No doubt we further require that this causal interaction occur within the body *and also* meet additional specifications. What these are need not be our concern, but clearly the event of arm rising must derive from the inner event of trying *as a further exemplification of the law*: 'In a person in a healthy state (etc.), trying to raise the arm is a sufficient condition of arm rising.' This law-like general truth could obtain only if there were proper or standard causal paths leading to arm rising and, therefore, only if there were improper or illicit or (so to say) accidental paths. In sum, when a man intentionally raises his arm, trying to raise the arm causes the act-neutral event of arm rising. That is, an inner active chosen event causes or brings about an outer or merely bodily event. I think we can take this to be the sense of the perfectly harmless and intuitively obvious truth, that, when a man raises his arm by intent, then *he* brings about the movement of his arm. We can now say *how* he brings this about: it is by trying.

4. THE SPECIAL STATUS OF TRYING

So much for one side of the dialectic. The antithesis is constituted of three important truths; and while they *are* antithetical truths, they synthesize all that precedes them; and this is already evident in the manner in which they ameliorate the more disturbing aspects of the thesis.

A preliminary word on trying itself. The ultimate psychological description of this act is: trying to raise the arm. Therefore this inner event relates in essence to a real or remembered or possibly merely imagined arm object and to an intended individual rising of that object. So far this is nothing special, for the same kind of relation, in which external entities are internally represented, holds if I image an existent material object. But those three further features of trying lift it clear of the ruck of other internal phenomena. This softens the blow of discovering in physical action a psychological event that is distinct from the act-neutral physical event; for resistance to the supposition of such an item might well stem from a confused discernment of its highly unusual character. Those three features are as follows. First, we can only try to do what we conceive of as at least a remote possibility. Second, while trying relates internally to the putative act, a correlative internal relation holds between both actual and putative act and trying. More, while trying relates internally to putative arm-object, a correlative general internal relation holds between the body and trying. Third, law-like generalizations link intending at the time with trying, and trying with the act-neutral event; that is, psycho-psycho and psychophysical laws obtain in this primeval region of the mind. Consider these claims in turn.

(A) *The putative goal of trying is: the possible*

If I point a gun at the sun, saying 'I am trying to hit the sun', you would interpret this as fantasy or as a joke; and that is because we both know that I know it is impossible to hit the sun. But a madman might try to shoot the sun, since madmen can think it a possibility, exactly as a young child might try to grasp the moon. Therefore, although the attempted act need not be possible, it must be located by the agent outside the realm of pure fantasy and within the bounds of possibility (as we say). For the putative goal of trying is: the possible.

The peculiar implications of this fact are most apparent in cases of paralysis. A man with a paralysed arm can try to raise it, and even if he fails can continue trying, but there is a *limit* to how much he can keep on trying. In the end, the capacity even to try just fades away. Odd as that may seem, this is simply because it will sink into most heads that, for the moment at least, the act is impossible. And yet it need not sink into the head of an idiot, who might indeed keep on and on dementedly trying. Immediately, this makes trying look to be a sheer myth. 'Keep on and on *what*?', one wishes to protest; for the idea of an internal event so hemmed in by cognitive restrictions seems ridiculous. Now I think this is because we take trying to be either like imaging or an internal straining, and therefore we construe it either as an internal representing or else as an autonomous undirected act. No matter. This section is, after all, dedicated to demonstrating *the unique status* of the act.

(B) *The essential mutual interdependence of trying and act-object*

The second peculiarity of trying resides in the fact that the (act that is the) object of trying itself internally depends upon trying. This is in contrast with mental imaging, for the imaged object exists independently of consciousness. Therefore imaging is a sheer internalization or introjection (as psychoanalysis would say). But the object of trying necessitates, and, as we shall see in section V, actually involves, itself. If I may anticipate the conclusions of that discussion, trying putatively relates to what involves an intimately and peculiarly related bodily movement *and* itself! Thus, it is almost like a sketch for a picture that includes itself! Therefore, neither trying nor the act itself is prior to the other. Trying is not an introjection of what is external, and neither is its putative object an externalization or projection (as psychoanalysis would say) of trying.

Now a further consideration shows the relation between trying and its act-object to be even more intimate and egalitarian. Schopenhauer (op. cit.) described the body as 'objectified will,' and I propose to interpret this in the following way. We single out a human body as one object of a certain kind, and the kind is: body of a human being; and this mammal is such that that object could not be what it is if it did not harbour the somewhere potential for being employed in action. An organism that contained *no* potential for action, howsoever deeply buried and inaccessible, could not be a human being (or a camel or a mosquito, for that matter). This does not guarantee that any part must have the function/ functions it has, but ensures that it is part of what is as such a vehicle of the will. 'I cannot really imagine this will without this body' can be supplemented by the equally interesting 'I cannot really imagine this body without this will'.

In sum: trying is neither post nor prior to action, and is a trying to do what involves itself. Neither it, nor the attempted act, relates to the other as introjection or projection; and even the physical event one aims at causing is change in what is itself of such a kind as necessarily to harbour the somewhere potential for being the immediate vehicle of trying. This absolute egalitarianism of trying and act, this essential interdependence between what is internal and what is a closely bound union of internal and external, takes us far from Cartesianism. It is the externalizing and synthesizing corrective to the antithesis to logical behaviourism.

(C) *Trying as mental 'pineal gland' (or: the psychophysical law)*

The inner event, trying, though merely internal and therefore lacking absolute guarantee of its object in the outer world, has no other existence than as a putative cause of a bodily event. Were the act of trying *independently specifiable*, an act like the imaging of a bodily event, then whereas that act would putatively relate to items in the outer world and also putatively be a cause of arm rising, it would retain its identity as a distinctive act of a certain kind. We would then merely *redescribe* the act as 'trying to raise the arm', and its causal efficacy would be a simple contingent property akin to that of the thought of a steak to cause watering of the mouth. *Now that would indeed usher in some version of Cartesianism; and its falsity must be very strongly emphasized.* For although trying to raise an arm *is not*: whatever causes arm rising; it *is* and is essentially: an x which in the state of psychophysical normality, world permitting, is sufficient to cause arm rising. This is an essentialist psychological analysis of trying. Because 'trying to raise an arm' is the ultimate psychological description of what causes arm rising when one raises one's arm, we do not *redescribe* any mental event as 'trying to raise the arm'. To repeat: were the causal power of trying an external property, like the power of fear to cause pallor, willing would be mythical. Thereupon the whole edifice of animal action, and with it consciousness itself, must inevitably collapse. Therefore trying, in being essentially a cause of a physical phenomenon *and* a linchpin of consciousness, serves a crucial bridge function between mind and body, not unlike that allotted by Descartes to the pineal gland. It is the key point at which the essential mutual interdependence of mind and body can be openly seen to be part of the scheme of things. It is like a psychic promontory that all but juts into the physical world.

In this respect it is to be contrasted with two other closely related primordial denizens of the mind: intention and desire. For in their case there exist no psychophysical laws like: in a body in a normal state, world permitting, necessarily trying is a sufficient causal condition of arm rising. After all, without fear of the charge of abnormality, one can always rescind an intention or be too anxious to attempt to fulfil a desire when optimal conditions for fulfilment present themselves. This alone obstructs the possibility of a law in the case of desire and intention. But the only impediments to the efficacy of trying are extrabodily constraints *or* bodily harm *or* severe mental pathology that doubtless has some sort of physical basis. For it would be a serious mistake to treat hysterical incapacity to move a healthy limb as on a par with common or garden manifestations of common or garden anxiety. The latter, but not the former, are part of the normal scene.

Because trying is mental, there can be no absolute guarantee of its object: that is, of its success. But because it is in essence normally a cause of its physical objective, its causal power cannot be an external property like the power of a thought to cause goose pimples. Thus, trying to perform a physical act falls between sheer physical movement and ordinary mental activity. The first is inconsistent with its internal character, and the second would make of the potential for physical action a merely contingent endowment of animal consciousness (for its causal status makes it unique in the mind). But we know that trying to move a limb is an internal event and that the potential for physical action is as primitive a feature of animal consciousness as perception (even as life itself). Are we seriously to envisage a conscious-type organism that nowhere in the depths of its bodily structure has ever harboured the most incipient of potentials for causing bodily change? In fact, trying to move a limb is a unique mental event simply in being *standardly* a cause of physical change; for all other examples of causal power on the part of the mental, like the power of an erotic thought to change the pulse rate, are either merely typical or haphazard powers. But even more important is the fact that trying is *in essence* normally a cause of bodily change. For in this we find the material for demonstrating that trying to move a limb is the mental 'pineal gland'.

Thus, it is a primitive constituent of animal consciousness, which yet constitutively cannot exist without bodily phenomena. For how could trying be real, and be no more than *the* event-cause of willed physical movement, without the guaranteed physical possibility of *some* willed movement?

Desire and imagination, while being free to range over the unreal, are tied none the less in various ways to the world; but the bond between trying to move a limb and the body is tighter. For it is one thing to say: I cannot embark upon what I take to be an act of moving the arm *without supposing there to be* an occurrent arm movement. It is quite another thing to say: I cannot embark upon what I take to be an act of moving the arm without there *actually existing* the organically based possibility of willed bodily movement. The shift from a purely thought-mediated relation to one that is both that *and causal*, accounts for this dramatic alteration. For how could a causal law have any reality if reality could provide *no* exemplifications of that law? Could it hang in the mid-air of thought? At the very least, the soul must as such be searching for its body!

That the dualistic account that we have given of physical action has not severed the mind from the body, is evident when we review the features of trying just considered. Thus, a primitive element of animal consciousness, the trying to perform a physical action, has as object that which involves both that act of trying *and* change in what necessarily harbours a potential for being the immediate vehicle of such trying acts; it is neither post nor prior to that object. Further, because it is essentially normally the cause of bodily phenomena, its reality depends constitutively upon the reality of such bodily phenomenal effects. It seems to me that we have here succeeded in closing the circle, in binding mind and body indissolubly together while recognizing their genuine diversity. It is a true synthesis.

(D) *Omnipotence and the psycho-psycho law*

Before leaving Section IV, I will briefly discuss the psycho-psycho law connecting intending with trying. That law postulates an entailment between occurrent knowledge that the instant of that realization is the time of intended action, and trying. The main problem that requires discussion is: what are the consequences of supposing the non-existence of this entailment? I believe them to amount to a form of omnipotence. By that I have in mind the pernicious idea that true self-determination must be answerable to *nothing* (as if people were like that Steinberg figure that was engaged in drawing itself!).

Certain entailments fail to go through. Thus, if I intend to perform act x at t', and now is t', it is not entailed that at t' I try to perform x; for it is not entailed that I know I *now* intend to perform x. Again, if at instant t'' I know I now intend to perform y, it is not entailed that at t'' I try to perform y; for 'now' can be a 'protracted now,' say a whole week, whereas t'' is an instant. Then what is the position if 'now' is an instant? Does an entailment hold? Or does some third possibility lie between a last-instant flagging of resolution and the entailment? Does that precious ingredient of the universe, self-determination, lurk in so slight a crevice? I think not, for if I tried to perform an intentional action then I must have intended to try. Does not intentional action express intention?

Immediately, this seems to deflate the law to nothing. And the truth is that the law is both of great importance, and also nothing to write home about. It is important because it disproves omnipotence and intelligibly links present action with past cogitation, and trivial because of its circularity. Concerning the latter: in formulating that law and speaking of 'occurrent knowledge', we *redescribed* a psychological event whose ultimate psychological description was 'at t' it seemed to me that that was an instant at which I intended to do x', as 'at t' I realized that I intended at that instant to do x'. Therefore it is only under redescriptions that an event-law holds; and, in addition, the logical bond between intentional-act-event and intention-state is a truism. Nevertheless, it is of great importance. *For this is how action takes place* and how it preserves its crucial link with the past. For the act emerges translucently out of an intention, and characteristically that *same* intention was at an earlier moment formed through deciding, and it persisted until the act. And there can be no mystery about how the intention leads into the action. For if at t' there occurs the realization that that instant is an instant at which one intends to act, then inevitably that instant is one in which the will is *beginning to move*. Necessarily, their time is one and the same. (Think how people begin to wheel around *as* they remember they have forgotten something.)

Yet it is natural to think that something more needs to be interposed between intending and trying if the act is to be one's own: something one might term 'an act of will'. But that creates a gap that could never be closed. It is a false account of self-determination. Certainly, as the setting for action comes into view, intentions require supplementation by subsidiary intentions *cast in the ostensive mode*, e.g. as I round the corner the intention to get *an* apple is supplemented by the intention to get *that* apple in the bowl before me. But that is *all* that is needed if the will is to move. And yet it is natural for action thus determined to seem automatic. For it seems to locate the originating force outside the self and within the intention. Thus, we find ourselves in the ridiculous position of playing off a person and his intentions one against the other! But that would make of that person: a nothing! Here, too, we stand in need of a dialectical synthesis: of the self as self-determining, and as determined by reason; and of the self as self-determining in the present, and of self-determining the present in the past. Being people, we are vehicles of reason and of our past reasonings.

Now I suggest that that seeming automatism amounts to no more than this: that in the instant in which actual time and intended-act-time are seen to coincide, *there is nothing left for one to do but act*. Small wonder, for their time is one; and the great error is to postulate a necessary temporal gap, as if to allow space for some unmotivated mental mid-air leap. But it is a parody of this position to suppose that in that instant of realization one has lost the power of choice, for that is precisely what one is exercising. We are running our head up against nothing but—commitment! Therefore we are seriously misled if we take that supposed automatism to signify, if only in the slightest degree, that the act was taken out of our hands—for example, if we make of the mind an alien force that precipitated us into action. If the mind gave a shove, that was *us* freely precipitating ourselves into action. It was self-determination. And, therefore, in deciding to act (and so forming an intention) and thereafter abiding by that intention, oneself determines (through *mental agreement* but through no further *willing*) what in a knowledge-context entails movement of the will. All one needs to do to ensure action, provided the world suitably co-operates, is knowingly to abide by one's intention until the chosen instant. Action inevitably ensues.[5]

The process of forming supplementary intentions can readily come to an end. All that is then required, if the will is to move, is the occurrent knowledge that a certain instant is the time of intended action. And so the transition from intention to will is entirely pellucid. Indeed, *what else* but intention could get the will on the move? A self-determination that is modelled on the miracle? That is, intervention as an outsider in the interior mental mechanics of one's own actions, breaking oneself free therefore from one's own desires and values? (From nature itself!) But this would be to conceive of self-determining as akin to the whims of a Deity responsible to nothing. Shakespeare, in depicting the sickness of omnipotence, was presumably thinking of this problem when he had Caesar say (concerning intended action): 'The cause is in my will: I will not come|That is enough to satisfy the senate.'[6] For this fantastically supposes the explanation of intended action to lie in the motion of the will, understood as an explanatory ultimate. But that would banish intelligibility from all action.

---

[5] In this I find myself in disagreement with none other than Franz Kafka, among whose aphorisms occurs the following daunting thought: 'It is conceivable that Alexander the Great, in spite of the martial successes of his early days, in spite of the excellent army that he had trained, in spite of the power he felt within him to change the world, might have remained standing on the bank of the Hellespont and never crossed it, and not out of fear, not out of indecision, not out of infirmity of will, but because of the mere weight of his own body.' (Franz Kafka (1933), 'Reflections on Sin', in *The Great Wall of China and Other Pieces* (London: Martin Secker) aphorism no. 36.)

[6] *Julius Caesar*, II. ii.

Thus, we have here a psycho-psycho law, linking intending and trying. It takes the following form: if a man at an instant in time realizes that that instant is an instant at which he intends to perform action x, then logically necessarily he begins trying to do x at that very moment of realization. This unconditional law joins the conditional law uniting trying with bodily phenomena, a psycho-physical law, and together they display, with absolute clarity, the transition from some earlier mental event of deciding to the bodily phenomena that are its natural outcome. The existence of such precise and simple laws shows that we are dealing with a rock-bottom primeval region of the mind.

5. THE ANALYSIS OF PHYSICAL ACTION

When a man intentionally raises his arm, the following happens. His arm rises; he tries to raise his arm; and the latter event causes, along acceptable bodily paths, the physical event of arm rising. These are the logically necessary and sufficient conditions of an intentional action of raising the arm. Then what analysis are we to give of that action? How does the act relate to these related phenomena? What *is* the act of raising an arm?

Four possible answers come to mind. (1) The action is identical with the mere rising of the arm: that is, with a rising of the arm that is suitably caused by a trying. (2) It is nothing but the causing of arm rising by the trying-act. (3) It is identical with the trying to raise that arm: that is, with a trying to raise the arm that succeeded in causing arm rising. (4) The act of raising the arm is a complex event, constituted out of a causally linked pair of events, the trying and the arm rising, which are (as we saw in Section IV) 'made for one another'. Consider these answers in turn.

(1) Is the act of raising the arm identical with a rising of that arm that was suitably caused by a trying to raise it? This has the disagreeable consequence that the act of raising the arm must have been caused by one's trying to perform that act and that this causation must be mediated by unknown bodily phenomena. But we know that the most immediate cause of trying to perform the action, say, a desire or a becoming aware of a physical situation, was the most immediate cause of the act itself. In any event that disagreeable consequence clearly shows alternative (1) to be false, and we can safely set (1) aside. Thereafter, however, the position is less clear.

(2) This is the doctrine that the act of raising the arm is the causing, by a trying, of a bodily movement of arm rising. But what *is* 'a causing'?

Presumably, it must be whatever one affirms to be the case, when one affirms that trying caused arm rising. Thus, it can hardly be some third distinct event, a distinctive causing-event, sandwiched between any two causally linked events. This would be to suppose it just another link in a causal chain—one that threatens to multiply itself to infinity! For if every event has a cause, so has the cause-event; and so on indefinitely. Therefore it cannot be a distinctive event. And it cannot be either of the causally linked events. Indeed, it simply is not an event at all.

But do we not allot times to causings? But do we not, in the same derivative sense, allot places to spatial relations? Think of the statement, given perhaps in the stage directions at the beginning of a play: 'Over in the corner of the room, a sofa stands next to a piano'. Is not this the same in structure as: 'At midnight, a flash of lightning caused an explosion'? But these sentences merely state the location of related items, and so we read the latter as saying that 'a flash of lightning and an explosion, the former causing the latter, both happened at midnight'. This does not require that we understand the causing as something which, though not an event, yet has a position in time that is uniquely its own. If it has a position in time, that position is uniquely that of the effect. Therefore it might be said that thesis (2) should be taken to say that the act *is* the effect, arm rising. And so there is a reading of thesis (2) that simply returns us to thesis (1).

Thus, we take (2) either to say what (1) asserts, or to say that the act is a distinctive causing-event, or that it is a causing that is not an event. The first two possibilities have been rejected, which leaves us with the claim that the act is not an event. But that is entirely unacceptable. After all, we know it has event-effects, such as the breaking of an electric-light globe, and event-causes, such as deciding or coming to believe that now is the time for the intended act; and we know it has an unrepeatable position in space-time, and was constituted through the ongoing of an activity of raising an arm. What more do we need if we are to demonstrate that it was an event? Therefore we also reject thesis (2).

Now all that is communicated by the sentence, 'He intentionally raised his right arm', is that two events that were suitably causally linked, a trying-event and an arm-rising event, happened together. Thus, it communicates that they were simultaneous. (I do not propose to discuss here the difficulties raised by the supposition that trying at t' to move an arm might cause arm movement at a later t''. Let me merely note that one might have the power to try at t' to move one's arm at t'', but that the normal power is to try at t' to move one's arm at t'.) Now if that is all that is communicated by the sentence, and if the act is an event, and if it cannot be the effect-event, then we are absolutely forced back upon theses (3) and (4). That is, (3) that the act is a trying that succeeds, or (4) that it is a complex event constituted out of a successful trying and an arm rising, suitably causally linked.

I will begin by discussing (3), not because I am certain it is wrong, but because I see difficulties in that position. Thesis (3) states that an intentional act of raising one's arm *is* an inner act of trying that succeeds. Now this drives physical action under cover, for it retreats in entirety into the realm of the mind; and it also expels it from the class of those events which can immediately cause effects beyond the body through (say) collision. More, it implies that the act of raising the arm causes arm rising, and so it follows that all the evident physical effects of the act must be mediated by arm rising. The act becomes literally invisible, and proves to be a pure and very special kind of mental act. All of these I take to be counter considerations to (3). One further counter consideration is this. While in an everyday sense I know why this trying caused this arm rising, there is another sense in which I am ignorant as to why it did; for there is much between brain and arm for scientists to investigate that should elucidate why any particular act of trying caused a particular arm rising. Therefore, if my act of arm raising knocked a vase off a pedestal, it should be possible for scientists to investigate the question, 'Why did his act of raising his arm knock over the vase?', in part, through searching for the causal link between brain and arm. And I should be able to say: there is a stretch in the causal chain linking my act and the movement of the vase, that is totally opaque to me. This looks implausible, seeing that I *saw* my elbow hit the vase! Taken in conjunction with the above difficulties, with the supposed invisibility and purely mental character of physical action, I believe it is enough to reject thesis (3).

Therefore we are forced back upon thesis (4), the doctrine that the act of raising an arm is a complex event constituted out of two causally linked simultaneous events that were 'made for each other'. Now no especial difficulty need arise in postulating such an item as a complex event; and anyhow examples abound. A short burst from a motorbike is constituted out of an array of discrete sounds linked in a certain relation; if a sudden blast of wind tears all the leaves off a tree at one go, then this denuding of the tree, an event of a certain kind with a phenomenal cause, is constituted out of many distinct events of leaf removal; and so on.

So much for the concept of complex event. Now if the act of raising an arm is constituted out of two event-parts, an act of trying and an arm-rising event, there exist unique binding forces between these events that should make of their union something more than a mere conventionally concocted parcel of events. The simultaneity, the uniquely law-like psychophysical causal link, the fact that the ultimate psychological description of trying is 'trying to raise the arm', the fact that the arm is part of an object that necessarily is a possible vehicle for the will, and so on. In short, all that we saw, in Section IV, that led us to say of these two events that they were 'made for each other'.

This analysis of physical action permits it to have immediate psychological causes and immediate physical effects. On the one hand, variously a desire or decision or intention or awareness that this is the intended time; on the other hand, a toppling vase. It also does justice to our intuition that in physical action, even more than in emotion, body and mind are united. It has the superficial confirmation that it implies that one directly perceives physical action without mediation by the body, yet cannot necessarily tell, merely by looking, that what one has seen *is* physical action. Now it is undeniably natural to suppose that physical actions exhibit these traits. That they have immediate psychological causes and immediate physical effects, unite mind and body as nowhere else, are directly witnessable and yet not immediately perceptually identifiable as action; and further, that they are both viewed from the inside (for only the person who tries knows in no way that he tries and acts), and from the outside (in being directly perceived), and are yet the one event appearing to different vantage points.

Now this last final observation is hardly *a proof* of thesis (4), but it emphasizes its plausibility. For *if* the action is an event; and *if* two distinct events, trying and arm rising, are entailed by the occurrence of the action; and *if* it can be neither of these two events; then, if only by elimination, we seem forced to accept thesis (4), which states that it is a unique union of both.

6. POSTSCRIPT

Two years after this article was written in 1972 I changed my views—along the following lines (see B. O'Shaughnessy, *The Will*, Cambridge: Cambridge University Press, 1980). The correct theory of instrumental action leads directly to the conclusion that *all* successful instrumental tryings ('attempts', 'shots at', 'go's at') *are* the succeeded-in act. This generality then suggests the universal principle that successful attempts *are* as such the deed succeeded-in (and other arguments confirm this claim). Now since walkings are openly visible phenomena, do not occur in the privacy of one's mind, and encompass leg movements, and since whenever we act we try to do so, trying to walk must encompass leg movements and must surely therefore be physical in status. Meanwhile, these tryings are known-of to their agent (under *some* description) with mentalistic immediacy, are absolutely immediately caused by act-desire and act-intention, and must therefore be psychological in status. (There being no ontological fence for them to sit upon!) Thus, this phenomenon must be of physical *and* psychological status. Then in the light of the nomic ('non-deviant') psycho-physical requirements for physical action, it is a small step to the further theory that physical actions are psychological events whose physical characterization is known *a priori*: namely, as the full activation of the motor system, which is to say as a single causally bonded developing event that begins in the brain and culminates in the desired limb movement (see O'Shaughnessy (1980), ii. 212–14, 286). This is a dual-aspect theory. It is so both ontologically *and* epistemologically—in a way Physicalism is not. What on this account is unique about physical action is that it is the only psychological phenomenon whose physical characterization is *a priori* known. This is the nub of a dual-aspect theory of bodily action. It is constitutionally specific where Physicalism—which is consistent with all sorts of quasi-Cartesian interiorist analyses of physical action as well as with the dual-aspect analysis—is not. The theoretical assets of this account are considerable.

4

ACTING FOR REASONS

ROBERT AUDI

If we do not know for what reasons a person acts, we do not fully understand that person. If we do not know any reason for which an agent does
something, we cannot adequately assess whether, in doing it, that agent is
acting rationally. And if Kant is right, unless we know the reason(s) for
which an action is performed, we do not know its moral worth. But what is
it to act for a reason? Clearly, acting for a reason is closely related to acting
intentionally, to acting rationally, and to acting on the basis of practical
reasoning. An action for a reason apparently must be intentional; an action
based on practical reasoning must be performed for a reason; and at least
the paradigms of rational action must be intentional. Whether there are
some equivalences among these notions will be discussed below. Let us
begin by laying out some guiding assumptions.

1. ACTIONS, REASONS, AND PRACTICAL REASONING

Consider an ordinary case in which a representative agent, *S* (Sue, let us
say), acts for a reason. In the course of mailing impersonal invitations to a
conference Sue has organized, she puts John's aside. Her reason: to delay
it until after she sends him a condolence letter (his mother has died). If this
case is *typical* of action for a reason, we may say the following. (1) Her
action is explainable by appeal to her reason; for example, she put the
invitation aside in order to delay it until after she sends condolences. (2)
She believes something to the effect that her putting it aside will delay it.
(3) If asked why she is putting it aside, she will tend to answer by appeal
to her reason. (4) Her action is, in some way, a response to, and occurs
because of, her reason. For instance, if she ceased to have the reason

From *Philosophical Review* 95 (1986). Copyright © 1986 Cornell University. Reprinted by
permission of the publisher and the author.

because she decided to send no condolences, then (assuming she had no other reason for the action) she would no longer put the invitation aside. (5). In putting it aside, she has a sense of what her reason for doing this is and of her action as a response to the reason. She may, for example, be aware of wanting to delay the invitation and of her action as delaying it. (6) She knows or believes that she is putting it aside, and knows why. (7) The action is, *relative* to her reason for it and her belief that the action will delay the invitation, prima-facie rational. And (8) she controls whether she carries the action out and, to some degree, how. It is up to her, for example, that she flips the invitation aside with her fingers rather than her pen. Generalizations of (1)–(8) do not apply to all actions for a reason; but they hold in paradigm cases, and an account of acting for a reason should both unify and refine them. The account I shall give will do this by exhibiting action for a reason as explainable by motivation embodying that reason, and as guided by S's beliefs, reflected in S's cognitive dispositions, and, in a special way, under S's control.

There are many kinds of reasons. My focus is reasons *for which* one acts. It should be uncontroversial that if S A's for a reason, her A-ing is motivated. For convenience, I also assume that if S A's for a reason, she A's because she wants something, in a very broad sense of 'want'.[1] Thus, a reason, r, for which one acts, can be expressed by an infinitive clause giving the content of the relevant want, Where A is, for example, phoning, S's reason might be to say that she is late, and the relevant want—to say that she is late—is what motivates her phoning. This is not to identify motives with wants; I simply assume that wants are pervasive motivating elements in action. Let us say that a reason for which S A's is, in part, a state of affairs r, which (a) expresses something she wants, and (b) is connected with her A-ing through an appropriate belief, for example that her A-ing will achieve r. Thus, S wants to say she is late, believes phoning will achieve this, and phones for that reason, that is, to say she is late.[2] These assumptions may well be neutral regarding a plausible internalism which says that certain judgements, for instance that one ought to A, can provide a sufficient reason for which one A's (and can explain one's A-ing); for such judgements may perhaps imply wanting in the broad sense. If they do not, then an internalist reading of the account of acting for a reason to be

---

[1] That 'want' has a sufficiently broad use is argued in my (1973), 'Intending', *Journal of Philosophy* 70. Other terms might suffice, however.

[2] It may seem that some reasons for action are not expressible infinitivally. Consider A-ing because one wants *that* Sam benefit. I believe that the reason here is (say) *to contribute* to his welfare, but no major point below turns on this issue.

developed may simply replace wanting by the relevant judgements or by other motivating elements, for example attitudes or intentions.

We sometimes refer to people's wants, beliefs, fears, and other states as reasons for which they act. S's wanting wine might be cited as her reason for leaving just before dinner. Such states express reasons as described above and might be called *reason states*. It is reason states, and not reasons proper, that I take to have causal power, though for convenience I shall sometimes speak of the latter in causal terms. Facts may also be cited as reasons: the fact that Tom has a fine record might be the reason for which S asks him to speak. But while many kinds of things are cited as reasons for which an agent acts, the context normally provides enough information for infinitival expression of the agent's reason.

It is important to distinguish reasons for which S A's from other kinds. *Reasons to A* are normative and impersonal. There can be reasons to keep one's promises, even if nobody wants to. *Reasons for S to A* are personal and normative. That A-ing would fulfil S's yen to visit China might be a reason for *her* to A. *A reason S has for A-ing* is personal, but need not be normative; it is also potentially motivating, whereas a reason there is for her to A need not be. Thus, if she *believes* A-ing will fulfil her yen, she *has* a reason for A-ing. *A reason for which S A's*, however, must be a reason she has *and* actually motivates her A-ing, in a sense implying that it is a *reason why she A's*, that is, one that at least partly explains her A-ing. But a reason why she A's need not be one for which she does so; the action could be simply due to drugs. When S A's for a good reason, for example writes a recommendation to keep a promise, all five kinds of reasons are involved: keeping her promise is a reason to write; a reason for her to do so; a reason she has to do so; a reason why she writes; and a reason for which she writes. Even A-ing for a bad reason involves at least the last four kinds of reason.

In construing reasons for which one acts as the contents of motivating wants, I am not denying that beliefs are also crucial. Indeed, a reason for which one acts can be conveyed by citing a belief—such as that by phoning one can say one is late—as effectively as by appeal to the motivating want. Intuitively, the want—or intention, judgement, or whatever plays the motivational role in our account—*moves* one to act; the belief *guides* one in acting. One's reason, through its relation to one's motivating want, is that for the sake of which, and on account of which, one acts; but given different beliefs one would not (other things equal) do what one does do. For these and other reasons, beliefs are as important as wants in the account to be developed.

Acting for a reason may seem equivalent to action based on practical reasoning.[3] Such action occurs when, for example, one considers one's goal, say to visit China, sees a way to realize it, decides on that way, and acts accordingly. Certainly (1)–(8) apply to actions based on practical reasoning, and one might think that S A's for a reason if *and* only if her A-ing is based on such reasoning. But not all actions for a reason are so based.[4] Moreover, even assuming we understand practical reasoning, it is very hard to explicate an action's being *based on* it.

There is, however, a correspondence between acting for a reason and acting on the basis of practical reasoning. If S A's for a reason, for example buys a ticket in order to visit China, we may construct a practical argument which represents, in its major premiss, S's motivating want (to visit China) and, in its minor, S's guiding belief (that she must buy a ticket). The correspondence holds whether or not S actually reasoned from these premisses to a conclusion. Indeed, we may construe acting for a reason as a concrete *realization* of such a practical argument. The point is not simply that S *instantiates* the argument, that is, has the want and belief expressed in its premisses and does the thing indicated by the conclusion. There are at least four other factors. First, the premisses represent the *structure* of the causal and explanatory basis of the action, viz. the relevant want and belief. Second, the explanatory relation which that want and belief bear to the action mirrors a kind of support (or prima-facie justificatory) relation which the premisses of the argument bear to its conclusion. Third, S is at the time disposed to appeal to the argument if asked to explain or justify her A-ing, rather in the way one appeals to a rule or practice one has been automatically following. If, for example, S is asked why she A-ed, she is disposed to say things like, 'Because I wanted to r and believed A-ing would enable me to r'. Fourth, where S's A-ing is a realization of a practical argument, then even if the action is not based on practical reasoning, the explanatory relation between her reason and action is just what it would have been if (other things equal) she had A-ed on the basis of actual reasoning from its premisses to its conclusion; she would, for example, have A-ed for the *same* reason, though perhaps more deliberately for it.

When S simply infers the conclusion of a practical argument from its premisses, I call the argument *inferentially realized*. My point here is that it may also be at once noninferentially and *behaviourally realized*, through a spontaneous action that expresses S's motivating want and is guided by

---

[3] This has been held or implied by a number of recent writers. I have cited some and discussed the rationale for the view in my (1982), 'A Theory of Practical Reasoning', *American Philosophical Quarterly* 19.

[4] I have defended this in 'A Theory of Practical Reasoning', cited in n. 3.

a belief which S need not entertain. Practical reasoning can also occur *without* S's acting on it.[5] There the practical argument is only partly realized, whereas its full realization implies S's doing what its conclusion favours. Thus, while acting for a reason is not equivalent to acting on the basis of practical reasoning, we may take as a guiding idea—which will help us interpret (1)–(8)—the view that action for a reason is a realization of a practical argument. Granted, this idea presupposes some understanding of practical reasoning, but the idea is clear enough to help explicate acting for a reason.

2. THE BASIC ELEMENTS OF ACTION FOR A REASON

In the light of the examples and guiding ideas set out above, we can begin to clarify acting for a reason. Initially, our focus will be on quite simple actions, and for the present we may ignore acting for more than one reason.

Explainability

Clearly, if S A's for a reason, r, she must act *on account of r*, and her wanting to r must move her to A. Thus, the motivating want, the want to r, plays a causal role in a sense implying that S A-ed at least partly because she wanted to r, where 'because' has explanatory import. This suggests an *explanatory condition*: if S A's for r, then her wanting to r is part of what explains why she A's. This in turn normally implies that S *also* A-ed partly because she believed an appropriate relation to hold between her A-ing and r. But neither the want nor the belief need be a necessary condition: S can A for a reason even if something other than the relevant want and belief (such as an alternative goal) is sufficient for her A-ing. The relevant want and belief, must, however, be important enough, for her A-ing, to have the appropriate explanatory power.[6] Moreover, if A-ing is temporally extended, they must *sustain* it and have comparable explanatory power: while A-ing is in progress, citing them must be adequate to explain why S *is* A-ing, in the same way it might explain why S did something that was

---

[5] An important case of such failure to act is weakness of will. In my (1979), 'Weakness of Will and Practical Judgment', *Noûs* 13, I have argued that the relevant kind of weak-willed action is possible.

[6] An action for a reason may be *overdetermined* in at least two ways: (1) there may be other reason states, *or* non-mental factors, that *would* have made S A if her want and belief had not; (2) other factors may, at the very same time, also *partly* cause her A-ing.

instantaneous. For instance, assuming there is no other reason for her *A*-ing, then just as, in the latter case, *S* would not have *A*-ed if, other things equal, she *had* not wanted to *r*, so, in the former case, *S* would not *continue* to *A* if, other things equal, she did not *still* want to *r*.[7]

Acting for a reason, however, takes far more than satisfying the explanatory sustaining condition. Imagine that *S* wants to wake Jan, a guest, and believes that a way to do it is just to open her bedroom door. Now suppose this want and belief evoke the thought of waking her, and that this thought makes *S* nervous. Her nervousness might cause her to drop the breakfast tray, and by dropping the tray against the door she might open it. It would then be (indirectly) because of *S*'s want and belief that *S* opens the door. Yet *S* does not do so for a reason. She does it *because of a reason* (strictly, because of a reason state), not for one. Her *A*-ing is an *effect* of her want, but not a *response* to it. To see these contrasts better, let us explore the role of beliefs.

Connecting beliefs

The example just given suggests the importance of belief in guiding an action for a reason to its goal. Suppose *S* had believed instead that dropping the breakfast tray was the best way to wake Jan, and had dropped it in order to wake her. Then *S* would have acted for, not merely because of, a reason. What has been added? When a *connecting belief*, together with a motivating want, brings about the action (in a suitable way), *S* acts not just because of but *in the light of* a reason. Such beliefs make *A* relevant, for *S*, to her reason. In the first case, it just happens that *S*'s opening Jan's door is an action for which she has a reason. But when *S A*'s for a reason, it is to be expected that *A* in some sense match her reason. This is largely due to the guiding role of connecting beliefs. Suppose *S* wants to saw a plank at right angles, pencils in a line, and carefully saws. She is guided by her belief that sawing straight down will yield a square cut. Thus, if she realizes she is cutting leftward, she pressures the saw to the right. Her motivation sets her goal; her connecting belief guides her to it. The guidance may involve other beliefs, say, that she is sawing left (and elements, such as perceptual

---

[7] In referring to *A*-ing as temporally extended I presuppose an intuitive notion of *performative extension:* reading a letter takes time in a way touching a button does not. But suppose *S*'s touching a button causes, days later, a boiler explosion. Then *S*'s exploding the boiler might be said to exhibit *generational extension*. Even if the bodily action at its base—*S*'s performative contribution to exploding the boiler—is instantaneous, her exploding the boiler is—arguably—not completed until the explosion that her bodily action causes. Performative extension is my concern. I leave open the possibility that generational extension is only a matter of the effects of action.

data, besides beliefs). Corrective adjustment may also be automatic, in the sense that the guiding is done without explicit awareness. And where the action is so routine that no guidance need be exercised, guidance may be simply a matter of readiness to adjust. Here the action itself is in a way automatic. In all three cases, what counts, for S, as a correction depends on her connecting belief; and that belief is essential to what we might call the *discriminative* character of action for a reason.

If acting for a reason implies acting in the light of it, must S *believe* she has a reason for A-ing, or believe the reason for which she A's to *be* a reason for which she A's? Often, acting for a reason satisfies these conditions. But it need not. Just as one can see a face in the light of a lamp, without believing that there is lamplight on it, or believing, of this lamp, that it lights the face, one can A for a reason, without believing that one has a reason to A or believing, of this reason, that it is a reason for which one A's. Moreover, presumably a child can act for a reason before acquiring the concept of a reason, and thus before acquiring beliefs like these, which entail having that concept.

The lighting example can mislead, however. For while S need not believe a lamp to bear some relation to an object she sees in the light of it, she must believe some appropriate relation to hold between her reason and any action she performs for it. For instance, S might believe her A-ing to be a means to r. Since a connecting belief may be *de re*, it does not require S's having the concept of a reason, or that of any specific connecting relation, such as causal sufficiency, nor, I think, any concepts beyond the grasp of the least conceptually advanced creatures that can act for a reason. Such relations might be called *conduciveness relations*; for example, if S's reason for opening the door is to wake Jan, S may simply believe her opening the door to be a way to wake Jan. S's connecting belief may also be *de dicto*, say, that opening it is the best way to wake Jan, or that if she opens it she will probably wake Jan, though in these cases S must perhaps also believe, of some appropriate bodily action (like grasping), that *it* is opening the door.[8] As these cases suggest, it may be impossible to specify the connecting belief or motivating want simply by using S's name and the relevant action-description, for example by speaking of Sue's opening the door. For what S wants is often self-referential, say, that *she* open the door; and S

---

[8] For a plausible less inclusive view of how one must conceive one's reasons, see Stephen L. Darwall (1983), *Impartial Reason* (Ithaca and London: Cornell University Press); he says, 'What distinguishes the agent's reasons [for acting] . . . is that they are considerations she took to be reasons *for* her *to* have acted, considerations that, in her view, were grounds for a positive rational appraisal of the act' (p. 205). Cf. pp. 206–7. Apparently, then, if S A's for r, she takes r to be a reason for her to A. I prefer a weaker view, but the cases Darwall describes are common and important.

need not conceptualize or have beliefs about her goal in terms of either her own name or any particular true description of herself.[9] It is hard to specify S's reason precisely, but no major thesis of this paper turns on how this problem is solved.

Our second requirement, then, is the *connecting belief condition: S A*'s for a reason, r, only if there is some connecting relation, C, such that (a) S believes C to hold between her A-ing and r, or believes something to the effect that C holds between her A-ing and r, and (b) this belief (or set of beliefs) guides, and partly explains, S's A-ing. Like S's motivating want, a particular connecting belief may not be a necessary condition for S's A-ing, but some connecting belief must play an actual part in producing or sustaining the action.

Attribution

The explanatory sustaining condition and the connecting belief condition are not all we need. Consider a variant of the guest example. Suppose that S's wanting to wake Jan, *together with* S's believing this to be best done by rattling the breakfast tray, makes S nervous, and that this nervousness, by making her rush, causes her to rattle the tray unintentionally. Our first two conditions could apparently hold, yet she does not rattle the tray for a reason. One might tackle the problem by requiring that the relevant want and belief produce A *directly*. But consider Ken, an aphasiac accident victim who habitually grunts when he wants food and believes grunting will get the nurse to bring it. Suppose he now takes a deep breath, gets ready to grunt, and then unexpectedly grunts at a pitch and loudness that surprise him and in a way that feels involuntary. The grunting might be a 'direct' result of the relevant want and belief, yet fail to be action for a reason.

We can understand such cases better by reflecting on how Ken might explain his grunt if his awakened room-mate asks why he grunted. Given that Ken realized he grunted unintentionally, he presumably would not think he did it because he wanted to call the nurse, nor anything else suggesting he did it for a reason. To be sure, if he is embarrassed and wants to rationalize doing it, he might cite the reason he *had* to grunt. But a natural answer would be something like, 'I don't know—I suddenly found myself grunting automatically.' Yet when one A's for a reason, one quite

---

[9] Hector-Neri Castañeda has developed this point. See, for example his (1979), 'Philosophical Method and Direct Awareness of the Self', in Ernest Sosa, (ed.), *Essays on the Philosophy of Roderick M. Chisholm* (Amsterdam: Rodopi), esp. 29–35. Also relevant is Lynne Rudder Baker (1982), *'De Re* Belief in Action', *Philosophical Review* 91. For criticism of Castañeda see Steven E. Boer and William Lycan (1980), 'Who, Me?', *Philosophical Review* 89. For a reply by Castañeda, see his Self-Profile, sect. IV, in James Tomberlin (1985) (ed.), *Hector-Neri Castañeda* (Dordrecht and Boston: Random House).

naturally cites the reason if asked why one A-ed. Indeed, the reason tends to occur to one without inference or observation, and so readily that even if one disapproves of it, self-deception or repression may be needed to block one's becoming conscious of it when asked why one A-ed. We have at least this much privileged access to the reasons for which we act. In acting for a reason one normally has a sense of one's agency; this sense, in turn, tends to give one knowledge or potential knowledge of the action (or of one's attempt at it) as causally grounded in the motivating want and the connecting belief(s). The beliefs constituting such knowledge are among the characteristic marks of acting for a reason. Ken lacks both the sense of agency and beliefs of this sort.

In the light of these points, one might think that in acting for a reason S *must* have a sense of acting in response to it, and that we should adopt some such phenomenal condition. Perhaps we should. There is surely some way one's A-ing for a reason is cognitively reflected. But suppose one A's for a reason with one's mind wholly on something else. On a walk one may be buried in thought, yet wave at a passing friend in order to greet him. It is not clear that one need have a sense of agency in so waving. I suggest a related thesis weaker than but consistent with the phenomenal condition: that if S A's for a reason, then, quite *independently* of seeking reasons she had or might have had for A-ing, she is disposed, *noninferentially*, to attribute her A-ing to the motivating want and connect-ing belief(s). This disposition *may* be based on a sense of agency; it cer-tainly seems rooted partly in the way A-ing for a reason is *belief-guided*. Indeed, it might be a kind of impression made by the action even if S lacked a sense of agency, as in absent-mindedly waving. That sense and this disposition could both be due to the same elements underlying the action, that is, to processes involved in its generation by the motivating want and connecting belief. By contrast, if Ken has any disposition to attribute his grunting to the reason he had for it, it is *derivative*; it depends on his seeking a reason (say, to rationalize his odd behaviour). Nor does his attribution seem noninferential: he very likely infers that his wanting food must have produced the grunt 'by itself'.

The sort of disposition in question is often not manifested, particularly in behaviour; only at certain times do we tend, for example, to explain our actions. But the disposition is especially likely to be manifested should S try to explain or to justify her A-ing. This is indeed part of the force of the idea that action for a reason is a realization of a practical argument: since the explaining want and belief—of whose causal efficacy S normally has a sense—correspond to the premises of the argument, it is natural that S be disposed (in effect) to invoke that argument if she tries to explain or to justify her A-ing. If , however, an action for a reason arises, as I assume it

may, from wants or beliefs that are in some sense unconscious, the disposition may be *inhibited*, perhaps by whatever keeps *S* from being conscious
that she has those wants or beliefs. But apart from, say, self-deception or
repression, we expect people who are acting for a reason to be able to tell,
noninferentially and very reliably—though by no means infallibly—for
what reason they are acting.

To capture some of what has emerged I propose an *attribution condition:*
if *S A*'s for a reason, *r*, then, independently of seeking reasons she had or
might have had for *A*-ing, she is noninferentially disposed to attribute her
A-ing to her wanting to *r* and her believing some connecting relation to
hold between her *A*-ing and *r*. (Connecting beliefs may also be *de dicto*,
and the disposition normally persists after *S A*'s; but we may ignore these
complications.) This disposition can be manifested not only in overt behaviour, for example speech or writing, but also in thinking or even belief. If
one has the thought that one *A*-ed because one wanted revenge, this may
suffice for attribution of the action to that want. Suppose, however, one is
acting routinely and simply forms the belief that one *A*-ed for revenge.
I take such belief formation to be a minimal case of attribution, though I
do not consider it (or belief) something one does. We do say things like,
'If you believe that, you are attributing ignoble motives to him.' Either
attribution need not be behaviour or believing is sometimes sufficiently
behavioural to count as attribution.

We might call the kind of attribution just illustrated *causal*, since *S*
conceives the want for revenge as causing her action. Similarly, attribution
may be *explanatory*. Our case might also illustrate that; for *S* might take
her wanting revenge to explain her *A*-ing (though one could regard a want
or belief as causative but not consider it explanatory, or vice versa). There
are at least two other kinds of attribution. Suppose Tom is removing
labels. We ask why. 'I'm recycling envelopes.' Call this kind of attribution
redescriptive, since he attributes his action to his (connecting) belief that he
is recycling, and implicitly to his wanting to recycle. He also explains both
what he is doing and why (though redescription is possible without explanation, and explaining action is possible without redescription). Since I
assume that attribution may be manifested in beliefs, and that knowing
entails believing, I regard the attribution disposition as manifested in the
(extremely common) case of *knowing what one is doing*, understood to
imply believing (or at least taking) one's action to be, as in Tom's case, a
realization of (or contribution toward) one's goal. The attribution here
may be redescriptive; but we should not assume that a linguistic description must figure in attributive beliefs. We might thus call such attribution
cognitive.

Cognitive attribution is conceptually elementary enough to occur in tiny children. Imagine Amy, who has just learned to talk, stretching toward a cookie and saying, 'Want cookie!' In the context, she expresses her wanting the cookie and her believing that (for example) reaching for it will get it. Moreover, she in some sense *sees* her stretching as getting (or trying to get) it. If so, she may be viewed as manifesting a disposition to attribute the action, cognitively, to the relevant belief and want. This disposition does *not* entail a further disposition to explain or justify the action in terms of them. (She might only partially grasp the concepts of wanting and believing.) To be sure, since the attribution may be *de re*, even if it is causal she need only to be taken to attribute, to the want and belief on one side, and to the stretching, on the other, an appropriate relation, such as making happen. I leave open whether she may be so described. I suggest only that she may believe her stretching to have a property—say, getting the cookie—appropriate to connect it with her guiding belief and motivating want. Perhaps even prelingual children and some animals may have such beliefs. I see no need to deny that. If they may, then they can act for reasons in the sense of our account. Some philosophers are inclined to say that for prelingual children and animals, talk of acting for reasons is metaphoric: while they may *have* reasons for acting—given suitable wants and beliefs—and while there surely are reasons, perhaps including wants and beliefs, *why* they act, they do not full-bloodedly act for reasons. Other philosophers think it obvious that such creatures act for reasons. I suspect these cases are borderline; if they are, it is appropriate that the account does not decisively include or exclude them. Moreover, any account of acting for a reason will encounter borderline cases at *some* point on the evolutionary ladder, and it may be a merit of the proposed account that borderline cases arise for it where reflective intuitions differ, and that the materials of which it is built—for example, the different sorts of reasons sketched in Section I—may be so arrayed that they are progressively acquired in the development of an agent. Perhaps the development of human agents mirrors the evolution from mentally lower to higher creatures, and any account that does justice to acting for a reason as applied to normal adults will encounter hard cases as we go back into infant and animal behaviour.

Preliminary account

The three conditions so far proposed account for most of the eight points set out in Section I. If S's putting the invitation aside satisfies the explanatory, connecting belief, and attribution conditions, then clearly her doing so is explainable by appeal to her reason, she has an appropriate belief connecting her reason with her action, and she is noninferentially disposed to attribute her action to her connecting belief and motivating want. Moreover, her action is a *response* to her reason. Not only does she act because of the corresponding want and the connecting belief; her putting the invitation aside is also sustained by them: if, for example, she ceased to have them, then (if she has no other reason for the action), she would stop putting it aside. The action is, then, subject to alterability due to change of reason. So much for points (1)–(4).

The three proposed conditions also accommodate (5)–(7). First, if S satisfies them, then typically she has an awareness both of the reason for which she is acting (delaying the invitation) and of acting in response to it (strictly, to the want expressing the reason). That awareness, in turn, indicates both why it is natural to explain one's action by redescribing it in terms of the reason for which one is acting, and why agents have a special authority regarding what they are doing. Secondly, the conditions enable us to see why, in typical cases of acting for reason, S knows she is doing (or at least that she is trying to do) the thing in question. Thirdly, they suggest why, at least normally, an action for a reason is prima-facie rational relative to S's motivating want and connecting belief(s). It in some sense serves her (motivating) reason: her A-ing is aimed at realizing a want (purpose, goal, etc.) of hers. S may overlook a conflicting want more important to her, but her A-ing may still be prima-facie rational.

The three conditions can also deal with a number of problematic examples introduced in the literature, for example by Chisholm, Goldman, and Davidson.[10] In Chisholm's case, a nephew accidentally runs over his uncle as an indirect result of nervousness produced by the motivating want (to inherit a fortune) and connecting belief (that by killing his uncle he would inherit it). The want and belief may not even sustain the action, since the nervousness has its own momentum; but clearly the agent has no sense of acting for a reason and is not noninferentially disposed to attribute the action to them. Goldman's agent wants to offend his host and believes that grimacing, upon tasting the soup, will do it; but he grimaces unintentionally because, as a result of (discovering) his want and belief, a friend befouls his soup. Here the want and belief do not sustain the grimace; and

---

[10] See Roderick M. Chisholm (1966), 'Freedom in Action', in Keith Lehrer (ed.), *Freedom and Determinism* (New York), 19–20; Alvin I. Goldman (1970), *A Theory of Human Action* (Englewood Cliffs: Prentice-Hall), 54; and Donald Davidson (1973), 'Freedom to Act', in Ted Honderich (ed.), *Essays on Freedom of Action* (London: Routledge and Kegan Paul). For critical discussion of these cases as challenges to a causal account of action, see Irving Thalberg (1984), 'Do Our Intentions Cause Intentional Actions?' *American Philosophical Quarterly* 21.

given the way it is involuntary and unexpected, he would doubtless be disposed to attribute it to something strange in the soup, not to his own motivation. Davidson's case of a climber whose want and belief unnerve him so that he loosens his hold on a dangling companion is similar to Chisholm's: it turns on an intermediary with its own momentum, and it does not satisfy all of our first three conditions.

So far, then, our conditions account for many important points about acting for a reason and show why so acting is not simply behaviour caused by appropriate wants and beliefs. The conception embodied in the conditions is roughly this: an action for a reason is a discriminative response to that reason, performed in the light of it, and such that one is noninferentially disposed to attribute it to that reason. Let me elaborate. Because an action for a reason is grounded in a guiding belief and a motivating want (normally one stronger than competitors—else one would not normally act on it), it expresses both one's intellect and one's will. This is in part why it is a response and not a mere effect. Because an action for a reason is performed in the light of a reason, it tends to change with alterations in that light: if one ceases to have the reason, one tends to cease doing the thing which expresses it; and if one senses that one is not acting in accord with one's guiding belief, one tends to make corrective adjustments, for example pressuring the saw to the right to get a square cut. Action for a reason thus expresses one's present make-up, not merely one's motivational history. And because we are disposed as we are to attribute our actions for a reason to that very reason, we tend to know noninferentially what we are about: our sense of agency is not just a consciousness of movement, but a (normally automatic) cognitive grasp of the direction—at least the psychological direction—of our behaviour. This is partly why, as agents, we are not merely well-placed spectators of our own actions. The attribution condition helps to capture this cognitive grasp that we tend to have of our own agency: without the self-knowledge it provides for, we would be cut off from what we do; it could, to be sure, be rather like acting for a reason, but if there is no such noninferential disposition at all, as opposed to one that is overridden by self-deception or undermined by error, then the behaviour falls short of acting for a reason. It might be a patterned result of our reasons, but not fully action for a reason.

Accidentality

We must now explore how an action for a reason is controlled. We might begin with an idea that emerged in discussing attribution: normally, if S

A's for r, then either she knows she A-ed for r, or at least is in a position to know this by virtue of her sense of her own agency. S *need* not know why she A-ed; she might have another reason for A-ing which, while she hopes not to be influenced by it, may still have motivated her. S may also not know she *is* A-ing, as where she calls a warning to distant swimmers, but cannot tell if they hear her. Even then, however, she knows for what reason she is calling out, and for what reason she is warning them *if* she is.

Consider, by contrast, a case where, unbeknownst to S, her right arm has become paralysed. She might still want to greet Jan and believe that waving is the way to do so. Now imagine that there happens to be a brain-affecting machine nearby so adjusted that her want and belief cause it to emit rare radiations; these just happen to affect her brain in the right way to overcome the paralysis, so that (indirectly) the want and belief produce her waving, after which the paralysis recurs. Imagine that the machine also induces in her a noninferential disposition to attribute the waving to the want and belief that caused it. Has she waved for a reason—to greet Jan? There is much to be said. Even assuming that the attribution condition can be satisfied in this way, the accidental genesis of the waving prevents S from knowing that she waved in order to greet her friend. For it is simply a lucky accident that the relevant want and belief (through the machine) produced the action; and if she believed that she waved *because* of them (taking the connection between them and her action to be normal), she would be mistaken, and her attribution of her action to the reason would not yield knowledge. We should also consider the observer's viewpoint: whereas we can normally know certain things about S's motivation from her behaviour, here our likely inference would not yield knowledge, but only justified (accidentally) true belief. The action is not an *expression* of her reason for it. That, in turn, helps to differentiate this case from acting for one of two competing reasons, say, one selfish and one unselfish, yet not knowing which is responsible for the action: there the connection between the explaining reason and the action is not accidental and the action *is* an expression of that reason.

If an action for a reason cannot be one produced by the reason (state) accidentally, how should we conceive nonaccidentality? May we say that the relevant want and belief(s) *reliably* produce the action? Consider an analogy. Suppose that, from a distance, Ann sees Joe in a shop window and believes him to be a man. Imagine that the figures usually in such windows are manikins. Being myopic, Ann would have taken one to be a man if she saw it instead. Her vision is unreliable, and even if she justifiably believes

Joe to be a man, she does not know him to be one.[11] Compare the greeting: S would have believed she waved because she wanted to greet her friend, even if her wanting to do so had not activated the machine and thereby her arm, but instead the machine had similarly raised her arm by itself. Observers, moreover, would form the same beliefs about her motivation whether it was efficacious or not. Such facts suggest that if S A's for a reason, the reason produces the action reliably: otherwise, neither S nor observers can know what they normally can about her motivation or belief. The action is a mere product, not an expression, of her reason.

Compare this case, however, with one in which Tom sinks a putt, yet, being a very poor golfer, succeeds only by great luck. Has he sunk it for a reason, say, to win? We are pulled in two directions. If we conceive sinking the putt as the same action—under another description—as hitting the ball, we tend to say yes, since clearly he hits the ball for a reason. If we conceptually isolate his sinking the putt and view it as a different action that he can bring off only by lucky accident, we tend to say that it is not for a reason. Notice, moreover, that if Tom is so inept that he is lucky even to hit the ball, we are much less inclined to say he sank the putt for a reason. For though there is something causally significant he does for a reason, viz. swinging *at* the ball, we do not view his sinking the putt *as* this (wild) swinging, under another description, for example 'hitting it'.

Let us explore reliability and accident through another case, Russian Roulette. Zed puts one bullet in a nine-chambered revolver, spins the magazine, and, hoping to kill himself, fires. If he shoots himself, is it for a reason? Again, there are conflicting inclinations; but his shooting himself is plausibly identified with his pulling the trigger, and one is inclined to say that he has shot himself for a reason: to kill himself. Now imagine a firearm with 2,000 chambers. Should we say the same? I think so, for given the actual causal route from the triggering, which is produced by his reason states reliably and in the usual way, to the shooting, the latter may be described *as* triggering; and this description of the shooting anchors it to his reason. By contrast, suppose Tom had missed the ball and hit it on his backswing, whereupon it struck a tree, bounced off a golf cart, and then rolled into the hole. It is doubtful that he sinks it for a reason, if only because it is not clear *what* action for a reason to view as his sinking it. The contrast indicates a further point: the issue is not mainly a matter of the probability with which, given what S clearly does do for a reason, the final

[11] For discussion of similar cases see Alvin I. Goldman (1976), 'Discrimination and Perceptual Knowledge', *Journal of Philosophy* 73.

outcome will occur, for example the putt's sinking. The probability of the shooting might well be even lower than that of the sinking, without the former's ceasing to be an action for a reason or the latter's becoming one. Low probability does not entail accidentality. Nor does *luck:* if I seek you in a crowd of 50,000, my finding you could be good luck yet nonaccidental. Perhaps where *S* contemplates an action of hers (say searching) as a possible way to achieve something, then, apart from untoward intervention, we tend not to call her succeeding accidental even when her chance is very slim. This case, too, suggests that even if normally an action for a reason has a description under which it is probable, or at least not highly improbable, given *S*'s reason states together with her abilities and circumstances, we cannot specify a cut-off or even a precise range of acceptable probabilities. Whether or not we may say that the relevant connections are reliable, they are at least nonaccidental.

One point we can add to clarify the relevant nonaccidental connections is that *for S* the causal link between her *A*-ing and any intermediaries there may be between them and her want to *r* not be abnormal, for example run in certain ways outside her body, especially through others' actions. But imagine that, to overcome paralysis, a brain aid is attached to *S*'s head and regularly produces appropriate intermediaries between her wants and beliefs and her actions; here there need be no unreliable connection or inadmissible intermediary, that is, intermediary that prevents *S*'s *A*-ing from being performed for a reason. The case also shows that an admissible intermediary need never have occurred: *S* can act for a reason the first time such a device aids her. Once properly installed, it becomes normal *for her*. Compare the effect, on our manikin viewer, of donning corrective glasses. Straightaway, she may know the man she sees to be one. As some of our examples suggest, the concept of acting for a reason is consistent with the existence of various sorts of intermediaries. What it rules out is that a crucial intermediary be only accidentally produced by the relevant want and belief, or only accidentally produce the action.[12]

---

[12] Such examples may suggest that *A*-ing for a reason is governed by a law to the effect that, given the relevant want, belief, *and* intermediary (say, the functioning of the brain aid) *S A*'s. But suppose Ken's wiggling his ears is hard for him, and he sometimes tries and fails. It might still be an action for a reason when they do produce it. This suggests that the strongest nomic connection plausibly affirmed here is something like this: if *S*'s wanting to *r* and believing her *A*-ing to bear a connecting relation *C* to *r* bring about her *A*-ing, via an intermediary, there is a law to the effect that a person in whom a want and belief of these types produce an intermediary of that kind *tends* to *A*. (This formulation leaves open whether the tendency generalization can be replaced by a universal one, perhaps formulated using quite different concepts.) But there may not even be a tendency (or probabilistic) connection here, unless—as is by no means clear—it is implied by our point that *A* must have a possible description under which it is nonaccidentally connected with reason states.

Accident can intrude at yet another place: in causing the disposition to attribute the action to the motivating want and connecting belief(s). When S A's for a reason, this disposition seems partly due to these same factors. That might explain why S has the disposition independently of seeking reasons she had for A-ing. *Must* the disposition be nonaccidentally produced by the relevant wants and beliefs? It seems so produced in paradigm cases of action for a reason, and the sorts of things one imagines accidentally producing the disposition from those wants and beliefs (for example, stray radiations) suggest that an action they also produce is not for a reason. I am inclined to think that where S acts for a reason the disposition is nonaccidentally produced. In any case, so far as one considers it accidentally produced, one is less inclined to regard the associated action as performed for a reason.

What emerges in this subsection, then, is a *nonaccidentality condition: S A's for a reason, r, only if her A-ing is nonaccidentally produced by her motivating want and connecting belief(s). Perhaps* nonaccidentality of the relevant sort, though a prima-facie weaker notion than reliability, is equivalent to reliable generation of the kind that some actions for a reason exhibit. More could certainly be said about accidentality and reliability; but our examples go some way toward clarifying the notions and seem to show that, sometimes, where it is doubtful whether S A's for a reason it is also doubtful, apparently for similar reasons, whether the connection between the relevant want and belief and her A-ing is nonaccidental, or reliable. We may at least conclude, then, that by clarifying these notions we can better understand acting for a reason.

Intermediaries

The nonaccidentality condition brings us closer to explaining the eight points set out in Section I, but we must clarify further how actions for a reason are controlled. One difficulty is wayward causal chains. It is no surprise that such chains plague an account of acting for a reason, since that entails acting intentionally and they are a well known obstacle to explicating intentional action.[13] Consider again a brain-affecting machine.

---

[13] Davidson suggests that philosophical reflection cannot solve the problem of wayward chains (op. cit.). Tuomela and Armstrong have proposed at least partial solutions. See esp. Raimo Tuomela (1977), *Human Action and Its Explanation* (Dordrecht and Boston: D. Reidel), esp. 256–8; and D. M. Armstrong (1981), 'Acting and Trying', in his *The Nature of Mind* (Ithaca and London: Cornell University Press). In my (1980), 'Tuomela on the Explanation of Action', *Synthese* 44, 300 ff., I have assessed Tuomela's proposal (making some points applicable to Armstrong's as well). For criticism of Armstrong's view see Harry G. Frankfurt (1978), 'The Problem of Action', *American Philosophical Quarterly* 15. For valuable recent discussions see

Imagine that Tom wants to shorten a conversation with Joe and believes that he can do so by looking at his watch. The machine might so affect this want and belief that they produce both his looking at his watch and a noninferential disposition to attribute his looking at it to them, yet do so just before Tom would have looked at it, so that he now looks at it abruptly. (The timing might surprise him without eliminating his disposition to attribute his action to this belief and want.) Imagine, too, that the machine regularly accompanies his doings, that its timing usually coincides with his, and that it systematically takes account of his wants and beliefs so as to produce his action from them nonaccidentally. Has he looked at his watch for a reason? This is not quite clear. That *may* indicate that our first four conditions come close to providing an account of acting for a reason. Perhaps the machine only affects *when* Tom acts for a reason, and one can *A* for a reason even if the timing of one's doing so is not based on that reason, or on any reason. It is not obvious, then, that cases like this undercut the first four conditions.

If, however, the proposed conditions do rule out wayward chains, more should be said about one's control over what one does for a reason. Perhaps the appropriate connection between reason and action may be undermined by intermediaries *apart from* the circuitous patterns we naturally call wayward chains (though we may simply use 'wayward' to mean 'of a kind incompatible with acting for a reason'). Suppose we alter our last example so that Tom's wanting to shorten his conversation and believing his looking at his watch would do this had caused Ann, who likes to think she is making people do things they would do anyway, to use the machine to cause him to look at his watch in just the way he intends and at the appropriate time. The action would then seem normal to him. But this is not mere overdetermination, as where one *A*'s for two reasons but would have *A*-ed for either alone. Ann uninvitedly exercises agency parallel to Tom's and in a way that seems to undermine his: he did what he wanted, but only *through* her action, and by a kind of short circuit. A guiding idea here is that actions one performs for a reason are *one's own*. From that point of view, Ann is a pre-emptive or at least diluting influence. It is not entirely clear that the dilution is sufficient to make her an *alien* intermediary: one that prevents *S*'s *A*-ing from being for a reason. If it is sufficient, then our four conditions may not rule out enough.

It is quite otherwise when someone is one's *instrument*, as where *S* uses Tom, on whom Ken is falling, as a means to support Ken. But there are

Myles Brand (1984), *Intending and Acting* (Cambridge, Mass.: MIT Press), esp. ch. 1; Christopher Peacocke (1979), *Holistic Explanation* (Oxford); and Michael Zimmerman (1984), *An Essay on Human Action* (New York: Peter Lang), esp. ch. 6.

intermediate cases. Recall *S*'s temporary inability to raise her arm, and suppose that Ron turns on a machine which counteracts the inability, so that *S* then raises the arm normally in order to greet Jan. Ron is not *S*'s instrument for *A*-ing, yet Ron's intervention seems friendly. Ron removes an obstacle; he *enables S* to *A*, but does not cause her *A*-ing. The distinction is difficult to explicate, and I shall not elaborate. But we may at least say that if the relevant want and belief bring about *S*'s *A*-ing via another agent's producing, rather than simply enabling, her *A*-ing, then *S* does not *A* for a reason. We have, then, one rough sufficient condition for an alien intermediary.

Another sufficient condition may be implicit in the idea that an action for a reason is *voluntary*, in the sense that, unlike reflex behaviour, it is under the control of one's motivational system. Even compelled action may be voluntary in this sense. Acting for a reason seems possible only if *S* can have opposing reasons that pull her in another direction. The notion of acting for a reason is, I suggest, *contrastive*. This is not to say (what is surely false) that *S* must have chosen *A*-ing from among alternatives. On one interpretation, the idea is that *S*'s *A*-ing is under the control of her *will* and is thus *reversible*. Let me illustrate. Imagine a drug that acts like a motivational step-up transformer: it is so affected by the want and belief that produce *S*'s *A*-ing that it strengthens her tendency to *A*, for example raises her resistance to dissuasion. It does not, however, do so independently of the reason states: its operation is sustained by them, though it increases their power. Now suppose the increase is so great that even if *S* had had an opposing want as strong as she is capable of, say to avoid causing nuclear war, she would still have *A*-ed.[14] Then her action is somewhat like a runaway car which, though one's foot is stuck on the accelerator, punctually stops where one wants it to go. The action seems not to be controlled by *S*'s motivational system, and hence not appropriately under *her* control. This idea may partly underlie the inclination to connect the voluntariness exhibited by action for a reason with freedom, and thus to consider any action for a reason free to *some* extent: degrees of freedom are largely a matter of what sorts of reasons would have led *S* to do otherwise, and actions reversible by *any* opposing reasons are not wholly

[14] It is not clear that the notion of maximal motivational strength applies to persons. Even if *S* could not want any one thing more than, say, to avoid causing nuclear war, surely she could acquire a belief linking that to something else she wants to avoid, for example breaking a promise. Could she not then want to avoid the conjunction of these more than to avoid causing nuclear war by itself? How could the aversive conjunct add no motivation? In any case, the sense that motivation can always be greater as *S* acquires further reasons is part of what makes the reversibility condition plausible: if she *A*'s for reasons, she might have abstained given sufficient counter-reasons.

unfree. Threat of death, for example, normally reduces freedom drastically; yet one might prefer death to lying, and hence even acting to save one's life may be believed not wholly unfree. (One is reminded of Aristotle's idea, in *Nicomachean Ethics* 1110ª, regarding an agent compelled to jettison cargo: 'when the origin of the actions is in him, it is also up to him whether to do them or not to do them'.) On this view, then, acting for a reason implies that minimal degree of freedom possessed by voluntary actions, conceived as those reversible by opposing reasons.

Arguably, then, action for a reason must be voluntary in a sense implying that the causal power of an intermediary may not exceed the causal power of *S*'s motivational system: roughly, that if *S* would have done it no matter what else she wanted, she did not do it in order to get what she wanted. But does voluntariness require reversibility? Imagine that *A*-ing is something *S* deeply believes in, for example preventing nuclear war, and *S* would be *glad* to be compelled to do this if that would help her to *A*. If she then irreversibly *A*'s because the transformer intervenes on the side of this deepest of all her desires, might she not do so for the relevant reason? This is perhaps not a clear case of acting for a reason, but it seems more like acting for a reason with a vengeance than like merely acting because of one.

There is, however, another way to view the contrastive aspect of acting for a reason. Suppose that instead of focusing on reversibility, we ask whether opposing reasons can reduce the strength of *S*'s tendency to *A*. Assuming that *S* wants more than anything to avoid causing nuclear war, would her tendency to act accordingly be reduced by her opposing reasons, such as its vanquishing the wicked? Imagine an intermediary that, while sustained by the relevant want and belief, *isolates* her reason for *A*-ing from the influence of opposing reasons so that they do not reduce *at all* her tendency to *A*. If *S* now acts because of the want to avoid causing nuclear war, her action is disconnected from opposing reasons, no longer seems suitably under her control, and is quite arguably not performed for a reason. On this view, voluntariness requires *integration* into one's motivational system, and thus susceptibility to counterinfluence.

Let us explore the relevant kind of voluntariness further. Perhaps if an action is performed *for* a reason, it must be under the control *of* reason, in the sense that it is appropriately responsive to the agent's reasons. This might explain why an action for a reason must at least normally be reversible should *S* develop a counter-reason with motivational strength as great as is within her capacity. But the reversibility and integration views of voluntariness differ importantly in where they locate the contrastiveness of acting for a reason: on the former, action for a reason implies the possibility of *alternative action;* on the latter, it implies the possible influence of *alternative reasons.* The first view, we might say, emphasizes being under the control of the will, the second, being under the control of reason. Thus, the reversibility view makes a kind of *freedom,* however unlikely its exercise, necessary for acting for a reason. The integration view makes a kind of *autonomy* necessary if, in virtue of one's reasons—for example, by bringing information about the bad effects of A-ing to bear to produce opposing motivation—one cannot even influence the motivation on which one acts, one's capacity to govern one's conduct is undermined, and one cannot act for a reason. One is reduced to a spectator: one can experience one's reason states' causing one's A-ing, but cannot bring reasons to bear in self-direction. Integration is the better candidate for a necessary condition on acting for a reason. If the strongest opposing reasons which S can have would not even weaken her tendency to A, then A-ing is presumably not under the control of her reason, nor appropriately integrated into her motivational system. In any event, autonomy and freedom must be distinguished; and when they are, it may turn out that the inclination to think that freedom persists to the point of irreversibility is based on the perception that a measure of autonomy, in the form of a capacity to marshal a degree of resistance to compulsion, can survive even when irreversibility is reached.

A second sufficient condition for an alien intermediary, then, is undermining the kind of voluntariness characteristic of acting for a reason. But does motivational integration (or even reversibility) belong to the concept of such voluntariness, and in a philosophical account of acting for a reason, or have we been just articulating psychologically important truths? Surely this distinction, if ultimately real, is not sharp. Perhaps acting for a reason should not be taken to include only actions subject to the influence of opposing reasons. But if not, such integration surely is implicit in a concept of acting for a reason very close to the non-technical one we are explicating.

There is a further aspect of control of one's actions for reasons. Normally, we control, within limits, not only *what* we do, but the *way* we do it.[15] We do not merely wave; we do it with a certain style, speed, and accent. Now suppose an intermediary causes S to wave with her elbow, and she is astonished. Actions for reasons typically occur against the background of one's beliefs about how one will (or can) act. An action that deviates enough from these is probably not under one's control. But how should we

---

[15] I assume here that A-ing in a particular way is not performing a different action, B; but if that is false my point could be re-expressed.

regard such deviations? Must *A* be carried out in a way *S* intends, or at least expects, to carry it out?[16] One might think so. When *S* waves with her elbow, she will tend to answer in the negative: 'Did you intend or expect to wave that way?' We must not infer, however, that *S* intended or expected to wave in a particular way, as where she means to flap her handkerchief. For her *not* intending or expecting to wave as she did does not imply her *having* an intention or expectation to wave in any specific, other way.

The parallel point holds for beliefs: even if, before waving, *S* would have assented to, for example, 'Do you believe you will wave in the usual way?' it does not follow that she believed she would (or intended to) do so, *before* being asked.[17] Moreover, supposing she did have the postulated intentions and beliefs before waving, there are problems for this approach. First, these intentions and beliefs could be waywardly caused (say, by accidental influences from outer space). Must a waywardly caused intention to wave with fingers together prevent *S*'s normal spread-fingered wave from being an action for a reason? That seems doubtful. Second, even where the postulated intentions are normal, the action need not match them to be performed for a reason. *S* may pleasantly surprise herself by the elegant way she recites a line of poetry she had intended simply to read unerringly. The elegant recitation may still be an action for a reason (even if its elegance is not due to a reason). Perhaps some way in which an action for a reason is carried out must be intended, but not every significant way need be intended, or even expected. Acting for a reason occurs in a (usually rich) field of expectations, purposes, and habits; but the extent to which it must follow a pre-existing plan or pattern—if indeed every action for a reason must follow such a plan or pattern—should not be exaggerated. The *control model* we are developing seems to give a better account of these points than the *preconception model* which, in one form, we are criticizing as too narrow. Creativity can come not only in what we do for reasons, but in the sometimes surprising ways we do it.

Even though the control appropriate to *S*'s *A*-ing for a reason does not entail *S*'s intending the specific ways in which she *A*'s, perhaps the manner of her *A*-ing must still have *some* correspondence with her intentions, beliefs, habits, or the like. But when might a departure from such elements warrant calling an intermediary that causes that departure alien? It is very

[16] This is suggested by Goldman in *A Theory of Human Action*, for example on p. 59, where he cites Chisholm as holding a similar view. A view of this sort is also suggested by Tuomela, op. cit. 256 f. Cf. John R. Searle (1983), *Intentionality* (Cambridge: Cambridge University Press), esp. ch. 3.

[17] I have argued for this in 'Tuomela on the Explanation of Action' cited in n. 12. pp. 301 f. Related supporting arguments are given in my (1982), 'Believing and Affirming', *Mind* 91.

difficult to capture the sense of 'control' appropriate to the *way* one acts for a reason. Perhaps we can extend the idea that an action for a reason is a belief-guided response to it. It may be that if S A's for a reason, the way S A's, for instance saws, is *alterable* by her (at least up to a certain time) should she try to alter it—and thus has a kind of reversibility of manner. It is partly this kind of control that we miss in some standard cases of waywardly caused behaviour. But there may be exceptions. After an accident, S might be able to move her hand in only one direction, for just one distance, and at just one speed. Even here, however, there would be a measure of integration: opposing reasons could weaken her tendency to move it in the relevant way.

We have now noted a number of necessary conditions for S's controlling the way she A's. An intermediary that undermines one of these is plausibly called alien. Notice that what is crucial is S's *exercising control*. Ann, with her brain machine, might *have control* over what S does: yet if Ann does not exercise supplantive control, we have at most a potential threat, not actual compulsion. May we now conclude, then, that an intermediary is alien if and only if it undermines S's appropriately controlling either her A-ing or the way she A's, that is, roughly, if *and* only if it (i) renders accidental the connection between the explaining want and belief(s) and the action; (ii) embodies supplantive action by another agent; (iii) undermines the voluntariness of S's A-ing; or (iv) produces a way of A-ing that S cannot suitably alter? This condition, taken with the four proposed above, seems to deal with both problematic intermediaries discussed in the literature and the examples used in this subsection. But the notion of an alien intermediary is elusive; (i)–(iv) provide a good sense of the notion, but they may not be strictly necessary and sufficient conditions.

To rule out alien intermediaries, then, I propose a *normal intermediaries condition: S A's* for a reason only if her motivating want and connecting belief(s) do not bring about or sustain her A-ing, via an alien intermediary, understood as just sketched. If (as I am inclined to think) voluntariness requires the integration of the explaining reason into S's motivational system, then we must construe alien intermediaries as including factors that *precede* formation of, or are somehow embodied in, the motivating want, and affect it so as to destroy integration. These might be considered intermediaries by virtue of intervening between S's motivational history and the want motivating A or A itself. Even with these qualifications, borderline cases persist. But those remaining seem to be just the sort one would expect given the points at which the notion of acting for a reason is itself vague.

If an action for a reason is conceived as proposed above, our account, with temporal variables added (and 'S' representing any agent), would be this:

I. S's A-ing is an action for a reason, r, at t, if and only if, at t, S A's, and there is a connecting relation, C, such that (1) S wants to r and believes C to hold between her A-ing and r, or believes something to the effect that C holds between her A-ing and r; (2) S's A-ing is at least in part explained by this motivating want and at least one connecting belief, and is guided by the belief(s); (3) S is noninferentially disposed, independently of seeking reasons she has had, or might have had, at or before t, for A-ing, to attribute her A-ing to the want and (explaining) belief(s); (4) S's A-ing is nonaccidentally produced by the want and (explaining) belief(s); and (5) the want and (explaining) belief(s) do not bring about (or sustain) S's A-ing via an alien intermediary.

Condition (1) expresses a reason S *has* to A, (2) a (guiding) reason *why* she A's, and (3)–(5) a reason *for which* S A's. One further point in order before we proceed is that while the account may seem to use the notion being explicated, it does not. It refers to reasons S had; but the kind of reason being explicated is one *for which* S acts, and this is not presupposed in explaining the conditions. Above all, (3) is explicated not by appeal to the notion of attributing an action to a reason for which it is performed, but in terms of attributing one's A-ing to the relevant reason *states*, and none of the kinds of attribution distinguished presupposes the concept of acting for a reason.

3. NON-BASIC ACTION, MULTIPLE REASONS, AND PARTIAL EXPLAINERS

So far, we have invoked no distinction between basic and nonbasic actions. Consider an example. Suppose Joe shoots wildly in the air and the bullet, which would normally miss Tom by 5,000 metres, is deflected by an aeroplane propeller so that it strikes his head and kills him. Does Joe kill Tom? *If* he does, it is doubtful that he does so for a reason, even if he shot because, in anger, he wanted to kill him and impulsively believed that somehow shooting in the air might do it. For one thing, the reason states seem to cause the death accidentally. At best Joe kills Tom *by* bouncing the bullet at him. But that is not an action for a reason either. There is a plausible principle here: if S A's for a reason, then either (i) A-ing is basic—roughly, it is not performed *by* performing any other action—and has its status as being for a reason directly, that is, other than through an action by (or in) which it is performed, or (ii) it *inherits* this status from a basic action *by* (or in) which S performs it. The distinction between basic and non-basic action (tokens) is controversial and need not be presupposed. We can put much the same point in terms of descriptions (or properties): if S's A-ing is, under that description, performed for a reason, then either it has the status of being for a reason directly, that is, simply as an A-ing, or it derives that status from fitting some description '*B*-ing', and thus is an A-ing because it is a *B*-ing.

Perhaps we may generalize: if A is a non-basic action for a reason, then no intervening agent not appropriately under S's control brings about the essential constituent in A, here, the victim's death. With von Wright, let us call this the (entailed) result of the action.[18] For moving a hand, it is the hand's moving; for pulling a trigger, the trigger's moving back; etc. Now if the propeller is an intervening agent, it is plainly not under Joe's control. For one thing, the connection between his shooting and Tom's death is accidental. But consider a different case. Suppose S delivers a gift to Ken through her son. It may be delivered for a reason even though her son brings about the result: Ken's receiving it from her. But now imagine that the boy is rebellious and throws the gift in a trash can, unaware that the can belongs to Ken's mother. If Ken now gets the gift, it would be wrong to say that S delivered it. Granted, he received it, but not *from her*. Not only does she lack appropriate control of the boy; her reasons only accidentally lead to Ken's receiving it.

We can further clarify the relevant kind of control by another contrast. In the first case, the boy is S's *means* of delivering the gift. In the second, S fails to deliver it by means of her son. Similarly, it seems wrong to say, in the shooting case, that Joe kills Tom by means of bouncing the bullet off an aeroplane propeller (at least where Joe is not even hoping to do so in that way). Doing one thing by means of another is closely associated with having or exercising appropriate control over an intermediary. Perhaps exercising this kind of control is typically a matter of being so related to the intermediary that one A's by means of it, or, at least, it is the (or a) means by which one A's. Typically, where S has no control of an intermediary agent or event, then even if it helps her A, it is not a means by which she A's; and if it is a means by which she A's, then even if she does not intentionally use it she typically has some control over it. Moreover, where we doubt whether one of these notions applies to an intermediary, we

---

[18] See G. H. von Wright (1971), *Explanation and Understanding* (Ithaca, NY: Cornell University Press), 66–7, 75, and 88.

often doubt whether the other does, and whether the relevant action is performed for a reason.

If we presuppose the distinction between basic and non-basic actions, non-basically acting for a reason may be construed as follows:

II. S A's non-basically, for a reason, at t, if and only if, at t, there is some action B such that (1) B is basic and is an action for a reason in the sense specified in I; (2) S A's by (or in) B-ing; (3) A satisfies the first four conditions of I; and (4) if S's B-ing generates her A-ing via an intermediary that causes the result of A-ing, then (a) S appropriately controls any such intermediary, and (b) S's B-ing *also* causes, or is a cause of, this result.[19]

An action *for* a reason must be suitably under the control *of* reason; and when its status as an action for a reason is derivative, whether owing to transmission across the by-relation or to its fitting certain descriptions, that control must be preserved. We have seen how the notion of a means can help to clarify (a). This notion itself needs further study, and both (a) and (b) need more explication; but some of the points made in Section II indicate various lines of inquiry which may clarify the notion of control.

There are other problems in action theory that can now be clarified. One is how to understand acting for a number of reasons. Another is how to conceive the extent of a reason's influence in producing or sustaining an action—a matter of much importance in evaluating people. Let us consider these problems.

We have not so far captured the idea of acting (wholly) for a single reason, only that of acting for at least one. But surely to act for one reason is to have just one reason with the properties specified in I. What we must add is an *explanatory uniqueness condition:* if S has any other reason, r_1, for A-ing, then the previous conditions do not hold with r_1 in place of r. Hence her A-ing cannot be (correctly) explained as performed in order to t_1. But where S acts for two or more reasons, an in-order-to explanation can cite any of them, though it might be misleading to omit any, at least if they are of equal weight.

To capture the notion of acting for multiple reasons, I suggest this:

III. S A's at t for reasons $r_1, r_2, \ldots, r_n$, if and only if, at t, S A's, and (i) each r_i satisfies (1)–(5) of I, and (ii) for each r_i, her wanting to realize

---

[19] II does not specify for *what* reason S A's. It need not be the same reason for which she B's, but what it is can be determined using I. II can be reformulated, moreover, in the terminology of action under a description.

it explains (adequately) why she A's, and explains it in such a way that it would be correct to say that she A-ed, for one thing, in order to realize it (or because, for one thing, she wanted it).

This implies that each motivating want is important in bringing about A-ing; but each is, since each expresses (unqualifiedly) a reason *for* which S A's. Moreover, while each want, together with the appropriate belief(s), is only *part of what explains* S's A-ing, it is not a merely *partial explainer* of that. For, together with the belief(s), it *adequately* explains it. Indeed, in a sense it fully explains it; for it enables one to understand why S A-ed. Yet the want is only part of what explains the action because other wants *also* adequately explain it.

There are many problems concerning the *importance* of a reason in producing an action. Our account can clarify this notion. First, consider reasons S has for A-ing which *contribute* to producing her A-ing, yet are not main reasons for which she A's. Call these *partially explaining reasons* for which she A's, to contrast them with fully (in the sense of 'adequately') explaining reasons:

IV.   A reason r, which S has, at t, for A-ing is a (merely) partially explain-ing reason for which she A's, at t, if and only if, at t, (i) r satisfies clauses (1), (4), and (5) of I; (ii) the relevant want and belief(s) *contribute* to bringing about S's A-ing; (iii) S has the disposition specified in (3) of I, except that normally she is disposed to attribute her A-ing only in part to the relevant want and belief(s); and (iv) it is not the case that S's A-ing is explainable by appeal to her wanting to r, or that she A's because she wants to r.

A number of partially explaining reasons working *together* can fully ex-plain S's A-ing: each want can partially explain it, and jointly they would adequately explain it. They might even be the only reasons that explain it. This can be so even if no one of them is necessary for A (none could be sufficient, even together with S's beliefs, or it would not be just a partially explaining reason).

Both partially explaining reasons *and* 'main' reasons may differ in *moti-vational influence:* in how much they contribute to producing or sustaining the action. Thus,

V.   Where r_1 and r_2 are reasons for which, at t, S A's, r_1 is more influential than r_2, at t, and relative to S's A-ing, if and only if, at t, S's wanting to r_1, together with the associated connecting belief(s), contributes more to bringing about or sustaining her A-ing than does her wanting to r_2 together with the connecting belief(s) associated with r_2.

The relevant contribution is in some sense causal, and the key idea is giving a more nearly adequate explanation of A-ing, or, for two fully explaining reasons, a more nearly complete explanation. A related 'measure' is how much a reason contributes to the strength of S's tendency to A. Such strength is difficult to explicate, but a central element is how hard S would try, say, how much work she would do, to overcome obstacles to A-ing. Clearly, then, the strength of S's motivating want(s) is crucial for how much influence her reason(s) have on her A-ing. But beliefs are also important: if S wants r_1 as much as r_2, yet believes A-ing is far more likely to realize r_2 than r_1, then other things equal r_2 gives her both a better reason to A and one that, if she A's, will be more influential in her doing so.

4. ACTIONS FOR REASONS, INTENTIONALITY, AND INTRINSIC MOTIVATION

How is acting for a reason, conceived as proposed, related to intentional action? Certainly intentional actions that are not intrinsically motivated, that is, are performed in order to realize a *further* end, are actions for a reason. If S A's in order to r, say, strolls to get fresh air, where r is not equivalent to A-ing, S A's for a reason. But suppose realizing r is logically equivalent, but not identical, to A-ing. Does S A for a further end? I shall assume so, at least if S does not believe the equivalence holds. If S does believe this, the issue may turn on whether she conceives realizing r as distinct from A-ing.

It is not clear whether intrinsically motivated intentional actions— roughly, actions performed just for their own sake—are actions for a reason.[20] Suppose Tom strolls simply because he feels like strolling. Asked his reason, he might say, 'No reason, I just feel like it.' However, he might have said, 'I just feel like strolling; I'm not avoiding you.' Thus, just feeling like it—roughly, wanting it for its own sake—can be offered as a reason. Tom might also have said, 'No particular reason, I just want to.' Here just wanting to is given as a reason, though not a 'particular' one. Perhaps the key contrast is not between intentional actions that are, and those that are not, for a reason, but between those for a *further* reason and those that are intrinsically motivated, for example performed because one just wants to.

---

[20] This question has received too little attention considering how often intentional actions have been conceived as actions for reasons. See, for example, G. E. M. Anscombe (1963), *Intention*, 2nd edn. (Ithaca, NY: Cornell University Press), 9; Donald Davidson (1969), 'How is Weakness of the Will Possible?' in Joel Feinberg (ed.), *Moral Concepts* (London and New York: Oxford University Press), esp. 110; and Goldman's *A Theory of Human Action*, 76–9.

If this is so, then Tom's 'No reason' may be a denial of a further reason for strolling. Since further reasons are far more common—and much more often the kind we have in mind in asking someone's reason for an action—there can easily be a point to Tom's saying this even if he is aware of acting for an intrinsic reason.

There is, then, some ground for taking intrinsically motivated intentional actions to be actions for a reason. But what is the connecting belief? *S* surely does not believe her *A*-ing is a *means* of realizing *r*, for example that her strolling is a means of strolling. Perhaps she believes strolling to have some desirable characteristic, such as being enjoyable. This view might explain the 'for' in 'for its own sake': one does want it for something, but not something extrinsic to it. Note, too, that there is a corresponding kind of practical argument: from premisses expressing one's wanting to stroll for some intrinsic property of it, and one's believing strolling would have that property, to a conclusion that favours strolling. The connecting belief, despite noninstrumental content, would *function* like an instrumental belief. But *must* there be connecting beliefs for intrinsically motivated actions? If we distinguish strolling intentionally from doing so merely voluntarily, as where one just meanders along, it is arguable that the strolling is intentional only if *guided* by a belief connecting it to a motivating want. Believing the strolling to be enjoyable can guide *S*, even if she does not conceive the action as a *means* to enjoyment. It would seem, in fact, that wanting to stroll for its own sake would cease to sustain strolling unless S took the strolling to be, for example, pleasurable.

This problem is important in part because, if intrinsically motivated actions are actions for reasons, then intentional action is equivalent to action for a reason. If it is, our account of acting for a reason should serve as an account of intentional action. I am not quite prepared to affirm the equivalence. But except possibly in cases of intrinsic motivation the account apparently applies as well to intentional action as to action for a reason. Granted, if intrinsically motivated actions are actions for a reason yet do not require a connecting belief, the account must be qualified. It is not clear, however, that the account does not apply to intrinsically motivated actions; and if it does, it applies to all intentional actions. This in itself would be an important result. But it might also lead to an account of action in general. Perhaps (as some philosophers hold) action may be viewed as behaviour, in the sense of what one *does*, that is intentional under some description. This is not obvious; but if it is so, we may well be able to understand action in general as behaviour which, under some description, is acting for a reason.

We can now better understand the relation of action for a reason and action performed on the basis of practical reasoning. If our account is correct, then apparently an action for a reason need not arise from, or be preceded or accompanied by, practical reasoning. For except on an implausibly weak account of practical reasoning, S could A for a reason, yet not have engaged in such reasoning about A-ing. This point is best seen by distinguishing action for a reason from *reasoned action*. The former does not entail the latter. Reasoned actions, however, are all actions for a reason, and actions based on practical reasoning are all in a sense reasoned. If so, we can clarify the relation between a piece of practical reasoning and an action *based* on it. Minimally, it is an action for one or more reasons that figure in the premises. Thus, given the motivating want and connecting belief(s) expressed in the premises, the account can partially explicate how the action is based on the reasoning. It will be *for* the reason(s) expressed in the major premiss.[21] It should be noted that similar points may hold for the relation of actions for a reason to actions arising from *volition*. For instance, an action arising from a volition might be performed for a reason underlying (or in some other way closely associated with) the volition, as where wanting to greet Tom may generate, when S sees him, her volition to raise her arm. Our account allows that at least a great many actions for a reason arise from volition, though it also allows that an action for a reason *need* not stem from a volition conceived as, say, a phenomenal event of trying. However, every action for a reason is such that a volition *could* produce it and S could be aware of the relevant mental event.

An action for a reason is one that is, in a special way, under the control of reason. It is a response to, not a mere effect of, a reason. It is nonaccidentally produced or sustained by a motivating want and a connecting belief. It is guided by these, and thereby discriminative; it is explainable by appeal to them, associated with a noninferential disposition to attribute the action to them, and, in a certain way, voluntary. In the light of this conception, actions for a reason, though they need not arise from a process of practical reasoning, may be viewed as realizations of practical arguments. Actions for a reason are intentional, and the converse holds except possibly for intrinsically motivated actions. Thus, our account of

---

[21] I have discussed how the major and minor premisses are to be construed, and examined a number of relevant works on practical reasoning, in 'A Theory of Practical Reasoning', cited in n. 3. A full account of an action's being based on practical reasoning must anchor A-ing to the reasoning process of S's from which it suitably arises. Only some of the crucial materials for such an account are provided in this paper.

acting for a reason constitutes at least a partial account of intentional action, and it applies unrestrictedly to most of its varieties. The account unifies and, in some cases, explains, many of the distinctive features of action for a reason; it helps us to explicate the sense in which an action may be based on practical reasoning; and it clarifies both acting for multiple reasons and a number of ways in which reasons for which one acts may be more or less important for understanding the action. Some of the concepts we have used to explicate acting for a reason need further clarification, but we have at least laid out what appear to be the major constituents of acting for a reason. If these need further explication, they are none the less conceptual materials well worth the effort of scrutiny. They are both intrinsically interesting and important for a number of topics in the philosophy of mind. If the account of acting for a reason is at points incomplete, it at least provides a structure within which further inquiry might progress.

This paper was originally written for presentation at the University of Helsinki, and I am grateful for that occasion and for a National Endowment for the Humanities Fellowship which supported part of my work. For detailed and very helpful comments, I thank William P. Alston, John G. Bennett, Michael Bratman, Hugh J. McCann, and readers for *The Philosophical Review*. I have also benefited from comments by Malcolm Acock, Albert Casullo, David Alan Johnson, John L. Longeway, Alfred R. Mele, Allison Nespor, John Tienson, Mark C. Timmons, Raimo Tuomela, and Michael Zimmerman. Earlier versions were given to a number of audiences and in an NEH Summer Seminar which I directed in 1981, and I profited from all of those discussions.

5

REASONS EXPLANATION OF ACTION: AN INCOMPATIBILIST ACCOUNT

CARL GINET

Incompatibilism is the thesis that any free action must be an undetermined event. By a *free* action I mean one such that until the time of its occurrence the agent had it in her power to perform some alternative action (or to be inactive) instead. By an *undetermined* event I mean one that was *not* nomically necessitated by the antecedent state of the world. (Hence, a determined event is one that *was* nomically necessitated by its antecedents.) By saying of an event that it was *nomically necessitated* by the antecedent state of the world, I mean that the antecedent state together with the laws of nature determined that that event, rather than some alternative, would occur.

I believe that a compelling argument for incompatibilism can be given but I will not undertake to give it here.[1] I want rather to rebut two arguments *against* incompatibilism that have been put forward from time to time. One of these, to which I will give by far the larger response, combines the consideration that a free action can be influenced by the agent's intentions, desires, and beliefs—can have an explanation in terms of reasons for which the agent did it—with the assumption that only a determined event can have such an explanation.[2] My response to this will

Carl Ginet, 'Reasons Explanation of Action: An Incompatibilist Account', *Philosophical Perspectives* 3 (1989), 17–46. Reprinted by permission of the Editor of *Philosophical Perspectives*.

[1] Versions of the argument that are substantially adequate though flawed in minor ways can be found, among other places, in Carl Ginet (1966), 'Might We Have No Choice', in K. Lehrer (ed.), *Freedom and Determinism* (New York: Random House); Peter van Inwagen (1975), 'The Incompatibility of Free Will and Determinism', *Philosophical Studies* 27: 185–99; Carl Ginet (1980), 'The Conditional Analysis of Freedom', in Peter van Inwagen (ed.), *Time and Cause: Essays Presented to Richard Taylor* (Dordrecht, Neth.: Reidel); id. (1983), 'In Defense of Incompatibilism', *Philosophicial Studies* 44: 391–400; and Peter van Inwagen (1983), *An Essay on Free Will* (Oxford: Clarendon Press).

[2] The earliest appearance of this argument, or one closely akin to it, that I know of is in David Hume (1739–40), *A Treatise of Human Nature*, Bk. II, pt. II, sect. 2.

be to counter the assumption by offering an adeterministic or *anomic* account of such explanations. The other argument does not assume that reasons explanations are deterministic (nor does it assume the contradictory) but simply claims that where we have an undetermined action we do not have an agent in control of (determining) what her action is to be: we do not have an action that the agent chooses, freely or otherwise.

I

Let me first dispose of this latter argument. It is contained (though mingled with and not clearly distinguished from the other argument) in the following remarks of Frithjof Bergmann:

> Would indeterminacy, even if its existence could be demonstrated, really vouchsafe freedom, or would it not fulfill this expectation? . . . Where or when would [the indeterminacy] have to occur to provide us with freedom? . . . Imagine Raskolnikov walking up the steps to the old pawnbroker woman's room and assume that his mind still vacillates, that with every tread he climbs his thinking alternates from one side to the other. . . . he mounts the staircase thinking 'I shall kill her', 'No, I shall not'. This continues till he stands right before her door. Now let us hypothesize that his last thought just as he pushes the door open is 'No, I shall not do it' and that the sought-for indeterminacy occurs right after these words crossed his mind. The thinking of this thought is the last link in a causal chain, but now there is a gap between this and the next event, which is his bringing the axe down on her head.
>
> What would this mean? Would the occurrence of a disjuncture in this place render Raskolnikov's act more free; would it provide him with a power or a control that he lacks otherwise? . . . The implication, if anything, would be the reverse. If his last thought really is 'No, I shall not do it' and this thought is somehow disconnected from the next event so that it has no causal influence on it and he then kills her, then one could only say that the indeterminacy has rendered his will ineffectual, that instead of giving him greater power or control the causal gap *decreased* it.
>
> . . . one could envision two alternatives: either something other than his own last thought 'influences' him so that he does commit the murder, or the last reversal was quite strictly not effected by anything whatever and occurred entirely 'by chance'. . . . in either case it was not *he* that made the decision, and *he* certainly did not exercise his freedom. We therefore can conclude that the occurrence of a causal gap in this particular location—between his last thought and his action—would not furnish him with freedom, but on the contrary would undermine the agent and make him a victim.[3]

Bergmann is suggesting that there is an absurdity in the thought that positing a break in the causal necessitation just before Raskolnikov's action helps to make it one that *he* chooses. In fact, he suggests, it would

---

[3] Frithjof Bergmann (1977), *On Being Free* (Notre Dame, Ind.: University of Notre Dame Press), 234–5. This is the central argument in an app. 'Freedom and Determinism'.

do just the opposite: it would go against its being the case that Raskolnikov determines whether or not he delivers the murdering blow. And if Raskolnikov does not determine that, then surely his delivering the blow is not his freely chosen action for which he can be held morally responsible.

Why exactly is the indeterminacy just before the action supposed to deprive the agent of control over his action? One reason, Bergmann seems to suggest, is that (as he thinks) if the action is undetermined then it is in no way influenced by his antecedent intentions or thoughts, and its being influenced by them is essential to its being controlled by the agent. But his words, particularly the last few sentences quoted, also invite the thought that the implication is more direct and does not depend on taking a deterministic view of how motives influence actions or on taking any particular view as to what agent control consists in: it is, one may think, just obvious that if an action is undetermined then the agent does not control (determine) it, has no say in whether or not it occurs.

We also find this latter idea in the argument that van Inwagen (1983) refers to as 'the third strand of the *Mind* Argument' for compatibilism. The premise of that argument, as van Inwagen phrases it (p. 144), is 'the principle that no one has any choice about the occurrence of an undetermined event'. I believe we adequately capture the idea here if we express it as follows:

(1)   For any time t and any undetermined event occurring at t: it is not possible for it to have been in anyone's power to determine whether that event or some alternative (undetermined) event instead would occur at t.

From this premise we can in two short steps derive a conclusion severely damaging to incompatibilism:

(2)   Therefore, for any time t and undetermined action occurring at t: it is not possible for it to have been in the agent's power to determine whether that action or some alternative (undetermined) action instead would occur at t.

(3)   Therefore, it is not possible for a free action to be undetermined.

It is impossible for the conclusion (3) and incompatibilism both to be true *if* it is also true that free action is at least possible (whether or not actual). The metaphysical possibility of free action is something that most incompatibilists assume, myself included, as of course do most compatibilists. That assumption conjoined with (3) does entail that incompatibilism is false. Since the argument is obviously valid, if free action is possible, either incompatibilism or the argument's premiss is wrong. A little reflection will show us that the latter is the problem.

Whatever plausibility this premiss has derives, I think, from ambiguity in sentences of the following form when they are about events that are actions.

(A) It was in S's power to determine whether undetermined event E or some alternative undetermined event instead would occur at t.

When the event E is *not an action of S's* a natural reading of this sentence does make it express a plainly impossible proposition:

(A1) It was in S's power so to act that S's action (in concert with other circumstances at the time) would have nomically necessitated that E would occur at t and have been undetermined; and it was in S's power so to act that S's action would have nomically necessitated that some alternative instead of E would occur at t and have been undetermined.

Here each conjunct is impossible, for it implies that it was in S's power to make the case something that is impossible, namely, that an event at t would have been both determined and undetermined. On this inconsistent reading of (A) the premiss of the argument, (1) above, obviously holds.

But when the event E is an action of S's, another reading of (A) is possible, one that is perfectly consistent:

(A2) It was in S's power to act in a certain way at t without being nomically necessitated to do so; and it was in S's power to act in some alternative way at t without being nomically necessitated to do so.

Here each conjunct attributes to S the power to make the case something that in itself is perfectly possible, namely, S's performing an undetermined action. If an undetermined action is possible then there is no reason to say that an undetermined action cannot be in the agent's power to perform.

To determine an event is to act in such a way that one's action makes it the case that the event occurs. Let us grant (for the sake of this discussion) that if the event is *not* one's own action then this requires that the event be causally necessitated by one's action (in concert with other circumstances) and thus that it not be an undetermined event. But if the event *is* one's own action then one's determining it requires only that one perform it; and one's performing it, which is just the action's occurring, is compatible with the action's being undetermined, not causally necessitated by antecedents.

Suppose that S's raising her arm at t did occur as an undetermined action: S raised her arm at t without being nomically necessitated to do so. In that case, it was open to S, in S's power, up to t to raise her arm at t without being nomically necessitated to do so. There is no reason to doubt it. Nor is there any reason to be puzzled as to how this can be so. But van Inwagen (in uncomfortable company with some compatibilists) seems to find a mystery here. He says:

> I must reject the following proposition:
>> If an agent's act was caused but not determined by his prior inner state, and if nothing besides that inner state was causally relevant to the agent's act, then that agent had no choice about whether that inner state was followed by that act.
>
> I must admit that I find it puzzling that this proposition should be false . . .
>
> Now I wish I knew *how it could be* that, for example, our thief had a choice about whether to repent [or instead rob the poor box], given that his repenting was caused, but not determined, by his prior inner states, and given that no other prior state 'had anything to do with'—save negatively: in virtue of its non-interference with—his act. I have no theory of free action or choice that would explain how this could be.[4]

As I understand him, what puzzles van Inwagen is how an agent could have a choice about whether or not his action occurred, i.e. could determine that it occurred rather than something else instead, *if* the only antecedent things causally relevant to its occurrence, the agent's motives for it (his 'prior inner state'), left it undetermined, nomically unnecessitated. How, by what means, van Inwagen seems to want to ask, did the thief ensure that that action (rather than some alternative) occurred? The answer is: by no *means*, by nothing distinct from and productive of the action, but simply by performing the action itself. If an event is S's action then S (but, of course, no one else) can ensure its occurrence, determine *that* it occurs and thus *whether or not* it occurs, just by performing it.

So I attribute the puzzlement van Inwagen feels here to failure to distinguish the two very different readings sentences of form (A) can have when E is one of S's own actions. He wants to say that (A) can be true in such a case but he wonders *how* it can be. His feeling that (A) can be true is traceable to the (A2) interpretation, which gives a proposition whose possibility is clear and straightforward. His conflicting feeling that there is no way (A) can be true in such a case is traceable to the (A1) interpretation, which gives an inconsistent proposition.

[4] van Inwagen (1983) op. cit., 149–50.

II

Let us turn now to the other argument against incompatibilism I mentioned earlier. This one crucially assumes that if an action is not a purely chance or random event, if it is influenced by or has an explanation in terms of the agent's reasons or motives for doing it, then it is *ipso facto* determined. A. J. Ayer (1946), for instance, says:

Either it is an accident that I choose to act as I do or it is not. If it is an accident, then it is merely a matter of chance that I did not choose otherwise; and if it is merely a matter of chance that I did not choose otherwise, it is surely irrational to hold me morally responsible for choosing as I did. But if it is not an accident that I choose to do one thing rather than another, then presumably there is some causal explanation of my choice: and in that case we are led back to determinism.[5]

J. J. C. Smart (1968) argues that:

the question of pure chance or determinism is irrelevant to the question of free will, though, so far from free will and determinism being incompatible with one another, a close approximation to determinism on the macro-level is required for free will.
   Some philosophers would . . . say that in free choice we act from reasons, not from causes, and they would say that acting from reasons is neither caused nor a matter of pure chance. I find this unintelligible.
   . . . the free choice is supposed to be not deterministic and not a matter of pure chance. It is supposed to be pure chance in the sense of 'not being determined' but the suggestion is that it is also not merely random and is 'acting from reasons'. The previous paragraph [not quoted here; see n. 16 for a description of its content] suggests, however, that acting from reasons is not merely random precisely because it is also acting from causes.[6]

We can formulate the argument these authors make as follows:

(1) Incompatibilism entails that an action cannot be both free and determined by an antecedent state of the world.

(2) If an action is not determined by an antecedent state of the world then it has no explanation in terms of its antecedents.

(3) But some free actions do have explanations in terms of their antecedents.

(4) Therefore, incompatibilism is wrong.

Premiss (1) is true by the definition of incompatibilism. Premiss (3) is obviously undeniable. We frequently give explanations of our own actions, and accept explanations of others' actions, like the following:

[5] A. J. Ayer (1959), *Philosophical Essays* (London: Macmillan), 275.
[6] J. J. C. Smart (1968), *Between Science and Philosophy* (New York: Random House), 300–1.

S opened the window in order to let the smoke out.
S wanted to get out of the country quickly and realized it would take days unless she gave the official a bribe, so she handed him all her roubles.

These are explanations of actions because they answer the question 'Why did S do that?' The first explains why S opened the window. The second explains why S handed the official all her roubles. These examples illustrate a category of explanations that apply only to actions: they are explanations that give us the agent's reasons for acting as she did. For most of our actions, or most that we have occasion to reflect on, we believe that they have such reasons explanations. Very often some of the intentions, desires, or beliefs that we bring into such an explanation are antecedents of the action. It would be preposterous to suggest that free actions can never have such explanations, to deny premiss (3).

Some philosophers seem to think that premiss (3) would be acceptable even if it were stronger and said that an action *must* have an explanation in terms of its antecedents, or that this must be true of *responsible* actions or of ones that the agent *chooses*, ones that are truly the agent's actions. Bergmann, for example, seems to suggest this in the remarks quoted above (p. 107). But I can see no reason to accept these much stronger claims. When I cross my legs while listening to a lecture, that action (usually) has no explanation in terms of reasons for doing it that I had antecedently. I just spontaneously do it. A spontaneous action, not arising from any antecedent motive, can even be undertaken with a further intention that begins to exist just when the action does. For example, a bird catches a person's eye and, without having antecedently formed the intention to keep watching it, she moves her head when the bird moves, in order to keep her eyes on it.

But premiss (3) itself is obviously true. As I said, it would be absurd to suppose that a free action could not have an explanation in terms of the agent's antecedent reasons for doing it. It is premiss (2), that an action has no explanation in terms of its antecedents if it is not determined by them, that is the substantive and deniable premiss in the argument. Ayer clearly assumes that there are only two alternatives: either an action is determined or it is a purely chance event. He says, 'if it is not an accident that I choose to do one thing rather than another, then presumably there is some causal explanation of my choice: and in that case we are led back to determinism.' Smart finds unintelligible the suggestion that there is a third alternative, 'that acting from reasons is neither caused [determined] nor a matter of pure chance'.

To assume premiss (2) is to assume that *all* explanations of events must be law-governed or *nomic*. That is to assume that an explanation can be true only if laws of nature guarantee that the explaining factors plus other circumstances are accompanied by the explained event. Applied specifically to reasons explanations of actions, this means the following:

(B)   A reasons explanation can be true only if laws of nature guarantee that the agent's reasons for performing the action plus other circumstances are accompanied by the explained action.

This bold, bald assumption is false.

III

Some philosophers have thought that the laws of nature that govern reasons explanations in the way required by assumption (B) are fairly obvious. J. S. Mill, for example, in his *Examination of Sir William Hamilton's Philosophy* says that 'Necessitarians', of whom he counts himself one,

affirm, as a truth of experience, that volitions do, in point of fact, follow determinate moral antecedents with the same uniformity, and (when we have sufficient knowledge of the circumstances) with the same certainty, as physical effects follow their physical causes. These moral antecedents are desires, aversions, habits, and dispositions, combined with outward circumstances suited to call those internal incentives into action.... A volition is a moral effect, which follows the corresponding moral causes as certainly and invariably as physical effects follow their physical causes.[7]

One may object that, in point of fact, the same volition or action does not invariably follow the same set of 'moral' antecedents and this is particularly clear in cases (which are common) where the moral antecedents include the agent's having two or more desires that conflict, so the agent can satisfy at most one of these desires. For example, on a Saturday afternoon I have a desire to spend the rest of the afternoon doing some philosophical work and also a desire to spend it watching a football game on television. Suppose this same set of conflicting motives recurs on several Saturday afternoons. Can't I choose to satisfy one of the motives on some of these occasions and the other on others of them, without there being any relevant difference in the antecedents on these several occasions? Mill says no.

When we think of ourselves hypothetically as having acted otherwise than we did, we always suppose a difference in the antecedents: we picture ourselves as having known something that we did not know, or not known something that we did know;

[7] J. S. Mill (1872) (ed. J. M. Robson, 1979), *An Examination of Sir William Hamilton's Philosophy* (Toronto: University of Toronto Press), 449–50.

which is a difference in the external inducements; or as having desired something, or disliked something, more or less than we did; which is a difference in the internal inducements.[8]

It is already clear to Mill what the general law must be in such cases of conflict of motives: the chosen action will be the one that satisfies whichever of the conflicting motives is stronger than all the others: the strongest motive prevails.[9]

Thomas Reid (writing more than sixty years before Mill) makes the following remarks about this way of dealing with conflict-of-motives cases.

When it is said, that of contrary motives the strongest always prevails, this can neither be affirmed nor denied with understanding, until we know distinctly what is meant by the strongest motive . . . when the motives are of different kinds, as money and fame, duty and worldly interest, health and strength, riches and honor, by what rule shall we judge which is the strongest motive? Either we measure the strength of motives, merely by their prevalence, or by some other standard distinct from their prevalence. If we measure their strength merely by their prevalence, and by the strongest motive mean only the motive that prevails, it will be true indeed that the strongest motive prevails; but the proposition will be identical, and mean no more than that the strongest motive is the strongest motive. From this surely no conclusion can be drawn . . . We are therefore brought to this issue, that unless some measure of the strength of motives can be found distinct from their prevalence, it cannot be determined, whether the strongest motive always prevails or not. If such a measure can be found and applied, we may be able to judge of the truth of this maxim, but not otherwise.[10]

This suggests that one can secure confidence in Mill's law only by making it true by definition: 'the strongest motive' *means* the motive that prevails. If this term is defined by some logically independent criterion, so that the proposed law will be a non-trivial proposition, then it is an open question whether the facts would give us reason for confidence in it. Reid presents Mill with a dilemma: either the strongest motive law is true by definition, in which case it is not the law of nature that was wanted, or some independent test of the strongest motive is to be found, in which case we do not know yet whether the proposed law holds.

Mill attempts to reply to this line of thought. He says there are two flaws in the argument that 'I only know the strength of motives in relation to the will by the test of ultimate prevalence; so that this means no more than that the prevailing motive prevails.'

First, those who say that the will follows the strongest motive, do not mean the motive which is strongest in relation to the will, or in other words, that the will

---

[8] Ibid. 451.   [9] Ibid. 451–3.
[10] Thomas Reid (1815), *Works*, iii–iv, quoted from Gerald Dworkin (1970) (ed.) *Determinism, Free Will, and Moral Responsibility* (Englewood Cliffs, NJ: Prentice Hall).

follows what it does follow. They mean the motive which is strongest in relation to pain and pleasure; since a motive, being a desire or aversion, is proportional to the pleasantness, as conceived by us, of the thing desired, or the painfulness of the thing shunned. . . . The second [flaw] is, that even supposing there were no test of the strength of motives but their effect on the will, the proposition that the will follows the strongest motive would not . . . be identical and unmeaning. We say, without absurdity, that if two weights are placed in opposite scales, the heavier will lift the other up; yet we mean nothing by the heavier, except the weight which will lift up the other. The proposition, nevertheless, is not unmeaning, for it signifies that in many or most cases there *is* a heavier, and that this is always the same one, not one or the other as it may happen. In like manner, even if the strongest motive meant only the motive which prevails, yet if there is a prevailing motive—if, all other antecedents being the same, the motive which prevails today will prevail tomorrow and every subsequent day—Sir W. Hamilton was acute enough to see that the free-will theory is not saved.[11]

This fails to wriggle out of the dilemma. Mill's proposed independent criterion of motive strength is the degree of pain and pleasure anticipated. On any ordinary understanding of this, the facts will not support the proposed law: people sometimes choose an alternative they believe will be more painful or less pleasant than another alternative they believe open to them, in order to keep a promise, for example. In his second point Mill seems to give the game away, apparently without quite realizing it. He says that, even if there were no other test of strongest motive but the one that prevails, this would make the strongest motive law no more absurd and unmeaning than 'the heaviest weight always lifts the other up'. To this Reid should reply: Exactly so. No more unmeaning *and no less tautologous*.

Mill goes on to claim that the proposition, 'The heavier weight lifts the other up', 'signifies that in many or most cases there is a heavier *and this is always the same one*, not one or the other as it may happen' (emphasis added). He implies that the corresponding proposition, 'The strongest motive prevails', implies a corresponding thing, that the prevailing motive in recurrences of the same set of conflicting motives is always the same one. But, of course, neither tautology can have the implication claimed for it. It is a contingent proposition, and therefore compatible with 'the heavier weight lifts the other up', that two objects should change over time with respect to which is the heavier of the two. Likewise it is contingent, and therefore compatible with the tautological interpretation of 'the strongest motive prevails', that when the same set of conflicting motives recurs a different one prevails from the one that prevailed earlier. And, more important, this is not only a logical possibility but actually happens, often. Sometimes when my desire to work conflicts with my desire to watch football the first motive prevails, and sometimes the other prevails. Sometimes when my desire to get an early start on the day conflicts with my desire to sleep a bit more the first desire prevails, and sometimes the other does. If there are laws of nature that explain why the prevailing motive does prevail in such cases, that explain this in terms of antecedents of the action, it is far from obvious what the contents of those laws are and it seems unlikely that they deal entirely in terms of 'moral' antecedents (i.e. the agent's antecedent reasons or motives), for it seems that we already know all the relevant facts about them: the agent had the conflicting motives and it seemed a toss-up which to satisfy.

There is another sort of case, noted by Reid, where the strongest motive law cannot apply at all, even on its tautological interpretation, because there is no motive that distinguishes the chosen alternative from another one.[12] On my computer's keyboard there are two keys such that if I press either of them the result is that an asterisk appears on the screen. I know this about these keys and I want to produce an asterisk, so I have a motive or reason for pressing one of them. Now suppose further that I have no desire such that pressing one but not the other of these two keys satisfies it. I have no motive for pressing one of them that is not also equally a motive for pressing the other. I am utterly indifferent between these two equally good means to my end of putting an asterisk on the screen. So I arbitrarily choose to press one of them. Here we cannot say that my pressing one rather than the other signified the prevailing of one over another of two conflicting motives I had. There *were no* conflicting motives such that one motive favoured the one key and the other motive favoured the other key. Yet I did press the key I pressed for a reason, namely, in order to produce an asterisk. The answer to 'Why did he press that key?' is 'Because he wanted to produce an asterisk'.

Of course, I did not have a reason for pressing that key *rather than the other*. There is no answer to 'Why did he press that key rather than this other one?', at least no answer that is a reasons explanation. I chose to press that key for a certain reason, but it is not the case that I had a reason for *not* pressing this other one instead. A similar thing holds in a conflict-of-motives case where it seems to the agent a toss-up which motive to satisfy. The answer to 'Why did he get out of bed just then?' is 'Because he wanted to get an early start on his day'. But to the question 'Why did he get out of bed rather than stay in it for a while longer?' there may be no

---

[12] Above n. 10, p. 87.

answer, because there may be no answer to 'Why did he choose to get an early start rather than to get more sleep?'.

In this case it is plausible to suppose that, *if* there is a *nomic* explanation of why he got out of bed rather than remaining in it, his desire to get an early start will figure in it, since it was a reason for that action but not a reason for the alternative. Of course it cannot be the only relevant antecedent in a nomic explanation here and the available reasons explanation affords little clue as to what might be the other antecedents that would subsume the case under laws of nature. In the indifferent means case, however, we have no good reason to suppose that, if there is a nomic explanation of why I pressed that key rather than the other one, my motive for pressing that key will figure in it, since it was an equally good motive for the other alternative. It seems that here the available reasons explanation for my action gives little hint as to what any of the antecedents of this nomic explanation might be if there is one.

So, contrary to what Mill appears to suggest, our reasons explanations for our actions do not always show us, or even give us much of a clue to, what the laws are (if any) that govern the determination of our actions by their antecedents.

IV

But to show that we do not know any causal laws governing our reasons explanations is not to show that no such laws obtain[13] or that their obtaining would be incompatible with the reasons explanations. Some philosophers have tried to make this latter claim of incompatibility,[14] but their arguments do not succeed, as Davidson (Ch. 1), among others, has shown.[15] But that issue is not relevant here, for assumption (B) makes a much stronger claim than that a reasons explanation of an action is *compatible* with the action's being nomically necessitated by its antecedents. Assumption (B) is that reasons explanations *require* such necessitation. That is something that Davidson (Ch. 1) does *not* argue for but simply assumes. Neither does Ayer or Smart argue for this requirement. Smart writes as if he has done so when he says, 'The previous paragraph

[13] As Donald Davidson, Ch. 1 this volume, points out.

[14] For example A. I. Melden (1961), *Free Action* (London: Routledge & Kegan Paul), and Norman Malcolm (1968), 'The Conceivability of Mechanism', *Philosophical Review* 77: 45–72.

[15] See Alvin Goldman (1969), 'The Compatibility of Mechanism and Purpose', *Philosophical Review* 78: 468–82.

suggests . . . that acting from reasons is not merely random precisely because it is also acting from causes', but in the paragraph he refers to he argues only that reasons explanations *can* be nomic.[16] That is not the same thing. The possibility of nomic reasons explanations does not imply the impossibility of anomic reasons explanations.

There are arguments that might be given for assumption (B). It might be said, for instance, that in giving a reasons explanation we are giving *causes* of the action—we do frequently use the word 'because' in giving reasons explanations—and where there are causes there must be nomic necessitation. But this last premiss amounts to just another way of stating assumption (B). A more worthy argument is this: in any explanation of an event in terms of its antecedents there must be some relation between explanans and explanandum in virtue of which the one explains the other. What else could this explanatory connection be if it is not that the explanans plus other antecedent circumstances nomically necessitates the explanandum?

That is a fair question. We can show that the right answer is *not* 'There is nothing else it could be' by showing that for paradigm reasons explanations there are conditions that

> are obviously sufficient for their truth,
> obviously do not entail that there is any true law covering
> the case (any nomic explanation of the action),
> but do involve another sort of obviously explanatory
> connection between the explained action and its explanans.

Any condition satisfying these criteria I will call an *anomic* sufficient condition for a reasons explanation. It is not difficult to specify such conditions.

Consider first a very simple sort of reasons explanation, the sort expressed in a sentence of one of the following forms:[17]

(1) a. *S* V-ed in order (thereby) to U.
    b. By V-ing *S* intended to U.
    c. *S* V-ed with the intention of (thereby) U-ing.

I take these different forms to give us different ways of saying the same thing.[18] Some instances of these forms:

---

[16] He argues (Smart (1968), op. cit., 300) that a computer programmed to select items from a set according to certain criteria can be said to have been 'programmed to act in accordance with what we would call "good reason" '.

[17] In these forms 'V-ed' is a variable ranging over past-tense singular forms of action verb phrases (for example, 'opened the door'), 'to U' ranges over infinitive forms ('to open the door'), and 'V-ing' ranges over progressive forms minus their auxiliaries ('opening the door').

[18] Certainly (1b) and (1c) are equivalent and each implies (1a), and in normal sorts of cases where (1a) is true (1b–c) will be true also. M. Bratman (1987), *Intention, Plans, and Practical*

S rubbed her hands together in order to warm them up.

By flipping the switch *S* intended to turn on the light.

S opened the window with the intention of letting out the smoke.

A statement of any of the forms (1a–c) is an answer to the question, 'Why did *S* V?'; it offers an explanation of *S*'s V-ing. It says that *S*'s reason for V-ing was that she believed and intended that by V-ing she would U. Actually, 'believed and intended' is redundant. *S*'s intending that by V-ing she would U implies that *S* believes that by V-ing she has enough chance of U-ing to make V-ing worth the effort, and that is all the belief that the explanation requires. So we can say that such an explanation says that *S*'s reason (or at least one of *S*'s reasons) for V-ing was her intention thereby to U.

The only thing *required* for the truth of a reasons explanation of this sort, besides the occurrence of the explained action, is that the action have been *accompanied* by an intention with the right sort of content. Specifically, given that *S* did V, it will suffice for the truth of '*S* V-ed in order to U' if the following condition obtains.

(C1) Concurrently with her action of V ing, *S* intended by *that* action to U (*S* intended *of* that action that by it she would U).

If from its inception *S* intended of her action of opening the window that by performing it she would let in fresh air (from its inception she had the intention that she could express with the sentence 'I am undertaking this opening of the window in order to let in fresh air') then *ipso facto* it was her purpose in that action to let in fresh air, she did it in order to let in fresh air.

This is so even in the possible case where there is also true some independent explanation of the action, in terms other than the agent's reasons. Imagine that by direct electronic manipulation of neural events in *S* (through, say, electrodes planted in the part of *S*'s brain that controls voluntary bodily exertion) someone else caused *S* voluntarily to open a window. Now the (C1) condition (where 'V' is 'open the window' and 'U' is 'let in fresh air') could also be true in such a case. The accompanying intention required by (C1) is at least conceptually compatible with the direct manipulation of *S*'s voluntary exertions by another. Indeed, there appears to be nothing incoherent in the supposition that the controllers of the implanted electrodes might arrange to produce both *S*'s voluntary

Reason (Cambridge, Mass.: Harvard University Press) ch. 8, describes unusual sorts of cases where it seems right to say that (1a) is true but (1b–c) are not, given the plausible assumption that, if one believes that ends E1 and E2 cannot both be achieved, one cannot (without being criticizably irrational) intend to achieve both, but one can both undertake action A1 in order to achieve (aiming at achieving) E1 and undertake action A2 in order to achieve E2.

exertion and the accompanying intention about it. If the (C1) condition were also true then it would be the case that S intended by her opening the window to let in fresh air. So it would be the case that S opened the window because of the other's manipulation of S's brain events *and* S opened the window in order to let in fresh air. There is no reason to think that the truth of either explanation must preclude the truth of the other.

Note that the content of the intention specified in (C1) refers *directly* to the action it is an intention about. That is, it does not refer to that particular action via a description of it but rather, as it were, demonstratively. The content of the intention is not the proposition, 'There is now exactly one action of V-ing by me and by it I shall U', but rather the proposition, 'By *this* V-ing (of which I am now aware) I shall U'.[19] It is owing to this direct reference that the intention is about, and thus explanatory of, *that particular* action. Such an intention, which is directly about a particular action, could not begin before the particular action does. In general, whether the propositional attitude be intending or believing or desiring or any other, for the proposition involved to contain direct or demonstrative reference to a particular requires that the particular have an appropriate sort of role in causing whatever constitutes the reference to it, a relation that is precluded if the reference comes before the particular begins to exist. (It is enough if the particular has begun to exist, even if it is an event: one can demonstratively refer to a particular event by demonstratively referring to a part of it.) This means that we have a factor, the agent's concurrently intending something of the action, that is sufficient to verify a reasons explanation of the action and that not only does not but could not be antecedent to the action. We have a sufficient condition that entails nothing about what happened before the action that is relevant to explaining it. We have a reasons explanation that is entirely in terms of a concurrent state or process and not at all in terms of any antecedent one.

Usually, some explanatory antecedent is in the background of this sort of reasons explanation, 'S V-ed in order to U'. Usually, the intention concurrent with S's V-ing is the outcome of an antecedent intention, or at least desire, to U in the very near future. Usually, maybe even always, when an agent opens a window in order to let in fresh air, or pushes on a door in order to open it, she has already formed the intention to perform

---

[19] George Wilson (1980) *The Intentionality of Human Action* (Amsterdam: North Holland), ch. V, calls attention to such directly referring intentions. He calls them 'act-relational' intentions and contrasts them with 'future action' intentions. To be exact, it is the statements attributing these two kinds of intentions, rather than the intentions themselves, that he calls 'act-relational' and 'future action'. An act-relational statement attributes, as he puts it, an intention *with which* the agent acts, an intention the agent has *in* the action.

such an action for such an end and the action is undertaken in order to carry out that antecedently formed intention, or at least she antecedently possessed a desire for that end and the action is undertaken in order to satisfy that antecedently existing desire. But, however common it may be, there is no necessity that it be so: one can quite spontaneously do such things with such intentions.

So we see that our sufficient condition for explanations of sort (1), in terms of a concurrent intention regarding the particular action, does not entail that the action has a nomic explanation in terms of its antecedents. We should also see that it does not entail that the action has a nomic explanation in terms of concurrent conditions. Of course the following generalization is true of such cases: for any agent S and time t, if S intends of her V-ing at t that she thereby U then S Vs at t. But this is logically necessary and not a law of nature. It may be, of course, that when S has an intention directly about a current action of hers, intends of *this* V-ing that by it she U, there is a mental state of S that is necessary for her having this intention but is compatible with the non-occurrence of the action of V-ing, a mental state that needs to be supplemented only by the right relation to the action for the whole to be her intending something *of* that action. But it will not be plausible to suppose that it is a law of nature that whenever an agent has this sort of mental state—ingredient in intending something of a concurrent V-ing but compatible with there being no V-ing—she does concurrently V. Her belief of her concurrent action that it is a V-ing could be false. Even if that belief could not be false (as might plausibly be held for the case where V-ing is a mental act of volition), there is no case for saying that our sufficient condition entails a nomic connection. Either there is an ingredient of the agent's direct intention about her V-ing that is compatible with her not V-ing or there is no such ingredient. If the latter, then the intention does not give us the non-entailing condition necessary for a nomic explanation. If the former then, although this aspect *could* be part of a nomically necessitating factor, there is nothing in the condition itself that entails that it must be so. There is, we have noted, a causal connection between the action and the intention required for the latter to refer directly to the former. But even if this must involve a nomic connection—and it is by no means clear that it must—the causation goes in the wrong direction, opposite to that from explaining intention to explained action. (In general, when one's thought contains a direct reference to a particular, it is in virtue of the particular's producing something in the thought, not vice versa.)

If the explanatory connection between the explaining intention and the explained action is not nomic necessitation then what is it? Well, it stares one in the face. In reasons explanations of sort (1) the concurrent intention explains the action simply in virtue of being an intention of that action that by or in it the agent will do a certain thing, in virtue, that is, of being that sort of propositional attitude (an intention) whose content has that feature (its being that by or in that action a certain thing will be done). That is all there is to it. It is simple but for the purpose of explaining the action it is sufficient. Aside from the relation required for the direct reference, this is an *internal* relation between the explaining factor and the explained action. It follows from the direct reference plus *intrinsic* properties of the relata, namely, the property of one that it is an action of *S*'s and the property of the other that it is an intention of *S*'s with a certain sort of content, namely, that the item to which it directly refers be an action with such-and-such properties. The explanatory connection is made, not by laws of nature, but by the direct reference and the internal relation.

Are reasons explanations of sort (1) *causal* explanations? They are if all one means by 'causal' is that the explanation can be expressed with a 'because' linking the explanandum and the explanans. ('She opened the window because she intended thereby to let out the smoke.') If, on the other hand, one requires that a case, properly so called, precede its effect, then these are not causal explanations. And it perhaps sounds odd to speak of a *concurrent* intention about an action as *causing* or *producing* or *resulting in* or *leading to* the action.

None of these expressions sounds odd, however, when speaking of a motive or reason the agent had prior to the action. One case where the explaining factor is antecedent to the action is the case where we explain the action as the carrying out of a decision the agent had made, an intention she had formed. One class of such explanations are expressible by sentences of the following form:

(2) a. *S* V-ed then in order to carry out her intention to V when F.
   b. *S* V-ed then because she had intended to V when F and she believed it was then F.

Here (2b) simply spells out more fully what (2a) implies. Some examples of this sort of explanation:

S opened the window in order to carry out her intention to open the window when people started smoking.
S raised her hand in order to carry out her intention to raise it as soon as the Chair called for the votes in favour of the motion.

What is an anomic sufficient condition for the truth of such an explanation? The wording of (2a) suggests that it should include, besides the explained action and the antecedent intention, an intention concurrent with the action to the effect that the action be a carrying out of the prior intention. This will make it the case that S performed the action *in order to* carry out that prior intention, performed it, that is, with the intention of carrying out that prior intention. So we can say that an explanation of sort (2) is true if (C2) is true.

(C2) (a) Prior to this V-ing S had an intention to V when F, and (b) concurrently with this V-ing S remembered that prior intention and its content and intended of this V-ing that it carry out that prior intention (be a V-ing when F).

Note that S cannot have the concurrent intention specified in (C2b) without believing that F now obtains; so it guarantees the second conjunct of (2b).

It is obvious that this sufficient condition is anomic. That is, it is obviously compatible with the truth of (C2) in a particular case of S's V-ing that there should be another case (involving S or some other agent) that is exactly similar in everything antecedent to the action (including other circumstances as well as the agent's intention to V) but lacks the agent's V-ing. Thus (C2) could hold even if there were no nomic explanation of S's V-ing in terms of the prior intention plus other antecedent circumstances. What then makes the explanatory connection here, if it is not nomic connection? Well, in the concurrent intention required by (C2) S intends of her current action that it be of just the sort specified in the content of the required prior intention (to which the content of the concurrent intention must refer), namely, a V-ing when F. It is this internal and referential relation between the contents of the prior and the concurrent intention, together with the explanatory relation of the concurrent intention to the action, which we have already discussed, that makes the explanatory connection between the prior intention and the action. The connection has two links, from prior to concurrent intention and from concurrent intention to action.

Following the model of (C2) for explanations of sort (2), it is not difficult to work out anomic sufficient conditions for other forms of reasons explanations in terms of antecedent states of the agent. Consider, for example, the sort expressed by sentences of the following form:

(3) a. S V-ed in order to carry out her (antecedent) intention to U.
b. S V-ed because she had intended to U and believed that by V-ing she would (might) U.

Here (3b) spells out more fully what is implied by (3a). Some examples of instances of this form of explanation:

S shouted in order to carry out her (antecedent) intention to frighten away any bears there might be in the vicinity.

S uttered, 'They're gone', because she had intended to let *R* know when they had gone and believed that by such an utterance she would do so.

The following is an anomic sufficient condition for the truth of explanations of sort (3).

(C3) (a) Prior to V-ing *S* had the intention to U and (b) concurrently with V-ing *S* remembered that prior intention and intended that by this V-ing she would carry it out.

S's having the concurrent intention specified in (C3b) requires that *S* believe that by this V-ing she would or might U, and thus it entails the second conjunct of (3b).

Still another sort of reasons explanation in terms of antecedents is expressible in sentences of the following form.

(4) *S* V-ed because she had desired that *p* and believed that by V-ing she would (might) make it the case that *p* (or contribute to doing so).

Examples of this sort of explanation:

S opened the window because she had a desire for fresher air in the room and believed that opening the window would let in fresher air.

S voted for the motion because she wanted it to pass and believed that her vote would help it to do so.

The following gives an anomic sufficient condition for explanations of this sort.

(C4) (a) Prior to V-ing *S* had a desire that *p* and (b) concurrently with V-ing *S* remembered that prior desire and intended of this V-ing that it satisfy (or contribute to satisfying) that desire.

Our anomic sufficient conditions for explanations of actions in terms of antecedent reasons, (C2)–(C4), require *S* to remember the prior mental state (of intention or desire) while engaged in the action that that prior state explains. This will be a feature of any anomic sufficient condition for a reasons explanation of an action in terms of a prior state of the agent. If at the time the agent begins the action she has no memory at all of the prior desire or intention, then it can hardly be a factor motivating that action. Now it is not necessary in order for (C4), for example, to be an anomic sufficient condition for the truth of (4) that this memory connection be anomic as well. Even if it were true that there is remembering of the prior desire only if there is a nomic connection between the prior state (plus its circumstances) and some current state, it would not follow from this and (C4) that there must be a nomic connection between the prior desire (plus its circumstances) and the action for which, given the truth of (C4), it provides a reasons explanation. But it is interesting to note, incidentally, that it is possible to specify an anomic sufficient condition for remembering, for the connection between an earlier state of mind and a later one that makes the latter a memory of the former. S's seeming to remember a prior intention to do such-and-such will be a memory of a particular prior intention *if* S had such a prior intention and nothing independent of that prior intention has happened sufficient to produce S's seeming to remember such an intention. More generally, one's having had prior experience of a certain sort is the *default* explanation of one's later seeming to remember having had such experience, in the sense that it is the explanation *unless* this role is pre-empted by something else, independent of it, that was sufficient to cause the memory impression.[20]

Like those in terms of concurrent intentions, our anomic sufficient conditions for reasons explanations in terms of antecedent motives are compatible with the truth of independent explanations in terms other than the agent's reasons. Consider again our example of S's voluntarily opening a window *both* as a result of another's manipulation of events in S's brain *and* in order to let in fresh air. Add to it that S had earlier formed a desire for fresher air in the room and concurrently with her opening the window remembered that desire and intended of that action that it satisfy that desire, making true the appropriate instance of (C4). Then you have a case where S opened the window both because of the signals sent to the volitional part of her brain and in order to satisfy her antecedent desire. Again there is no reason to think that the truth of either explanation excludes the truth of the other.

A noteworthy fact about (C4), the anomic sufficient condition for an explanation of the form 'S V-ed because she had desired that *p* and believed that by V-ing she would satisfy that desire', is that it suggests a way of distinguishing between (i) a desire that was a reason for which the agent acted as she did and (ii) a desire that was *not* a reason for which the agent acted as she did although it was a reason for so acting that the agent was aware of having at the time. A desire of the agent's fits description (i) if the agent acts with the intention that that action satisfy that desire; and a desire of the agent's fits description (ii) if, and only if, the agent has no such intention concurrent with the action despite being aware of the desire and of the fact that it is a reason for acting as she did (given her beliefs).

---

[20] I have argued this point more fully in Carl Ginet (1975) *Knowledge, Perception, and Memory* (Dordrecht, Neth.: Reidel), 160–5.

One may wonder, however, if and how there *could* be cases that fit description (ii). Our account does not answer this question, but only turns it into the question whether it could be that an agent at the time of acting believes that her action will satisfy a certain desire she has without intending of the action that it satisfy that desire. Suppose S urgently needs her glasses which she left in R's room where R is now sleeping. S has some desire to wake R, because she would then have R's company, but also some desire *not* to wake R, because she knows that R needs the sleep. S decides to enter R's room in order to get her reading glasses, knowing as she does so that her action will satisfy her desire to wake R. Could it nevertheless be true that S did not intend of her action that it wake R? Bratman (1987) offers an illuminating account of how this could be so.[21] It seems right to say that S did not intend to wake R if S was so disposed that, had it turned out that her entering the room did not wake R, S would not have felt that her plan had failed to be completely realized and she must then either wake R in some other way or decide to abandon part of her plan. And S's being thus *uncommitted* to waking R is quite compatible with S's expecting and desiring to wake R.

V

The anomic sufficient conditions we have given for explanations of actions in terms of antecedent reasons allow the possibility that the very same antecedent state of the world could afford a reasons explanation for either of two or more different alternative actions. Suppose, for example, that there have been two different occasions when I have formed the intention to produce an asterisk on my computer screen and have known that either of two keys will do the job. If on one of those occasions I pressed one of those keys, my action can be explained by saying that I pressed that key in order to produce an asterisk; and if on the other occasion I pressed the other key, that action can be explained by saying that I pressed *that* key in order to produce an asterisk. The only differences we need to suppose in the two situations are in the action explained (my pressing the one key rather than the other) and its concurrent intention (which I

---

[21] See Bratman (1987), op. cit., 155–60. The example he discusses differs from mine in that the agent in his example believes that the expected but unintended effect (the 'side' effect) will help to achieve the same end that his intended means is intended to achieve, whereas in my example S does not believe this but desires the expected side effect, waking R, for reasons independent of her intended end, getting her glasses. But this difference seems immaterial to Bratman's account of how the side effect can, though expected and even desired (or believed to promote desired ends), still be unintended.

could have expressed, 'By this pressing of *this* key I intend to produce an asterisk'). We need suppose no differences at all in the relevant *antecedent* intention. On both occasions it was just an intention to produce an asterisk.

In that example the agent was indifferent between alternative means to an intended end. In another sort of example the agent chooses arbitrarily between incompatible desired ends. Suppose S desires the motion to pass and at the same time desires to avoid offending her friend who opposes the motion. Whether she votes for the motion or votes against it, the explanation can be that S did it in order to satisfy the relevant prior desire. Again, the only differences in the two alternative situations that we need to suppose, in order to make the alternative explanations hold in them, are differences in the actions and their concurrent accompaniments. We need suppose no difference in the antecedents.

Here we have a striking difference between the anomic explanatory connection we have found in explanations of actions in terms of antecedent reasons and the nomic explanatory connection in deterministic explanations of events. The nomic, deterministic connection, by its very nature, can go from a given antecedent state of the world to just one subsequent development. If the antecedent state of the world explains a subsequent development via general laws of nature then that same antecedent state could not likewise explain any alternative development. Given fixed laws of nature, a given antecedent situation has the potential to explain nomically and deterministically at most one subsequent alternative development. But the same antecedent state can explain in the anomic, reasons way any of several alternative possible subsequent actions. If the antecedent situation contains the agent's having desires for two or more incompatible ends or her being indifferent between alternative means to an intended end, then it has the potential to explain in the reasons way whichever of the alternative actions occurs. The one that occurs needs only to have the right sort of accompanying memory and intention.[22]

---

[22] We have here a solution to another puzzle of van Inwagen's, concerning how an agent can have a choice about, can have it in her power to determine, which of competing antecedent motives will cause her action, be the reason for which she acts. He expresses this puzzle in a footnote appended to his remarks I quoted above:

Alvin Plantinga has suggested to me that the thief may have had a choice about whether to repent owing to his having had a choice about whether, on the one hand, DB [a certain complex of desire and belief in the thief] caused R [the thief's repenting], or, on the other, his desire for money and his belief that the poor-box contained money (DB*) jointly caused the event *his robbing the poor-box* (R*). We should note that the two desire-belief pairs, DB and DB*, both actually obtained; according to the theory Plantinga has proposed, what the thief had a choice about was which of these two potential causes became the actual cause of an effect appropriate

It is true, as we noted earlier, that when an agent chooses arbitrarily between incompatible ends or between alternative means to an intended end we do not have an explanation of why the agent acted as she did *rather than* in one of the other ways. Nevertheless, we do have an explanation of why the agent acted as she did: she so acted in order to carry out the intention or to satisfy the relevant desire. The truth of that explanation is not undermined by the agent's not having any reason for, there not being any explanation of, her not doing one of the other things instead.

But now one may wonder about cases where the antecedents explain an action in the reasons sort of way but do *not* have the potential to explain alternative actions equally well, where the antecedents give the agent's reason for acting as she did and also explain why she did not act in any alternative way instead. If such explanations must be nomic, must imply that sufficiently similar antecedents will (as a matter of the laws of nature) always lead to the same sort of action rather than to any alternative, then incompatibilism is still in serious trouble. For it would be absurd to say that any such reasons explanation of an action renders it unfree.

Incompatibilists need not worry. Such explanations need not be nomic either. Consider again reasons explanations of sort (3).

(3)   *S* V-ed in order to carry out her intention to U.

Our anomic sufficient condition for such an explanation was (C3).

(C3) (a) Prior to V-ing *S* had the intention to U and (b) concurrently with V-ing *S* remembered her prior intention and its content and intended that by this V-ing she would carry it out.

What sort of enriched condition will be sufficient for the truth of a similar explanation of why *S* V-ed *and* did not do something else instead (either some other sort of action or being inactive)? A commonly occurring condition that accomplishes this is the following.

(C3*) (a) Just before V-ing the agent intended to U at once and pre-ferred V-ing then to any alternative means to U-ing then that

to it. This may for all I know be the correct account of the 'inner state' of a deliberating agent who has a choice about how he is going to act. But if this account is correct, then there are two events *its coming to pass that DB causes R* and *its coming to pass that DB* causes R** such that, though one of them must happen, it's causally undetermined which will happen; and it will have to be the case that the thief has a choice about which of them will happen. If this were so, I should find it very puzzling and I should be at a loss to give an account of it. (van Inwagen (1983), op. cit., 239, n. 34)

The proper account seems to me straightforward. The thief determines which of the antecedent motives he acts out of simply by acting in the way recommended by one of them while concurrently remembering the motive and intending his action to satisfy it. His doing so is obviously compatible with his action's being nomically undetermined by the antecedent state of the world.

occurred to her that she thought she could then perform, and (b) concurrently with V-ing she remembered her prior intention and intended by this V-ing to carry it out and she continued to prefer V-ing to any alternative means of U-ing that occurred to her that she thought she could then perform.

It is obvious that (C3*) is sufficient for the truth of a reasons explanation of the sort under consideration, one of the form:

(3*) S V-ed then rather than doing something else or being inactive instead because she intended to U at once and she preferred V-ing to any other means of U-ing that occurred to her that she thought she could then perform.

It should be equally obvious that (C3*) does not entail that S's V-ing was nomically necessitated by its antecedents. There certainly is no plausibility in the proposition that the antecedents given in (C3*a) must always issue in S's V-ing. Often enough such antecedents are followed by S's doing something else instead, owing to some new alternative occurring to S at the last minute, or to S's changing her mind about what alternatives are open to her, or to S's suddenly abandoning (perhaps even forgetting) her intention to U at once, or to S's weakness of will (though S believed that V-ing was definitely the best means to U-ing and therefore intended to take that means, there was in some other means a temptation that she was in the end unable to resist). As with the antecedents that explain why S V-ed (those given in (C3a)), the antecedents that explain why not any other alternative instead (added in (C3*a)) do so completely only in conjunction with conditions concurrent with and not antecedent to the action explained (specified in (C3*b)). To suppose that there occurs another case where the antecedents are exactly the same but S does not V but is inactive or does something else instead is not to suppose anything incompatible with the truth of the explanation entailed by (C3*).

VI

I hope to have made it clear that incompatibilism does not entail certain absurdities it has been alleged to entail. The thesis that a free action cannot be nomically determined by its antecedents does not entail that an agent cannot determine which free action she performs or that an agent cannot perform a free action for reasons. When one sees how easy it is to give anomic sufficient conditions for reasons explanations of actions, one may find it surprising that many philosophers should have subscribed to the assumption that such explanations must be nomic. (Even some incompatibilists have been guilty of this assumption; they have typically also been 'hard' determinists, denying that we in fact have free will.[23]) Perhaps the error is less surprising if we see it as a case of over-generalizing a well-understood and highly respected paradigm, in this case the explanatory paradigm of the natural sciences where laws of nature are what make explanatory connections. Fascination with this paradigm can, it seems, blind one to the fact that the explanatory paradigm of our ordinary reasons explanations of action is quite different. There an internal and referential relation is sufficient to make the explanatory connection and has no need of a nomic connection. Neither does it rule out a nomic connection. Reasons explanations are not *in*deterministic, only *a*deterministic; but that is all that the defence of incompatibilism requires.

[23] For example: Paul Henri Thiry, Baron d'Holbach (1770) *Système de la Nature* (London), chs. XI–XII; Paul Ree (1885) *Die Illusion der Willens Freiheit* (Berlin), chs. I–II (Eng. trans, in P. Edwards and A. Pap (1973) (eds.), *A Modern Introduction to Philosophy*, 3rd edn. (New York: Free Press)); Clarence Darrow (1922), *Crime, Its Cause and Treatment* (New York: Crowell).

6

A CAUSAL THEORY OF INTENDING

WAYNE A. DAVIS

My goal is to define intending. I defend the view that believing and desiring something are necessary for intending it. They are not sufficient, however, for some things we both expect and want (e.g. the sun to rise tomorrow) are unintendable. Restricting the objects of intention to our own future actions is unwarranted and unhelpful. Rather, the belief involved in intending must be based on the desire in a certain way. En route, I argue that expected but unwanted consequences are not intended, examine the two senses of 'desire', distinguish intending from being willing, and relate intending to a variety of other propositional attitudes.

I

The topic of intention has three subtopics: *simple intention*, or *intending*, as expressed in '*S* intended to miss'; *intentional action*, as in '*S* intentionally missed'; and *further intention*, as in '*S* missed with the intention of losing'. They form a natural hierarchy. Doing *A* intentionally entails intending to do *A*; and doing *A* with the intention of doing *B* entails doing *A* intentionally and intending to do *B*. Intending to do *A*, however, does not entail doing *A* intentionally (or unintentionally), nor does it entail doing anything else with the intention of doing *A*: simple intentions need not be acted on. Our subject is intending.

The verb 'intends' and its synonyms (*means*, *plans*, the uncommon *purposes*, and the progressive form *is intending*[1]) take various complements:

Wayne A. Davis, 'A Causal Theory of Intending', *American Philosophical Quarterly* 21 (1984), 43–54. Reprinted by permission of *American Philosophical Quarterly*.

[1] 'Means' in (a) or (d) expresses speaker's meaning rather than intending. 'Means' and 'plans' in (c) require *for*. 'Planning' is ambiguous, meaning *intending* or *making plans*.

    (a) *S* intends *NP*
    (b) *S* intends to *VP*
    (c) *S* intends *NP* to *VP*
    (d) *S* intends that *NP* (should) *VP*

The complements are transformationally related. 'The composer intended a grand finale' can be expanded to 'The composer intended the finale to be grand', which is a syntactic variant of 'The composer intended that the finale be grand'. 'Sue intends to sing' can be expanded to 'Sue intends that she should sing'. The subjunctive auxiliary 'should' is optional. 'Intend' also occurs with *compound* complements: negations, conjunctions, disjunctions, conditionals, and so on.[2] To achieve greatest generality, therefore, we should take as our definiendum *S intends that p*, where *p* stands for any sentence (in the appropriate grammatical form).

There are two ways to *express* our intentions. 'I intend to come' or its expansion 'I intend that I should come' is an *explicit* expression of intention. 'I will (or shall) come', in *oratio recta*, is an implicit expression of the same intention. If I say I will come, you can normally infer that I intend to come even though I did not explicitly say so. Many sentences have as an utterance implication that the speaker intends what they describe. Most, however, have no such implication: consider 'The sky is blue' or even 'I will die someday'. In the second or third persons, 'shall' must be used to express intention: compare 'My opponent will win' with 'My opponent shall win'. Despite the utterance implications connecting them, corresponding explicit and implicit expressions of intention are logically independent: I may intend to win even though in fact I will lose.

II

According to a long tradition, intention can be analysed into cognitive and motivational components.[3] Among the synonyms, the cognitive element is

---

[2] The complements in '*S* intends to bring it about that . . .' (R. M. Chisholm (1970), 'The Structure of Intention', *Journal of Philosophy* 67: 633–47), '*S* intends to bring about state of affairs φ by doing action *A*' (R. Audi (1973), 'Intending', *Journal of Philosophy* 70: 387–403), and '*S* intends to act in a certain way on a certain occasion under certain conditions' (M. Bratman (1979), 'Simple Intention', *Philosophical Studies* 36: 245–59), are compounds of a less familiar sort.

[3] See J. Austin (1873), *Lectures on Jurisprudence*, i (London); O. W. Holmes (1881), *The Common Law* (Boston); Sir J. Salmond (1930), *Jurisprudence*, 8th edn. (London), 393; B. N. Fleming (1964), 'On Intention', *Philosophical Review* 73: 301–20; A. Kenny (1966), 'Intention and Purpose', *Journal of Philosophy* 63: 642–51; H. P. Grice (1971), 'Intention and Uncertainty', *Proceedings of the British Academy* 57: 263–79; Audi (1973) op. cit.; G. Harman, 'Practical Reasoning', Ch. 7 this volume 149–77; D. Davidson (1978), 'Intending', in Y. Yovel (ed.),

stressed by 'plan', the motivational by 'purpose'. I think *belief* is the cognitive component: *S intends that p only if S believes that p.* Jack intends to call only if he believes he will call (he thinks he will, he expects to). Otherwise Jack only wants to call, hopes to, intends to try, or intends to call if he remembers. Jack could express his intention by asserting that he will (definitely or probably) call, which would also express the belief that he will call. As I understand it, believing *p* is equivalent to being more certain of *p* than of not-*p*. When someone's degree of belief is very low, i.e. when he is only slightly more certain of *p* than of not-*p*, he is inclined to believe *p*. Jack must at least be inclined to believe that he will call.

Unlike hoping, intending that *p* requires more than not being certain that not-*p*. While anyone buying a lottery ticket hopes to win, he cannot without exaggeration say 'I intend to win', unless he is either deluding himself or in on a fix. Of course, 'I don't intend to win' would be equally misleading, suggesting that he intends *not* to win. 'Don't intend' is like 'don't want' or 'don't believe', which commonly express aversion or disbelief rather than mere lack of desire or belief.

The belief condition explains why 'I will call' is an utterance implication of 'I intend to call', and why the statement 'I intend to call but I won't', while not logically inconsistent, is nevertheless most odd.[4]

The belief condition also explains why the requirements of rationality apply to intending, such as consistency, respect for evidence, and explanatory coherence.[5] It is irrational to have incompatible intentions and unreasonable to intend to do something in the face of conclusive evidence that you won't. In contrast, there is nothing irrational about conflicting or unrealistic desires. Similarly, the principle 'If *S* expects to do *A* and believes that he will do *A* only if *p*, then to be consistent *S* must believe *p*' holds when 'expects' is changed to 'intends', though not to 'desires'. Finally: 'Other things being equal, a given conception of the future, containing plans as well as predictions, is more coherent than another to the extent that the first leaves less unexplained than the second. As the point applies to theoretical reasoning, it is reflected in the slogan, "Inference is inference to the best explanation". As it applies to practical reasoning, it is reflected in the slogan, "To will the end is to will the means"' (Harman, Ch. 7 this volume, 153).

A variety of mental states exclude belief and therefore intention, such as: disbelieving, doubting, being pessimistic, having no hope, and wishing

Philosophy of History and Action (Dordrecht, Neth.), 41–60; and M. C. Beardsley (1978), 'Intending', in A. Goldman and J. Kim (eds.), *Values and Morals* (Dordrecht, Neth.), 163–84.

[4] Cf. Audi (1973), op. cit. 388.   [5] Cf. Harman, op. cit. 152 ff.

that p; having no idea whether p; being surprised if p, and believing it impossible than p. If Alan has no idea whether he will succeed, or is pessimistic that he will, or wishes that he would, he must not intend to succeed. Someone can intend to do what *in fact* cannot be done, such as turn on a light which unbeknownst to him is burned out.[6] But no one can intend to do what he *thinks* cannot be done.[7] Since disbelieving that p is believing that not-p, it follows that intending to do something is incompatible with intending not to do it.

Since we can *try* to do what we do not expect to do, *trying something does not entail intending it.*[8] A beginner can try to hit the bull's-eye. But only an expert marksman, or someone who thinks he is, could properly be described as intending to hit the bull's-eye. I know I cannot press 1000 pounds, but I might try if only to prove to you that I cannot. The same examples show that someone can intend to try to do something without intending to do it.

If I intend to buy a house someday, I must not *doubt that* I will. I may of course *have some doubts* about the matter. But having some doubt, or being in doubt, only means being uncertain. *Intending that p does not require being certain that p.*[9] I intend to play tennis this afternoon even though I realize there is a 10 per cent chance of rain, a remote chance I will change my mind, and so on. 'I intend to but I may not', while crying for further comment, is not odd. If intention did require certainty, there would only be firm intentions. And intention would be incompatible with *hope.* Intending that p only requires being more certain that p than that not-p. As Audi observed (1973: 388), I might intend to speak to someone in Boston, even though I think the chances of him being there are barely better than even.

A fortiori, intending that p does not entail *knowing* that p.[10] Besides certainty, knowledge requires true and justified belief. If Kathy does not go shopping later, then she cannot now know that she will go no matter how firmly she intends to. And many things that we intend to do, such as turn

---

[6] Contrast A. C. Baier (1970), 'Act and Intent', *Journal of Philosophy* 67: 648–58 and H-N. Castañeda (1971), 'Intentions and the Structure of Intending', *Journal of Philosophy* 68: 462.

[7] Cf. S. Hampshire (1967), *Thought and Action* (London), 650; J. W. Meiland (1970), *The Nature of Intention* (New York), 44 ff.; and Audi (1973), op. cit. 397. Contrast I. Thalberg (1962), 'Intending the Impossible', *Australasian Journal of Philosophy* 40: 49–56; C. G. Hedman (1970), 'Intending the Impossible', *Philosophy* 45: 33–8.

[8] Cf. Beardsley (1978), op. cit. 178; contrast Thalberg (1962), op. cit.; Hedman (1970), op. cit.; and Meiland (1970), op. cit. 44, 67.

[9] Cf. Davidson (1978), op. cit. 49, who erroneously concluded that intention does not imply belief. Contrast S. Hampshire and H. L. A. Hart (1958), 'Decision, Intention, and Certainty', *Mind* 67: 1–12 and Grice (1971), op. cit. 264–6.

[10] Contrast Hampshire and Hart (1958), op. cit. and Hampshire (1967), op. cit.

on a light in an unfamiliar room, we simply *assume* we'll do, without adequate evidence. Other things we irrationally expect to do despite strong evidence to the contrary. Bob may plan to use his car even though an expert mechanic said there is only a slight chance it will be drivable. Of course, intention does not exclude knowledge or certainty either.

III

Belief is obviously not a sufficient condition of intention. I believe that I will die someday, and make a mistake today, but I intend to do neither. What is lacking is *desire*, the motivational element in intention: *S intends that p only if S desires that p*. Jack intends to call only if he desires (wants, wishes) to call. I believe desiring *p* is equivalent to preferring *p* rather than not-*p*. Jack must at least be inclined to call, i.e. have a slight preference for calling. The desire must exist *when* the intention does. The fact that later in life someone will want to die does not prove that he currently intends to. The desire condition makes intending that *p* incompatible with being sorry, being angry, regretting, and fearing that *p*, and hoping that not-*p*. If Ted is sorry that his wife is going to leave him, he cannot intend that she leave him. If Bob intends to order diet dessert he must not regret that he will though he may regret that he *has to*. The belief and desire conditions jointly entail that intending implies being glad or optimistic that *p*.

The desire condition explains why, whenever someone expresses an intention, saying perhaps that he is going to church, or to Florida, it is appropriate to ask 'Why do you want to do that?' In contrast, if someone said he is going to jail, or to Hell, the same question would be out of place, suffering from an erroneous presupposition. The condition explains why implicit expressions of intention resemble commands:[11] both express desire. The desire condition also explains why intentions have many of the same properties as desires: e.g. people tend to do, and to think about, what they intend or desire to do; intentions and desires explain actions; intending or desiring to do something provides a reason to adopt the means of doing it;[12] and reasons for intending to do something are reasons for wanting to do it.

---

[11] Cf. G. E. M. Anscombe (1963), *Intention*, 2nd edn. (Ithaca, NY), 2; A. Kenny (1963), *Action, Emotion, and Will* (New York), 219–21; and H-N. Castañeda (1972), 'Intentions and Intending', *American Philosophical Quarterly* 9: 145.

[12] Contrast M. Bratman (1981), 'Intentions and Means-End Reasoning', *Philosophical Review* 90: 254 ff.

Philosophers often distinguish *intrinsic* from *extrinsic* desire. To desire something intrinsically is to desire it *for its own sake*, whereas to desire something extrinsically is to desire it *for the sake of something else*. Either sort of desire will satisfy the desire condition: it does not matter *why* we want what we intend. I may intend to have a good time (intrinsic desire) or to flip the light switch (extrinsic desire).

'Desire' is also ambiguous.[13] In the sense intended in the desire condition, 'desire' is synonymous with *want, wish*, and *would like*, and appears as a *transitive verb* in sentences like 'I desire to eat' and 'I desire food'. I call this *volitive desire*. In another sense, 'desire' has the near synonyms *appetite, hungering, craving, yearning, longing*, and *urge*, and appears as a *noun* in sentences like 'I have a desire to eat' and 'I have a desire for food'. I call this *appetitive desire*. Objects of appetitive desire are *appealing*, things we *view with pleasure*. The two senses are logically independent. We often want to eat, for social or nutritional reasons, when we have no appetite and view the prospect of eating without pleasure. We desire to eat, but have no desire to. On the other hand, we may have a ravenous appetite and find the prospect of eating terribly appealing, and yet not want to eat because we are on a diet. We have a desire to eat, but don't desire to. While distinct, the two sorts of desire tend to coincide: an appetitive desire to do something tends to generate and motivate a volitive desire to do it. An appetite for food tends to make people want food. Note that the intrinsic-extrinsic distinction cuts across the appetitive-volitive distinction.

'Want' is unambiguous, expressing volitive rather than appetitive desire. The phrase *really want*, however, is multiply ambiguous. In one sense, 'really want' means *actually* want. If a salesman says he wants to get you the best deal possible, you may wonder whether he really wants to or whether he is just trying to deceive you. In another sense, 'really want' means want *very much*. Every student wants to get an A. We nevertheless might tell a senior that if he really wanted an A he would study harder. In a third sense, what we really want is what we have an appetitive desire to do. At a dinner party, after answering 'Yes' to the question 'Do you want dessert', and then starting in on it, I may confide to you that I don't really want anything more to eat, since I am stuffed. Sue, who answered 'No', may explain that she really wants some, but is on a strict diet. Emphasis on 'want' is also used to express appetitive desire. We must really want what we intend only in the first sense.

---

[13] I defend this claim at length in W. A. Davis (1983), 'The Two Senses of Desire', *Philosophical Studies* 44.

The desire condition has been widely rejected. The problems fall into three distinct groups: actions motivated by duty or necessity; expected but unwanted consequences of intended acts; and circularity.

I intend to teach today, because I feel obligated to do so. Nevertheless, I have no desire to teach. I'm not in the mood. What I really want to do is play tennis. It is natural to conclude that intention does not entail desire.[14] But 'desire' is ambiguous. It has its appetitive sense in such examples. In the volitive sense, I *do* desire to teach; my reason for wanting to is that I have an obligation. The conclusion to draw, therefore, is that intention entails volitive rather than appetitive desire.

The principle that intention entails desire can be expressed as follows: someone intends to do something only if he is *motivated* to do it. But this is also ambiguous. In one sense, I am not motivated to teach, since I'm not in the mood. I may need to 'get motivated' in order to lecture effectively. In another sense, though, I am motivated to teach, by the fact that I am obligated to. Intending only entails being motivated in the volitive sense. This does not mean that all intentional action is motivated by desire. For an action to be motivated *by* desire, it is not enough that the agent should want to perform it. His motivation, that is, his *reason* for wanting to perform it, must be that he has a desire to perform it. I want to teach, but my action will be motivated by obligation rather than desire. For my reason for wanting to teach is that I am obligated to rather than that I have a desire to (that I find the prospect appealing or view it with pleasure).

Many have countered that the alleged sense in which people want or desire to do whatever they intend to do is abnormal, extended, or even contrived.[15] Not true. The following sort of dialogue is quite common and perfectly normal. '*Al*: Where are you going? *Bob*: To the zoo. *Al*: Why on earth do you want to go to the zoo? *Bob*: I promised my son I'd take him.' Bob's final remark served to answer, not reject, Al's second question. (Contrast: '*Al*: Why are you beating your wife? *Bob*: She's my mistress.'

---

[14] Cf. J. Jenkins (1965), 'Motive and Intention', *Philosophical Quarterly* 15: 165; J. Rachels (1969), 'Wanting and Willing', *Philosophical Studies* 20: 10; Chisholm (1970), op. cit. 645; Baier (1970), op. cit. 651ff.; W. F. Hare (1970), 'Trying', *Kinesis* 3: 46; Meiland (1970), op. cit. 117; and R. Lawrence (1972), *Motive and Intention* (Chicago), 86. Contrast T. F. Daveney (1961), 'Wanting', *Philosophical Quarterly* 11: 135–44; P. M. Churchland (1970), 'The Logical Character of Action Explanations', *Philosophical Review* 79: 231; A. Goldman (1970), *A Theory of Human Action* (Englewood Cliffs, NJ), 50; T. Nagel (1970), *The Possibility of Altruism* (Oxford); Audi (1973), op. cit. 389; and Beardsley (1978), op. cit. 167 ff.

[15] See R. Norman (1971), *Reasons for Actions* (New York), 19; Lawrence (1972), op. cit. 88; S. Hampshire (1975), *Freedom of the Individual* (Princeton), 40; W. Neely (1974), 'Freedom and Desire', *Philosophical Review* 83: 32ff.; and A. R. Miller (1980), 'Wanting, Intending, and Knowing What One is Doing', *Philosophy and Phenomenological Research*, 4: 339.

Here Bob's response rejects the question without answering it.) What *would* be abnormal and completely inappropriate for Bob to say is: 'I *don't* want to go to the zoo. What made you think I did?' Of course, he might answer: 'I don't *want* to go, but I promised.' But the emphasis on 'want' changes its meaning to appetitive desire.

Audi (1973: 390) has stressed the appropriateness of 'What do you want?' when asked of anyone who intrudes. The answer might be 'To deliver a message', even though the intruder is embarrassed to interrupt and does so only because he feels obligated. The answer 'Nothing' would be extraordinary to say the least. Similarly, suppose you have to do something unpleasant that you do not know how to do, such as commit your wife to a mental institution or file for bankruptcy. You could always ask for instructions by saying 'I want to do such-and-such; how do I go about it?' The response, 'How could you *want* to do something like that?' would be puerile.[16]

Reflect also on cases where a man refrains from doing something out of a sense of obligation even though he 'really wants' to do it. Suppose Alan suppresses a burning desire to kiss Monique, because he feels he ought to be faithful to his wife. Later, to show just how virtuous Alan was, we might observe that he had the ability and the opportunity, so that he could have kissed Monique if he had wanted to. The use of the *counterfactual* subjunctive here—if he *had* wanted to—presupposes that Alan did *not* in fact want to kiss Monique.[17] Note finally that any reason for doing something can be said, in perfectly standard English, to be a reason for wanting to do it.

At this point, the charge of circularity arises. Some have contended that 'desire', in the sense in which intention entails desire, is simply a synonym of 'intention'.[18] But we saw above that intention, unlike desire, entails belief. I desire to finish this paper today, but I cannot be said to intend to because I am certain that I won't. Other differences will emerge below.

Harman (Ch. 7 this volume, 154 ff., 165) holds that desire can be defined in terms of intention, which consequently cannot be defined in terms of

---

[16] Cf. J. Gosling (1969), *Pleasure and Desire* (Oxford), 93, 105.   [17] Cf. ibid. 87 ff.

[18] See Daveney (1961), op. cit. 135–44; W. Sellars (1963), 'Imperatives, Intentions, and the Logic of "Ought"', in H-N. Castañeda and G. Nakhnikian (eds.), *Morality and the Language of Conduct* (Detroit), 217; E. Bedford (1966), 'Intention and Law', *Journal of Philosophy* 63: 654 ff.; Fleming (1964), op. cit. 307 ff.; Chisholm (1970), op. cit. 654; G. H. von Wright (1971), *Explanation and Understanding* (Ithaca, NY), 103; P. Foot (1972), 'Reasons for Action and Desire', *Proceedings of the Aristotelian Society* 46: 204; and Miller (1980), op. cit. 339. Contrast Meiland (1970), op. cit. 74; Audi (1973), op. cit. 390–1; Harman, op. cit. 150; Davidson (1978), op. cit. 58 ff.; and Beardsley (1978), op. cit. 169.

desire. A desire, he says, is definable as a *disposition* to intend: S desires p provided S intends p or would if 'given a choice' between p and not-p. It is possible, however, that Tom desires not to aggravate his tennis elbow, is given the choice of aggravating it or not, and yet does not intend not to aggravate it because he wants even more to play tennis. And Jack may not want or intend to kiss Jill for the simple reason that he has never even heard of her, even though he *would* intend to kiss Jill *if* he were given the chance. Moreover, to define something, in the sense in which I seek to define intention, is to produce an interesting and illuminating set of necessary and sufficient conditions. Hence even if desire could be defined in terms of intention, it would not follow that intention could not also be defined in terms of desire.

Finally, the principle that intention entails desire has been rejected on the grounds that expected but unwanted consequences of intended acts are themselves intended.[19] I disagree, for the following reasons. (1) I intend to practise the piano today. Disturbing the neighbours and making mistakes are expected but unwanted consequences. It sounds wrong to say that I *intend* to disturb my neighbours. It is positively absurd to say that I intend to make mistakes. It is very natural though to say that I am *willing* to do these things. But that does not entail that I intend to. (2) My intention in practising is to improve my playing, not to disturb anyone. Indeed, the expected disturbance is one reason I have for *not* practising, albeit an insufficient one. But the fact that if I did A I would as a consequence do something I intend to do could surely never be a reason not to do A. (3) I hope that I will not disturb the neighbours. But the statement 'I intend to though I hope I won't' is odd to say the least. (4) I do what I can (such as closing windows) to minimize the possibility of disturbing the neighbours. I make a great effort to avoid errors. But no one tries not to carry out their intentions. (5) If I tell someone that I will make a mistake today, I would be understood as making a prediction, not as expressing an intention. Consequently, the question 'Why do you intend to do that?' would be out of place. Indeed, it seems that no one ever expresses an intention to bring about expected but unwanted consequences, which

---

[19] See J. Bentham (1948), *The Principles of Morals and Legislation* (Oxford), ch. vii; H. Sidgwick (1966), *The Methods of Ethics*, 7th edn. (New York), 202; B. Aune (1966), 'Intention and Foresight', *Journal of Philosophy* 63: 652–4; Meiland (1970), op. cit., ch. 1; Castañeda (1971), op. cit. 458–66; and Miller (1980), op. cit. 334–43. Contrast Kenny (1966), op. cit., esp. p. 644; Bedford (1966), op. cit. 654–6; H. L. A. Hart (1968), *Punishment and Responsibility* (Oxford), ch. v; G. Pitcher (1970), 'In Intending and Side Effects', *Journal of Philosophy* 67: 659–68; H. Oberdiek (1972), 'Intention and Foresight in Criminal Law', *Mind* 81: 391; R. F. Stalley, 'Intentions, Beliefs, and Imperative Logic', *Mind* 81: 18–24; Audi (1973), op. cit. 396–7; Harman, op. cit. 151; and J. M. Boyle and T. D. Sullivan (1977), 'Diffusiveness of Intention Principle', *Philosophical Studies* 31: 357–60.

would be most surprising if they were always intended. If I *did* announce that I intend to disturb the neighbours, you would immediately begin wondering why I wanted to disturb them. You might suspect that I had something against them.

In support of the principle that expected but unwanted consequences of intended acts *are* intended, it might be observed that I would be held *responsible* for disturbing the neighbours. But responsibility is not restricted to intended acts, as cases of negligence demonstrate. In particular, lack of intention is no excuse when we are willing to perform the evil deed. Miller (1980) has recently argued that lack of intention is at least a *mitigating* circumstance. But so is lack of desire.[20]

I granted above that people are willing to bring about the expected but unwanted consequences of intended actions. Miller (1980) for one sees no difference between being willing to do something and intending to do it, so he would conclude that side-effects are intended. There are, however, at least three further differences between intending and being willing to do something besides the one at issue, namely, that the former but not the latter entails desiring to do it. First: S may be willing both to do A and not to do A, but S cannot intend both. Kathy says she wants to go to a movie. I tell her I am willing to see *Star Wars* or *Jaws*. Then I am willing to see *Star Wars*, but I am also willing not to see *Star Wars*. I could not intend to see *Star Wars*, however, if I intended not to see it. In light of the belief condition on intending, the first difference is a consequence of the second: if S does not expect to do A, S may be willing to do A but cannot intend to do A. Until Kathy makes up her mind, I do not expect to see *Star Wars* and so cannot intend to see it. I am however perfectly willing to see *Star Wars*. Third: wanting to do A implies being willing to do A for a wide range of A, but does not imply intending to do A. If I want to see *Deep Throat*, then I must be willing to see it; but I need not intend to see it.

Intending to do something entails being willing to do it. But the facts cited show that being willing to do something does not entail intending to do it. Willingness is opposed to *un*willingness. To be unwilling to do something, I believe, is to intend *not* to do it. Hence being willing to do something entails not intending not to do it. While my willingness to disturb the neighbours does not prove that I intend to disturb them, it does prove that I lack the intention to avoid disturbing them.

---

[20] I discuss this fully elsewhere; see W. A. Davis (1982), 'Miller on Wanting, Intending, and Being Willing', *Philosophy and Phenomenological Research* 43.

IV

Belief and desire are not jointly sufficient for intention.[21] Many things are simply *unintendable*, such as, generally, past events and the actions and states of other people and objects. I may want Borg to win at Wimbledon again, and expect him to; but I could hardly intend Borg to win there again. I believe that the weather will be warm tomorrow, and want it to be; but I cannot intend the weather to be warm. I believe, and want it to be the case, that I ate yesterday; I cannot today, however, intend it to be the case that I ate yesterday.[22]

A familiar suggestion is that S intends that p only if p describes a possible future action of S himself.[23] This is *too strong*, even though only actions are either intentional or unintentional, and even though action is required to carry out an intention. We intend to be or have many things: Ali intended to be champion; I intend to have a Steinway someday. We often intend other people to do things, and as result make, help, or let them do it: my parents intended that I go to college. We intend objects to have various properties and build them accordingly. Even past events are sometimes intendable. I might at 8:15 intend to meet Kathy at 8:00 if I didn't realize how late it was. Perhaps even eating yesterday could be intended if someone had a time machine and believed he could change the past. More importantly, however, the suggestion is *too weak*. John was pushed out of a helicopter over a trout pond. He expects to scare away the fish when he hits the water. He wants to scare them, because his arch-enemy is fishing. But he could hardly intend to frighten them, and his doing so will not be intentional. Yet scaring fish is an action, something John will do, and something others intend to do. Similarly, someone alone and immobilized may expect to perspire and want to (to cool off) without intending to.

I believe intention is lacking in the above cases because the belief and the desire are not *connected* in the appropriate way. For one thing, the belief is not a *consequence* of the desire. John believes that he will scare the fish, not because he wants to, but because he realizes he is falling into a trout pond. My belief that I ate yesterday is a result of memory, not of current desire. In cases of intention, however, the belief is a consequence

---

[21] Cf. Lawrence (1972), op. cit. 84.

[22] 'I intend that I ate' is ungrammatical. The main verb in the complement of 'intend' (or 'desire') cannot be in the past tense. So we must use the circumlocution 'intend *it to be the case* that I ate' or 'intend *that it be the case* that I ate'.

[23] See Anscombe (1963), op. cit. 2; Fleming (1964), op. cit. 301; Jenkins (1965), op. cit. 175; Baier (1970), op. cit. 649; Audi (1973), op. cit.; and Beardsley (1978), op. cit. 174.

of the desire. I intend to finish this paragraph. And I expect to finish it at least in part because I want to finish it. So we have: *S intends that p only if S believes that p at least in part because S desires that p.* This condition, of course, entails both the belief and the desire conditions.

The connection condition marks a major difference between intending and other propositional attitudes with cognitive and motivational components, such as hoping, being optimistic, and being glad or happy. For example, being glad that *p* also entails believing and desiring that *p*, but the belief need not be a consequence of the desire. Hence I may be glad that I ate yesterday, and John may be glad that he will scare away the fish. The connection condition perhaps explains why intending is thought of as an act of the will, while hope, optimism, and happiness are thought of as emotional reactions.

Hampshire and Anscombe observed that while beliefs entailed by intentions are based on reasons for *desiring* or *doing*, other beliefs are based only on reasons for *believing*.[24] This was regarded as mysterious, but isn't in light of the connection condition. Anything supporting the desire involved in an intention will indirectly support the belief. Their assertion that beliefs entailed by intentions are *not* based on reasons for believing is incorrect, however. I intend to get some exercise tomorrow, and one of my reasons for believing that I will is that I am going to play tennis. Jennifer may intend to get married someday even though *part* of her reason for expecting to is that nearly everyone gets married.

We have seen that if *S* intends *p*, then *S* believes *p because* he desires *p*. We may now observe more generally that if *p* is intendable for *S*, then *S*'s believing *p depends on* his desiring *p*, except when there is overdetermination. I intended to turn on the light. If I hadn't wanted to, I would not have expected to. Such counterfactual dependence is a normal by-product of causation. Raising your arm is intendable. If you should want to raise your arm, you would as a consequence expect to raise it. If you should not want to raise your arm, you would as a consequence not expect to raise it. Other cases are less straightforward. Letting his elbow heal is intendable for Tom, but he does not expect (or intend) to let it heal even though he wants to. For his desire to play tennis is greater. However, if Tom wanted to let his elbow heal *badly enough*, more than any competing desire, then Tom would expect (and intend) to let it heal. In contrast,

---

[24] Hampshire and Hart (1958), op. cit.; Hampshire (1967), op. cit., ch. 2; and Anscombe (1963), op. cit. See also K. W. Rankin (1966), 'Wittgenstein on Meaning, Understanding, and Intending', *American Philosophical Quarterly* 3: 1–13; B. Powell (1967), *Knowledge of Actions* (New York); Meiland (1970), op. cit., chs. 8 and 9; Grice (1971), op. cit. 266; Hampshire (1975), op. cit., ch. 3; and Harman, op. cit. 167.

no matter how much I wanted to grow six inches, I would not expect to; growing six inches is unintendable.

Another unstraightforward case. I expect to disturb the neighbours even though I am averse to disturbing them, because I am more averse to not practising. However, if I were *sufficiently* averse to disturbing the neighbours, so that my aversion exceeded every competing aversion, then I would not expect to disturb the neighbours (I'd give up practising). In contrast, no matter how averse I were to dying someday, I would not expect to live forever. Finally, a case of overdetermination. A captured spy might intend to die (by taking cyanide) even though he would still expect to die (by firing squad) even if he did not want to.

Furthermore, when p is intendable the *degree* to which S believes p is a function of the *degree* to which S desires p (except when there is overdetermination). Making Tom more desirous of playing tennis would tend to make him more certain of playing. And diminishing his desire would tend to reduce his certainty. We realize that the more we desire something, the less likely we are to change our minds or forget, or let obstacles stand in our way. In contrast, you cannot change Tom's desire by changing his belief. Tom would be more certain of playing if he were more certain he would be able to play (suppose he is concerned about the availability of partners). But that would not make him any more desirous of playing (though it would presumably make him more desirous of getting ready, going to the courts, and so on). One case in which increasing the desire will not increase the belief is when the belief is already maximal. If Tom is completely certain he will play tennis, increasing his desire to play obviously could not make him any more certain of playing.

The *firmness* of an intention is a function of the degree of the entailed belief. My intention to play tennis next Wednesday is weak, for while I believe to some extent that I will, I am uncertain. My intention to play tennis tomorrow is firmer, since I am more certain I will. Note that 'I will definitely (or certainly) do it' expresses certainty as well as firm intention, while 'I will probably do it' expresses uncertainty as well as weak intention. It follows that the firmness of an intention is also directly related to the strength of the entailed desire. The greater my desire to play tennis tomorrow, the firmer my intention.

V

Our first connection condition is insufficient. *Wishful thinking* entails believing something because you want it to be the case. Yet not all cases of wishful thinking are cases of intending. Compare Clay, who wants to beat Tom in tennis, and through a little wishful thinking actually expects to, with Maura, who wishfully expects the Red Sox to win the World Series. Clay may intend to beat Tom, but Maura could not intend the Red Sox to win. One difference lies in their *reason for believing* what they do. Part of Clay's reason for believing that he will win is undoubtedly that he wants to. But even though Maura has engaged in strenuous wishful thinking, the fact that she wants the Red Sox to win is not part of her reason for believing that they will.[25] This suggests: *S intends that p only if part of S's reason for believing that p is that he desires that p.* It may also be true that part of *S*'s reason for believing *p* is that he *intends p*.[26] But this cannot be used without circularity to define 'intends'. The second connection condition implies the first (at least normally). For if part of *S*'s reason for believing *p* is that he desires *p*, then *S* must believe *p* at least in part because he believes he desires *p*; and *S* (normally) believes he desires *p* at least in part because he does desire *p*.

Tom intends to play tennis at 3:00, so he wants to. He consequently does not want to play basketball or baseball then (though he may have wanted to before he decided not to). He does have some *competing desires*, though. He would like to have time and energy to play basketball, and wishes not to aggravate his tennis elbow. Consequently, the fact that he desires to play tennis is only part of Tom's reason for believing that he will play. Another important part is that he would rather play tennis than have time for basketball or let his elbow heal. *S* must prefer what he intends only to alternatives he has *considered at the appropriate time*. Tom may have temporarily forgotten an important appointment he would rather keep than play tennis. Furthermore, only *intendable* alternatives are competitors. Tom intends to play with Clay even though he would rather play with Mike, because Tom knows Mike has to work. And of course, competing alternatives must be *believed incompatible*. Tom's desire to exercise does not compete with his desire to play tennis. Unlike Audi (1973: 395), I shall not impose a separate necessary condition requiring that *S* have no stronger competing desires. For if he did, the belief condition and the second connection condition would undoubtedly not be satisfied.

The connection condition will also be false, typically, if *S* expects his desires to change. That he desires *now* to play tennis at 3:00 would not be

---

[25] The familiar distinction between '*S*'s reason for believing *p* is that *q*' and 'The reason why *S* believes *p* is that *q*' is obviously crucial here. That he is prejudiced against women may be the reason why John believes Ann is unsuitable for the job, but it will presumably not be his reason for believing that she is unsuitable.

[26] Cf. Grice (1971), op. cit. 274 ff.; and Harman, op. cit. 167 ff.

part of Tom's reason for believing that he will if Tom believed that by 3:00 he will no longer want to play, or that by 3:00 his desire to let his elbow heal will be stronger. Under either condition, Tom would not intend to play at 3:00.[27]

We still do not have the whole story. Suppose that Maura has kept records showing, amazingly, that in past World Series the team she wanted to win always did win. So given that in the current Series she wants the Red Sox to win, Maura predicts confidently that they will. This is no longer just a case of wishful thinking, but it is not yet a case of intending either, even though Maura's reason for believing the Red Sox will win is that she wants them to. There is no intention here, I believe, because Maura knows her desires will have no influence over the outcome. While her believing that the Red Sox will win is a consequence of her wanting them to win, she realizes their winning will not be even in part a consequence of her wanting them to win. Clay, in contrast, undoubtedly realizes that if he does win, he will do so in no small part because he wants to. We have, then, a third connection condition: *S intends that p only if S's reason for believing that p is that his desiring that p will have as a consequence the fact that p.* S need not believe that his desire will *cause* what he intends. Bob has been poisoned. Intending to die, he is not going to take the antidote. As Bob realizes, the poison, not his death-wish, will be the cause of death. It is nevertheless true that Bob will die at least in part *because* he wanted to die, and that his death will be a *consequence* of his death-wish. Not all consequences or explanations are causal in the narrow sense.[28] The title, therefore, is to be interpreted broadly.

We must now confront the possibility of *wayward causation*. Suppose John wanted to scare away the fish, but had no intention of trying to do so or of manifesting his desire in any way. Suppose he knows, however, that despite his best efforts at concealment, someone else will learn of his desire and push him out of the helicopter, resulting in his scaring away the fish. Then John expected that his desire to scare away the fish would result in his scaring them away, but we could hardly say that he intended to scare away the fish. The causal chain John expected was of the wrong sort. He did not expect his desire to *motivate* him to scare away the fish, or to do anything that would have as a consequence his scaring away the fish, or even to refrain from doing anything that would have as a consequence his not scaring away the fish. In short, he did not expect his desire to motivate him to act in such a way that he would scare away the fish. As a contrasting

[27] Cf. D. Pears (1964), 'Predicting and Deciding', *Proceedings of the British Academy* 50: 211; Grice (1971), op. cit. 279; and Harman, op. cit. 162.
[28] Contrast Harman, op. cit. 156; and Grice (1971), op. cit. 278.

case, suppose John expected that his desire would motivate him to reveal that he wanted to scare away the fish, since the knew that such a revelation would lead the pilot to push him out of the helicopter. In this case John expected his desire to motivate him to act in such a way that he would scare away the fish; and I think that John intended to scare them, albeit in an unusual fashion.

We should therefore strengthen the connection condition once more: *S intends that p only if S's reason for believing that p is that his desiring that p will motivate him to act in such a way that p.* I take motivation to be a specific explanatory relation linking desires (and beliefs) to other desires and actions. It is very familiar, though difficult and perhaps impossible to define. 'S's desire will motivate him to act' should be understood as entailing that S's desire will persist until he acts. 'Acting in such a way that p' is quite broad, covering bringing it about that p, seeing to it that p, and letting it be the case that p, as well as simply performing the action described by p. It is not so broad, though, that my writing this paper counts as acting in such a way that the sky is blue. The phrase has no mentalistic implications. The circuitry in my calculator acts in such a way that the calculator turns off automatically, and pistons in cars act in such a way that gasoline explosions are converted into mechanical energy. Note that S may be acting in such a way that the light will remain on, say, in virtue of *not* doing various things, such as turning a switch to the off position. And S may be motivated to act in that way in virtue of being motivated *not* to turn the switch. Finally, S may believe that a desire will motivate him to act in such a way that p even though S has no idea what *specific* actions his desire will motivate. Thus I might intend that my wife enjoy her birthday without yet knowing exactly what I will do to see that she does.

Our odyssey through the connection conditions began by asking why S cannot intend the weather to be warm even though he wants and expects it to be warm. A natural answer is that S does not believe it is *up to him* whether it is warm. What this means is now easy to explain. Something is up to S, I believe, if it depends on his desires in a certain way. Specifically, it is up to S whether p provided if S desired p to a sufficient extent, the desire would motivate him to act in such a way that p. Thus it is up to me whether I go for a picnic today. For if I had a sufficiently strong desire to go for a picnic (I don't), it would motivate me to do so. But it is not up to me whether the weather is warm. For no matter how much I want warm weather, that could not motivate me to act in such a way that it is warm. The past is not up to me at all, since current desires can only influence future actions.

If the fourth connection condition is correct, intending requires a significant background of knowledge and self-consciousness. Someone who intends to do something must know the most elementary motivational
psychology and be able to apply it to himself. This would explain why we
are even more hesitant to ascribe intentions to animals, the very young,
and the severely retarded, than desires or expectations. The requisite
knowledge, however, does not seem beyond the reach of any human being
with minimal intelligence and experience.

VI

The following case may suggest that we still do not have sufficient conditions for intending.[29] Alan is weak-willed when it comes to women. In
particular, he has a strong desire to continue seeing his mistress. Recognizing his weakness, Alan knows that he will continue to see her. However, he
despises himself for this, knowing that it will hurt his wife and ruin his
marriage. He is even taking steps to change, visiting a psychiatrist, and less
constructively, being cold and mean to his mistress. Being realistic, however, he does not expect these measures to work immediately. Alan seems
to satisfy all the conditions laid down so far. He expects to continue seeing
his mistress because he has a desire to do so which he believes will motivate him to continue seeing her. But Alan clearly does not *intend* to
continue seeing his mistress. He is not settled on continuing. On the
contrary, he is trying to stop. At this point, we need to recall a distinction
drawn above. Alan's desire to see his mistress is *appetitive*, not volitive.
Even though Alan has a strong desire, a craving even, to continue seeing
his mistress, he wants to stop seeing her in order to preserve his marriage
and avoid hurting. Because he wants to change, he is getting psychiatric
help. Alan therefore does not satisfy either the desire condition or the
connection conditions, which require *volitive* desire.

I believe the necessary conditions we have discussed are jointly sufficient. Combining them and simplifying, we obtain a manageable definition:
*S intends that p iff S believes that p because he desires that p and believes his
desire will motivate him to act in such a way that p.* 'Because' is to be
understood here as introducing both the reason *why S* believes that *p* and
the reason *for which* he does, i.e. both the explanation and the grounds for
his belief. The proposed definition holds when *p* is a compound sentence as
well as when *p* is simple.

---

[29] See Bratman (1981), op. cit., fn. 5.

Harman (Ch. 7 this volume, 150, 165) has implied that if we define intentions in terms of beliefs and desires, then we are 'analysing away' intentions rather than 'taking them seriously as psychological states'. Intentions become 'constructs' rather than 'real attitudes that are part of the causal and explanatory order'. Defining something, however, neither brings it into existence nor robs it of reality. In defending a set of necessary and sufficient conditions for having an intention, I have sought to analyse, not analyse away. My hope is that by showing how intentions, beliefs, and desires are related, our understanding of all three mental states will be improved.

I would like to thank Baruch Brody, Peter French, David Cole, Eric von Magnus, Robert Audi, and an anonymous reader for many helpful comments.

7

PRACTICAL REASONING

GILBERT HARMAN

Reasoning is here taken to be distinguished from proof or argument in the logician's sense. Reasoning is a process of modifying antecedent beliefs and intentions, perhaps by adding some new ones, perhaps by deleting some of the original ones—normally by adding some and deleting others. An argument or proof is sometimes relevant to reasoning in this sense but is never an instance of it. An argument or proof is more like an explanation than an instance of reasoning. It has premises, intermediate steps, and a conclusion. Reasoning has no premises and no conclusion, unless we are to say that the 'premisses' comprise all of the antecedent beliefs and intentions and that the 'conclusion' is the resulting set. But that way of speaking might be misleading, since reasoning often leads to abandoning some 'premisses.'

The theory of reasoning is therefore not the same as logic, which is a theory of argument or proof. Logic is relevant to reasoning only because there is a connection between reasoning and explanation, and explanation often takes the form of an argument. But logic is not directly a theory of reasoning. There is deductive logic, but strictly speaking there is no such thing as deductive reasoning; given a deductive argument, one can always abandon a premiss rather than accept the conclusion. There is inductive reasoning (perhaps better called theoretical reasoning) but no such thing as inductive logic. Again, there is practical reasoning, but no such thing as a practical logic and no such thing as the practical syllogism.

Let us distinguish practical reasoning from theoretical reasoning in the traditional way: practical reasoning is concerned with what to intend, whereas theoretical reasoning is concerned with what to believe. As is argued elsewhere,[1] theoretical or inductive reasoning is an attempt to improve one's overall view of the world by increasing its explanatory

Gilbert Harman, 'Practical Reasoning, *Review of Metaphysics* 79 (1976), 431–63. Reprinted with permission.

[1] G. Harman (1973), *Thought* (Princeton, NJ: Princeton University Press).

coherence. The present paper argues, among other things, that similar considerations are relevant to practical reasoning.

An important aspect of the view of practical reasoning defended here is that intentions are taken seriously as psychological states on a par with beliefs. Intentions are, therefore, treated as primitive in the sense that they are not to be analysed away in terms of reasons, beliefs, desires, and behaviour. A great deal will be said below about the nature of intentions, because we must understand what intentions are if we are to understand practical reasoning.

I

It is therefore essential to distinguish intentions from desires, wishes, hopes, and aims. One important difference, which we will now discuss, is that intention involves belief in a way that these other attitudes do not. If one intends to do something, it follows that one believes that one will do it; such a belief is not similarly involved in wanting to do something, wishing to do it, hoping to do it, or aiming at doing it.

It is true, of course, that the future is always uncertain and that anything can happen. Knowing that, one may still have definite intentions as to what one is going to do, which may seem to indicate that intention does not always involve belief. But one may also have beliefs about what one is going to do, despite knowing that anything can happen. Does that show that belief does not involve belief? Of course not: the point, then, is that intention involves belief only in the way in which belief involves belief.

To take a specific instance of the point: Albert intends to be in Rome next summer, although he does not believe that he will be there no matter what. He believes, for example, that he will not be there if he changes his mind and he will admit that he might change his mind. This may seem to indicate that, although Albert now intends to be in Rome next summer, he does not believe without qualification that he will be in Rome next summer. But he does not intend without qualification to be in Rome next summer, either. A description of his intention that is accurate for one context must not be compared with a description of his belief that is accurate only for a different context. In as much as it is true that Albert now intends to be in Rome next summer, although he admits that there is a chance that he may not be there, it is also true that Albert now believes that he will be in Rome next summer, although he admits that there is a chance that he may not be there. In as much as it is true that Albert does not flatly believe that he will be in Rome next summer but believes only that he will be in Rome next summer provided that he does not change his mind, it is also true that Albert does not intend flatly to be in Rome next summer but intends only to be there provided that nothing happens that would give him a sufficient reason to change his mind. Either way, intention involves belief.[2]

It might still be objected, nevertheless, that someone may intend to do something without being sure of success. A sniper shoots at a soldier from a distance, trying to kill him, knowing that the chances of success are slim. Does he not intend to kill the soldier, even though he does not positively believe that he will kill him? If he succeeds, despite the odds, the sniper kills the soldier intentionally and, if he kills him intentionally, must he not intend to kill him?

The answer to this objection is that, in the case described, the sniper does not flatly intend to kill the soldier, although, if he succeeds, he does kill him intentionally. It is a mistake to suppose that whenever someone does something intentionally, he intends to do it. Things someone does as foreseen but unintended consequences of what he intends, for example, are sometimes things he does intentionally. In firing his gun, the sniper knowingly alerts the enemy to his presence. He does this intentionally, thinking that the gain is worth the possible cost. But he certainly does not intend to alert the enemy to his presence. Similarly, if someone tries to do something and succeeds, he sometimes does it intentionally, even if, not being sure of success, he does not, flatly, intend to do what he succeeds in doing. Our sniper is again a case in point.

In order to see the point, consider apparently similar cases in which one tries and succeeds but does not do something intentionally. Henry tries to win a game of chess and succeeds. Does Henry win intentionally? Only if it was up to him whether he would win. Similarly, it would be true to say that the winner of a lottery wins intentionally only if he had rigged things so that he would win. In the more normal case a winner does not win intentionally, even though he tries to win and succeeds. Again, at the firing range the sniper intentionally shoots a bull's-eye only if that is something he can do at will. If it is just a lucky shot, he does not intentionally shoot a bull's-eye.

The reason why we say that the sniper intentionally kills the soldier but do not say that he intentionally shoots a bull's-eye is that we think that there is something wrong with killing and nothing wrong with shooting a

---

[2] For a related argument see H. P. Grice (1972), *Intention and Uncertainty* (Oxford: Oxford University Press), 4–6.

bull's-eye. If the sniper is part of a group of snipers engaged in a sniping contest, they will look at things differently. From their point of view, the sniper simply makes a lucky shot when he kills the soldier and cannot be said to kill him intentionally.

The same sort of consideration leads us to say that, in firing his gun, the sniper intentionally alerts the enemy to his presence. We say this because the sniper acts in the face of a reason not to alert the enemy to his presence. On the other hand, we will not say in any normal case that the sniper intentionally heats the barrel of his gun, even though in firing his gun he knowingly does heat the barrel, because there is no reason for the sniper not to heat the barrel of his gun. One can do something intentionally even though one does not intend to do it, if one does it in the face of what ought to be a reason not to do it and, either one tries to do it, or one does it as a foreseen consequence of something else that one intends to do.

If we are to appeal to facts about when someone does something intentionally in order to support claims about what someone intends to do, we must restrict our attention to intentional actions that the agent has no reason not to do—actions like winning at chess or shooting a bull's-eye rather than actions like killing a soldier or alerting the enemy to your presence. But consideration of such actions indicates that intention involves belief. As we have seen, one intentionally wins at chess or intentionally shoots a bull's-eye only if it is up to oneself whether one will do it, only if one can do it at will, only if it is something that one knows that one can do if one chooses to do it. One intentionally wins a chess game or shoots a bull's-eye only if one does so knowing that one is going to do so. But knowing involves believing. In such cases, then, one intends to win or to shoot a bull's-eye only if one also believes that one will win or shoot a bull's-eye.

This thesis, that intention involves belief, helps to explain certain similarities between theoretical and practical reasoning. Recall that we have defined the distinction between theoretical and practical reasoning as a distinction between reasoning concerned with what to believe and reasoning concerned with what to intend or desire. So defined, the distinction cannot be a sharp one, given that intention involves belief. Practical reasoning that affects intentions must in that case also have an effect on beliefs. Similarly, theoretical reasoning must often have an effect on intentions, since, if one concludes that one will not be able to do what one has been intending to do, that conclusion must change one's intention. Since intention involves belief, theoretical and practical reasoning overlap.

In theoretical reasoning, one seeks to increase the explanatory coherence of one's overall view of the world (see footnote 1). Since intention involves belief, and theoretical and practical reasoning overlap, explanatory coherence must be relevant to any sort of reasoning about the future, theoretical or practical. One's conception of the future therefore consists in both plans and predictions; and, in reasoning about the future, one must seek to make one's total conception of the future coherent with itself and with one's other beliefs and desires, where the coherence aimed at is, at least partly, explanatory coherence. Other things being equal, a given conception of the future, containing plans as well as predictions, is more coherent than another to the extent that the first leaves less unexplained than the second. As this point applies to theoretical reasoning, it is reflected in the slogan, 'Inference is inference to the best explanation'. As it applies to practical reasoning, it is reflected in the slogan, 'To will the end is to will the means'. The point is the same in both cases. If intentions or predictions involve doing something, one's total system of intentions and predictions will be more coherent, other things being equal, if it also includes an explanation of one's doing that thing. When what one is going to do is something intended, such as winning at cards, and the explanation cites one's means, e.g. cheating, one's reason for accepting the explanation is not different in kind from one's reason when what one is going to do is not something intended, such as falling down, and the explanation, for example, that someone will pull on the rug, does not cite one's means.

The thesis that intention involves belief therefore associates practical reasoning about means and ends with theoretical reasoning. It brings these two sorts of reasoning under a single principle. It does this, moreover, in a way that illustrates an important difference between intentions and, say, desires. The various things that one intends to do should be consistent with each other. If, for example, one has a choice between doing A, B, or C, knowing that only one of these things can be done, then it would be inconsistent to intend to do A and, at the same time, to intend to do B, just as it would be inconsistent to believe both that one was going to do A and that one was going to do B. The analogous point does not hold for desires. One can, in the situation described, want to do A and also want to do B, without inconsistency. This is easy to understand, given that intention involves belief in a way that desire does not. For this means that intentions, but not desires, are subject to the same demands of joint consistency to which beliefs are subject.

Intention, of course, involves desire as well as belief. If one intends to do something, there is a sense in which one must want to do it, even if there is also another sense in which one does not want to do it. Practical reasoning that affects intentions therefore also affects desires. Even if there is nothing one can do about a situation, moreover, the belief that a given event would promote a desired end can lead one to desire that event. How can we account for this fact about the way in which practical reasoning can affect desires?

In order to answer this question we must distinguish intrinsic desires from others. Intrinsic desires are basic in the following sense. When planning what to do, one's plan should be not only internally coherent but should also, as far as possible, promote one's intrinsic desires. Other desires, let us call them extrinsic desires, are derived from or motivated by intrinsic desires, just as intentions are. To say that one's plan should promote extrinsic desires as well as intrinsic desires would be to encourage one to count certain intrinsic desires several times, which would be misleading. Furthermore, if one learns that an event extrinsically desired is not, after all, going to promote intrinsic desires, one should ordinarily abandon one's extrinsic desire for that event rather than one's intrinsic desire for the end that had been previously thought to promote the event. The two types of desire are, then, in a sense, really two different attitudes, even though both are called desires.

Now, it would seem that intentions are primitive in the sense that they are not to be analysed away in terms of reasons, beliefs, desires, and behaviour. Similarly, beliefs and intrinsic desires are primitive, unanalysable attitudes. However, extrinsic desires, unlike the other attitudes mentioned, are usefully treated not as primitive attitudes but as analysable in terms of intentions and dispositions to intend. An extrinsic desire is a disposition to choose; more exactly, it is an intention or a disposition to intend. This would explain why something like means–ends reasoning can affect extrinsic desires. Such reasoning can affect intentions and dispositions to intend, which is what extrinsic desires are. This sort of practical reasoning, as it affects extrinsic desires, can in this way be brought under the same principle that connects means–ends reasoning as it affects intentions and inference to the best explanation as it affects beliefs. This can be done, furthermore, in such a way that desires are not made subject to the same demands of joint consistency to which intentions and beliefs are subject. To want A, in other words, to have an extrinsic desire for A, is to be disposed to choose A, in other words, to be disposed to intend to take A, given a choice between getting A or not. Knowing that one cannot have both A and B, one may still want A and want B in the sense that one would choose A, given a choice between getting A or not, and would also choose B, given a choice between getting B or not.

An important unsolved problem in this connection is what to say about hopes. Unlike desires, hopes seem to be subject to the same requirements of joint consistency as intentions and beliefs. If one knows that one cannot have both A and B, it is irrational to hope for A and at the same time to hope for B. This cannot be because hope involves belief in the way that intention does, for hope does not involve belief at all; in fact, hope apparently excludes belief. It is not clear what the explanation of this requirement on hopes is. It is not even clear whether hopes are basic primitive attitudes, like beliefs, intentions, and intrinsic desires, that play a role in the causal order, or are constructs analysable in terms of other attitudes and dispositions, in the way that extrinsic desires are.

This ends our discussion of the thesis that intention involves belief. No real proof of this thesis has been given. But certain objections have been answered and some indication has been given concerning how the thesis might account for a similarity between theoretical and practical reasoning. The discussion that follows will assume that this thesis is true. Indeed, it is unclear how the following argument could be given without such an appeal to the thesis that intention involves belief. The resulting theory, therefore, supports this thesis to the extent that the theory is independently plausible and to the extent to which the argument really does depend on this thesis.

II

The next thing to be shown is that forming an intention is something one does, which, like other things one does, can be done for a reason, can have a purpose, and can serve as a means to one's ends. In particular, forming the intention to do A settles in one's mind the question whether one is going to do A. It can be useful to settle that question because, having done so, one will no longer need to consider whether or not to do A and one can turn one's mind to other issues. Furthermore, in any additional theoretical or practical reasoning, one will be able to take it for granted that one will be doing A. Sometimes one forms the intention to do A simply to settle what it is one is going to do; settling that question is one's reason for forming the intention. Forming that intention is, moreover, one's means of settling that question and of enabling oneself to think about other matters while taking it for granted that one is going to do A.

There is also a second way in which forming an intention can serve as a means to one's ends. Judy is going to a party. Should she go by subway or by cab? Should she walk to the nearby cab-stand or walk in the other direction to the subway entrance? After brief thought, she decides to take a cab rather than the subway. In other words, she forms the intention of walking to the cab-stand. Now, forming that intention is something she does and, furthermore, something she does for a reason. She does it in order to get to the party in the quickest and most convenient way. She supposes that, because of having formed that intention, she will walk to the cab-stand where she will be provided with the needed transportation. Forming the intention to take a cab is therefore part of her means of getting to the party. It is something that she does because she thinks that it will lead to her actually taking a cab and obtaining a ride to the party. She supposes that if she did not form that intention she would not take a cab and would not get to the party that way.

In fact, forming the intention to take a cab is also her means of getting herself to take a cab, although that sounds odd and suggests that forming that intention is something like making an effort of will. Forming an intention to hail a cab is certainly not the same thing as making an effort of will; nevertheless, it is for Judy her means of getting herself to take a cab. For she supposes in this case that she must form that intention if she is to take a cab and she supposes that, if she does form the intention, she will take a cab, and will do so because of that intention. Therefore, there is a sense in which she views her intention as a means to what she intends.

A similar thing is true of Judy's original intention to go to the party. In forming the intention to go to the party tonight, she supposed that she would arrive at the party at an appropriate time because of her intention. She supposed that she would not be going to the party except for having intended to go. Furthermore, she foresaw that, because of her intention, she would leave home and be guided in an appropriate route to the relevant place. Her intention helps to get her to the party by guiding her actions in such a way that she arrives at the party when the time comes. So, there is a sense in which her intention to go to the party is part of her means of getting to the party.

On the other hand, if Judy had decided to stay home tonight and not go to the party, she would then have intended to stay home but, normally, she would not have supposed that she was going to stay home because of her intention.[3] She would not have thought of her intention as leading her to stay home or as guiding her actions or nonactions in such a way that she stayed home—at least not in any normal case. Her intention to stay home would not have been part of her means of staying home unless she would have gone to the party except for that intention—for example, if, being continually assailed by the temptation to go to the party, she had firmly

---

[3] Here I am indebted to Judith Jarvis Thomson. Her example shows that Grice is wrong when he suggests that ' "X intends to A" is very roughly equivalent to the conjunction of (1) X accepts that he will do A and (2) X accepts that his doing A will result from (the effect of) his acceptance that he will do A' (op. cit. 13). There is a similar suggestion in a paper by G. F. Stout to which Grice refers, 'Voluntary Action', originally published in *Mind* (1896) and reprinted in his (1930) *Studies in Philosophy and Psychology* (London: Macmillan), 59. The same suggestion appears much earlier in St Thomas Aquinas, *Summa Theologica* IaIIaeQ.3, a.5, Obj. 1 (reference in G. E. M. Anscombe (1957), *Intention* (Oxford: Blackwell), 87.

resolved that she would resist temptation and stay home. Normally, though, she would stay home even if she did not intend to stay home, as long as she did not intend to do something else. Normally, therefore, her staying home would not have been a consequence of her intending to stay home; at best it would have been a consequence of her not intending to go out.

Now, although Judy's intention to stay home is not normally part of her means of staying home, it is her means of doing something else—namely, guaranteeing that she will stay home. She forms the intention of staying home because she does not take it to be otherwise certain that she will stay home. She forms the intention in order to eliminate the possibility that she will not stay home, to settle the issue, so that she can think about other things and can rely in her later deliberations on her presence at home this evening.

The 'act' of forming an intention is always a means to an end. It is always a means of guaranteeing that one will do what one intends to do. Sometimes it is also a means of actually doing what one intends to do, as when Judy intends to go to the party. Let us call such an intention a 'positive intention'. Sometimes, on the other hand, one's intention is only a conditional means to doing what one intends. Judy intends, for example, to go to the party if Harry calls. If Harry then calls, her intention will become operative in getting her to the party. If Harry does not call, her intention will remain inoperative. Let us call this sort of intention a 'conditional intention'. Sometimes, finally, one's intention is not so much a means or conditional means to doing what one intends to do, as it is a way of ensuring that one will not do something else, as when Judy forms the intention of staying home, which then settles that question and keeps her from the further consideration that might conceivably lead her to form the intention of going out. Let us call this last sort of intention a 'negative intention'. All three sorts of intention are at least means of guaranteeing that one will do what one intends.

Forming an intention is something one does as a means of doing something else. So, forming an intention is itself something one does intentionally. This does not, however, give rise to an infinite regress.[4] When one forms the intention to do A, one intends to intend to do A; but these are not distinct intentions. The intentions are inseparable. One cannot intend

[4] The threat of regress is noted by Grice, op. cit. 16; Wilfrid Sellars (1966), 'Fatalism and Determinism', in Keith Lehrer (ed.), *Freedom and Determinism* (New York: Random House) 156–7; Gilbert Ryle (1949), *The Concept of Mind* (London: Hutchinson), 67; and H. A. Prichard (1949), *Moral Obligation* (Oxford: Oxford University Press), 192. Prichard refers, tantalizingly, to an unpublished essay by Cook Wilson in which Wilson apparently identifies willing X with willing the willing of X.

to do A without intending to intend to do A. So, the intention to do A contains the intention of intending to do A. Intentions are therefore self-referential.[5] The intention to do A is in part the intention that one have that very intention. The intention to do A is the intention that, because of that very intention, it is guaranteed that one will do A. More specifically, a positive intention to do A is also the intention that, because of that very intention, one will do A. A conditional intention to do A, if C, is also the intention that, if C, one will, because of that very intention, do A. And a negative intention to do A is also the intention that that very intention to do A will ensure that one will not decide to do something other than A.

The second thesis, then, is that intentions are self-referential. It is now time to present reasons for thinking that this thesis is true. The argument that follows will proceed by stages and will concentrate on positive intentions.

First, it is clear that in the normal case a successful positive intention to do A is in fact instrumental in one's doing A. It leads one to do A and is part of the explanation of one's doing A. This can be denied only if intentions are not taken seriously as real attitudes and are treated as epiphenomenal constructs to be analysed away in terms of desires, beliefs, and behaviour. But no plausible analysis of this sort has ever been suggested, and it is, therefore, much more reasonable to take intentions to be a real part of the causal and explanatory order. Indeed, it seems quite obvious that actions cannot be explained in terms of beliefs and desires alone; these attitudes must be translated into intentions before one can act. And, if intentions have the sorts of effect we normally suppose they have, a successful positive intention will normally be instrumental in one's doing what one intends to do.

Furthermore, one can rationally form a positive intention to do A only if one can at the same time justifiably conclude that one's intention will be instrumental in one's doing A. For, as has already been argued, one's intention to do A involves the belief that one will do A. One can rationally form that intention, therefore, only if one can rationally form the corre-

---

[5] It might be wrongly objected, by the way, that a child can intend to do something before it has the concept of an intention and, therefore, before it can have self-referential intentions. But there is no reason why the child must have a theoretically adequate concept of intention before it can have self-referential intentions. Who of us has a theoretically adequate concept of intention? Furthermore, it is not clear what the test is for saying that the child has a concept of intention. If the test is whether the child knows how to use the word 'intend' or some equivalent word, then to be sure it would seem that the child can intend to do things before it has the concept of intention. But how does that show that the child does not have self-referential intentions? If the test is whether the child does things that require the use of the concept of intention, and if the child can have self-referential intentions only if it uses the concept of intention, and if the thesis in the text is right, the child who intends to do something already has the concept of intention.

sponding belief. Since one's intention is a positive intention, moreover, one cannot rationally believe that one is going to do A whether or not one intends to. One can rationally believe that one will do A, therefore, only if one can rationally believe that one intends to do A and that this intention will lead to one's doing A. It follows that one can rationally form a positive intention to do A only if one can rationally conclude that one's intention will be instrumental in leading one to do A.

The same point can be put another way. As the result of practical reasoning, one forms the positive intention of doing A. It has been noted above that practical reasoning and theoretical reasoning overlap and that considerations of explanatory coherence are relevant to both sorts of reasoning. Furthermore, one's intention to do A involves the belief that one will do A. Since one's intention is a positive intention, one's practical conclusion has explanatory coherence only if it involves the supposition that one's intention to do A will lead to one's doing A. Without that supposition, one has no reason to think that one will do A. So, for reasons of explanatory coherence, one can form the positive intention to do A only if one can also conclude that one's intention will be instrumental in one's doing A.

None of this needs to be conscious, by the way. Reasoning is not the conscious rehearsal of argument; it is rather a process in which antecedent beliefs and intentions are minimally modified, by addition and subtraction, in the interests of explanatory coherence and the satisfaction of intrinsic desires. One is not ordinarily aware of all of the relevant beliefs, desires, and intentions—nor is one ordinarily aware of the details of the change that reasoning brings about. One may not even be conscious that any reasoning at all has occurred.

So far, then, we have seen that one can form the positive intention of doing A only if one can also conclude that this intention will be instrumental in one's doing A. The next thing to see is that one must also draw a conclusion about *how* one's intention will lead one to do A. This is true even in the limiting case in which A is something immediately within one's power. In such a case, the intention to do A (now) will, without further ado, lead one to do A. Let us call the way in which one's intention produces one's action in such a case the 'normal simple way'. For example, Ludwig forms the simple intention of raising his arm; that leads him to flex his arm muscles in such a way that he raises his arm. Now, in order rationally to form this simple intention, Ludwig must conclude not only (as has been previously argued) that his intention will be instrumental in getting him to raise his arm, but also that it will do so in the normal simple way. Otherwise Ludwig's conception of the immediate future will lack explanatory coherence. If he cannot conclude that his simple intention will in the normal simple way lead him to raise his arm, he cannot coherently form the simple intention of raising his arm. If he sees, for example, that Alice is holding his arm down, he must adopt either a weaker intention, for instance to *try* to raise his arm, or a more complex intention, for instance to push Alice away and then raise his arm. Even if A is immediately within one's power, therefore, one can coherently form the positive intention of doing A (now) only if one has some idea about how one's intention will lead to one's doing A.

If A is not immediately within one's power, one may develop a plan of more or less complexity for doing A. Or one may simply rely on one's ability at a later time to plan accordingly and take whatever steps will be necessary to do A. More will be said about this below. The present point is that, even though one can intend to do A without having yet planned in detail how it is to be done, one can in that case coherently form the positive intention to do A only if one can now conclude that one's intention will later lead one to make plans and take appropriate steps. Even in such a case, therefore, one can coherently intend to do A only if one has some idea about how one's intention will lead one to do A—namely, that it will lead one at some later time to make plans and take whatever steps are necessary to do A.

But to have a more or less definite idea of this sort about how one's present intention to do A will lead to doing it, is to have a more or less definite plan about how one is going to do A. A positive intention to do A includes a more or less definite plan concerning how the intention is (or is going to be) instrumental in doing A. One's plan is that one's intention will lead in such and such a way to one's doing A. Furthermore, one's plan says what one intends to do. Whenever one has a positive intention to do A, therefore, one intends that one's intention will lead in such and such a way to one's doing A. This means, as has already been said, that one's positive intention to do A must be the self-referential intention that that very intention will lead (in such and such a way) to one's doing A; otherwise, there would be an infinite regress.

This conclusion is further supported by consideration of the conditions under which someone does something intentionally. We have already seen that one can do something intentionally even if one does not intend to do it, if one has a reason not to do it and, either one tries to do it and succeeds, or one foresees that one will do it in consequence of doing something else that one intends to do. There are also cases in which one intends to do something and does it, but not intentionally.

For example, Mabel intends to drive to Ted's house, to find him, and to kill him. By chance, Ted happens to walk by as Mabel backs out of her driveway and she runs him down without even seeing him. She intends to kill him and does kill him, but she does not kill him intentionally.

The difficulty in this case is clearly that Mabel does not kill Ted in anything like the way in which she intends to kill him. But it will not be enough simply to say that one kills someone intentionally if one intends to kill him, does kill him, and does so in the way in which one intends. That is too vague. For perhaps Mabel's intention was to bring Ted back to her driveway where she was going to run over him. Then she does kill him in the way in which she intends to kill him, namely by running over him in her driveway, but she still does not kill him intentionally.

The point is that, even though she intends to kill him by running over him and does kill him in that way, she does not do what she intends. One kills someone intentionally if one intends to kill him, does kill him, and thereby does what one intends; but in this case Mabel does not do what she intends. Her intention is not simply 'to kill Ted' or 'to kill Ted by running over him'. It also includes a plan specifying how that intention will lead her to do what she intends to do. She does not in the example do what she intends, because what she does differs significantly from the plan that is part of her intention.

This illustrates a way in which positive intentions differ from desires and hopes. Mabel can want and hope simply to kill someone, but she cannot in the same simple way intend simply to kill someone. Her intention must be the intention that that very intention will lead in a certain way to her killing the person in question. Her intention to kill him cannot be separated from her intention that her intention will lead in a certain way to her killing him. Desires and hopes are different. Mabel's desire or hope that she will kill Ted can easily be separated from a desire or hope that her hope or desire will lead in a certain way to her killing him. That is why it is appropriate to say that in running Ted down Mabel gets what she wants and what she hopes for but does not do what she intends, even though she wants, hopes, and intends to run Ted down.

Here is another example. Betty intends to kill someone. She aims her gun and, at the crucial moment, a noise startles her, leading her to contract her finger so that she shoots and kills him—but not intentionally. Although she intends to kill him and does kill him, she does not do what she intends. For her intention to kill him is the intention that that very intention will lead her to pull the trigger at the crucial moment; and that does not happen. So, she does not kill him intentionallly. Notice, furthermore, that her intention must lead in the normal simple way to her pulling the trigger. If Betty's intention makes her nervous and nervousness causes her to pull the trigger, her intention leads her to pull the trigger but not in the intended way; so she does not do what she intends and does not kill him intentionally.[6]

All these examples confirm the claim that a positive intention to do something is the intention that that very intention will lead in a more or less explicitly specified way to one's doing the thing in question.[7] An additional reason for accepting this claim must be deferred until the next part of this paper, namely that the claim is needed in order to distinguish intentions from predictions. First, more must be said about the ways in which intentions incorporate plans.

Now intentions typically have more than a momentary existence; it is often essential to an intention that it be conceived as existing for a period of time. If Carol intends to meet Jim for lunch, she intends that her present intention to do so will lead her to do so. She envisions herself as arriving at the appointed place and time because of her present intention to do so; and typically she would envision this happening because she envisions herself as continuing to have the intention to meet Jim at that place and time. Exceptional cases can be imagined; she might now arrange to have herself taken by force to Jim at the appropriate time. In that case, her intention to meet Jim for lunch would not involve the assumption that she would continue to have that intention. But, in the more normal case, an intention does involve the assumption that one will continue to have it.

Intentions often involve planning and co-ordination. If Carol intends to meet Jim in St. Louis and she is now in New York, she must envision some way of getting from New York to St. Louis. She cannot wait until the last minute. She may, for example, decide to fly to St. Louis. Then she must plan to order tickets and she must plan to pick up her tickets when they are ready. She must arrange to get to the airport. And so forth. She envisions an intention or plan that will exist over a period of time which will be responsible for various things when they become appropriate: ordering the tickets, picking them up, arranging for a taxi, and so forth.

Typically, Carol's plan is not spelled out in detail from the beginning. She may, for example, accept an invitation to read a paper to some economists in St. Louis in a year's time. She decides that she will read a paper at their meeting; she now intends to read a paper there. Her participation in

---

[6] Donald Davidson (1973), 'Freedom to Act', in Ted Honderich (ed.), *Essays on Freedom of Action* (London: Routledge and Kegan Paul).

[7] The various points made in this section and in section II about what is involved in doing something intentionally suggest a rather complex analysis: X intentionally does A if and only if, for some A', (1) X does A', either intending to do A' and thereby doing what he intends, or trying to do A' in the face of what ought to be a reason not to and thereby doing what he is trying to do, and (2), either A = A', or X knows that doing A' will involve doing A and X has some reason not to do A.

the meeting will involve a number of things. She must write the paper, perhaps revise it, send a copy to her commentator, purchase plane tickets, reserve a hotel room, and so forth. At first, little of this is settled. She will not have decided yet what hotel to stay at or exactly when she will want to arrive in St. Louis. She may not even know where she will be coming from. She may not know who will be the commentator to whom a copy of her paper must be sent. Indeed, she may not have decided what she will say in her paper or even what the general topic of the paper will be.

This vagueness in her plans is not an objectionable incoherence in them since she can rely on her ability to add to her plans and modify them as appropriate. In planning to read a paper in St. Louis at next year's meeting she sees her plan developing in a natural way. She conceives her plan as existing for a period of time and as changing over time by becoming more specific in ways that have the result that she reads a paper at next year's meeting in St. Louis. If she could not count on that, for example, if she could not count on her ability to develop in the time available a more detailed idea of the paper she must write, she could not now intend to read a paper at the St. Louis meeting. Intention involves belief.

Actually, this is still oversimplified in at least two important respects. First, what is relevant is not just a single plan evolving over time towards a single final goal, but an evolving system of plans aiming at various goals. In reasoning one must co-ordinate different plans with each other, and, in intending, one relies on one's ability to be able to continue to do this. For example, when Carol intends to read a paper at next year's meeting, she relies on her ability to co-ordinate her system of plans and intentions in such a way that she will read a paper in St. Louis next year. If she intends to read several different papers at several different places next year, she counts on being able to plan the writing of each in a way that leaves time and thought for the writing of others; she counts on her ability to co-ordinate her travel plans so that she will arrive at the right place at the right time. In one respect, then, the unit of intention is not a momentary attitude or even a growing plan aimed at a single goal; it is the whole evolving system. (Of course, in another respect, the unit of intention is not one's whole evolving system of intentions, since one can intend to do something, do what one intends, and thereby do something intentionally, without having to do everything that one intends in one's whole system of intentions.)

A second complication is that one's system of plans changes, not just by becoming more detailed and explicit in response to new information and approaching deadlines, but also through the forming of new plans and intentions in order to satisfy new desires. Becoming hungry, one forms the intention of eating; desiring entertainment, one decides to go to the movies or to play chess; asked to read a paper in Chicago, Carol decides to do that in addition to the paper for St. Louis; and so forth. One's changing system of plans is constituted by one's present intentions along with the relatively routine ways one has of adapting one's plans to deadlines, to new information, and to new desires. Carol's intention to read a paper to the St. Louis meeting is part of her system of plans and routines, and it involves the supposition that she will end up reading a paper there because of that system.

III

Let us return now to the problem of distinguishing intentions from predictions. As we have seen, a positive intention differs from most predictions in virtue of being a self-referential conception that something is going to happen as a result of that very conception. Now, it is possible that some predictions should take the same form. An insomniac may find that the belief that he is going to stay awake is a self-fulfilling belief, which may lead to his being able to make the self-referential prediction that he will stay awake because of that very prediction, although he does not intend to stay awake.[8]

This insomniac concludes that he will stay awake because of his having reached that very conclusion. Someone who intends to stay awake has reached a similar self-referential conclusion. What is the difference?

---

[8] I owe this point to Derek Parfit. It illustrates a second way in which the suggestion of Grice's mentioned in n. 2, above, is inadequate.

This is a good place to say something about Grice's main thesis. He argues that, if one intends to do A, one must believe that one is going to do A; and he is concerned with how one could be justified in believing that. His answer is (1) there is a state of mind that he refers to as 'willing to do A' which one is in both when one intends to do A and also when one wishes wholeheartedly that one could do A; (2) to intend to do A is to will to do A and to believe that this willing will lead to one's doing A; and (3) one's belief rests on inductive evidence that, under certain conditions, when one wills to do A, one almost always does A.

This answer is counter-intuitive. For one thing, the notion of willing that Grice introduces is clearly an artificial rather than a natural notion. Furthermore, his theory of willing is not needed to answer his problem. The problem arises from supposing that the justification of a belief represents a way that someone might reach that belief as a conclusion. But it is also plausible to suppose that one is justified in believing what one believes as long as it coheres with other things that one believes in an explanatorily plausible way. If the belief that one is going to do A is part of one's positive intention to do A, that belief is justified as long as one is justified in intending to do A. For one can be justified in intending to do A only if the belief that one will do A coheres in an explanatorily plausible way with other things that one believes, such as that one intends to do A, that this intention will lead to one's doing A, that positive intentions normally lead to the doing of what is intended, and so forth.

One difference is that the person who intends to stay awake does so because he wants to stay awake, while the insomniac does not in the same way base his prediction on a desire to stay awake. We might say, then, that intentions and practical reasoning aim at satisfying desires in a way that predictions and theoretical reasoning do not.

In saying this, however, there is a danger of circularity since we have been assuming that extrinsic desires are to be explained in terms of intentions and dispositions to form intentions. To intend to do something is, in a sense, to want to do it. But it would be circular to appeal to this fact in order to distinguish intentions from mere predictions.

On the other hand, intrinsic desires are basic unanalysable attitudes in their own right. Intrinsic desires, unlike extrinsic desires, are not to be explained in terms of intentions and dispositions to intend. It is true that, whenever one has an intrinsic desire for something E, one will be disposed to intend to take E if given that choice. But one's intrinsic desire cannot be identified with that particular disposition, since one's intrinsic desire has implications for one's whole system of intentions and practical reasoning. A new intrinsic desire will bring about many new dispositions to form intentions and cannot be identified with any of them. Intrinsic desires are real attitudes that are part of the causal and explanatory order. They are not constructs out of intentions and dispositions to form intentions. Intrinsic desires, such as hunger and thirst, come and go in ways that are not to be explained by changes in one's beliefs, intentions, and dispositions to form intentions. On the contrary, changes in intentions and dispositions to form intentions are themselves to be explained by changes in such intrinsic desires. The intrinsic desire for E explains, for example, the disposition to take E if given the choice. That particular disposition is also identifiable as an extrinsic desire for E; it is the limiting case of extrinsic desire. Whenever one has an intrinsic desire, one will also have a disposition to choose, a disposition which constitutes a corresponding extrinsic desire; but the intrinsic desire explains the corresponding extrinsic desire and is not to be identified with it.

We have been trying to say what distinguishes intentions from mere predictions. Self-reference is not enough, because some predictions are self-referential in the way that intentions are. Nor is it enough to say simply that intentions aim at satisfying desires in a way that predictions do not, since the relevant desires might be extrinsic desires, which are themselves to be explained in terms of intentions. We must limit the relevant desires to intrinsic desires and say that intentions and practical reasoning aim at satisfying intrinsic desires in a way that predictions and theoretical reasoning do not.

What does it mean to say that intentions aim at satisfying intrinsic desires? Someone can intend to stay awake without wanting to stay awake for its own sake. He may want to stay awake only because he needs to stay awake in order to finish an essay that he is writing. In that case, he intends to stay awake but does not have an intrinsic desire to stay awake. So, we cannot say that intentions always aim at satisfying an intrinsic desire to do the intended thing.

Can we say, then, that intentions aim at satisfying some intrinsic desires, in the sense that, whenever someone intends to do something, he intends to do it either because he intrinsically wants to do it or because he thinks that doing it may contribute to his getting something that he intrinsically desires? We cannot say exactly this. Sometimes one forms the intention of doing something, not because doing that thing may contribute to the satisfaction of intrinsic desires, but because forming that intention may contribute to the satisfaction of intrinsic desires. Judy forms the intention of staying home tonight, not because staying home will serve her purposes, but because forming that intention will serve her purposes by allowing her to turn to other issues, taking this issue as settled.

Can we say, then, that intentions aim at satisfying intrinsic desires in the sense that, whenever someone intends to do something, he intends to do it because he thinks that intending to do it may contribute to getting something that he intrinsically desires? That is almost right, but it leaves out the fact that the system of intentions has an inertia that keeps it going when desire fades. One may form certain intentions, because of one's intrinsic desires, and retain those intentions even when one no longer has the desires, as long as retaining those intentions does not interfere with the satisfaction of intrinsic desires one now has. The retained intentions will specify ends that do not correspond to any of one's current intrinsic desires, and means-ends reasoning may lead one to form new intentions on the basis of those ends. So it is not even true that, whenever someone forms an intention, he does so because he thinks that doing so may contribute to the satisfaction of his intrinsic desires.

The connection between intention and desire is an indirect one. Intentions arise from practical reasoning, predictions from theoretical reasoning, and intrinsic desires are relevant to practical reasoning in a way that they are not relevant to theoretical reasoning. In theoretical reasoning one attempts to improve the explanatory coherence of one's beliefs. Explanatory coherence is also relevant to practical reasoning, but so is coherence with intrinsic desires. Sometimes this involves forming an intention to do something that one intrinsically wants to do or that one thinks may contribute to getting something one intrinsically desires; but there are also the other cases mentioned above. Sometimes it involves forming an intention that contributes to the satisfaction of one's intrinsic desires, although doing what one intends does not, and sometimes it involves retaining an intention even though one no longer has the desires that were originally responsible for that intention.

In other words, one thing that distinguishes an intention from a prediction is the kind of reason one has for intending to do something, as compared with the kind of reason one normally has for predicting. An intention is an idea of the future for which one has one sort of reason; a prediction is normally an idea for which one has a different sort of reason. This is simply to say that an intention is an idea arrived at and maintained by practical reasoning, whereas a prediction is normally an idea arrived at and maintained by theoretical reasoning; reasons are specified by reasoning. To say how desire is relevant to reasons for intentions, but not to reasons for predictions, is to say how coherence with intrinsic desires is a factor in practical but not in theoretical reasoning.[9]

This point is not by itself sufficient to distinguish intentions from mere beliefs. It is necessary also to add that when someone intends that something will happen he thinks of his intention as guaranteeing that it will happen. One cannot intend that something will happen if one thinks that whether it will happen or not is entirely outside of one's control. It is necessary to add this point because it may be possible for someone to adopt mere beliefs for practical reasons. Pascal argued that this is true of belief in God. He argued that there is a good practical reason to believe that God exists, namely that, if God exists, He will reward believers and, if God does not exist, little has been lost. As a result of this reasoning, Pascal undertook to get himself to believe in God. His resulting belief was not an intention, however, even though his reasons for it were practical rather than theoretical.

Now, Pascal's belief in God was not itself part of the conclusion of his practical reasoning nor of any reasoning at all; it was the consequence of a course of action he undertook as a result of his practical reasoning. But suppose (perhaps impossibly) that he had been able simply to believe at will that God exists, in the way that he could at will intend to do one thing or another, so that no elaborate process of conditioning was needed in order to get himself to believe in God. Although his practical reasoning would then have led immediately to his believing in God, that belief would still not be an intention that God exists. For Pascal certainly did not suppose that

---

[9] There is a respect in which coherence with intrinsic desires *is* a factor in theoretical reasoning. See Gilbert Harman (1986), *Change in View* (Cambridge, Mass.: MIT Press), ch. 6.

God's existence could depend in any way on what he, Pascal, thought about it, so he could not think of his belief as in any sense guaranteeing that God exists. His belief would therefore not be an intention.

To see how this makes a difference, let us suppose that Pascal already believes in God and believes that God will send him to Heaven if Pascal believes that He will. Pascal therefore has a strong practical reason to get himself to believe that he will go to Heaven. Let us suppose, furthermore, that Pascal can form this belief at will and that he does so as the result of his practical reasoning. In this case, his belief is not distinct from the intention to go to Heaven, since he forms his belief with that intention and the intention already involves the belief. For Pascal to intend to go to Heaven by forming the belief that he will go is for him already to believe that he will go to Heaven. In this case, then, the question whether Pascal can at will come to believe that he will go to Heaven is not to be distinguished from the question whether he can simply decide to go to Heaven.

Contrast that example with a slightly different one in which Pascal believes merely that God is more likely to send him to Heaven if he believes that God will do so than if he does not believe it. Again Pascal has a practical reason to get himself to believe that he will go to Heaven, but this time his belief can be distinguished from his intention. His intention is, perhaps, to try to go to Heaven by forming the belief that he will go to Heaven. That intention does not by itself involve the belief that he will go to Heaven; it involves only the belief that he will try to go. Pascal then forms the belief that he will go to Heaven as the result of his practical reasoning. But, since in this case Pascal does not suppose that his forming that belief guarantees that he will go to Heaven, that belief cannot be identified with an intention to go to Heaven.

Returning now to an earlier example, the insomniac believes that he will, as the result of that very belief, stay awake. His belief is that his belief guarantees that he will stay awake. But his belief is not an intention, because it is not a conclusion of practical reasoning.

This suggests, then, that an intention is a conclusion of practical reasoning that says that that very conclusion guarantees that something will happen.

Let us apply this suggestion to the problem of distinguishing intended means to ends from merely foreseen consequences of actions. This will also enable us to note two important requirements on reasoning.

Recall that reasoning is often a combination of theoretical and practical reasoning, resulting in both intentions and predictions. The sniper decides to try to kill the soldier by shooting at him now, so he decides to pull the trigger now, even though he foresees that this will have certain consequences, namely, that he will heat the barrel of his gun and will alert the enemy to his presence. He therefore concludes that he will do a number of things. He will try to kill the soldier, he will pull the trigger, he will shoot his gun, he will heat the barrel of the gun, he will alert the enemy to his presence. Some of these conclusions are intentions, others are predictions. What is the difference?

There is, in fact, an apparent difficulty here for our suggestion concerning the difference between intentions and predictions. The sniper has an intention which he supposes will lead him to pull the trigger and therefore to shoot and therefore to alert the enemy to his presence. As a result of his practical reasoning, he concludes that his conclusion will lead him to alert the enemy. He does not, however, intend to alert the enemy. How, then, can it be suggested that an intention is a conclusion of practical reasoning that says that that very conclusion guarantees that something will happen? This suggestion would seem to imply, falsely, that the sniper intends to alert the enemy to his presence.

Clearly, in order to save the suggestion, it is necessary to suppose that the sniper reaches two conclusions, one practical, the other theoretical.

(1) (Practical Conclusion) This conclusion (1) will lead me to try to kill the soldier by pulling the trigger of my gun, thereby shooting at him.
(2) (Theoretical Conclusion) Because the conclusion (1) will lead me to shoot, it will lead me to alert the enemy and to heat the barrel of my gun.

The theoretical conclusion (2) is not self-referential and does not count as an intention, according to our suggestion. Our suggestion, therefore, does not imply that the sniper intends to alert the enemy.

But this merely pushes the problem back one step. Why does the sniper have to draw conclusions (1) and (2)? Why doesn't his practical reasoning lead him to the following single conclusion?

(3) (Practical Conclusion) This conclusion (3) will lead me to try to kill the soldier by pulling the trigger and therefore shooting at him, thereby heating the barrel of my gun and alerting the enemy to my presence.

Our suggestion implies that he does not reach this conclusion, for then he would be intending to alert the enemy and to heat the barrel of his gun, which he is not intending. But why does he not reach this conclusion?

In order to answer this question, we must assume that there is a requirement on reasoning that favours theoretical reasoning over practical reasoning. If a conclusion can be reached by theoretical reasoning alone, it is not to be reached instead as a conclusion of practical reasoning. Let us call this the *minimality requirement* on practical reasoning. Because of the minimality requirement, the sniper must reach conclusions (1) and (2) rather than conclusion (3). As much of his total conclusion (as possible) is to be on the theoretical side of that conclusion rather than on the practical side.

There is one exception to the minimality requirement, or, if not an exception, at least a complementary principle which favours practical reasoning over theoretical reasoning in certain cases. Given a choice between reaching a particular practical conclusion or reaching the theoretical conclusion that one will reach that practical conclusion in that way and will therefore do what one's practical conclusion says one will do, one should reach the practical conclusion directly. Let me call this the requirement of *not predicting decisions* that one can make instead. Because of the requirement of not predicting decisions, the sniper must form the intention of trying to kill the soldier and cannot simply predict that he will intend to try to kill the soldier. For he can predict that he will try only if he can predict that he will intend to try; and he is required actually to form that intention if he can now do so as a consequence of practical reasoning, rather than simply to predict that he will do so.

Notice, by the way, that this requirement does not rule out all mere predictions of one's decisions. It only rules out predicting decisions that one could now make. More specifically, it rules out reaching the theoretical conclusion that one will reach a certain practical conclusion for certain reasons, if one could instead now reach that practical conclusion directly for those reasons. It is probably an instance of a more general principle that would rule out any conclusion to the effect that one will reach another conclusion, theoretical or practical, on the basis of certain specified reasoning, if one could now instead reach the latter conclusion directly on the basis of that reasoning.

These two requirements, of minimality and of not predicting decisions, lead the sniper to draw conclusions (1) and (2) rather than, say, the following two conclusions.

  (4) (Practical Conclusion) This conclusion (4) will lead me to try to kill the enemy soldier.
  (5) (Theoretical Conclusion) The conclusion (4) will lead me to pull the trigger and therefore to shoot and therefore to heat the barrel of my gun and alert the enemy to my position.

For reasons of explanatory coherence, the sniper can suppose that his conclusion (4) will lead him to pull the trigger only if he also supposes that his conclusion (4) will lead him to form the intention of pulling the trigger, which will in the normal simple way lead him to pull the trigger. For the sniper to reach conclusions (4) and (5) would, therefore, be for him to violate the requirement of not predicting decisions.

Now consider what keeps the sniper from drawing the following conclusions.

(6) (Practical Conclusion) This conclusion (6) will lead me to try to kill the soldier by pulling the trigger of my gun.

(7) (Theoretical Conclusion) Because the conclusion (6) will lead me to pull the trigger, it will lead me to shoot and therefore to heat the barrel of my gun and alert the enemy to my presence.

Given our suggestion about how to distinguish intentions from mere beliefs, the sniper cannot draw these conclusions, since it would then follow that he would not be intending to shoot and would merely foresee that he was going to shoot. Since he must in this example intend to shoot, he cannot draw conclusions (6) and (7). It would, however, be circular to assert that these conclusions violate the requirement of not predicting decisions, because what is now at issue is why the sniper must decide to shoot at all. Why can he not see his shooting as a foreseen but unintended consequence of his pulling the trigger?

The answer must be that, given his intention of trying to kill the soldier, practical reasoning can lead him to form the intention to pull the trigger of his gun only as part of the intention to shoot the gun. Pulling the trigger would not by itself count as trying to kill the soldier. It counts as trying to kill the soldier only on the assumption that it is required in order to shoot the gun. If the sniper were to suppose that the trigger was not connected to the firing pin so that pulling the trigger would not be a way of shooting the gun, he could not and would not suppose that pulling the trigger was a way of trying to kill the soldier.

In other words, the sniper's practical reasoning cannot lead him simply to the conclusion (6). He begins with the intention of trying to kill the soldier. He then has a practical reason to form the intention of shooting at the soldier. For reasons of coherence, he can form that intention only if he also includes an intention to pull the trigger of his gun. Because of the requirement of not predicting decisions, furthermore, he reaches the practical conclusion (1) rather than a theoretical conclusion saying merely that he will form that intention. Considerations of explanatory coherence along with the minimality requirement, moreover, lead him to reach the theoretical conclusion (2) rather than adding to his practical conclusion intentions to alert the enemy and heat the barrel of his gun. That is why the sniper reaches conclusions (1) and (2) rather than any of the other possibilities mentioned.

Now, Kant and many philosophers since Kant have suggested on intuitive grounds that there is something like the requirement of not predicting decisions. The minimality requirement is less familiar, although it is also intuitively plausible. What is striking about the present argument is that it shows that there is a reason to accept such requirements which is not simply an appeal to intuition. Such requirements are needed in order to distinguish what is intended from what is not intended.

IV

There is a popular theory of human motivation sometimes called 'psychological hedonism'. According to this theory, the source of motivation is always desire for pleasure and the absence of pain. This theory has seemed plausible to many psychologists and others who have thought about the development of motivation. For it seems fairly evident that a newborn baby is a selfish pleasure-seeking hedonist, and it is not clear how, from that beginning, a person could develop any nonselfish ends which are not ultimately based on his desire for pleasure and the absence of pain.

Psychological hedonism is, of course, notoriously implausible as a description of adults in society. People seem to want things to happen that cannot bring them pleasure. The clearest examples involve desires concerning what will happen after the death of a person who does not believe in survival after death. Such a person may make a will, because he wants his property to be distributed in a certain way after he dies, although he will not be around to enjoy that distribution. Similarly, most people, including those who do not believe in any sort of afterlife, desperately hope that they will be remembered after they are gone, although again they will not get any pleasure out of being remembered. Various heroic sacrifices that people have made for other people are also often mentioned in this connection.

It is, however, not very helpful to point to the implausibility of psychological hedonism unless we can also show how desires could have arisen that are not ultimately desires for pleasure or the satisfaction of bodily needs. In the absence of an alternative theory, a psychological hedonist will be justified in reinterpreting the data. He will be justified in saying that the person who makes the will does so in order to get pleasure from showing the will to others or from looking at it himself, and that, even if in some sense people believe that they will not survive their own death, when they imagine what the future will be like they illegitimately imagine themselves as hidden spectators reacting to what happens. So, in order to evaluate psychological hedonism, it is not enough simply to assert that an adult has acquired ends that are not ultimately based on his desires for pleasure and the absence of pain. Some account of how this can happen is needed.

Nor is it enough simply to deny the hedonistic premiss that a baby is a selfish pleasure-seeking hedonist. Perhaps it can be argued that the child's desire to eat is not a desire for the pleasure of eating or for the absence of the pains of hunger; and similarly for thirst, etc. But this is quibbling. It is, for one thing, by no means obvious how we could decide whether the child's desire is ultimately a desire to eat or ultimately a desire for the pleasure of eating. And, even if the point were conceded, it would not really matter. Psychological hedonism could easily be modified accordingly. The basic claim of psychological hedonism is that there is no way for a person to develop new ultimate ends; one is stuck with the ends that one is born with. As one gets older, the hedonist argues, one does not learn new ultimate ends; one learns new ways of satisfying the intrinsic desires that one was born with. If these original intrinsic desires include not only desires for pleasure but also desires for food, water, etc., then the hedonistic thesis should be restated to say that one's motivation is always ultimately to satisfy one's desires for pleasure, for the absence of pain, for food, for water, etc. This is still to say that motivation is basically selfish, and it is not very different from the original claim that one is motivated always to get pleasure and avoid pain.

Two further modifications in the thesis of psychological hedonism are needed in order to accommodate the indirect connection between motivation and desire discussed above. First, there is the fact that intentions have an inertia that allows them to survive the desires on which they were originally based. The desire for food leads Sam to form the intention of eating a steak. Half-way through, the desire is satisfied; he finishes the rest of his steak out of the inertia of his original intention. While he is eating the rest of his steak, his motivation does not derive from a current desire of his for pleasure or for food, although such a desire originally motivated that intention.

A second point is that, as previously indicated, one may form the intention of doing something, not because of the benefits of doing it, but because of the benefits of forming the intention. This happens, for example, when one forms an intention simply in order to settle an issue, so that one can go on to other things.

But neither of these modifications seriously undermines psychological hedonism, which sees the ultimate source of motivation in intrinsic desires for pleasure, for the absence of pain, and possibly for food, water, etc. As argued previously in this paper, the connection between desire and motivation is an indirect one, depending on the role that intrinsic desires play in practical reasoning. Psychological hedonism is, at bottom, the claim that the intrinsic desires that play that role in the adult are essentially the same as the intrinsic desires of the infant. If psychological hedonism is to be seriously challenged, therefore, some account must be given of how new kinds of intrinsic desires might arise.

Actually, the answer is simple. One can often simply adopt at will a new intrinsic desire. And, if one regularly adopts the same intrinsic desire under certain conditions, one will develop a habit of doing so—a disposition to have that desire under those conditions. One adopts a new desire in this way because adopting a new intrinsic desire can often promote one's antecedent ends.

In watching a game, for example, one may temporarily adopt a desire for a particular team to win—not because of any benefits one expects from that team's winning, but because it is more fun to watch a game when one wants a particular team to win. Or, at a party, one may take an interest in a topic of conversation, not because one supposes that further information about that subject is of any use, given one's prior interests, but because the conversation will be found enjoyable only if one is interested in the topic of conversation.

It has often been observed that pure hedonism is self-defeating because a person whose ultimate desires are desires for pleasure will not, in any usual case, get as much out of life as someone with a variety of interests who genuinely cares for other people. The present point is that a variety of interests and a concern for others can be derived from an initial desire for pleasure—not because these concerns and interests have pleasure as their ultimate object (in the sense that they are ultimately concerns for and interests in one's own pleasure, which they are not), but because having those interests and that concern can be a means to one's own pleasure. This is the sort of thing that the child learns as it grows from a selfish hedonistic infant to a loving adult with a concern for society and interests in the arts. Psychological hedonism may be right in seeing the ultimate source of adult desires in the primitive desires of the infant but is wrong in taking this to show that adult intrinsic desires are ultimately desires for the same sort of things that the infant intrinsically desires.

One can have a selfish reason to develop a genuinely unselfish concern for others. For, if one has an unselfish concern for others, it is likely that the others will reciprocate. Furthermore, and more importantly, one's life will be richer and more interesting. But, given such a concern, one may also acquire, for example, an unselfish desire about the distribution of one's property at one's death, which can lead one to write a will in order to bring about that distribution, even though one will not be around at that point to be affected by that distribution.

Similarly, it is often useful, for reasons of efficiency, to develop an intrinsic interest in something in which one already has an instrumental interest, for example, money or physical fitness. When such intrinsic interests have developed, they may lead to actions that go beyond what would have been needed to satisfy one's original purposes. One may come to want to amass a large fortune, more than anyone would 'need', or one may wish to retain the sort of physical fitness only an athlete ordinarily has. An analogous point helps to explain why one may hope to be remembered after death. It is often in one's interest that others should think of one and not forget one; fame has its uses. It is, therefore, useful to acquire an intrinsic interest in being remembered and thought well of. Having acquired that interest, however, one may well want to be remembered after one has died, even though being remembered at that point will not be useful in terms of one's original purposes.

All this is based on the assumption that it is within one's power to adopt new intrinsic desires at will. Let us now consider some reasons for thinking that this assumption is true.

Observe, first, that we sometimes hold a person responsible for the attitude that he takes toward what he is doing. In such a case, we must be supposing that his attitude is to some extent within his control. Now, in particular, we sometimes blame the person playing Monopoly with us for not being interested in winning, and that is to hold him responsible for the attitude with which he is playing. We therefore must be supposing that he could change his attitude at least temporarily by an act of will.

Furthermore, and more importantly, if we suppose that a person can adopt a temporary desire by an act of will, we can give a better explanation of the acquisition of dispositions to have new intrinsic desires than if we do not make this supposition. Given this supposition, we can account for dispositions to have new intrinsic desires in terms of simple habit formation. Without this supposition, we must either accept psychological hedonism or appeal to some sort of novel *ad hoc* psychological mechanism in order to account for new intrinsic desires and dispositions.

It is true that we avoid the supposition that there is such an *ad hoc* mechanism only by making a different supposition. But we do not have to invoke any new *ad hoc* mechanism. We appeal to a mechanism that is needed in any event. Any theory must allow that there are certain attitudes that one can adopt more or less at will. One can, for example, direct one's thoughts in various ways, one can imagine various things, and one can attend to various aspects of things at will. More to the point, one can temporarily suspend one's disbelief, one can suppress hostility, and one can even decide that one will, for the moment, believe someone or accept a particular hypothesis. To say that one can also adopt a temporary desire for something is, therefore, just to add another item to this list. It is not to invoke a wholly new mechanism.

This is not to say that one can always take a temporary interest in something. Sometimes one cannot—just as sometimes one cannot concentrate on what one is doing.

There is another way in which practical reasoning can lead one to adopt new ends. Sometimes one adopts an end so that things that one had already done or plans to do can gain significance as means toward the end that one now adopts. This is how some people choose careers—so that their earlier training will not be wasted. The typical teacher of physics, for example, did not originally study the subject with the purpose of becoming a physics teacher. He studied the subject because it interested him or perhaps because it was a required subject. Later he decided to become a teacher of physics; at that point he was able to see his earlier study as part of the means by which he is able to become a physics teacher—and that is part of his reason for becoming a physics teacher: so that his earlier study will not have been wasted.

It is true that he enjoys physics (let us suppose), so he is choosing a career that will allow him to do something that he enjoys doing. But that is only one consideration. It is also relevant that in becoming a physics teacher he gives significance to his earlier study and to that extent helps to unify his life. If he had chosen instead to do something else, he might always have felt some unhappiness over his decision, even if he fully enjoyed his life. His training in physics might in that case have had no significance—it would have been wasted. It would have lost connection with his later life, a connection that could have helped to give his life unity. In the same way, someone who is musical or athletic in his youth will often feel unhappy if he does not continue those activities as he grows older.

People create their lives, at least to some extent. They adopt purposes which give their lives meaning. But they do not adopt these purposes ahead of time—only after the fact. To choose a career is for many people to drift into a career. Past acts done for other reasons assume a pattern in the light of ends adopted only now.

We adopt ends that help to rationalize and give significance to what we have been and are doing—not only in large decisions, as in choosing careers, but even in our smallest and most insignificant acts. A dramatic illustration of this occurs when someone who has been hypnotized is told that later, after he 'comes out of it', at a given signal, he is to open a window. When he does later open the window and is asked why, he will be found to have constructed some appropriate end that will rationalize what he is doing. This is no mere curiosity, worthy of interest only as a parlour trick. It represents an important aspect of rationality, an aspect that promotes stability in one's plans and allows one to assume that one's long-range plans will be carried out. For in the midst of them, one will be strongly motivated to continue so as not to waste what has gone before. In the midst of some minor activity one may forget what one intends to be doing, but one will often then reconstruct an end on the basis of what is being done at the moment, and one will finish—simply for the sake of finishing what one is doing. One does something because that was what one was doing. Otherwise, one's earlier activities would be pointless.

The same idea keeps one going in more serious activities. A student continues in graduate school, for example, because he has gone this far already and, if he stops now, the earlier years would amount to nothing. This is, of course, not always for the best. Some people irrationally continue careers, political or religious activities, or their families because they do not want to have to count what they have been doing so far as a waste of time. The aspect of practical reasoning that we are now discussing is not its only aspect and it should not always prevail. But it is an important aspect, and an account of practical reasoning that ignores it is incomplete.

Practical reasoning is, like theoretical reasoning, holistic. In practical reasoning, one seeks a conception of one's life that is both explanatorily coherent and coherent with one's desires. One can increase coherence by adopting means to already existing ends—but that is not the only way. One can also increase coherence by adopting new ends, either because the adoption of those ends will help get one something previously wanted, or because adopting those ends gives a significance to things one has already done or plans to do.

8

TWO FACES OF INTENTION

MICHAEL BRATMAN

We do things *intentionally*, and we *intend* to do things. Our common-sense psychology uses the notion of intention to characterize both our *actions* and our *mental states*: I might intentionally start my car, and I might intend to start it. My intention to start it clearly does not guarantee that I do. But beyond that it is not obvious how these two phenomena *are* related. A central problem for a theory of intention is to provide a plausible account of this relation.

One thing seems clear: it is part of our common-sense psychological framework that these phenomena are not completely *un*related. In classifying both our actions and our states of mind in terms of some root notion of intention, common-sense psychology clearly assumes that there is some important commonality. Our problem is to say what this commonality is, by spelling out the relation between intentional action and intending (or, having an intention) to act.

There are two common approaches to this problem. The first—the *desire-belief model*—sees intentional action as action that stands in appropriate relations to the agent's desires and beliefs.[1] This is a reductive model: it sees intentions to act as reducible to certain desires and beliefs.[2] On this

From *Philosophical Review* 93 (1984). Copyright © 1984 Cornell University. Reprinted by permission of the publisher and the author.

[1] This is one of the guiding themes in Donald Davidson's classic paper, 'Actions, Reasons, and Causes'. First published in 1963 and reprinted as Ch. 1 in this volume. See also A. Goldman (1970), *A Theory of Human Action* (Englewood Cliffs: Prentice-Hall). Davidson's commitment to this tradition has waned in recent years. I discuss this change in Davidson's theory of action, and its relation to some of the issues discussed in the present paper, in my 'Davidson's Theory of Intention' (1984) in a Festschrift in honour of Donald Davidson, ed. Merrill Hintikka and Bruce Vermazen, (Oxford: Oxford University Press).

[2] Philosophers who explicitly defend a reduction of the state of intention to certain desires and beliefs include R. Audi (1973), 'Intending', *Journal of Philosophy* 70: 387–403; M. Beardsley (1978), 'Intending', in A. Goldman and J. Kim (eds.), *Values and Morals: Essays in Honor of William Frankena, Charles Stevenson and Richard Brandt* (Dordrecht, Neth.: Reidel); and P. Churchland, (1970) 'The Logical Character of Action-Explanations', *Philosophical Review* 79: 214–36.

approach, the problem of the relation between acting intentionally and having an intention to act becomes the problem of the relation of the complex of desires and beliefs constitutive of the latter to those desires and beliefs necessary for the former.

I think this approach is mistaken. We are planning creatures. We frequently settle in advance on plans for the future. On occasion, this even involves settling on one of several conflicting options each of which is, in light of our desires and beliefs, equally attractive. These plans help guide our later conduct and co-ordinate our activities over time, in ways in which our ordinary desires and beliefs do not. Intentions are typically elements in such co-ordinating plans. Once we recognize this central role intentions play in our lives the natural view to take, I think, is that intentions are distinctive states of mind, not to be reduced to clusters of desires and beliefs.

So I have argued in several recent papers.[3] Here my argument against the desire-belief model will be only indirect. I will try to show what a part of a theory of intention would look like once we reject that model. Insofar as the account sketched is plausible, it will constitute an indirect argument against that model.

This brings us back to our problem of the relation between intending to act and acting intentionally. Once we see intentions as distinctive phenomena, how should we understand this relation? Here is where the second common approach comes in. I may intend to start my car later today: this is a *future-directed* intention. But I may also intend to start my car now: this is a *present-directed* intention. Such a present-directed intention does not guarantee that I actually start my car. But if I do start my car intentionally then, it seems plausible to suppose, I have such a present-directed intention to start it. After all, while starting the car I surely intend to do *something*. Given that what I do intentionally is start it, it seems that what I intend will include starting it.

This suggests a general solution to our problem: for me intentionally to A I must intend to A; my mental states at the time of action must be such that A is among those things I intend. I will call this the *Simple View*.[4]

---

[3] M. Bratman (1981), 'Intention and Means-end Reasoning', *Philosophical Review* 90: 252–65; id. (1983), 'Taking Plans Seriously', *Social Theory and Practice* 9: 271–87; id. (1984), 'Davidson's Theory of Intention', op. cit. I discuss slightly different, but related matters in (1983), 'Castañeda's Theory of Thought and Action', in James Tomberlin (ed.), *Agent, Language and the Structure of the World: Essays Presented to Hector-Neri Castañeda, with His Replies* (Indianapolis: Hackett).

[4] Note that the Simple View does not say that there must be a separate *event* of intending to A for each intentional A-ing. The Simple View only imposes a requirement on one's mental states. Philosophers who accept something tantamount to the Simple View include B. Aune

The Simple View is a special case of a more general conception, the *Single Phenomenon View*. On this more general view, intentional action and the state of intention both involve a certain common state, and it is the relation of an action to this state that makes that action intentional. The Simple View adds to this more general conception the requirement that this state is just an intention so to act.

The Simple View has its virtues. It recognizes the distinctiveness of intentions, and provides a straightforward and initially plausible account of the relation between such intentions and intentional action. It is a view towards which common sense initially leans, as well as a view implicit in many discussions of intention in moral philosophy.[5] Nevertheless, while I will be accepting a version of the more general, Single Phenomenon View, I find the Simple View unacceptable. Our conception of the state of intention is that of a single state tied to two very different sorts of phenomena. Intention is Janus-faced, tied both to co-ordinating plans and intentional action. The Simple View does not allow sufficient theoretical room for both these faces of intention.

In Sections 1 and 2 of this paper I explain why. In Section 3 I show how one might naturally be led to the Simple View by an unacceptable reduction of another kind: a reduction of present-directed intention to volition.

(1977) in *Reason and Action* (Dordrecht, Neth.: Reidel, 1977), ch. II, esp. 89–102, and J. Searle (1983) in *Intentionality* (Cambridge: Cambridge University Press), ch. 3. Searle says that the rejection of what I have called the Simple View is 'a mistake that derives from a failure to see the difference between prior intentions [what I have called future-directed intentions] and intentions in action [what I have called present-directed intentions]' (p. 94 n). But, as will be seen, my objection to the Simple View does not depend on such a failure.

In J. Bentham (1984), *The Principles of Morals and Legislation* (New York: Hafner), 84, Bentham famously distinguishes between consequences which are 'directly' intentional and consequences which are only 'obliquely' intentional. This distinction suggests a view according to which bringing about X may be intentional, even if one does not intend to bring X about, so long as one intends something one expects will (or, will likely) result in X. Such a view is intermediate between the Simple View and the more complex view I will be sketching below in Sections 4–6. This intermediate view is represented in contemporary discussions by, among others, H.-N. Castañeda (1975) in his important book, *Thinking and Doing* (Dordrecht, Neth.: Reidel), esp. 313. Here I will just note that this intermediate view is also subject to the objection against the Simple View to be developed in Sections 1 and 2.

The Simple View is rejected in passing by Georg Henrik von Wright (1971) in his *Explanation and Understanding* (Ithaca, NY: Cornell University Press): 89–90. More recently, Gilbert Harman has criticized the Simple View in 'Practical Reasoning', Ch. 7 this volume, 149–77. I discuss Harman's criticism, and my reasons for preferring my alternative approach, below. Despite this and other differences in our views, my thinking about intention has been influenced by this paper and by Harman's other two recent papers on this subject: 'Willing and Intending' (1986), in R. Grandy and R. Warner (eds.), *Philosophical Grounds of Rationality* (Oxford: Oxford University Press); and (1983), 'Rational Action and the Extent of Intentions', *Social Theory and Practice* 9: 123–41.

[5] See, for example, Charles Fried (1978), *Right and Wrong* (Cambridge, Mass.: Harvard University Press), esp. 20–4.

Finally, in Sections 4–6 I sketch a route between the desire-belief model and the Simple View, a route that remains within the framework of the more general Single Phenomenon View. My proposal sees intentions as distinctive, and sees the intentionality of an action as dependent on its relation to such intentions. But it rejects the account of this relation provided by the Simple View. It holds, instead, that while to *A* intentionally I must intend to do *something*, I need not intend *to do A*. This leads to a distinction between *what* I intend and the *motivational potential* of my intention. I conclude by arguing that this distinction has a further virtue: it allows our concern with the ascription of responsibility to shape our classification of actions as intentional without thereby distorting our classifications of mental states in ways which undermine critical regularities.

1. CONSISTENCY OF INTENTION AND THE SIMPLE VIEW

My argument against the Simple View is rooted in my conception of intentions as elements in co-ordinating plans. So I need to say more about that conception.

We have been speaking of present-directed intentions. But there is a tension in saying that I intend to do what I am *now* doing: talk of what I intend to do seems normally reserved for my attitude towards my *future* conduct. When I am actually starting my car it may seem natural to say that I no longer *intend* to start it, I *am* starting it. I think we should take this strain as a philosophical hint: not that there are not present-directed intentions, but that to understand what intentions are we should begin by concentrating on the future-directed case.[6] This is the *methodological priority of future-directed intention.*[7]

Future-directed intentions are typically elements in larger plans.[8] Such plans help me to co-ordinate my activities over time, and my activities with

[6] Note that even my present-directed intention to start my car is an intention to perform an action that continues somewhat into the future. Indeed, I doubt whether it is possible to have a present-directed intention to perform an instantaneous action, for reasons outlined by Brian O'Shaughnessy (1980) in *The Will* (Cambridge: Cambridge University Press), ii. 312–13.

[7] Here I diverge from a long-standing tradition in the philosophy of action. This tradition begins with Anscombe's decision in her ground-breaking monograph to treat intentional action, rather than intending to act, as the basic case in terms of which to understand intention. See G. E. M. Anscombe (1963), *Intention* (Ithaca, NY: Cornell University Press), esp. 9.

[8] There is a certain ambiguity in talk about plans. Sometimes we are talking about *states* of the agent—states of *having* certain plans. Other times we are talking about an appropriate abstract structure—some sort of partial function from circumstances to actions, perhaps—that may be used to describe the planning-states of different people. A more careful usage might reserve

yours. The ability to settle in advance on such plans enables us to achieve complex goals we would not otherwise be able to achieve. This ability to settle on co-ordinating plans is a kind of universal means: it is of significant use in the pursuit of goals of very different sorts.

Intentions aid co-ordination as elements in larger plans. The concern with co-ordination exerts pressure towards unification of our various intentions. So if our intentions are to be well-suited to aid co-ordination, we should be able to put them together into a larger plan which can serve this co-ordinating role well. But to co-ordinate my activities over time a plan should be, other things equal, internally consistent. Roughly, it should be possible for my entire plan to be realized.[9] Further, a good co-ordinating plan is a plan for the world I find myself in. So, assuming my beliefs are consistent, such a plan should be consistent with my beliefs, other things equal. Roughly, it should be possible for my entire plan to be realized while my beliefs are true.[10]

Let us say that my intentions are *weakly consistent* if they could all be put together into an overall plan that is internally consistent. My intentions are *strongly consistent, relative to my beliefs* if all my intentions could be put together into an overall plan that is consistent with those beliefs. To be well-suited to aid co-ordination, my intentions will need to be, other things equal, strongly consistent relative to my beliefs. Since it is largely to aid such co-ordination that we bother with future-directed intentions in the first place, we have a pragmatic rationale for a rational demand that future-directed intentions be strongly consistent, relative to the agent's beliefs.

'plan' for the latter and 'having a plan' for the former; but this is frequently stylistically awkward. In this essay I use 'plan' to mean 'having a plan'—that is, a state of mind. Thus plans are in the same category as (though different from) desires and beliefs.

It is worth noting that the importance of plans, and the associated phenomenon of planning, to our understanding of intention is sometimes blocked from view simply by the terminology we employ. For example, in his paper (1968), 'Intention and Punishment', in *Punishment and Responsibility* (Oxford: Oxford University Press), H. L. A. Hart writes:

Intention is to be divided into three related parts. . . . The first I shall call 'intentionally doing something'; the second 'doing something with a further intention', and the third 'bare intention' because it is the case of intending to do something in the future without doing anything to execute this intention now (p. 117).

This scheme forces us to see most future-directed intentions merely as 'bare intentions', and this tends to block from view the roles of such intentions in plans, and the resulting constraints on these intentions.

[9] I assume a broad notion of realization such that a conditional intention to A if p is realized if not-p.

[10] I do not think that these brief explanations of the relevant notions of consistency are without their difficulties. There are deep problems here analogous to problems that arise when we try to say, for example, in what sense our beliefs about the morning star (that is, the evening star), or Cicero (that is, Tully) should be consistent. But I think this gloss on consistency will suffice for my purposes here.

This is a demand that should be respected in our further practical reasoning and planning.

This demand for strong consistency distinguishes intentions from ordinary desires. I might, without irrationality, both desire to play basketball today and desire to finish this paper today, all the time knowing I cannot do both. In contrast, intentions to play and to finish would, given my beliefs, convict me of a criticizable form of irrationality.

The demand for strong consistency provides the basis of my argument against the Simple View. But first I need to make one more point about that view. Suppose I intentionally start my car. On the Simple View it follows that

(1) I intend to start my car.

The point to note is that I can have the intention reported in (1) whether or not I actually do start my car. As we might say, the form of (1) is *not*

(2) aRb

where b is replaced by a singular term denoting an actual, particular action of starting my car.[11]

This clarification in mind, let us turn to a series of three examples.[12] In the first case I am playing a video game in which I am to guide a 'missile' into a certain target. I am quite skilled at such things, but it is a difficult game and I am doubtful of success. Still, I aim at the target and try to hit it. As it happens, I succeed in just the way I was trying. My success was not merely a matter of luck; it depended heavily on my considerable skills at such games. Further, hitting the target was what I wanted to do; I was not just aiming at the target as a way of ensuring that the 'missile' would go several inches to the right.[13]

Do I hit the target intentionally? It seems that I do. I want to hit it and so am trying to hit it. My attempt is guided by my perception of the target. I hit the target in the way I was trying, and in a way that depends on my relevant skills. And it is my perception that I have hit it that terminates my attempt. So even though I am doubtful of success while I am trying, if I do succeed in hitting the target I hit it intentionally. On the Simple View,

---

[11] This explains why I did not include Donald Davidson among those who accept the Simple View, even though he comes close to endorsing the view that if I intentionally start my car then I must intend my particular act of starting it. See his essays, 'How Is Weakness of the Will Possible?' and 'Intending', both in (1980), *Essays on Actions and Events* (New York: Oxford University Press).

[12] These examples take off from an example sketched by Robert Audi (1973), op. cit. esp. 401.

[13] In this last sentence I am indebted to Harman's discussion of such examples in 'Willing and Intending', op. cit.

then, I must intend to hit the target. And this is, for all we have said, an acceptable result.[14] Even though I am doubtful that I will hit the target, the intention to hit it need not violate the demand for strong consistency.

Suppose now that a second game is added, a game which also involves guiding a 'missile' into a certain target. Since I am ambidextrous and can play one game with each hand, I decide to play both games simultaneously. As before, the games are difficult and I am doubtful of success at either of them. As it happens, I miss target 2 but I do succeed in hitting target 1 in the way I was trying and in a way that depended on my relevant skills. Here again, it seems to me, I hit target 1 intentionally. The mere fact that I was also trying unsuccessfully to hit target 2 does not prevent me from intentionally hitting target 1.

The Simple View must say, then, that I intend to hit target 1. And this seems plausible. But what about my intentions concerning target 2? I was trying equally hard, and with equal skill, as well as with equally weak confidence of success, to hit target 2. It seems clear from the symmetry of the case that if I intend to hit target 1 I also intend to hit target 2. Of course, in the example I do *not* hit target 2, whereas I do hit target 1. But, as we noted above, this difference does not prevent me from intending to hit target 2.

So the defender of the Simple View must suppose that in this case I intend to hit each target. This sets the stage for my argument against this view, an argument which requires one more addition to our example.

Let us how suppose that the two games are known to me to be so linked that it is impossible to hit both targets. If both targets are about to be hit simultaneously the machines just shut down. Both targets remain visible to me, so I can see which target I hit if I hit either target. And there is a reward for hitting either target. But I know that while I can hit each target, I cannot hit both targets. Still, I know it is difficult to hit either target, so I again decide to play both games simultaneously; I see the risk of shutting down the machines as outweighed by the increase in my chances of hitting a target. I proceed to try to hit target 1 and also to try to hit target 2. I give each game a try.

Suppose I do hit target 1 in just the way I was trying to hit it, and in a way which depends heavily on my considerable skills at such games. It seems, again, that I hit target 1 *intentionally*. So, on the Simple View, I must intend to hit target 1. Given the symmetry of the case I must also intend to hit target 2. But given my knowledge that I cannot hit both targets, these two

[14] One might even here object to the Simple View if one thought that to intend to hit the target I must believe I will. Below I discuss this line of argument against the Simple View, and why I do not take it.

intentions fail to be strongly consistent. Having them would involve me in a criticizable form of irrationality. But it seems clear I need be guilty of no such irrationality: the strategy of giving each game a try seems perfectly reasonable. If I am guilty of no such irrationality I do not have both of these intentions. Since my relevant intentions in favour of hitting target 1 are the same as those in favour of hitting target 2, I have neither intention. So the Simple View is false. If it were true I would be guilty of a form of criticizable irrationality; but I need be guilty of no such irrationality. The Simple View imposes too strong a link between intention and intentional action, a link that is insensitive to differences in the demands of practical reason.

This argument against the Simple View appeals to constraints on intention that do not apply in the same way to intentional action. In this respect it is similar to an alternative argument that has been sketched in the literature. It will be useful to discuss this argument briefly.

Suppose I intend now to go to the concert tonight. What must I believe about my future concert-going? Some philosophers[15] accept the strong thesis that I must now believe I will go. Their reasons for this strong thesis tend to be of two sorts. There is, first, the need to explain the apparent oddness of remarks like: 'I intend to go to the concert, but I may not go'.[16] Second, there is the idea that by seeing intention in this way we can best explain the role of intentions in various kinds of practical thinking.[17] I will not examine such arguments for this strong belief condition here. It suffices for my purposes to note that once we are given this strong belief requirement on future-directed intention it will be natural to suppose that present-directed intentions are subject to a similar belief condition; and this leads directly to an argument against the Simple View.[18]

This argument has two premisses. The first is just this strong belief requirement. The second is the observation that a person can do something intentionally even though, at the time of action, he is in doubt whether he is so acting. We have already seen an example of this: I might intentionally hit the target even while being doubtful of success. Donald Davidson offers another example.[19] A person might try hard to make ten carbon copies on a typewriter, while being sceptical of success. Still, if this is what he wants to do, and if he does, in fact, make ten copies in the way

---

[15] For example, H. P. Grice (1971), 'Intention and Uncertainty', *Proceedings of the British Academy* 57: 263–79; and G. Harman (1976), 'Practical Reasoning', op. cit.

[16] Grice, op. cit. 264–6.

[17] For example, one of Harman's arguments in favour of this strong thesis is that it allows for a natural account of the role of intentions in means–end reasoning, (Ch. 7 this volume, 153).

[18] As Harman explicitly notes (ibid. 151).   [19] In Davidson (1980), 'Intending', op. cit.

he was trying and in a way that depends on his relevant skills, then it seems that he intentionally makes ten copies. Again, we have intentional action despite lack of belief.

So we have two premises: a strong belief requirement on intending to act, and the observation that one may *A* intentionally even while doubting that one is *A*-ing. These two premises entail that the Simple View is false. Given the strong belief requirement, when I act intentionally in a way in which I do not believe I am acting I will not intend so to act.

Like my initial argument, the present argument tries to cite a constraint on intention that does not similarly apply to intentional action. But whereas I cited the constraint that rational intentions are to be strongly consistent, given the agent's beliefs, the present argument cites a strong belief condition on intention. Now it seems to me that this strong belief condition is problematic in ways in which the demand for strong consistency is not. It seems plausible to suppose that sometimes intentions just do not satisfy such a strong belief condition. For example, I might intend now to stop at the bookstore on the way home while knowing of my tendency towards absent-mindedness—especially once I get on my bike and go into 'automatic pilot'. If I were to reflect on the matter I would be sceptical about my stopping there, for I know I may well forget. It is not that I believe I will not stop; I just do not believe I will. Still, my plan is to stop.

Examples like this seem at least to show that the strong belief requirement is no more obvious than the Simple View itself. So a philosopher committed to the Simple View could plausibly resist the present argument by turning it on its end and seeing it as an objection to the strong belief requirement. One person's *modus ponens* is another's *modus tollens*.[20]

In contrast, the demand for strong consistency of intentions is more difficult to avoid. First, instead of requiring an actual belief that I will *A* for me to intend to *A*, it demands only that (other things equal, and if my intentions are to be rational) I not have beliefs inconsistent with the belief that I will *A*. Second, this constraint is even compatible with the possibility of my intending to stop at the bookstore and believing I will not. It just requires us to say that, other things equal, I would then be guilty of a form of criticizable irrationality. Finally, it will be more difficult to turn the tables on my argument, rejecting the requirement of strong consistency in order to hold onto the Simple View. This is because this consistency

---

[20] Of course, if we reject the strong belief requirement, we will need alternative explanations of the linguistic data and the data about practical reasoning originally summoned in its support. I sketch an alternative explanation of the latter in my (1981) 'Intention and Means-End Reasoning', op. cit. I think an alternative explanation of the former can also be constructed, though I will not try here.

constraint seems to be firmly grounded in a basic feature of intentions: their role in co-ordinating plans.

Nevertheless, objections to my argument remain. I turn now to consider some of these.

2. OBJECTIONS AND REPLIES

My argument depends on two claims about the final video games case in which the games are known to be linked and I succeed in hitting target 1:

(i) If in this case I had present-directed intentions which failed to be strongly consistent, I would be criticizably irrational.

and

(ii) I hit target 1 intentionally.

Let us consider some ways in which a defender of the Simple View might try to challenge these claims.

Begin with (i). It might be urged that, for all that I have said, only *future*-directed intentions are subject to the strong consistency requirement. So I can intend to hit target 1 *now*, and similarly concerning target 2, without being criticizably irrational, contrary to (i).

This objection is inadequate for two reasons. First, the argument for the demand for strong consistency depended on the observation that intentions typically play a co-ordinating role. Now, while this is clearest in the case of future-directed intentions, this is also an important role of some present-directed intentions. Suppose my intentions concerning the video games are embedded in a larger plan for the day. I begin the day with what are then future-directed intentions concerning these games. When the time comes these become present-directed intentions. But they continue to be part of my coordinating plan. So they continue to be subject to the demand for strong consistency.

Second, the very idea that some present-directed intentions escape the consistency demands to which most other intentions are subject seems to me not very plausible. After all, they are all equally intentions. Notice that we do not think belief works this way. That is, we do not see certain beliefs about the present as subject to weaker demands of consistency than beliefs about the future.

A second objection to (i) grants that there is a general presumption against such inconsistency, but urges that this presumption can sometimes be overridden and, indeed, is overridden in the present case. I have strong pragmatic reasons for intending to hit each target, since that is how I best pursue the reward. Given these pragmatic reasons to have both intentions, the fact that they fail to be (given my beliefs) strongly consistent need not convict me of criticizable irrationality, contrary to (i).[21]

My response is to reject the contention that I must intend to hit each target in order best to pursue the reward. What I need to do is to *try* to hit each target. But this does not mean that I must *intend* to hit each target. Perhaps I must intend *something*—to try to hit each target, for example. But it seems that I can best pursue the reward without intending flat out to hit each target, and so without a failure of strong consistency.[22] Given a presumption against such a failure, that is what I should do. If I nevertheless do intend to hit each target I am criticizably irrational. So (i) remains plausible.

What about (ii), the claim that what I do intentionally is *hit target 1*? Here the defender of the Simple View might urge that what I do intentionally is only to *hit one of the two targets*. So all that the Simple View requires is that I intend to hit one of the two targets. And that intention is not threatened by the demand for strong consistency.

In assessing this objection we must be careful to distinguish my case from other, superficially similar cases. For example, suppose there is a single target in front of you and you know it is either target 1 or target 2. But since the targets are labelled on the back you do not know which target it is. Still, you do know that you get a reward for hitting target 1 or for hitting target 2. So you shoot at, and hit the target in front of you, which turns out to be target 1.

Now, on one natural reading of 'trying', you were not trying specifically to hit target 1. You were only trying to hit whichever target it was that was in front of you. Further, on a natural reading of 'knowingly', you did not hit target 1 knowingly; for you did not know that it was 1, rather than target 2, that you were hitting. Such observations make it plausible to say that while in hitting target 1 you intentionally hit one of the two targets, you did not intentionally hit target 1.

Again, suppose there are two targets close together, and one gun. You only have enough skill to aim in the vicinity of the pair of targets, trying to hit one or the other. And that is what you do. Suppose you hit target 1. Then it is plausible to say that in hitting target 1 you have intentionally hit one of the two targets without intentionally hitting target 1.

---

[21] I am indebted both to Kwong-loi Shun and to the editors of the *Philosophical Review* for forcing me to discuss this objection explicitly.

[22] Perhaps there are other cases of trying to achieve each of two goals known to be incompatible in which, due to peculiarities of one's character, one really must intend to achieve each goal in order best to pursue each goal. But we need not suppose that my case is like this.

In both these cases, then, it might plausibly be insisted that you do not intentionally hit target 1. It is important to note, however, that my case is different from these. I am trying to hit each of two targets (though I am not trying to hit both). I am not just trying to hit a single target which, for all I know, is one or the other of two different targets. Nor am I just aiming the same shot at both targets in the attempt to hit one or the other. Rather, each of the two targets separately guides my attempt to hit it. Further, I know that if I successfully hit target 1 my endeavour to hit it will be terminated by my knowledge that I have hit that very target. So my case differs from yet a third variation in which I know, rather, that the machine will only tell me if one of the targets is hit, without telling me which one.[23] In this third variation it may be plausible to insist that all I do intentionally is hit one of the targets. But, again, my case is importantly different.

These contrasts with variant cases highlight features of my case which argue for the claim that I intentionally hit target 1. First, I want to hit target 1 and so am trying to do so. Second, my attempt to hit target 1 is guided specifically by my perception of that target, and not by my perception of other targets. Relevant adjustments in my behaviour are dependent specifically on my perception of that target. Third, I actually hit target 1 in the way I was trying, and in a way that depends on my relevant skills. Fourth, it is my perception that I have hit target 1, and not merely my perception that I have hit a target, that terminates my attempt to hit it. Granted, if I had instead hit target 2 that also would have terminated my endeavour to hit target 1, given my knowledge of how the games are linked. Nevertheless, what actually does terminate my attempt to hit target 1 is my perception that I have hit that target. When all this is true it seems to me too weak just to say that I have intentionally hit one of the targets. Rather, I have intentionally hit target 1.

Both crucial claims in my argument against the Simple View are, then, quite plausible. But this is not the end of the matter. We need also to know the larger theoretical advantages and disadvantages of giving up the Simple View. The remainder of this paper pursues some of these larger issues. In so far as the alternative framework it sketches is independently plausible, it provides further support for the rejection of the Simple View.

3. INTENTION AND VOLITION

I have followed the Simple View in eschewing the reduction of intention to desire and belief. But I have also rejected the Simple View's detailed

---

[23] Example courtesy of the editors of the *Philosophical Review*.

conception of the relation between intentional action and the state of intention. I now want to examine one natural way of arriving at the Simple View, a way that depends on a different sort of reduction—this time, of intention to volition. I want to do this for two reasons. First, such a reduction is a natural way of arriving at the Simple View, and so deserves some comment here. Second, this will allow me to show how one can be led to an alternative conception of what is common to both intention and intentional action. This alternative conception accepts the Single Phenomenon View, but supposes that the element common to both intentional action and the state of intention is volition, rather than intention itself. Since I will be defending a version of the Single Phenomenon View which sees intention as the common element (though, of course, not the version expressed in the Simple View), it is important for me to say why I reject this alternative.

When I *A* intentionally—and not merely by accident, by mistake, unwittingly, inadvertently and so on—it may seem plausible to say that I am in a sense 'committed' to *A*-ing. There may seem here to be a kind of 'practical commitment' to *A*-ing that goes beyond mere desire. This suggests that all cases of intentionally *A*-ing share a special pro-attitude in favour of *A*-ing, a pro-attitude distinct from an ordinary desire to *A*. The presence of this pro-attitude in favour of *A* guarantees the kind of commitment to *A*-ing characteristic of intentionally *A*-ing. We may call this special attitude *willing* or, alternatively, *volition*, and this suggestion the *Volitional Thesis*. On the Volitional Thesis, then, in intentionally *A*-ing I will to *A* (or, perhaps, that I *A*): I have a volition to *A* (that I *A*).

If one accepts the Volitional Thesis one needs to say more about willing. In particular, one needs to say what the relation is between willing to *A* and intending to *A*. Here we are faced with an important theoretical decision. On one conception willing and intending are completely distinct mental elements: my volition to *A* is itself neither an intention to *A* nor a necessary part of such an intention. When we see willing this way the Volitional Thesis, while compatible with the Simple View, provides no direct support for that view and could be accepted by one who rejected the Simple View. In this paper I leave open the question of the acceptability of the Volitional Thesis when willings are understood, in this way, as completely distinct from intentions.

More germane to present concerns is a second conception which supposes there to be a much tighter connection between intention and volition. One version of this second conception sees the volition to *A*, required by the Volitional Thesis for intentionally *A*-ing, as at least a necessary component of a present-directed intention to *A*. This is the *Necessity*

Thesis. Finally, on an even stronger version of this conception a volition to *A*, in the sense of the Volitional Thesis, *just is* a present-directed intention to *A*. This is the *Identification Thesis*. And with the Identification Thesis we have arrived at the Simple View.

The Identification Thesis amounts to a reduction of present-directed intention to volition. Such a reduction seems fairly natural.[24] Yet, taken together with the Volitional Thesis it leads to the Simple View. Having rejected the Simple View we must block this reasoning at some point. Where?

Return to the last video games example. This example does not threaten the Volitional Thesis taken by itself. It remains open, for all that that thesis says, that I both will to hit target 1 and will to hit target 2. This is because by itself the Volitional Thesis offers no reason for supposing that willings are subject to the same demands of strong consistency to which intentions are subject. Nor does the example directly challenge the idea that willings, of the sort required by the Volitional Thesis, are necessary components of corresponding intentions. What the example precludes is that willings of the sort required by the Volitional Thesis be *identified with* corresponding intentions. If my willings to hit each target were just present-directed intentions to hit them, I would be criticizably irrational; but I am not. To avoid the Simple View we must reject the reduction of present-directed intentions to volitions of the sort required by the Volitional Thesis.

In light of our discussion, we can see what goes wrong with such a reduction. The Volitional Thesis introduces the notion of volition to capture the special commitment it supposes to be characteristic of intentional action. In contrast, the idea of an intention to act is partly tied to future-directed intentions and plans—and to their characteristic commitment to future action. When we identify present-directed intentions with such volitions we implicitly assume that these two roles do not bring with them conflicting demands. But what we learn from the video games example is that they do. So we should reject this reduction.

---

[24] Aune accepts the Identification Thesis in Aune (1977), *Reason and Action*, op. cit., ch. II, sect. 4. Searle (1983) also seems to be guided by some such reduction in *Intentionality*, op. cit. His initial arguments for the presence of an 'intention in action' in all intentional action are just the arguments commonly used to argue for the presence of volitions, for example: James's case of the anaesthetized patient who mistakenly thinks that he is raising his arm (p. 89). Such cases suggest that intentional action involves volitions in roughly the sense of the Volitional Thesis. By labelling this volitional element 'intention in action' Searle takes the *further* (and, so far as I can see, unargued) step of identifying it with present-directed *intention*. Finally, Castañeda (1975) explicitly says that present-directed intentions are volitions (*Thinking and Doing*, op. cit. 277), though in this book he accepts only the weaker view (described above in n. 4) of what present-directed intentions (i.e. volitions) are required in intentional action.

Having rejected the Identification Thesis, could we still retain the Necessity Thesis, the view that a volition to A is a necessary part of a present-directed intention to A? This would be to see a volition to A, rather than a full-blown intention to A, as the element common to both intentionally A-ing and having a present-directed intention to A. This would lead naturally to an alternative version of the Single Phenomenon View. On this alternative version the basic, single phenomenon is volition; it is a volition to A that is common to both my intentionally A-ing and the intention to A. While I may intend to A in intentionally A-ing, I need not: I need only will to A. An intention to A is a volition to A *together with something else.*

What else? In his important British Academy lecture H. P. Grice[25] in effect pursues a version of this strategy. Grice first introduces a general notion of willing which has the feature that I will that I A whenever I either intentionally A or intend now to A later. Gricean willings, while embodying (in the present-directed case) the special commitment characteristic of intentional action, are not confined to the present. Grice then goes on to claim that my intention to A is my willing that I A together with my belief that I will, as a result, A. There is a single phenomenon involved in both intentional action and the state of intention, but it is not intention itself. It is, rather, volition—understood as a proper part of intention.

This view has several virtues. It avoids the identification of present-directed intention and volition that we have seen to founder on the demand for strong consistency of intention. At the same time it provides an explanation of why intentions are subject to such consistency demands, namely: because beliefs are, and an intention to A includes the belief that one will. In this way it provides for a more complex connection between the commitment characteristic of intentional action, and that characteristic of future-directed intentions and plans, than is allowed by the Simple View.

The problem is that this view requires a return to the strong belief requirement on intention. And we have seen reason to be doubtful of that requirement. Further, there is no obvious way to weaken this belief requirement without creating other difficulties. For example, suppose we try saying that an intention to A is a volition that one A together with a belief that, as a result, one is more likely than not to A. The problem now will be that we have undermined the general capacity of rational intentions to be unified into larger, rational plans. This is because we have now blocked the inference from:

[25] Grice (1971), op. cit.

(a) I rationally intend to A and rationally intend to B.

to

(b) It would not be irrational for me to intend to A and B.

It is not generally true that if I rationally believe of *each* of A and B that I am more likely than not so to act, I can rationally believe the same of my performing *both* actions. So the inference from (a) to (b) will not go through. But, as we have seen, intentions are at least potentially elements in larger co-ordinating plans. To be rational my intentions should at least be capable of combining into a larger plan that is not irrational. So we will want to retain the inference from (a) to (b).

In light of these difficulties perhaps we should put aside such belief requirements on intention and appeal directly to the constraint of strong consistency. One way to do this might be to say that my intention to A is my volition to A together with my disposition to impose this constraint on that volition.

The problem now is that we make the step from volition to intention appear arbitrary. Recall that it is not generally appropriate to impose the demand for strong consistency on one's volitions: this is the lesson of the video games example. So, on the suggested view, to intend to A I must be disposed to treat my volition to A in a special way, a way not generally appropriate for volitions. But, having given up the belief condition on intention, the suggested view leaves us with no explanation of why this special treatment is appropriate in this case. We have no explanation of why I should impose the demand for strong consistency on this volition but not on others.

The strategy of constructing intentions out of volitions and other things, we now see, faces a dilemma in providing for the consistency constraints characteristic of intention. If it tries to account for these constraints by adding to volition a further belief condition, this condition will be too strong. If it tries just to tack onto volition a disposition to impose the relevant consistency constraints, it makes the step from volition to intention seem arbitrary. Faced with this dilemma, I propose taking a different tack.

4. INTENTION AND MOTIVATIONAL POTENTIAL

Both the Simple View and the Volitional Thesis agree in supposing that—*pace* the desire-belief model—intentional action involves a special pro-attitude, distinct from the agent's desires and beliefs. The problem has been to say more precisely what that special attitude is. On the Simple View it is an intention to act in the way one acts intentionally; and we have seen this idea to be at odds with the requirement that intentions be strongly consistent. On the Volitional Thesis all intentional action involves a distinctive volition so to act. I have not criticized this view directly. I have instead focused my critical attention on attempts to weld such a view to either a reduction of present-directed intention to volition (which just returns us to the Simple View) or the Gricean view of volitions as proper parts of intentions.

Both the Simple View and the Volitional Thesis share a common assumption. They both assume that if there is a distinctive pro-attitude involved in intentionally *A*-ing, it will be a pro-attitude specifically in favour of *A*—that there must be a tight fit between what is done intentionally and what is intended (willed). This is the *assumption of tight fit*. Together with our video games example, this assumption leads us to reject the idea that intentional action generally involves an intention, that intention is the element common to both the state of intention and intentional action.

I propose to give up the assumption of tight fit and to distinguish between what is intended, and the sorts of intentional activity in which an intention may issue. Making this distinction, we can say that when I *A* intentionally I intend *something*, but I may not specifically intend *to A*. Our notion of intentional action embodies a complex scheme for the classification of actions (or, perhaps, actions 'under a description'). To understand the relation between intention and intentional action we must recognize that the factors that determine what is intended do not completely coincide with the factors that, on this scheme, determine what is done intentionally.

Recognizing this, we can accept a version of the Single Phenomenon View which sees intention as the common element in both intentional action and the state of intention. To find a common element we need not retreat to some proper part of intention, volition. Actions are intentional in part because of their relations to intentions. But the admissible relations are more complex than those envisaged by the Simple View.

In the theory of action one can be led into two different mistakes (among others!). The first, built into the desire-belief model, is to suppose that intentional action involves no distinctive state of intention at all. The second, made by the Simple View, is to suppose that intentional action always involves an intention *so to act*—a supposition that does not do justice to the role of intentions in coordinating plans. I am proposing a way between. In acting intentionally there is something I intend to do; but this need not be what I do intentionally.[26]

Supposing, then, that there are cases in which I intentionally *A* and yet do not intend to *A* but only intend to *B*, for some appropriate *B*, a full account of our scheme for classifying actions as intentional will need to sort out just when this can be so. Whatever its details, such an account will implicitly specify a four-place relation between intentions, desires, beliefs, and types of actions. It will say what types of actions may be performed intentionally in the course of executing a certain intention, given a certain background of desires and beliefs. This allows us to define a useful notion, that of the *motivational potential* of an intention. *A* is in the motivational potential of my intention to *B*, given my desires and beliefs, just in case it is possible for me intentionally to *A* in the course of executing my intention to *B*. If I actually intend to *A* then *A* will be in the motivational potential of my intention. But we need not suppose that if *A* is in the motivational potential of an intention of mine then I intend to *A*.

Consider the last video games example. My intention includes my hitting target 1 in its motivational potential: it is possible, given my desires and beliefs, for me to hit target 1 intentionally in the course of executing my intention. Nevertheless, I do not intend flat-out to hit target 1. While hitting target 1 is in the motivational potential of my intention, it is not *what* I intend.

What then do I intend? There are several possibilities. I might intend to try to hit target 1, and also to try to hit target 2. I might intend to hit target

[26] Are there cases of spontaneous activity that, while plausibly classified as intentional, do not involve anything reasonably identifiable as an intention to act? If you unexpectedly throw a ball to me I might reach up and catch it. I catch it intentionally, but perhaps my catching it involves no intention to do something.

My worry here is not based on the false assumption that all present-directed intentions are preceded by corresponding, future-directed intentions. My worry, rather, is that once we see what a present-directed intention is (in part by reflecting on future-directed intentions) it may not be obvious that all spontaneous action that is intentional (and not mere reflex behaviour, as when I blink at the oncoming ball) must involve such a state. Perhaps our scheme for classifying actions as intentional, while treating as central actions involving intentions, is more inclusive than that. If this were so then we would have to limit my version of the Single Phenomenon View to those central cases of intentional action. Such a limitation on the Single Phenomenon View would still be compatible with (though it would not require) the claim of the Volitional Thesis that what distinguishes my intentional catching of the ball from my blinking is the role played by an appropriate volition.

It is not possible to address this worry in a definitive way without a more detailed specification of the relations between intention and action that can make that action intentional, without a full account of what I will be calling *motivational potential*. For example, lacking such an account it is unclear whether we can appeal to a general intention to protect myself from flying objects to explain, compatibly with the present account, why my catching the ball is intentional. Since I do not offer such a full account of motivational potential here, I leave the resolution of this matter to another occasion.

1 if I can, and similarly concerning target 2. I might even just intend to hit one of the two targets; though we must be careful to distinguish this case from the cases discussed in Section 2 in which, though I intend to hit one of the two targets, my intention does not include hitting target 1 in its motivational potential. The important point is just that my intention may include hitting target 1 in its motivational potential without including it in what is intended.

That my intention includes hitting target 1 in its motivational potential, even though it is not an intention to hit target 1, does not by itself *explain* why it is true that I hit target 1 intentionally. This is clear from the definition of motivational potential. The notion of motivational potential is intended to *mark* the fact that my intention to *B* may issue in my intentionally *A*-ing, not to explain it. It is a *theoretical placeholder*: it allows us to retain theoretical room for a more complex account of the relation between intention and intentional action while leaving unsettled the details of such an account. Such an account would not itself use the notion of motivational potential but would, rather, replace it with detailed specifications of various sufficient conditions for intentional conduct.

Let me put the point this way. On the theory just sketched, if I *A* intentionally then I *A* in the course of executing some intention to *B* and, given my desires and beliefs, this intention contains *A* in its motivational potential. This means that there will be some true statement(s) along the lines of:

If *S* intends to *B* and *S A*'s in the course of executing his intention to *B* and——, then *S A*'s intentionally.

A full-blown theory of intentional action will tell us how such blanks should be filled in. For example, our discussion of the video games example suggests that one such specification of sufficient conditions would be roughly along the lines of the following:

S intentionally *A*'s if
(1) *S* wants to *A* and for that reason intends to try to *A*, and
(2) *S A*'s in the course of executing his intention to try to *A*, and
(3) *S A*'s in the way he was trying to *A*, and
(4) (2) and (3) depend, in an appropriate way, on *S*'s relevant skills.

Without working out the details, we can see that such a specification would use conditions like (3) and (4) to fill in the theoretical space opened up by our distinction between what is intended and what is in the motivational potential of an intention.

This new theoretical space allows us to formulate a more satisfactory alternative to the desire-belief model than those so far considered. In contrast with the desire-belief model, we can grant that intentional action at least typically involves a distinctive pro-attitude that is not reducible to the agent's desires and beliefs. In particular, intention is a distinctive pro-attitude involved in intentionally A-ing, though it need not be an intention *to* A. By allowing this flexibility in what is intended we do better than the Simple View in providing for the consistency demands on intentions. We can allow, for example, that when I intentionally hit target 1 what I intend need not involve me in inconsistency.

This flexibility also takes away a main source of motivation for accepting the Necessity Thesis and treating an intention to A as consisting of a volition to A plus something else. Having given up the assumption of tight fit, we no longer must choose between an intention to A and a volition to A—understood as a proper part of such an intention—in order to locate a distinctive pro-attitude generally involved both in an intention to A and in intentionally A-ing. Further, since all intentions are subject to a demand for strong consistency, we avoid an analogue of the puzzle, faced by the defender of the Necessity Thesis, about why we should impose such constraints on only some proper sub-set of our volitions.

In response one might still worry that the distinction, between what is intended and what is in the motivational potential of an intention, is illusory. As Anscombe famously remarks, 'the primitive sign of wanting *is trying to get*'.[27] But what is true about wanting seems even more clearly true about intention: the 'primitive sign' of an intention to A is trying to A. In the face of this I have tried to drive a wedge between an intention whose execution may involve both trying to A and intentionally A-ing, and an intention to A. I have claimed that one might have the former intention and yet still not intend to A. But how is that possible? Differences in what I intend should reveal themselves in differences in the roles played by my intentions. But the basic role present-directed intentions play is in motivating and guiding present conduct. So it may seem unclear that there is a real difference between intending to A and having an intention whose role includes the motivation of intentionally A-ing.

The response to this worry is that intentions play other important roles. Differences in these roles can discriminate between two intentions, both of which include A in their motivational potential but only one of which is an intention to A. That there are these other important roles is clear from the methodological priority of future-directed intention; for a basic role played

---

[27] Anscombe (1963), op. cit. 68.

by future-directed intentions is as elements in coordinating plans. There are differences in the role played in such plans by an intention to A and that played by other intentions which include A in their motivational potential. Included among these will be differences in the constraints imposed on yet other intentions, given the demand for strong consistency. What I intend, when I have a future-directed intention, will be in part reflected in the ways in which my intention constrains my other intentions by way of this consistency demand. Thus, if my future-directed intentions concerning targets 1 and 2 do not convict me of criticizable inconsistency then, given my beliefs, they are not intentions to hit target 1 and to hit target 2. This is so even though my intention concerning target 1 includes hitting it in its motivational potential, and similarly with my intention concerning target 2.

A similar point applies to present-directed intentions. What I intend when I have a present-directed intention will not be simply a matter of the sorts of intentional conduct in which my intention might issue. I can have a present-directed intention which includes hitting target 1 in its motivational potential even though I do not intend flat-out to hit target 1. For my intention to be an intention *to hit target 1* it must constrain my other intentions accordingly, by way of the demand for strong consistency. And, as we have seen, my intentions concerning targets 1 and 2 may have hitting each target in their motivational potential without constraining each other in the ways characteristic of intentions to hit these targets.

5. MOTIVATIONAL POTENTIAL EXTENDED

Let us sum up so far. Desires, beliefs, and intentions are basic elements in the common-sense psychology underlying intentional action. Intentions are typically elements in plans. Intentional action generally involves an intention to act. The state of intention is itself the common element in both the states and the actions included within our conception of intention: the Single Phenomenon View is correct. The intention involved in intentional action need not, however, be an intention so to act. My intention may include A in its motivational potential even though I do not, strictly speaking, intend to A. The coherence of this latter idea is ensured by the role intentions play in co-ordinating plans. All this is neutral on the question of whether intentional action involves a special volitional element that is completely distinct from intention. But it does eliminate the need to introduce volitions as special psychological elements related to intentions as part to whole, and serving as the common element in intentional action and intending to act.

This approach depends on driving a wedge between what I intend and the motivational potential of my intention. Now, the wedge I have so far argued for has been rather thin: it has directly concerned only certain special cases in which the demand for strong consistency created problems for the Simple View. But once we have this wedge we can widen it in ways that promise to be useful. Let me briefly sketch two such ways.

Suppose I intend to run the marathon and believe that I will thereby wear down my sneakers. Now it seems to me that it does not follow that I intend to wear down my sneakers, and in a normal case I will not so intend. One sign of the absence of such an intention will be the fact that I am not at all disposed to engage in further reasoning aimed at settling on some means to wearing down my sneakers. In contrast, if I intended to get to the track by 9 a.m., as a means to running the race, I would be disposed to engage in reasoning aimed at figuring out how to do that.[28] My attitude towards wearing down my sneakers does not play the role in further means-end reasoning that an intention to wear them down would normally play.

Even so, if I proceed to run the marathon and actually do wear down my sneakers then I might well do so intentionally. Perhaps this is clearest in a case with two further features.[29] First, I not only believe I will wear them down; I consciously note this while I am running. Second, wearing them down has some independent significance to me; perhaps they are a family heirloom. In a case with these two further features I think we would classify my action as intentional. Yet it does not seem that these further features must change *what I intend* in running the race. Given my relevant beliefs and desires, in executing my intention to run the race I may intentionally wear down my sneakers; and this even though I do not intend to wear them down. So while *what* I intend does not include wearing down my sneakers, the motivational potential of my intention does.

[28] I introduce this further intention to make it clear that I am not just denying that I intend to wear down my sneakers 'as an end'. I do not intend to get to the track by 9 a.m. as an end; but I still do intend to do so. In contrast, I may not intend at all to wear down my sneakers. For probing discussions of related matters see Jonathan Bennett (1980), 'Morality and Consequences', *The Tanner Lectures on Human Values*, ed. Sterling M. McMurrin (Cambridge: Cambridge University Press), lecture III; and Gilbert Harman (1983), 'Rational Action and the Extent of Intentions', op. cit.

[29] As Allan Gibbard helped me see. Note that I do not say that I run the race *with the intention* of wearing down my sneakers. I do not discuss acting with a further intention in this paper. The basic point of the example derives from Harman's discussion of a similar example in his 'Practical Reasoning', Ch. 7 this volume, 151–2.

Generalizing, we can expect a full theory of intentional action to generate true statements along the lines of:

> If S intentionally B's in the course of executing his intention to B, and S believes that his B-ing will result in X, and his B-ing does result in X and——, then S intentionally brings about X.

For present purposes we can leave aside the subtle issue of just how the blank should be filled in (e.g. must it add that S is aware that he is bringing about X and is not indifferent as to whether or not he does bring it about?). The important point is that these sufficient conditions will not include the requirement that S actually intends to bring about X. This means that motivational potential can be extended by our beliefs about the upshots of what we intend, even when what we intend is not thereby extended.

Consider a second sort of case. I intend to shoot a jump shot. I know that my jump shot will have to contain certain sub-components, for example: stopping on my left foot. But as a skilled jump-shooter I need not intend all this, for my intentions and plans are typically at a level of abstraction appropriate to my skills. I may just intend to shoot the jump shot, perhaps as part of a larger plan to score and then to try to steal the in-bounds pass.

We may say that my stopping on my left foot is a *necessary constitutive means* of my shooting the jump shot. What this case suggests is that I may, while guilty of no criticizable irrationality, intend to B, know that A is a necessary constitutive means of B-ing, and yet not intend to A. Rational intention need not be transmitted along the lines of known, necessary constitutive means.

Nevertheless, it seems that the motivational potential of my intention may be transmitted along such lines even when what I intend is not. If I successfully execute my intention and shoot the jump shot, and if in so doing I stop on my left foot, then I may well have stopped on that foot intentionally. So the motivational potential of my intention to shoot the jump shot may include stopping on my left foot.

Here again this may be clearest for cases which have two further features. First, I not only know I must stop on my left foot; I consciously note this as I am shooting. Second, stopping on my left foot has some independent importance to me; perhaps I have recently injured it and it behoves me to go easy on it. In a case with these two further features I think we would classify my stopping on my left foot as intentional. Yet it does not seem that these further features force a change in what I intend. What I intend may remain just to shoot the jump shot. But given my background of beliefs and desires my intention includes stopping on my left foot in its motivational potential: it is possible for me to stop on my left foot intentionally in the course of executing my intention.

Generalizing again, we can expect a theory of intentional action to issue in true statements along the lines of

> If S intentionally B's in the course of executing his intention to B, and S believes that his A-ing is a necessary constitutive means of his B-ing and S A's in the course of executing his intention to B and——, then S intentionally A's.

Here again the important point is not the details concerning how to fill in the blank, but just that an intention to A is *not* required. This means that motivational potential can be extended by means-end beliefs, even when what is intended is not thereby extended.

These cases illustrate some of the complexities of our scheme for the classification of actions as intentional. The Simple View forces us to read these complexities back into the agent's intentions: it includes in what is intended everything done intentionally. Our view loosens the connection between what is intended and what is done intentionally: it sees what is intended as a fact about the agent's mind which need not reflect all the complexities of our scheme for classifying actions as intentional. It does this by using the notion of motivational potential to provide a buffer between the considerations that influence the intentionality of action and those that influence what a person intends.

6. MOTIVATIONAL POTENTIAL AND THE DISTINCTIVENESS OF INTENTION

I now want to argue that this buffer helps support the central claim that intentions are distinctive states of mind. It does this by protecting regularities important to the defence of this claim.

The classificatory schemes involved in our common-sense framework play certain roles in our lives, and we can expect the details of such schemes to be shaped by those roles. An important role played by our scheme for classifying actions as intentional is that of identifying ways of acting for which an agent may be held responsible: our concern is not limited to the description and explanation of actions, but extends to the assessment of agents. This is why it seems natural to classify as intentional my wearing down my sneakers. After all, as Sidgwick notes in defending his proposal to 'include under the term "intention" all the consequences of an act that are foreseen as certain or probable: ... we cannot evade responsibility for any foreseen bad consequences of our acts by the plea that we felt no desire for them'.[30]

Now, the case for seeing intentions as distinctive states of mind depends on locating them in an explanatory system connecting environment and behaviour, and on identifying their distinctive role in this system. To do this there need to be underlying regularities connecting intentions with each other and with other states and processes.[31] Further, these regularities must be significantly dependent on *what* is intended; a regular connection between, say, intentions formed during winter quarter and nervousness is not the sort of regularity we need. To the extent to which our scheme for determining what is intended is shaped by our concern, not only with explanation of action, but with the assignment of responsibility, it will be harder to find such regularities. This is because such a concern would tend to lead to the ascription of intentions which do not play their normal roles in motivation and practical reasoning.

To see this, consider again my intention to get to the track by 9 a.m., as a means to running the race. This intention plays a pair of roles important to attempts at explanation. First, it triggers further means-end reasoning concerning how to get to the track by then. Second, when the time comes it motivates activity guided by my beliefs (many of them perceptual) about where the track is.[32] In these respects it contrasts with my mere expectation that I will wear down my sneakers as a result of running. I am neither disposed to engage in reasoning aimed at settling on a means to wearing them down, nor do I guide my running of the race by keeping track of the state of my sneakers.[33]

There are, then, distinctive regularities connecting what is intended with further practical reasoning and with what beliefs guide our activity. The Simple View undermines such regularities. By reading back from the intentionality of my wearing down my sneakers to an intention to wear

---

[30] H. Sidgwick (1966), *The Methods of Ethics*, 7th edn. (New York: Dover), 202. For a useful discussion of such matters, and their relations to some views of Harman's, see Neil Lubow, 'Acting Intentionally', unpub. MS.

[31] It is not to my purpose here to discuss how strict these regularities need be, but I would expect them only to be of a sort involved in what Grice calls '*ceteris paribus* laws'. See H. P. Grice (1974–5), 'Method in Philosophical Psychology (From the Banal to the Bizarre)', *Proceedings and Addresses of the American Philosophical Association* 48: 23–53.

[32] Of course, to play this motivational role my intention need not be an intention to get to the track by 9 a.m. It might just be an intention to try, or to get there by then if my old car holds up. Still, if I do intend to get there by 9 a.m. (and do not merely expect that I will) my intention will normally play the cited role.

[33] I *might* guide my running of the race by keeping track of the state of my sneakers—for example, if I use them as a pedometer. Since even then I would not intend to wear them down, the presence of such guidance does not ensure intention. My point here is only that its absence indicates an absence of intention.

them down, it ascribes to me an intention which is outside the web of these regularities; for my attitude toward wearing down my sneakers does not play the roles characteristic of an intention to do so. To support such regularities we need to allow our concern with responsibility to shape what is done intentionally without similarly shaping what is intended. We need to allow our concern with responsibility to lead us to classify my wearing down my sneakers as intentional, without forcing us to say that I intend to wear them down. This is what the notion of motivational potential allows our theory to do.

Returning to our video games example, we can make a similar point. Here the relevant regularity is a general tendency towards equilibrium. Generally, when an agent notices that his intentions fail to be strongly consistent there will be an attempt at revision, aimed at achieving consistency. But this regularity is undermined if we suppose that in cases such as our video games example there are strongly inconsistent intentions and yet no tendency towards appropriate revision. The notion of motivational potential allows us to protect this regularity and yet still grant that I hit target 1 intentionally.

7. TWO FACES OF INTENTION

Intention is Janus-faced, tied both to intentional action and co-ordinating plans. I have tried to sketch a version of the Single Phenomenon View that provides room for both of these faces of intention, and for an appropriate link between them. In doing this I have tried to avoid the over-simplifications of the Simple View and the Identification Thesis, as well as the difficulties that arise when we try to construct intentions out of volitions and other things. I have also tried to leave room for the different effects which our concern with the ascription of responsibility has on the different classificatory schemes included within our conception of intention. And, finally, I have tried to do this in a way that recognizes, exploits and supports the distinctiveness of an agent's intentions and plans.

An ancestor of this paper was read at a conference on practical reasoning held at the University of Dayton in March, 1983. I benefited from the careful remarks of my commentator, Donald Gustafson. Other versions have been read at colloquia at Stanford University and at San Jose State University. John Perry's detailed comments on a late version of this paper helped me to clarify several important points, as did comments from the editors of the *Philosophical Review*. Among the many other people who helped me with this paper I want particularly to thank Gerald Barnes, Arnold Davidson, John Dupre, Allan Gibbard, Gilbert Harman, David Hilbert, David O'Conner, Denis Phillips, Adrian Piper, Kwong-loi Shun, and Howard Wettstein. Some of the initial work on this paper was done with the support of a NEH summer research grant.

9

SETTLED OBJECTIVES AND
RATIONAL CONSTRAINTS

HUGH J. McCANN

We may daydream about doing anything, even the impossible; but when we form intentions, they typically embody objectives we expect to obtain. This alone is enough to suggest there are constraints on what we may intend, and a number of authors have posed such requirements. One view has it that in order to intend to A a person must, at least on pain of irrationality, believe she will (probably) A.[1] Others claim this is too strong, and demand only that she not believe she will not A.[2] And there is a related requirement that one not have intentions that are mutually inconsistent, in that if one is fulfilled the other cannot be.[3] Such constraints are of interest partly for their antireductionist implications, since other motivational states, in particular states of desire, are not similarly encumbered. Part of the human condition is to have incompatible desires, and we are not criticizably irrational if we want to do what we believe we cannot. Equally important, however, are the implications for the theory of practical rationality. Very roughly, whether an intension is rational would seem to depend first and foremost on whether the objective it embodies is one whose pursuit offers an acceptable chance of our changing things in ways we take to be for the better. Constraints like those cited may be viewed as instructions on when the chance is acceptable: that inconsistent objectives are always unreasonable, and that it is never rational to pursue a goal unless

Hugh J. McCann, 'Settled Objectives and Rational Constraints', *American Philosophical Quarterly* 28 (1991), 25–36. Reprinted by permission of *American Philosophical Quarterly*.

[1] See, for example, Robert Audi (1973), 'Intending', *Journal of Philosophy*, 70: 387–403; Wayne A. Davis, 'A Causal Theory of Intending', Ch. 6 this volume, 131–48; and Gilbert Harman, 'Practical Reasoning', Ch. 7 this volume, 149–77.

[2] Michael Bratman has defended this view in a number of places, but see especially M. Bratman (1987), *Intention, Plans, and Practical Reason* (Cambridge, Mass.: Harvard University Press), chs. 3 and 8. A similar position is presented in Alfred R. Mele (1989), 'Intention, Belief, and Intentional Action', *American Philosophical Quarterly* 26: 19–30.

[3] Bratman (1987), op. cit.

we think the chances favour success—or, on the weaker view, unless we at least do not expect to fail. Any of these latter claims would, if true, constitute an important principle of practical rationality.

Unfortunately, all are false. There are a number of examples in which it is rational for agents to try to achieve goals they believe they will not accomplish, and some of the examples involve mutually incompatible objectives. Moreover, it turns out that when, unexpectedly, such attempts succeed, the sought-after goals are achieved *intentionally*, notwithstanding the fact the above constraints would forbid their being intended. Now ordinarily at least, we expect a person who *A*'s intentionally to have intended to *A*. Thus a plausible response to the examples in question is to treat them as exceptions to the norm, and allow that in them we may intend objectives that would ordinarily be ruled out. But some authors balk at this, and instead reject what they call the 'Simple View'—i.e. the principle that anyone who *A*'s intentionally intends to *A*.[4] My purpose here is to defend this principle. Rejecting the Simple View, I shall claim, forces us to assign to other mental states the functional role of intention: that of providing settled objectives to guide deliberation and action. A likely result is either that entities will be multiplied, or that the resultant account will invite reassertion of reductionist theories. In any case, the account must drive a wedge between intention and practical rationality, by forbidding agents to intend goals it is rational to seek. Worse yet, the states it 'substitutes' for intention turn out to be subject to the same constraints that prompted the substitution, and hence are indistinguishable from intention in the very respect in which they are alleged to differ. Thus, I shall argue, there is no evidence to justify such supposed distinctions, and the Simple View is to be preferred.[5]

1. THE FUNCTIONAL ROLE OF INTENTION

The best way to understand intention is by comprehending its functional role in deliberation and action—a role which sets it apart from other states to which it is sometimes alleged intention can be reduced. Unlike someone

    [4] The term is owing to Bratman, who argues against this principle in M. Bratman 'Two Faces of Intention', Ch. 8 this volume, 178–203, and in (1987), *Intention, Plans, and Practical Reason*, ch. 8. See also Mele (1989), 'Intention, Belief, and Intentional Action', 21. The same principle is rejected by Harman, 'Practical Reasoning'.

    [5] I have defended the Simple View in H. J. McCann (1986), 'Rationality and the Range of Intention', *Midwest Studies in Philosophy* 10: 191–211, but without exploring the theoretical issues pursued here. See also Fred Adams (1986), 'Intention and Intentional Action: The Simple View', *Mind and Language* 1: 281–301.

who merely desires to attain some end, a person with an intention has a *settled objective*: he is committed to a goal, which guides his deliberation and which, in the normal case, he will eventually act to achieve. This attitude of commitment qualifies intention for a functional role to which desires, even predominate desires, are unsuited. For one thing, it does not always occur that one of the alternatives over which an agent deliberates elicits a predominate desire in him. In such cases, forming an intention is the standard way to resolve the issue: it settles the agent on one course or another.[6] This same resoluteness characterizes intension generally. Someone who intends, say, to go to the library this afternoon is committed to that course of action regardless of how the commitment arose. It may be grounded in a prior, predominate desire to go to the library, or it may not; and even if it is, that desire need not presently persist. The agent may, so to speak, be 'locked into' the project of going to the library, without time to plan for an alternative that has since come to appear preferable. All the same, he is committed, and the commitment manifests itself in a number of ways.

The most emphasized dimension of intentional commitment concerns the initiation and sustaining of action. Suppose I intend to go to the Deluxe Burger Bar for lunch. If that intention survives to the time for action, and if I see that the time has arrived, and if nothing interferes, then I will act in accordance with the intention, and set out for the Deluxe. And as long as I retain the intention I will sustain my activity accordingly. I will monitor and adjust my behaviour in appropriate ways—make the correct turns, obey traffic signals, etc.—to insure my timely arrival.[7] Desires, however strong, do not carry this sort of commitment. I may desire to go to the Deluxe for lunch yet not do so. There is nothing irrational in this, since this desire needs to be weighed against others, such as my desire to finish grading an examination. As Michael Bratman has put it, desires are only potential influencers of conduct; intentions, by contrast, are conduct controlling.[8]

But there is a second dimension of intentional commitment, also emphasized by Bratman. Future-directed intentions have an important influence on rational processes—that is, on the thinking in which agents are apt to

---

[6] Such Buridan-type cases appear more frequent than might be supposed. See Bratman (1987), *Intention, Plans, and Practical Reason*, 11; and Edna Ullmann-Margalit and Sydney Morgenbesser (1977), 'Picking and Choosing', *Social Research* 44: 757–85.

[7] The role of intention in guiding behaviour has been emphasized by Myles Brand (1984), *Intending and Acting* (Cambridge, Mass.: MIT Press), ch. 7. See also Irving Thalberg (1984), 'Do Our Intentions Cause Our Intentional Actions?', *American Philosophical Quarterly* 21: 249–60; and Mele (1989), 'Intention, Belief, and Intentional Action', 22.

[8] Bratman (1987), *Intention, Plans, and Practical Reason*, 16.

engage after the intention is formed.[9] First, they introduce a characteristic stability or settledness into practical thinking: once in place, they are not readily subject to reconsideration. If I intend to go to the library this afternoon, I will not normally continue to deliberate about whether to go. But if I have only a desire to go, even a predominate one, this need not be so. I may still deliberate about whether to go to the library or, say, take the afternoon off and garden. This is not to say that intentions are somehow harder to get rid of than predominate desires. On the contrary: strong desires tend to be all but impossible to dislodge, whereas intentions have the reputation, at least, of being changeable 'at will'. Once I have an intention to A, however, I am normally of a settled disposition about A-ing: I am unlikely to consider the matter further, especially in the absence of new information. With desires this is not so. I may have a desire to take the afternoon off—a desire, in fact, that I will eventually act to fulfill—yet not consider the matter settled at all. Indeed, I may not even have thought about the issue, and may still have a lot of deliberation to go through before I form the intention. If so, I can hardly be said to have a settled objective.

Secondly, future-directed intentions often set problems for further deliberation, thereby prompting the formation of additional intentions. If I intend to go to the library, I must settle on a means of getting there, on the specific details as to when I will leave, etc., and on any preparatory steps I shall take before going. To solve such problems is to elaborate a plan of action, which is likely to involve a number of steps. And the steps of a plan are not developed haphazardly or in isolation from each other. For besides posing problems for further deliberation, future-directed intentions limit the admissible alternatives for solving those problems. The most important of these limitations, for purposes of this discussion, have to do with consistency. Plans should first of all be *internally consistent*, other things being equal. We would not normally expect a plan to include intentions that contradict, in that if one is fulfilled the other cannot be. In addition, however, there is a demand that plans be *consistent relative to the agent's beliefs*. To paraphrase Bratman, other things equal, it should be possible for an entire plan to be successfully executed without any of the agent's beliefs being false.[10]

I shall call these the requirements of *internal consistency* and *epistemic consistency*, respectively. The latter is, of course, a version of the weaker epistemic constraint cited earlier, and it is the more sweeping of the two

---

[9] The points that follow are based largely on discussion in Bratman (1987) *Intention, Plans, and Practical Reason*, 16 ff.

[10] See ibid. 31, where both these requirements are articulated.

requirements. Indeed, any case of internal inconsistency in which the agent recognizes the conflict will also be a case of epistemic inconsistency, since to be aware that a pair of intentions are inconsistent is just to believe that they cannot both be successfully executed. And if we view the requirements as arising out of considerations of rationality, we can see a clearcut justification for both of them. The rationality of intentions, it was suggested above, depends on whether the goals they embody are such that, by pursuing them, we gain an acceptable chance of changing the world in ways we believe are for the better.[11] But surely we will not normally be able to bring about desirable change by pursuing objectives that conflict either with each other or with our beliefs about what we will in fact achieve. I would be criticizably irrational, other things being equal, if I intended both to attend your seminar at 2:00 tomorrow and to play golf at that time. Similarly, though I might intend courses of action whose anticipated difficulty prevents my believing I *will* succeed, I would not normally be expected to have intentions I positively believe I will *not* carry out. I might, for example, intend to go to your seminar tomorrow, yet fear that I am coming down with the flu, and hence have no belief as to whether I will actually go or not. But if I am convinced I will *not* go, how could it be rational of me to intend to do so? The requirements of internal and epistemic consistency do, then, normally constrain intentions. Finally, we should remind ourselves that these constraints also militate against reductionism. There is nothing irrational about my desiring both to go to your seminar at 2:00 tomorrow and to play golf at that time, even though I would be irrational to intend both. Nor is it irrational of me to desire to go to your seminar when I am convinced I will not. Rational agents regularly desire to do lots of things they believe they will not do.

2. CONSISTENCY AND THE SIMPLE VIEW

If this account of the functional role of intention is correct—and there is a great deal that can be added to it—we have the basis for a strong antireductionist position. Intention appears to play an indispensable role both in practical thinking and in the genesis of action, and hence to deserve independent status in theories of rational agency. The position is jeopardized, however, by an apparent conflict between the consistency demands

---

[11] I prefer this formulation to Bratman's which bases the rationality of intentions on whether they maximize expected satisfaction of the agent's desires. But I agree with him that differences over what is fundamental to practical rationality are unlikely to affect the present discussion, since similar standards of reasonableness are likely to emerge on any plausible theory. Ibid. 52 f.

on intentions and the so-called *Simple View*: the principle that in order for me to perform an action *A* intentionally, I must at the time intend to *A*. On first hearing, at least, it seems hard to imagine a less offensive principle. Surely if I intentionally mow my lawn, or call you up, or slice a golf shot, the natural supposition is that at the time, I was in a state of intending to do those things. But the Simple View is threatened: there are a number of cases in which strict adherence to consistency requirements would preclude agents from intending actions which, as it turns out, they perform intentionally. When this occurs, it has been alleged, the Simple View fails.

A pair of examples of Bratman's will illustrate the point. The first is of a common phenomenon: an unexpectedly successful attempt. These occur because there are times when it is rational for us to pursue enterprises we expect will fail. Suppose that owing to a storm last night there is a large log blocking my driveway, and that I plan to make an effort this morning to move it. The log is large enough, however, that I believe it will prove too heavy for me, so that in fact I will not move it. Here it is not just the case that I have no belief that I will move the log; rather, I positively believe I will not. Still, I have nothing to lose by trying, as planned, to do so. And if to my surprise I succeed, we would say I had moved the log intentionally. By the requirement of epistemic consistency, however, it seems I cannot rationally intend to move it, for that would be to hold an intention inconsistent with my beliefs. And Bratman offers a further consideration to reinforce this prohibition. If indeed I believe I will fail to move the log, he says, then I should be able to plan on the basis of this belief, and intend to have the tree company move it this afternoon. But if my plan to try first to move the log myself involves intending to move it myself, then my total plan for the day would include both moving the log myself and having the tree company move it. And, as Bratman points out, 'it seems folly to plan to cause the log to be moved twice'.[12] Finally, we may cite a point recently emphasized by Alfred Mele—namely, that I would be unlikely to avow an intention to move the log. Noting its size you might say to me, 'Surely you do not intend to move that yourself!' I would probably not answer 'Yes'. I might say something like, 'No, but I intend to try.'[13]

A second sort of case is less common, but still perfectly possible. Consider an ambidextrous video game player who simultaneously plays a pair of video games, one with each hand. Each game involves directing a 'missile' toward a target. The targets are difficult to hit, and there is a reward for hitting either one. The games are, however, linked in such a way

---

[12] Ibid. 39.

[13] See especially Alfred R. Mele (1989), 'She Intends to Try', *Philosophical Studies* 55: 101–6. Also id. (1989), 'Intention, Belief, and Intentional Action', 28.

that if either target is hit, both games end, and if both targets are about to be hit simultaneously, both games simply shut down. Despite this last possibility, the player sees it as worthwhile to have a go at both games at once; she is highly skilled, and the risk of shutting down both appears to her to be outweighed by the greater chance simultaneous play provides of hitting one target, and thereby gaining the reward. Now suppose the player hits target 1. If so, she will have done so intentionally, since her success would be owing to her skill and effort. And the Simple View would then say that she had intended to hit target 1. The example is, however, symmetrical with respect both to the games themselves and to the agent's attitudes toward them. Hence she would also, if the Simple View is correct, have had to intend to hit target 2. This violates both consistency requirements, since these two intentions are consistent neither with each other nor with the player's knowledge that she cannot hit both targets. Hence, Bratman claims, to have both intentions would involve the player in a criticizable form of irrationality. Yet, given the facts of the case, it seems clear that the player need *not* be guilty of irrationality. Her strategy of giving both games a try appears perfectly reasonable. Now if she is not irrational, Bratman argues, then she does not have both intentions. And given the symmetry of the case, this would have to mean she does not have either of them. But then the Simple View has to be false. It has to be possible for the player to play both games, hit target 1 intentionally, yet never have intended to hit either target.[14]

It is important to realize that such cases need not be taken as refuting the Simple View. The alternative is to claim them as exceptions to the constraints of internal and epistemic consistency. Indeed, in Bratman's formulation both requirements carry clearly stated *ceteris paribus* clauses, and he claims that both are defeasible, in that 'there may be special circumstances in which it is rational of an agent to violate them'.[15] Now my having a go at removing the log from my driveway certainly seems rational, as does the game player's behaviour of firing at the targets of both games. And although more needs to be said on the matter, it may be possible to explain the hesitancy of agents in such cases to avow the relevant intentions on pragmatic grounds. Perhaps, then, the game player and I should be taken as intending to achieve what our behaviour is aimed at achieving, and what

---

[14] Bratman (1987), *Intention, Plans, and Practical Reason*, 114 f. Once having abandoned the Simple View, Bratman goes on to apply the distinction between intentional and intended action to cases of oblique intention, where otherwise unacceptable consequences are brought about as unavoidable accompaniments of the agent's main objective (ch. 10). Space does not permit treatment of such cases, which in any case have received other accounts. But they do not form part of Bratman's main argument against the Simple View.

[15] Ibid. 32.

we will in fact have done intentionally if our endeavours are successful. This, however, is not the strategy chosen by opponents of the Simple View. Instead, they hold that it is *irrational* for me and the game player to intend to achieve objectives that we *are* rational in pursuing. The effect is to introduce considerable strain into the theory of intentional action.

3. INTENTION SURROGATES

If we are to have blanket enforcement of consistency rules, we need a plausible account of what happens when the agents in our examples succeed in their efforts. That is, we need an explanation of how it is possible for an agent to intentionally A without intending to A. Now surely a person who intentionally A's must have intended to do *something*: otherwise, the theory would have to call for intentional behaviour to occur in cases where intentions are in no way operative. Opponents of the Simple View agree, but insist that the intention in virtue of which one A's intentionally need not be an intention to A. For Bratman, one must distinguish *what* is intended from the *motivational potential* of an intention. The latter is broader in scope, and it is the primary determinant of what acts are intentional. Provided its occurrence is not owing to such factors as deviant causal chains, blind luck, etc., an action A may be intentional simply by falling within the motivational potential of an intention one is executing. But the intention may be an intention to B, where B is different from A.[16] Similarly, Mele holds that A-ing intentionally requires having some pertinent intention, but not necessarily an intention to A.[17] And the appropriate intention for cases such as those we are considering, it is claimed, is the intention to *try* to A. That is, it is suggested that someone who manages to A in the course of carrying out an intention to try to A will, assuming other conditions standard for an intentional action are satisfied, have intentionally A'd.

On such a view, the correct explanation of how the game player comes to hit target 1 intentionally would be roughly as follows. She wants to hit target 1, and for that reason intends to try to hit it. She executes this intention by firing missiles at the target, and thereby hits it. This result is not due to blind chance or a deviant causal chain. The player hits the target in the way she was trying to, and her success is owing to her skill as a player. Accordingly, she hits the target intentionally. But she never intended to hit it; that would have yielded a violation of the requirements of

---

[16] Ibid. 119 f.   [17] Mele (1989), 'Intention, Belief, and Intentional Action', 21.

rational consistency, since she had to have the same attitudes toward hitting both targets. The treatment of the log-moving case is similar. I want to move the log, and for that reason intend to try to do so. I carry out my intention by tugging on the log, and to my surprise succeed in moving it. Again, the outcome is not fortuitous or owing to causal deviance. Hence I moved the log intentionally. Yet I could not rationally have intended to move it given my belief that I would not, for to do so would have been a violation of epistemic consistency.

There is considerable plausibility to these explanations, as far as they go. Our willingness to say both of my act of moving the log and of the game player's act of hitting target 1 that they are intentional certainly has something to do with the fact that each of us was trying to do exactly what we did. Other things being equal, that is enough to secure intentionality, despite my belief that I will fail, and despite the inconsistency of the 'wants' that ground the game player's intentions to try to hit each target. But this account of our examples is not yet sufficient to overthrow the Simple View. It depends on the crucial assumption that it is possible for a person to intend to try to A without intending to A. That assumption is difficult to defend, for the fact is that 'trying' is not a name for a kind of action. No matter what skills I have or what experience I can draw from, a bare intention to try to move the log is not an intention I can act upon; the same applies to the game player's intention to try to hit target 1. This is because there is no particular type of change we can bring about in the world that counts as a 'try'. Rather, 'trying' is a term that signifies the general business of acting in pursuit of some objective, a term that tends especially to be used when the objective is difficult to achieve. Thus my intention to try to move the log must be carried out by doing something else, aimed at achieving the objective of moving it. In this case, that turns out to be my act of tugging on the log. And the game player's intention to try to hit target 1 is executed by firing missiles at it.

But now it begins to appear that the agents in our examples may yet have the intentions opponents of the Simple View would forbid. For clearly, it can only be the agent's attitudes toward the actions constituting their attempts that make them count as such. Suppose, for example, that by tugging on the log I also succeed in straining my back. What makes my tugging on it count as an attempt to move it rather than an attempt to strain my back? And why is it that the game player's firing missiles counts as an attempt to hit the target rather than, say, to burn out the firing mechanism? The answer in each case is clear. It is because I tug on the log *as a means to the end of moving it* that my act counts as an attempt to move the log, and similarly for the game player's act of firing missiles at target 1. It is the place of the actions in our respective *plans* that determines what they are attempts to achieve. Furthermore, there is nothing in our consistency constraints that forbids me from *intending* to tug on the log, since I did believe I would do that; nor does anything prevent the game player from intending to fire at each target, since these intentions are perfectly consistent. But this situation does not differ at all from what we would expect if, confident of success, each of us had adopted the intention of *doing* what, in the examples, we are said only to intend to try to do, and had then chosen the actions constituting our attempts as means to fulfilling our intentions, and proceeded to carry out our respective plans. As far as planning and execution are concerned, our examples differ not at all from standard cases of intentionally *A*-ing. All that is missing, supposedly, is the intention to *A*. But if the agents in our examples do not intend their objectives, what exactly is their attitude toward them?

The problem here is that regardless of whether the game player and I intend to achieve our ends, we are still committed to them as settled objectives, which guide our deliberation and action. Hence theories that reject the Simple View must find some other mental state to play the functional role of intention in our examples. One option here is to claim there are mental states that count as a class of quasi-intentions: that is, mental states of having a goal or purpose which are able to guide deliberation and action, but which fall short of being full-fledged intentions in that they do not carry consistency constraints. Thus Mele speaks at one point of what he calls *intention**, characterizing it as, 'whatever is left of *S*'s intention to *A* when we substitute for her belief that she probably will *A* a belief that she probably will not *A*'.[18] For Mele, either an intention to *A* or an intention* to *A* may guide deliberation and action, and both involve having a plan the *goal* of which is to *A*. An intention* on my part to move the log from my driveway would involve a plan in which moving the log is represented as a goal, and some suitable act such as tugging on it is represented as the means.[19] On this account, then, to have a settled objective is to have a goal. But it should not be thought that to have a goal must in turn be to have an intention in the full sense. That, Mele argues, is false: 'When Lydia purchases a lottery ticket with the goal of winning a million dollars and the knowledge that her chances of winning are less than one in a million, surely she does not *intend* to win.'[20]

Bratman too is attracted by a theory of purposive states that fall short of being full-fledged intentions. There are, he says, two senses in which one

---

[18] Ibid. 20. On this characterization, of course, intention* need be nothing other than plain old intention, but Mele's presentation makes clear that he thinks otherwise.

[19] Compare Mele's example of shooting a free throw, ibid. 21.   [20] Ibid. 22.

may act 'with the intention of A-ing', and only the stronger sense entails that one intends to A. The weaker entails only that I act *in order to* A, which will occur provided I act with the purpose or goal or aim of A-ing. This, however, does not require that I intend, strictly speaking, to A.[21] Again, the suggestion is that there are mental states of having a goal or purpose which may guide planning and action, but which unlike intention are exempt from the demands of rational consistency. Unlike Mele, however, Bratman does not leave it at this. He seems not to want to treat merely having a goal or purpose as a mental state with full ontological standing. Instead, he speaks as though the functional role that usually belongs to intention is carried out in our examples by a state of desire— what he calls a *guiding desire* to A:

When I endeavor to A, I act in order to A, my aim or purpose in acting includes A. Even if I do not, strictly speaking, intend to A, I do desire to A, either as a means or for itself, or both. Further, I do not *merely* desire to A. My desire is guiding my attempt to A: it is a *guiding desire*. Now, in this case my guiding desire guides present conduct. But a desire may also be a guiding desire by virtue of guiding planning for the future.[22]

For Bratman, it is guiding desires that embody our goals and purposes when rational consistency forbids us to intend them. Like intentions, guiding desires frame settled objectives, which direct the planning of anticipated behaviour, and prompt its occurrence when the time for action comes. Our game player, then, may be taken to have a pair of guiding desires to hit target 1 and to hit target 2, which lead her in deciding to play the games simultaneously. Unlike the case with intending, however, there is no rational pressure for one's desires to be consistent, either internally or epistemically. Accordingly, the game player can allow her planning and her conduct to be guided by these desires without any failure of rationality. Similarly, I can rationally allow my desire to have the log out of my driveway guide my planning and conduct, thereby setting for me the goal or purpose of moving the log without my ever having the intention, properly so called, of doing so.

4. THE SIMPLE VIEW AND PRACTICAL RATIONALITY

On the Simple View, my act of moving the log from my driveway and the game player's act of hitting target 1 are straightforward intentional acts, in which an intended end is achieved by intended means. Our initial beliefs

---

[21] Bratman (1987), *Intention, Plans, and Practical Reason*, 129.   [22] Ibid. 137.

that our attempts would fail may have the pragmatic consequence of inhibiting avowals of our full intentions; but they call for no alteration in the standard structure of intentional behaviour. On the alternative approach, the intentionality of the game player's and my acts is held owing to our intentions to try, and our planning and behaviour is viewed as mediated by purposive states which are not intentions, and which on one account turn out to be embodied in the agent's desires. Rejecting the Simple View can lead, then, to considerable complication in the theory of intentional action. I think, however, that the postulation of other purposive states to fill the functional role of intentions is neither demanded by our examples nor justified by pre-analytic data.

That they are unnecessary is especially evident if, with Bratman, we view the requirements of internal and epistemic consistency as constraining only the *rationality* of intentions. Such a view does not hold it impossible for me and the game player to intend our objectives: it says only that we would be irrational to do so. But if the foundations of practical rationality are anything like what has been suggested above, this is a mistaken claim. In the case of the game player, firing at both targets maximizes expected gain, since it increases the chance of hitting one target, thereby winning the reward. As long as they are viewed only as principles of practical rationality, a more obvious exception to the requirements of internal or epistemic consistency could hardly be found. The log-moving example is similar. What makes tugging on the log sensible for me is the fact that I *may* thereby move it, thus clearing the driveway sooner and saving the expense of calling in the tree company. The cost of a failed attempt is, by contrast, remarkably low: some lost energy is all. Now it is perfectly consistent for me to believe both that I will not move the log, and that there is a slight chance I *will* move it. Why not, then, adopt the *intention* of moving the log myself, since I can pursue this objective at minimal cost, and with a chance of considerable gain? Indeed, if this case does not fall under the *ceteris paribus* clause of the epistemic consistency requirement, one wonders what would.

It turns out, then, that far from it being irrational for the game player and me to intend our settled objectives, we would in fact be irrational to intend anything less. Nor should we accept the argument that if I believe I will fail I cannot intend to move the log, since my belief should then support an intention to have the tree company move it, putting me in the foolish position of planning to cause the log to be moved twice. This argument is far too strong, for it applies equally to my intention to *try* to move the log, and to my supposedly weaker 'goal' or 'purpose' of moving it. If I believe I will not move it, then clearly I believe that my attempt will fail, and my purpose be frustrated. By a similar argument, therefore, I ought to intend right now to call in the tree company. But whether we call moving the log my 'purpose' or my 'intention', this again puts me in the unacceptable position of having two plans for moving the log. So what is wrong here is not my intending to move the log, but the demand that I be committed unconditionally to a plan that presumes failure. There is no reason for me to decide to call in the tree company before my attempt is made. The most I need have is the conditional intention to call the tree company if I fail.[23]

Principles of practical rationality offer no basis, then, for the claim that the intentionality of the game player's and my behaviour is owing to the operation of purposive states other than intention. Furthermore, such states would be theoretically redundant, for it turns out that in the end they too must be restricted by conditions of internal and epistemic consistency. Otherwise, anyone faced with an accusation of irrationality for having inconsistent intentions could circumvent the charge simply by forming 'goals' or 'purposes' instead. That would be far too permissive. Indeed, the entire idea that there are states of having a settled objective which are exempt from consistency constraints is wrong. Suppose you ask me my plans for tomorrow. I reply that I am looking forward to the afternoon, since at 2:00 I am going to play golf, and to attend your seminar. Since your seminar is not scheduled for the golf course, you find this a bizarre plan. Gently, you point out to me that I cannot do both. 'It's all right,' I reply, 'I'm not being irrational. Granted, I would be irrational if I were to intend to do both, but I don't have an *intention* either to go to your seminar *or* to play golf at 2:00 tomorrow. It is only my *purpose* to do both—my aim or goal, as you might say. So you can see everything is okay.' I do not think this reply would set your mind at ease. Similarly, suppose I tell you that at the next meeting of the APA in Chicago I plan to jump over the Palmer House. That, you might protest, is a silly plan to have, since I can't succeed at it. And it wouldn't change things if I respond that my only *intention* is to *try* to jump over the hotel, that actually jumping over it is merely a goal or purpose of mine. Here, the chances of success are so remote that unless there is some special reward just for trying, there is no point in my making any move toward the objective.

Unless special circumstances obtain, then, it is irrational to have settled objectives that are mutually inconsistent, or conflict with one's beliefs about what one will achieve. And the irrationality is not diminished by

---

[23] Bratman responds that if my belief that I will fail does not support planning it is not truly a belief (ibid. 40). I would disagree, but in any case this argument too would have to apply to all purposive states, and hence must fail in the end.

treating the having of such objectives as a purposive state that is supposedly weaker than intending. It is the commitment that goes with having a settled objective that is irrational in these cases, and it remains irrational regardless of what we call it. Nothing worth achieving can be accomplished by my committing myself both to going to your seminar and to playing golf. Unlike the game player's objectives, these cannot even be *pursued* simultaneously. So unless there were something to be gained simply by *having* both purposes, I can proceed more efficiently and with less frustration by dropping one of them. The other case is similar. If the APA were offering a prize for the most convincing attempt to jump over the Palmer House, I would have a good reason to try to do so. In fact, however, there is no reward just for trying, and the chances of actually succeeding are so vanishingly remote that they do not outweigh the effort and embarrassment of the attempt. The entire project is therefore irrational.

The mistake of seeking an alternative route to intentional action is compounded if, with Bratman, one associates it with a special operation of the agent's desires. Such a step cannot avoid consistency demands, but it does invite a reassertion of the sort of reductionism most current theories of intention are at pains to avoid. Unless 'guiding desires' play exactly the functional role usually reserved for intention, they cannot yield intentional behaviour. My guiding desire to move the log from my driveway must be able to prompt and sustain action on my part when the right time comes. It must be able to call for the selection of a fitting means, since it cannot otherwise be pursued. In order to fulfil these tasks efficiently, guiding desires cannot be constantly open to reappraisal, or viewed by the agent as embodying less than a settled objective. And of course guiding desires must carry constraints of internal and epistemic consistency. It would not do for me to be guided by a pair of desires to attend your seminar at 2:00 tomorrow and to play golf at the same time. But then, the reductionist might argue, guiding desires constitute at least as good a starting point for the rational planning and direction of behaviour as intentions. Why not, then, simply get by with them? In the normal case, we can safely suppose that the agent's strongest desire is what serves to guide his deliberation and behaviour. Cases where no single desire predominates are less clear, but surely a first approximation would have it that in them a desire gets to be 'guiding' through whatever mechanism non-reductionists would claim is responsible for the formation of an independent state of intending. In short, if desires are able to assume the functional role of intentions on some occasions, why not have a theory according to which they regularly do so?

The way to avoid this conclusion is not to let the argument get started. We have already seen that the functional role of intention is different from that associated with desire. What jeopardizes the non-reductionist position is not anything about the way desires usually operate, but rather the effort to adapt desires to the task of providing settled objectives. But this will seem necessary only if, contrary to the evidence, we insist it would be irrational for the agents in our examples to intend what they do intentionally. That insistence is what leads to the postulation of purposive states other than intention, and the resultant temptation to ground them in special operations of desire. There is no need, however, to start down this path. It is perfectly rational for the agents in our examples fully to intend their objectives. In short, these problems arise only because we abandon the Simple View, when a correct understanding of practical rationality indicates we should hold fast to it.

5. THE SIMPLE VIEW AND AVOWALS OF INTENTION

There is, however, a reply available to the opponent, for the requirements of internal and epistemic consistency can be interpreted another way. Instead of constraining the rationality of intentions, they may be taken as conceptual or ontological in import—i.e. as limitations on when the purposive states of agents *count as* intentions.[24] On this type of view, to have the settled objective of A-ing is always to have the goal or purpose of A-ing, and having a goal is not an 'alternative route' to intentional action. It is the fundamental purposive state, with ontological standing independent of desire. It is bound by consistency constraints, but our examples illustrate that in exceptional cases one may have goals that fail to be consistent. Such goals cannot, however, be *intended* by the agent (even though they are achieved intentionally), for while internal and epistemic consistency bind only the rationality of goals or purposes, they are now taken as strictly binding on when a purpose counts as an intention. It is a conceptual impossibility for me to intend to remove the log from my driveway, or for the game player to intend to hit target 1. And the evidence for this is simply what was said earlier about avowals: the fact that if asked whether I intended to move the log, I would avow only an intention to try.

If this view is adopted, the problems raised in the last section can be minimized. The notion of guiding desire with its reductionist overtones has

---

[24] Though he would not be committed to all that follows, Mele inclines toward a view of this second sort. For him, epistemic consistency is a 'confidence condition' on intention, one that must be satisfied before an agent can properly intend at all. Mele (1989), 'Intention, Belief, and Intentional Action', 28.

been dropped. Nor is it supposed that states of having a goal or purpose are exempt from being rationally consistent. The strictures of consistency apply, but with a *ceteris paribus* clause that is now clearly understood to cover our examples. Finally, this position does not proliferate entities, since it does not treat having a goal or purpose as a second way of having settled objectives besides intending. On the contrary, my having the goal of moving the log would count as a state of intending but for my belief that I will fail; and the game player's purpose of hitting target 1 would count as an intention if only she did not have the incompatible purpose of hitting target 2.

In one respect, this account parallels the Simple View exactly: it treats all intentional action as arising out of the same sort of mental state, regardless of consistency constraints. It insists, however, that those constraints be satisfied before an agent may be said to intend, rather than just to have a goal or purpose. The issues here are, of course, partly verbal. One is always free to define one's terms in such a way that the game player and I cannot 'intend' our objectives. But the Simple View cannot thereby be undone, for it pertains to the everyday concept of intending, not a stipulated one. And there are good reasons for not construing the everyday concept so narrowly. I for one would resist the suggestion that given my epistemic state, it is impossible for me to intend to move the log from my driveway, or to jump over the Palmer House. For one thing, such a view makes whether I intend depend on what beliefs I do *not* have. A heedless person could have either intention simply by failing to address the prospect of failure. But intention is not usually taken to be a negative concept, and it is supposed to attend the actions of the judicious at least as much as the foolish. If it does, then I *can* have these intentions; it is just that only the former would be rational. Indeed, to forbid this is to begin to separate intention from the foundations of rationality, by making it impossible for the game player and me to intend goals we are rational to pursue. But we judge the rationality of agents by considering their intentions, not by inquiring about supposedly weaker goals or purposes.

Finally, we need to note that the argument from avowals, by which this understanding of our consistency constraints sets such store, will not withstand scrutiny. Not that the conversation it envisions could not occur: asked whether I intend to move the log, I *can* reply, 'No, but I intend to try.'[25] The problem is, however, that I can give exactly the same sort of reply no matter how my settled objective is described. You might say to me, 'Surely it is not your purpose (goal, plan) to move that yourself.' And

[25] I might, but I need not. It is at least as plausible for me to opt for a weaker response like, 'Well, I intend to try in any case', thereby avoiding the appearance of denying that I intend my objective.

I could respond, 'No, but it is my purpose (goal, plan) to try.' Yet we have seen that to be set on trying to *A* must be to have the purpose or goal of *A*-ing. The 'No' in these replies cannot, then, be a denial that I have the objective in question, however it is described. Indeed, if we attempt to spell out the supposed denial, we get a reply I submit would *not* be given—i.e. 'No, I do not intend to move the log from my driveway, but I do intend to try to do so.' The trouble here is that the second conjunct asserts what the first denies: that I have the settled objective of removing the log from my driveway. Instead of taking the 'No' as a *dis*avowal of an intention, therefore, we should take it as a pragmatic weakening of the avowal, aimed at diminishing audience expectations about my success. Such weakening is of value precisely because our consistency constraints do normally bind the rationality of intentions. Since this is so, my avowals of intentions can normally be taken as indicative of what I believe I will accomplish and, since such beliefs are usually correct, as a basis for others to develop their own plans. By avowing only the intention to try to move the log, therefore, I signal my awareness of the difficulty, and implicitly warn others not to base their own deliberations on a belief that I will succeed. But I do not completely disown the intention of moving the log, since it is implicit in the intention to try to do so. Furthermore, the same considerations that make it equally misleading for me to avow outright the intention to move the log would also make it misleading for me baldly to avow the goal or purpose of moving it. And as we see above, the pre-analytic data indicate I would not do so.[26]

The evidence from avowals provides no reason, then, for thinking that to have a goal or purpose is to be in a mental state on a different conceptual footing from intending. Settled objectives are always subject to consistency demands, but only as regards their rationality, and only with a *ceteris paribus* clause that exempts agents like the game player and me. A similar point applies to the case of Lydia. If we are willing to accept the hortatory 'Surely she does not intend to win', this is in part because we would not expect her to avow such an intention. But we can also imagine digging in our heels: 'If she does not intend to win, she shouldn't be buying the ticket.' There are, however, dimensions to this example that are absent from the others. The fact is that winning a lottery is not so much something one does as something that happens to one. It requires a fortunate concatenation of circumstances, many of which depend on the actions of agents other than the winner. Viewing Lydia's situation in this light, we may well balk at talk

---

[26] For my further discussion of this issue, see H. J. McCann (1989), 'Intending and Planning: A Reply to Mele', *Philosophical Studies* 55: 107–10.

of her intending to win. But if we do then we should also reject saying that her goal is to win, or that her purpose is to win. A better description might be that her goal or purpose is to become the winner, or to put herself in a position to win. But of course that is also her intention. Notice, too, that the very considerations that tell against saying Lydia intends to win will also count against saying, if the prize falls to her, that she won intentionally. So even if this case does disclose some weak sense in which winning is Lydia's 'goal', it is not a sense that supports intentional action, and hence not a sense that threatens the Simple View.[27]

I would venture to submit, finally, that there is no ordinary sense in which terms like 'goal' or 'purpose' signify objectives that guide deliberation and behaviour, but fall short of being intentions. I can think of no plausible case where, *in the same breath*, one explicitly disavows the intention of *A*-ing while avowing the goal or purpose of doing so. (After forty-seven years of faithful participation in the lottery, Lydia finally has her day in the sun. Dazed with euphoria, she accepts the congratulations of the reporters: 'Oh, thank you so much! I knew all along that winning the lottery was practically impossible, so of course I never intended to win it. But naturally that's been my goal all along.') Ears differ, but to mine this scenario has standing only as an excerpt from a journalist's nightmare. If that is right, then any goal that guided Lydia's planning and behaviour is one she intended to achieve.

6. CONCLUSION

If the foregoing arguments are correct, we should not abandon the Simple View. There is every reason to endorse the requirements of internal and epistemic consistency, but only as constraining the rationality of intentions, and only in a form that allows cases like those of the game player and me to count as exceptions. We need not claim the intentional actions that occur in these cases are anything but fully intended. Instead of excluding such a state of affairs, the requirements of rationality actually demand it, and the very same requirements would have to apply to states of having a settled objective that are alleged to fall short of intending. Such states also turn out to be on an equal footing with intention as regards the conditions under which agents may be expected to avow them. Hence they appear not to fall short of being intentions at all. We have every reason to believe,

[27] It should be noted that Mele does not present the example as upsetting the Simple View, only as showing there are purposive states weaker than intending.

then, that to have a settled objective is to have an intention, and we need not complicate action theory in the ways rejecting the Simple View would require.

I am indebted to Michael Bratman, Alfred Mele, and Robert Audi for helpful discussions of these issues, as well as to the comments of an anonymous referee. An earlier version of this paper was presented at the 1989 meeting of the Central Division of the APA, and I also benefited from the discussion on that occasion.

10

INTENTIONAL ACTION

ALFRED R. MELE AND PAUL K. MOSER

We dedicate this paper to the memory of Hector-Neri Castañeda

Action theory revolves around the concept of *intentional* action. The same is true of much philosophical work on moral and legal responsibility, including work on conditions for blame and praise. Remove the intentional altogether from intentional action, and you have mere behaviour: brute bodily motion not unlike the movement of wind-swept sand on the shores of Lake Michigan.

We shall formulate an analysis of the ordinary notion of intentional action that clarifies a common-sense distinction between intentional and non-intentional action. Our analysis will build on some typically neglected considerations about relations between lucky action and intentional action. It will highlight the often overlooked role of evidential considerations in intentional action, thus identifying the key role of certain epistemological considerations in action theory. We shall also explain why some vagueness is indispensable in a characterization of intentional action as ordinarily understood.

Since a proper understanding of 'intentionally' in '*S A*-ed intentionally' does not require a controversial stand on how actions are to be individuated, we shall leave this matter unresolved. A number of competing views on individuation are now in circulation, and we shall allow for a wide range of them.[1] The action-variable '*A*', as used here, may be read by fine-grained individuators as a variable for actions and by coarse-grained individuators as a variable for actions under *A*-descriptions. The term 'action' may be read in the same manner.

From *Noûs* 28 (1994), 39–68. Copyright © 1994 Basil Blackwell, Inc. Reprinted by permission.

[1] For discussion of some competing views, see H.-N. Castañeda (1979), 'Intensionality and Identity in Human Action and Philosophical Method', *Noûs* 13: 235–60; see also Carl Ginet (1990), *On Action* (Cambridge: Cambridge University Press), ch. 3.

1. OPENING PROBLEMS

Detailed instructive analyses of intentional action have been advanced recently by Carl Ginet (1990) and Myles Brand (1984), *Intending and Acting* (Cambridge, Mass.: MIT Press). With a view to identifying some desiderata for a successful analysis, we shall show that their analyses fall prey to counterexamples.

Ginet's analysis includes the following alleged *sufficient* condition of a 'complex' action's (*V*'s) being intentional:

> *S*'s *V*-ing at *t* consists of some action, *S*'s *A*-ing at *t*, plus that action's causing certain results or its occurring in certain circumstances, where
> (a) *S*'s *A*-ing at *t* was intentional and
> (b) (i) At *t*, *S* believed of her *A*-ing that she would or might thereby *V* and
> (ii) At *t*, in what *S* knew that had not slipped her mind, *S* had justification for this belief that was not, at the same time, justification for believing a proposition too far from the truth as to how she was going thereby to *V*.[2]

Consider the following case. A nuclear reactor is in danger of exploding. Fred knows that its exploding can be prevented only by shutting it down, and that it can be shut down only by punching a certain ten-digit code into a certain computer. Fred is alone in the control room. Although he knows which computer to use, he has no idea what the code is. Fred needs to think fast. He decides that it would be better to type in ten digits than to do nothing. Vividly aware that the odds against typing in the correct code are astronomical, Fred decides to give it a try. He punches in the first ten digits that come into his head, in that order, believing of his so doing that he 'might thereby' shut down the reactor and prevent the explosion. What luck! He punched in the correct code, thereby preventing a nuclear explosion.

Fred's shutting down the reactor and his preventing the explosion satisfy Ginet's conditions for being intentional actions. Fred intentionally typed a certain ten-digit sequence into the computer. By so doing, he shut down the reactor, thereby preventing a nuclear explosion. If actions are constituted along the lines suggested by Ginet, Fred performed a shutting down of the reactor (and a preventing of an explosion) that consisted of a certain intentional typing action 'plus that action's causing certain results'. Fred believed of the typing action that he 'might thereby' shut down the reactor and prevent the explosion. Further, 'in what [Fred] knew that had not

---

[2] Ginet (1990), op. cit. 87. Ginet's analysis is recursive. His view divides actions into 'simple', 'complex', and 'aggregate[s] of simple or complex actions' (p. 73). The condition cited pertains to complex actions only.

slipped [his] mind, [he] had justification for this belief that was not, at the same time, justification for believing a proposition too far from the truth as to how [he] was going thereby' to shut down the reactor and prevent the explosion. His justification for the relevant belief was not also justification for a false belief about how he would or might (or 'was going' to) shut down the reactor and prevent the explosion.

Ginet's analysis implies that Fred *intentionally* shut down the reactor and *intentionally* prevented the explosion. That is implausible. When luck plays this great a role in the success of an attempt at A-ing, the A-ing is generally deemed too coincidental to count as intentional.

Our story continues. Suppose that Fred knew that if his typing were to shut down the reactor, there would be a one in a million chance that by so typing he would release a lethal chemical into the air, thereby killing hundreds of people. He believed of his typing that he 'might thereby' release a lethal chemical into the air (in addition to shutting down the reactor) and kill many townsfolk. He knew, moreover, just what the mechanism would be: a certain alignment of items that are extraordinarily unlikely to be aligned at any given time. Fred had no idea, however, whether they would be aligned at the crucial moment. As luck would have it, they were aligned when Fred typed the ten-digit code into the computer: By typing his sequence of numbers, Fred released a deadly chemical into the air and killed hundreds of people. Here, again, Ginet's conditions are satisfied, implying that Fred intentionally released the lethal chemical and intentionally killed hundreds of people. This consequence plainly is unacceptable.

We turn to Brand's analysis ((1984), op. cit., 28), which includes the following claim: 'S's A-ing during t is an intentional action [if] (i) S's A-ing during t is an action; and (ii) ... S has an action plan P to A during t such that his A-ing is included in P and he follows P in A-ing'. This claim, too, has the result that Fred intentionally shut down the reactor and intentionally prevented the explosion. Fred's shutting down the reactor and preventing the explosion are actions, and they were included in the plan that Fred followed, a plan that involved his typing into the computer the first ten digits that came into his head, in that order.

Consider a variant of the original case. This time it is Fred's job to shut down the reactor. Recognizing the threat of explosion, he opens a safe and looks inside for the needed handwritten code. As nervous as Fred is, it is not surprising that he misreads the code. He transposes two digits and mistakes a 4 for a 9 and a 7 for a 1. Fred thus thinks that he sees 2435465169, but the code before him is 2453465764. He puts the code down and approaches the computer with a plan to shut down the reactor and prevent an explosion by typing the sequence 2435465169. The typing goes exactly according to plan. Amazingly, the code in the safe was incorrect, and the code Fred typed happened to be right. When typing, Fred followed perfectly the plan that he had *at that time* to shut down the reactor and to prevent an explosion. So, on Brand's analysis, Fred's shutting down the reactor and his preventing a nuclear explosion were intentional actions. Given the crucial role that Fred's earlier mistakes played, however, his shutting down the reactor and his preventing the explosion are too coincidental to count as intentional.[3]

We need an analysis of intentional action that skirts problems from coincidental action, and thereby avoids deficiencies of the sort just illustrated. Such an analysis will deliver a much improved understanding of what distinguishes intentional from nonintentional action. To this we now turn.

2. ACTION PLANS

Consider Laura, a typical young child, who flips a switch, not knowing or even believing that this will (or might) turn on the heat lamp overhead which, in turn, will raised the room's temperature to 82 °F. Given no prior familiarity with a heat-lamp switch, Laura in fact has no representation whatever of a connection (causal or probabilistic) between her flipping the switch, the lamp's lighting, and the temperature's increasing. Laura thus did not *intentionally* increase the room's temperature, even if she intentionally flipped the switch.

On a common notion of intentional action, a person performs a certain action of type *A* intentionally only if she has a representation of *that* action type. Representations can come in various forms, accompanied by different kinds of propositional attitude. Under conditions of more information, Laura might have believed that flipping the switch would probably increase the room's temperature, or simply that flipping it would increase the temperature. The representational attitude provided by believing is, on standard construals, dispositional rather than merely episodic. It can exist even when unmanifested in actual events of assenting. Representational attitudes need not be dispositional. Given more information, Laura might have accepted, non-dispositionally, that her flipping the switch would increase the room's temperature. Acceptance of this sort is just non-dispositional assenting. It does not amount to

---

[3] For a related case, and its bearing on causal accounts of intentional action, see Alfred Mele (1987), 'Intentional Action and Wayward Causal Chains', *Philosophical Studies* 51: 55–60.

belief of the standard, dispositional sort.[4] Both belief and acceptance, however, are *affirmational* propositional attitudes. Both are functionally defined relative to the affirmation, actual or dispositional, of propositional items.

Not all representational attitudes are affirmational. Laura's representation of flipping the switch need not consist in her believing or accepting that she will, probably will, or even can, flip the switch. Laura might dispositionally *have a plan* for flipping the switch, where this amounts to her understanding and having dispositional access to a strategy (i.e. a plan) for reaching a goal that includes flipping the switch. An *action plan* need not be complex, and can in fact be deflationary. In the case of a basic action, *A*, one's having a plan might be just one's having a prospective representation of one's *A*-ing. Laura's intentionally raising her arm might rest, so far as plans are concerned, only on her having a prospective representation of her raising her arm in a normal manner. In more complex cases, one might have a plan that includes complex means for achieving a goal. For example, Laura might have a plan for increasing the room's temperature by using a rod to flip the switch to turn on the heat-lamp.

Having an action plan does not require believing that one will, or even probably will, perform the relevant action. Laura can have a plan for flipping the switch, but not believe that she will, or even probably will, flip the switch. Perhaps she knowingly is often frustrated in such cases by her ever-watchful energy-conserving parents. A state of having a plan can, however, be dispositional in the way belief is. It can exist even while unmanifested in an event of planning, and even while absent from awareness or consciousness. Laura need not be constantly aware of her plan or continually engaging in *acts* of planning to flip the switch.

We should not confuse one's being in a dispositional state of having a plan and one's merely *being disposed* to be in such a state. Laura's dispositionally having a plan for flipping the switch requires her having *come to be* in that state, her having *come to have* the plan in question. Agents are not in dispositional attitudinal states without having somehow come to be in those states. One's coming to be in a dispositional attitudinal state is an event, and not itself another dispositional state. One's merely being disposed to have a plan for flipping a switch does not entail either one's having a plan for flipping a switch or one's having any other sort of

---

[4] On the distinction between dispositional and nondispositional propositional attitudes, with regard to believing, see Robert Audi (1982), 'Believing and Affirming', *Mind* 91: 115–20; William Lycan (1988), *Judgement and Justification* (Cambridge: Cambridge University Press), ch. 3; Paul Moser (1985), *Empirical Justification* (Dordrecht, Neth.: Reidel), 12–13.

representation of flipping a switch. Since one's intentionally flipping a switch requires one's somehow representing flipping a switch, intentional action here requires more than a mere disposition to have a plan for flipping a switch.

What sort of event initiates a dispositional state of having a plan for acting? One proposal is that the initiator comes from an event of planning where one *plans to perform* the action in question. This proposal is too demanding, if we aim to capture the components of the ordinary notion of intentional action. On that notion, one might have an action plan that was passively acquired, without performing a planning action. Even if certain events (e.g. neural events) must initiate a dispositional state of having an action plan, those events need not themselves be actions. This consideration blocks a regress of required actions that might otherwise threaten.

One may have a plan *episodically* or *non-episodically*. Laura would episodically have a plan for flipping the switch if she instructed, or directed, herself to flip the switch, where such self-directing requires adopting a directive *de se*. The *de se* ascription, 'Laura directs herself to flip the switch', is true if and only if Laura gives herself a directive to flip the switch.[5] Intentional action can, but need not, include episodic action plans. Often we just dispositionally have plans that represent the actions we perform. Such habitual intentional action as answering one's ringing deskphone upon hearing it does not ordinarily include giving oneself a directive to answer the phone. Al dispositionally has a simple plan for answering his ringing phone. He extends his arm, grasps the receiver, raises it to his ear, and says 'Hello'. He habitually executes this plan upon hearing his deskphone ring. Typically he executes this plan without directing himself to execute it. Talk of having a plan must, then, allow for dispositional and non-dispositional having.

An agent's action plans are not themselves *motivational* items. Suppose that you once encountered a plan for making a doll's house in *Childlife Magazine*. You committed it to memory and are now mentally reviewing it, purely as a mnemonic exercise. The plan in the magazine plainly had no motivational component; nor does the plan in your memory now. You are not the least bit motivated now to execute the plan or to make a doll house. This scenario is quite coherent. Having a plan does not entail motivation for executing the plan Alfred Mele (1992), *Springs of Action* (New York: Oxford University Press): 144.

We can now introduce our first condition for intentional action:

---

[5] On the logical differences between *de se*, *de re*, and *de dicto* ascriptions, see David Lewis (1979), 'Attitudes *De Dicto* and *De Se*', *Philosophical Review* 87: 513–43; Mark Richard (1983), 'Direct Reference and Ascriptions of Belief', *Journal of Philosophical Logic* 12: 425–52.

(1) A person, S, intentionally performs an action, A, at a time, t, only if at t, S has an action plan, P, that includes, or at least can suitably guide, her A-ing.

(Our use of 'at a time t' can pick out temporal intervals as well as moments.) The basis for the disjunct 'or at least can suitably guide' will become clear in Section 3. Condition (1) preserves the conceptual platitude that our performing an action of type A intentionally requires our having some representation of that action type, or at least some representation that can suitably guide our performing an action of that type. It steers clear, however, of the excessive requirement that the needed representation must come from a belief that one (probably) will A.

Monroe Beardsley has claimed that 'to perform an action $A1$ intentionally [is] to perform $A1$ with the concurrent intention to perform an action of the kind A at that time', and that having such an intention requires that one 'believe that one will perform (or is performing) an action of kind A at that time'.[6] Beardsley thus holds that an agent performs an action intentionally only if she believes that she will perform (or is performing) an action of that kind. Laura, however, might fully appreciate the frequent vigilance of her parents toward preventing her from flipping the heat-lamp switch. As a result, Laura might not believe that she will flip the switch. On this occasion, Laura—acting in the dark and with extreme haste, as is her normal procedure concerning the switch—might not even believe that she *is* flipping the switch. Perhaps she believes that there is a very good chance that her finger is in contact with another item on the wall, but feels that she must act at once if she is to have a chance of flipping the switch before her parents stop her. The following conditions could still obtain: Laura has a definite plan for flipping the switch, tries to flip it in accord her plan

[6] Monroe Beardsley (1980), 'Motives and Intentions', in M. Bradie and M. Brand (eds.), *Action and Responsibility* (Bowling Green, Oh.: Philosophy Documentation Center), 72. Both claims are controversial, as subsequent discussion shows. Our immediate concern is with an implication of this pair of claims. A dispute about whether intention is reducible to belief/desire complexes merits mention. On the reductionist side, involving various construals of the belief condition, see Robert Audi (1973), 'Intending', *Journal of Philosophy* 70: 387–402; Monroe Beardsley (1978), 'Intending', in A. Goldman and J. Kim (eds.), *Values and Morals* (Dordrecht, Neth.: Reidel), 163–84; Beardsley (1980), op. cit.; Wayne Davis (1984), Ch. 6 this volume, 131–48. For criticism see Myles Brand (1984), *Intending and Acting* (Cambridge, Mass.: MIT Press), ch. 6; Michael Bratman (1987), *Intention, Plans, and Practical Reason* (Cambridge, Mass.: Harvard University Press), chs. 8–9; Donald Davidson (1980), *Essays on Actions and Events* (Oxford: Clarendon Press), ch. 5; Gilbert Harman (1976), Ch. 7 this volume, 149–77, and id. (1986), *Change in View* (Cambridge, Mass.: MIT Press); Hugh McCann (1986), 'Rationality and the Range of Intention', *Midwest Studies in Philosophy* 10: 191–211; Alfred Mele (1989), 'Intention, Belief, and Intentional Action', *American Philosophical Quarterly* 26: 19–30, and id. (1992), *Springs of Action* (New York: Oxford University Press), chs. 8–9; John Searle (1983), *Intentionality* (Cambridge: Cambridge University Press). Our view is nonreductionist.

(with familiar child-like incorrigibility), and directly succeeds in so doing. Suppose also that Laura has such success nearly half of the time she tries. This seems to yield a case of intentional action where no belief of the identified kind is present. (1), however, is satisfied in such a case.[7]

Condition (1) fits the popular claim that intentional action is somehow 'goal directed'. Action plans are action strategies that represent goals and often means to those goals as well. Since one's having an action plan does not incorporate motivation, however, it cannot fully account for the idea that intentional action is goal *directed*. The directedness of intentional action depends on a motivational condition that goes beyond (1). We turn now to a motivational condition that handles some troublesome cases of causal deviance.

3. INTENTIONS, ACTION PLANS, AND DEVIANCE

Intentions figure importantly in a great many intentional actions. On the so-called 'simple view', an agent intentionally A-s only if she intends to A (Frederick Adams (1986), 'Intention and Intentional Action: The Simple View', *Mind and Language* 1: 281–301; Hugh McCann, op. cit. and (1989), 'Intending and Planning: A Reply to Mele', *Philosophical Studies* 55: 107–10, and Ch. 9 this volume). Less daring souls have argued that in any case of intentional A-ing, *some* pertinent action is intended, but not necessarily an A (Bratman 1987; Mele 1989, 1992). The latter argue that (a) owing to belief constraints on intentions, or on *rational* intentions, an agent who intends to *try* to A might lack an intention to A, and that (b) under certain conditions, an agent who succeeds in A-ing in such a case has A-ed *intentionally*, the absence of an intention to A notwithstanding.

We shall remove some obstacles to the following thesis: An agent intentionally A-s only if she has an intention that encompasses, perhaps subconsciously, a plan that guides her A-ing. Intuitions about a species of behavioural 'side effect' pose a noteworthy problem for this thesis. Consider the following from Gilbert Harman:

In firing his gun, [a] sniper [who is trying to kill a soldier] knowingly alerts the enemy to his presence. He does this [i.e. alerts the enemy] intentionally, thinking that the gain is worth the possible cost. But he certainly does not intend to alert the enemy to his presence. (Ch. 7 this volume, 151)

Since the sniper does not unknowingly, inadvertently, or accidentally alert the enemy, it is natural to insist that he does not *unintentionally* alert the

---

[7] For further considerations against a positive belief-condition on intentional action, see the paper by Audi cited in the preceding note and much of the anti-reductionist literature cited there.

enemy. Such insistence does not entail, however, that the sniper *intentionally* alerts the enemy. There is a middle ground between *A*-ing intentionally and *A*-ing unintentionally. We locate 'side-effect actions' of the kind in question on that ground. In so far as such actions are not done unknowingly, inadvertently, or accidentally, they are not unintentional. In so far as the agent is not aiming at the performance of these actions, either as ends or as means to (or constituents of) ends, they are not intentional either. We shall say that they are *non-intentional*. The ordinary concept of intentional action requires the agent of an intentional *A*-ing to be aiming at *A*-ing (in a sense to be made more precise).

Another apparent problem for our thesis comes from sudden or impulsive intentional actions. Sometimes, certain theorists argue, things move too quickly for the agent to form the pertinent intentions (see Lawrence Davis (1979), *Theory of Action* (Englewood Cliffs, N.J.: Prentice-Hall): 59–60; Norman Malcolm (1968), 'The Conceivability of Mechanism', *Philosophical Review* 77: 61; John Searle op. cit., 84; George Wilson (1989), *The Intentionality of Human Action* (Stanford: Stanford University Press): 238–9). A driver might straightaway hit her brakes upon seeing a dog dart into her car's path; and a man angered by an insult may immediately and impulsively strike the offending party—in both cases, *intentionally*. The suddenness of the relevant reactions might suggest that the agents lacked sufficient time to *form* an intention to hit (respectively) the brakes or the offending person. If forming an intention is an *action*, however, an agent can *acquire* an intention without forming one. Some intentions are *passively* acquired, as are many beliefs and desires. If intention-acquisition can occur at something approaching the speed of thought, the problem dissolves. In that case, sudden and impulsive intentional actions are plausibly viewed as products of suddenly or impulsively acquired intentions—or, more precisely, as products of the *acquisition* of such intentions (see Frederick Adams and Alfred Mele (1989), 'The Role of Intention in Intentional Action', *Canadian Journal of Philosophy* 19: 511–31; Mele, *Springs of Action*, ch. 10, sect. 3). (This is not to say that our agents lack a general standing intention or policy of braking for animals or immediately striking insulting parties. Such intentions differ, however, from intentions to brake for this animal now or to strike this man now. Intentions of the latter kind—*proximal* intentions—will be discussed shortly.)

A third problem arises from what John Searle has termed 'subsidiary' actions. Searle contends that 'even in cases where I have a prior intention to do some action there will normally be a whole lot of subsidiary actions which are not represented in the prior intention but which are none the less performed intentionally' ((1983), op. cit., 84). In driving to work, an experienced driver shifts gears, checks his mirrors, and the like, with a kind of automaticity suggesting that he lacks specific intentions for the specific deeds. When so acting, he moves his limbs and eyes in various ways, even more 'automatically'.

Exactly how deep the representational content of intentions runs is a difficult question. Even when what is intended is routine and very simple behaviour for the agent (e.g. a professor's writing her name on a chalkboard), a great deal is going on representationally. Some psychologists take the representational content of motor schemata to run quite deep. Donald MacKay has argued that motor schemata involved in handwriting have 'lower-level components' that represent 'the neuromuscular activity required to achieve' the movement represented by their 'higher-level components' (Donald MacKay (1981), 'Behavioral Plasticity, Serial Order, and the Motor Program', *Behavioral and Brain Sciences* 4: 630). Are such representations included in *plans* for writing one's name? If so, one might well suppose that a normal experienced driver's normal driving plan includes representations even of the neuromuscular activity required to shift gears—not to mention gear shifting itself. In any case, particular gear-shifting actions and associated bodily movements need not themselves be intended to be intentional. Actions are intentional in virtue of their being suitably guided by an intention-embedded plan. On the view under development, the content of one's intention to drive to work, say, is a plan for driving to work. In normal cases, that plan is—by default—the agent's normal plan for that activity.

Low-level representations, on MacKay's view, can figure in the production of minute muscle movements that occur in the execution of a normal driving plan. Standard conceptions of intention do not countenance such representations as parts of the representational content of the agent's intention to drive to work—probably owing to the apparent inaccessibility of these representations to consciousness. On standard conceptions, intentions guide behaviour in a way that depends on their representational content. (Guidance, here, is not an *activity*. Road maps guide drivers via drivers' use thereof; but maps do not guide by *acting*.) The issue is one of degree: How deep does the representational content of intention run? This question is partly empirical and partly conceptual. We shall leave it open. If normal driving plans do not incorporate representations of low-level neuromuscular activity, they can provide guidance at a higher level, with the assistance of intention-extrinsic motor schemata.

The idea that intentions play a guiding role in a way that depends on intention-embedded plans is now popular (see John Bishop (1989), *Natural Agency* (Cambridge: Cambridge University Press): 167–72; Brand

(1984), op. cit. pt. IV; Heinz Heckhausen and Jurgen Beckmann (1990), 'Intentional Actions and Action Slips', *Psychological Review* 97: 36–48; Mele (1992), op. cit.; Irving Thalberg (1984), 'Do Our Intentions Cause Our Intentional Actions?', *American Philosophical Quarterly* 21: 249–60). For our purposes, a full account of guidance is unnecessary. A proper analysis of acting intentionally does not depend on a detailed theory of the *etiology* of intentional action. Still, guidance requires some attention. Guidance by a plan is required for *following a plan*, as distinct from merely *acting in accord with a plan*. This distinction resembles a familiar one between a bit of behaviour's according with a rule and the agent's following a rule.[8] Paul's moving a knight in a certain L-shaped pattern on a chessboard accords with a rule of chess even if Paul, ignorant of the rules of chess, is simply fiddling with the knight. We follow rules, however, only when our behaviour is appropriately *guided* by them. This holds of plan-following too.

The guiding function of intention depends on its plan-component. Consider Al's intention to start his computer now. The intention incorporates a plan for so doing: First, plug the surge protector in; then switch on the surge protector; then flip the power switch on the computer. In executing the intention, Al is guided by the plan. This guidance depends upon Al's *monitoring* progress toward his goal. The information (or misinformation) that he has plugged the machine in, for example, figures in the etiology of the continued execution of the plan.[9] A plausible requirement for an agent's *following* an intention-embedded plan in *A*-ing is that his acquiring or having the pertinent intention play a causal role in the production of his *A*-ing. (See, on this requirement, Brand (1984), op. cit., 25; Mele (1992), op. cit., ch. 11.)

Many theorists distinguish between intentions for the non-immediate future and intentions for the specious present. We shall call them *distal* and *proximal* intentions, respectively.[10] Although the temporal content of proximal intentions typically ranges into the future, part of any proximal intender's plan is to begin acting appropriately at once. Many intentional actions are initiated by acquisitions of proximal intentions. (Such *acquisitions* are events, and thus can provide for event-causation. Intentions themselves are states, not events.) Al's starting up his computer was initi-

---

[8] On the distinction regarding plans and the analogy with rules, see Brand (1984), op. cit. 240–1.

[9] Some have ascribed the monitoring function to intention itself: Brand (1984), op. cit., pt. IV; Thalberg (1984), op. cit., 257–9. See Searle (1983), op. cit., ch. 3, on the presentational nature of 'intentions in action'. For resistance, see Mele (1992), op. cit., ch. 11.

[10] The terminology varies. See Beardsley (1978), op. cit. 174; Brand (1984), op. cit. 148; Bratman (1987), op. cit. 4; Mele (1992), op. cit. 173.

ated by his acquiring a proximal intention to do so. His starting the computer was sustained by the continued presence of that intention. If, after plugging in the surge protector, he had ceased to intend to turn on his computer, he would not have executed the next step in the plan, other things being equal.

The view taking shape can handle familiar problems that *deviant causal chains* pose for causal analyses of intentional action.[11] The alleged problem is this: Whatever psychological causes are deemed both necessary and sufficient for a resultant action's being intentional, cases can be described where, owing to a deviant causal connection between the favoured psychological antecedents and a pertinent resultant action, that action is not intentional. Common examples of deviance are twofold, depending upon what portion of the causal chain gets attention. Some cases—instances of *primary deviance*—raise a problem about a relatively direct connection between mental antecedents and resultant bodily motion. Cases of *secondary deviance* focus on behavioural consequences of intentional actions and on the connection between these actions and their consequences.

The following are, respectively, exemplary instances of the two types of deviance:

C1. A climber might want to rid himself of the weight and danger of holding another man on a rope, and he might know that by loosening his hold on the rope he could rid himself of the weight and danger. This belief and want might so unnerve him as to cause him to loosen his hold [unintentionally].

C2. A man may try to kill someone by shooting at him. Suppose the killer misses his victim by a mile, but the shot stampedes a herd of wild pigs that trample the intended victim to death. (Davidson (1980), op. cit., 79, 78)

Both cases can be recast in terms of intentions. Suppose that in *C1* the climber intends to loosen his hold straightaway, and that his acquiring this intention so unnerves him that his hands tremble uncontrollably, with the result that he loses his grip on the rope. Here the climber does not perform an *action* of loosening his hold. The rope, rather, slips from his trembling hands (Brand (1984), op. cit., ch. 1; Searle (1983), op. cit., chs. 3–4; Thalberg (1984), op. cit.). If this is right, *C1* is not an obstacle to a causal analysis of an action's being intentional, unless the analysis entails that a pertinent action has occurred—e.g. the climber's loosening his hold on the

---

[11] A full rebuttal of arguments against *causal* analyses of intentional action is beyond our scope. For recent criticisms of 'causalism' about intentional action and about action generally, see Ginet (1990), op. cit.; Wilson (1989), op. cit. For rebuttal, see Mele (1992), op. cit., ch. 13. For responses to earlier criticisms of 'causalism', see Bishop (1989), op. cit. Our analysis of intentional action does not require that intention-acquisition itself be caused. Incompatibilists holding that free intentional actions are caused by uncaused intentions have no cause for worry. See Alan Donagan (1987), *Choice* (London: Routledge & Kegan Paul), chs. 7 and 10.

rope. The climber's acquiring the relevant intention proximately causes nervousness, which in turn issues in the motions of his hands. An increasingly popular view is that actions are proximately initiated by intention-acquisition (Brand (1984), op. cit.; Mele (1992), op. cit.; Thalberg (1984), op. cit.).

Concerning intentional action, George Wilson contends that the requirement of proximal initiation by intention-acquisition is too strong. Occasionally, he observes 'intentions cause states of nervous agitation that positively enable the agent to perform the type of action intended' ((1989), op. cit., 252). He offers the example of a weight-lifter whose 'intention to lift the weight then caused a rush of nervous excitement that was, in fact, necessary for him to budge the great weight even slightly from off the floor'. What is required, however, is not that intention-inspired nervousness, agitation, and the like, play no role in producing intentional actions, but rather that they not fill a temporal gap between intention-acquisition and action, lest intention-acquisition figure only *mediately* in the production of relevant behaviour. In Wilson's example, there is no gap, filled by nervousness, between the agent's acquiring a proximal intention to lift the weight and the beginning of the lifting. Rather, intention-acquisition proximately initiates the lifting—which action, on our view, begins prior to the weight's rising[12]—while also producing nervousness required for the agent's even budging the weight.

Proximal intentions typically are not momentary states. Presumably, the intention to lift the weight, in the case at hand, is at work as long as the lifting continues. If the agent were to cease intending to lift the weight, he would stop lifting it (other things being equal). Even if nervousness were required for the occurrence of the agent's muscular movements, acquisition of a nervousness-producing intention to lift the weight that results in an intentional lift would, in conjunction with the nervousness, figure in the proximal initiation of those movements.[13] If, alternatively, the causal role of intention-acquisition were exhausted by its issuing in nervousness, and the nervousness were somehow to result in the upward movement of limbs and weight independently of *any* pertinent intention at the time, the 'weight-lifting' would not be intentional. We would then have a case that, aside from its failure to produce an intuitively appealing mechanistic ex-

---

[12] See Brand (1984), op. cit., ch. 1; Davidson (1980), op. cit., ch. 3; Lawrence Davis (1979), *Theory of Action* (Englewood Cliffs, NJ: Prentice-Hall); Jennifer Hornsby (1980), *Actions* (London: Routledge & Kegan Paul); Colin McGinn (1982), *The Character of Mind* (Oxford: Clarendon Press), ch. 5.

[13] We set aside cases where a nervousness-producing intention to lift the weight results in another intention to lift the weight that has a more direct causal role in the lifting. Such cases pose no special problems now.

planation of the pertinent occurrence, is on a par with familiar instances in the literature of non-intentional occurrences caused by intention-inspired nervousness: e.g. *C1* above.

The observation about the *continued* functioning of proximal intentions bears on a case of deviance formulated by John Bishop. Bishop ((1989), op. cit., 139) notes that deviance can break in after intention-acquisition has (properly) initiated a causal chain but before bodily movement occurs and can deprive the agent of control over his motions. In that case, although an agent's bodily motions might accord with his intention, he does not act intentionally. On our view, the proximal intentions to A whose acquisition initiates intentional A-ings *sustain* and *guide* the A-ings.[14] In Bishop's case, the bodily motions are not guided by an intention. This accounts for the motions' not being intentional.

Our suggestion that many intentional actions are proximately initiated by the *acquisition* of a proximal intention requires clarification. Compare two cases. (1) Al, having formed at 7:30 a.m. an intention to turn his computer on at 8:00 a.m., has at 8:00 a proximal intention to turn his computer on. (2) Paul, who had no distal intention to turn his computer on this morning, forms at 8:00 a proximal intention to switch it on. In acquiring a proximal intention to start his computer, Paul comes to have an intention that he previously lacked. What about Al? *Must* his proximal intention to turn the computer on be a distinct intention from his distal intention? Or might the latter in some way evolve into the former? Might Al's distal intention have become a proximal one? We shall leave the issue open for current purposes. If distal intentions cannot become proximal intentions, the acquisition of the proximal intention in case (1), as in case (2), is partly a matter of the agent's coming to have an intention that he did not previously possess. If, alternatively, Al's distal intention evolved into his proximal intention, his *acquisition* of the proximal intention consists in a change of another sort—his distal intention's having become a proximal one. On either view, it is true of the agent at one time, and false at another, that he proximally intends to A. As we use 'intention-acquisition', this is sufficient for the acquisition of a proximal intention. If distal intentions can evolve into proximal ones, acquiring a proximal intention need not involve acquiring a *new* intention.

Actions can come in various lengths. Hitting the 'save' key on a compu-

---

[14] For details on this view, see Frederick Adams and Alfred Mele (1989), 'The Role of Intention in Intentional Action', *Canadian Journal of Philosophy* 19: 511–31; William Alston (1986), 'An Action-Plan Interpretation of Purposive Explanations of Actions', *Theory and Decision* 20: 275–99; Brand (1984), op. cit.; Mele (1992), op. cit., ch. 10; Thalberg (1984), op. cit.

ter takes a fraction of a second; running a marathon takes hours. Consider John's hiking up a mile-high mountain without stopping. John hikes from the foot of the mountain to the top. He also hikes the last half-mile, the last quarter-mile, and so on. His hiking the last quarter-mile, say, is intentional, since he intentionally climbs the mountain. It would be too demanding to suppose that each such segment of the hike must be initiated by acquisition of a proximal intention for that segment. Here again, we contend, these actional segments are intentional actions in virtue of their being appropriately guided by a relevant intention—e.g. an intention to climb the mountain.

When proximal intentions issue in overt intentional actions, how long does the presence of the intentions continue to *sustain* the actions? A plausible (if oversimplified) answer is that the sustaining generally continues through the completion of the bodily movement(s) involved in executing the intention.[15] The extent of these movements depends upon the content of the proximal intention, and there are restrictions on the latter. John, realizing that he cannot climb the entire mountain at once, will not (other things being equal) have a proximal intention to climb the entire mountain. Even actions performed straightway take time—even if less time than ordinary folks set aside for climbing a mountain.

John's hike might be sustained by a single intention to climb the mountain. His climbing the mountain need not begin, however, with a proximal intention that is distinct from his intention to climb it. He might have an intention to climb the mountain, *beginning now*, and not have a distinct intention to begin climbing the mountain now. If so, intentions do not neatly divide into proximal and distal. Some intentions will have both proximal and distal features. We call them *temporally mixed intentions*. A temporally mixed intention is an intention whose plan-component identifies both behaviour to be engaged in now and behaviour to be engaged in later. When an agent *executes* such an intention, proximal features typically figure in the initiation of an action, and distal features figure in the sustaining of whatever portion of the actional process falls outside the scope of the proximal aspect. The proximal and distal features of John's intention to climb the mountain beginning now may figure, respectively, in the initiation of the hike and in the sustaining of the continued hiking.

[15] A more refined answer would accommodate *ballistic* movements. When a person kicks a ball, for example, the leg is 'flung' by the quadriceps muscle, which ceases its activity before the leg stops moving and before the foot comes into contact with the ball (Martin Sheridan (1984), 'Planning and Controlling Simple Movements', in M. Smyth and A. Wing (eds.), *The Psychology of Human Movement* (London: Academic Press), 54). Once the leg is flung, its movement in the kicking is no longer guided. This need not concern us now.

We turn to secondary deviance, which admits of a quick response to be elaborated in due course. Suppose that the gunman in *C2* intended to bring about the man's death. He succeeded in doing just that. He did not, however, *intentionally* bring about the death. A common diagnosis is that the killing did not go 'according to plan' (Brand (1984), op. cit., ch. 1; Harman, Ch. 7 this volume; Searle (1983), op. cit., ch. 3; Thalberg (1984), op. cit.)—in which case, the agent did not follow his intention-imbedded plan. Agents follow their plans more and less closely. The question how closely a plan must be followed if the agent is to perform the relevant actions intentionally requires discussion.

Suppose that the gunman had intended to kill his victim by shooting him directly through the heart, but that, owing to a slight inaccuracy in his aim, he killed him instead by shooting him between the eyes. Most people would plausibly claim (given natural assumptions about the killer) that the killing was intentional. A reasonable preliminary diagnosis of the correctness of this claim is that the killing only moderately diverged from the intention-embedded plan. If (holding his intention fixed) the gunman had instead killed his victim with a stray shot that ricocheted off a rock into the victim's heart or head, intuitions would be more mixed. This is one of many indications of vagueness in common-sense conceptions of intentional action.

Philosophers sometimes overlook that common-sense judgements about what is and is not intentional are significantly influenced by background assumptions about the agents involved. Suppose that Arnold, an expert marksman, was convinced in Assassins' School that one can kill people by shooting them *only* by shooting them through the heart. He is now quite confident that all bullets carry special heart-destroying material, that they kill by causing that material to enter the heart, and that they can in no way injure any other part of the human body. Arnold, intending to kill Bob by shooting him through the heart, aims and fires. Uncharacteristically, he misses his intended victim's heart, and kills Bob by shooting him between the eyes. (Seeing that he has missed Bob's heart, Arnold is amazed to find Bob dead.) Was Arnold's killing Bob an intentional killing?

We shall want to hold Arnold responsible for killing Bob (other things being equal). Responsibility for one's *A*-ing does not, however, require that one *A*-ed intentionally. A drunk driver might be responsible for his running over a pedestrian, even if the driver did not intentionally run over the pedestrian. In Arnold's case, we are not surprised by the judgement that his killing Bob was not an intentional killing—even though the divergence of his behaviour from his intention-embedded plan is no greater than that in the initial heart/eyes case. This suggests that common-sense assessments of actions as intentional or nonintentional are conditioned by considerations about the agent's own *evidential* condition, a condition extending beyond the agent's intentions.

Consider a morally neutral case. Young Thor grew up in a distant land in which a game, 'hoops', remarkably similar to basketball is the national pastime. The chief difference is that hoops is played without a backboard. On a visit to Los Angeles, Thor encounters basketball for the first time, noticing some skilled young men playing a hoops-like game in a park. He is surprised by the wooden slab to which the hoop is attached. It strikes him as simply a device to minimize running after wayward balls. He has not seen a shot banked off the backboard; nor does it occur to him that the wood can serve this purpose. After joining the game, Thor is fouled and goes to the foul line with his standard hoops plan—a plan involving his shooting the ball *directly* into the hoop. He misses by a foot, hitting the backboard above the basket, and the ball bounces smoothly through the hoop. Thor is dumbfounded.

Did Thor sink the free throw intentionally? A natural answer is 'No'. If a skilled basketball player, Earvin, had approached the basket with the same plan, and had sunk the shot in just the way Thor did, most readers would count his sinking the shot as intentional—even though his shot diverged from his plan no less than Thor's shot diverged. The difference lies in the agents' respective evidential conditions. Earvin's evidential condition leaves open, as a real possibility and even a significant probability, a banked sinking of his shot. Thor's, by hypothesis, does not. A proper understanding of following a plan for *A*-ing 'closely enough' for the *A*-ing to be intentional must thus be sensitive to considerations of agents' evidence. We shall soon return to evidential considerations and address further varieties of deviance.

We now propose two additional requirements for an action's being intentional.

(2) *S A*-s intentionally at *t* only if, at *t*, *S* has an intention, *N*, that includes action plan *P*.

(3) *S A*-s intentionally at *t* only if, at *t*, *S* suitably follows her intention-embedded plan *P* in *A*-ing.[16]

Condition (3), we intimated in Section 1, will not block all cases of deviance. We turn now to some of the troublesome cases.

---

[16] For similar conditions on intentional action, see Brand (1984), op. cit. 28. Our subsequent conditions go substantially beyond Brand's account as well as other available causal accounts of intentional action.

4. EVIDENCE, SKILL, AND LUCKY ACTION

Consider a litmus test-case for an account of intentional action. Ann works as an admissions supervisor at an orchestra hall. She gives red admission slips to women and blue slips to men. Since the orchestral concerts are formal occasions, Ann always wears white gloves while working. Without examining the slips, she efficiently gives the men blue slips from her left pocket, and the women red slips from her right pocket. All goes as planned until Ann hands Harry an admission slip from her left pocket. Unbeknown to all concerned, Ann's admission slip for Harry is actually a white piece of litmus paper that instantaneously turns blue when touched by a human hand. Harry's hand turns Ann's white litmus paper blue. Consequently, Ann gives Harry an appropriate admission slip.

Ann's giving Harry an appropriate admission slip is an action. Ann has a plan for giving Harry an appropriate admission slip (by handing him a slip from her left pocket), and she is motivated to execute this plan. Does Ann *intentionally* give Harry an appropriate slip? It seems not. Her giving Harry an appropriate slip seems too coincidental. In *what* way—in virtue of *what*—is it too coincidental?

It might be tempting to answer with this condition: A person performs an action intentionally only if she either knows, believes, expects, or has evidence that she (probably) will perform that action *in the way she does perform it*. Ann does give Harry an appropriate admission slip, but she neither knows, believes, expects, nor has evidence that she (probably) will do so by giving him white litmus paper that will turn blue. Clearly, the proposed condition is strong enough to handle the litmus-test case.

Is the proposed condition *too* strong? Consider another case. Sarah, a typical six-year-old child, turns on her Atari computer to bring her favourite tic-tac-toe game to the screen, with just a flip of the switch. Sarah knows that the computer is set up to display this game whenever turned on, and she knows how to play this game with considerable skill; but she knows nothing more about the workings of the computer. She neither knows, believes, expects, nor has evidence concerning anything about such things as the computer's electronic circuitry, digital processor, random-access memory, or, more generally, the electronic way in which her flipping the on/off switch will bring her favourite game to the screen. She none the less flips the switch and brings her favourite game to the screen.

Sarah's bringing her favourite game to the screen is an action if anything is. She had a plan for bringing the game to the screen by flipping the on/off switch, and she is motivated to execute this plan. As a direct result, she does bring her favourite game to the screen. Sarah intentionally does so, but has no knowledge, belief, expectation, or evidence about the electronic way in which her flipping the switch brings her favourite game to the screen. The way in which Sarah brings her game to the screen involves an abundance of electronic detail. It would be excessive, however, to demand that she have knowledge, belief, expectation, or evidence about such detail to bring her game to the screen intentionally. The proposed condition would preclude much intentional behaviour. We have, moreover, no obvious way to avoid this problem by refining talk of 'the way in which an action was performed'.

We still need a plausible condition to handle the litmus test-case. Ann, recall, gives Harry an appropriate admission slip, but there is something 'coincidental' about her doing so. The coincidental aspect does not arise from anything objectively fortuitous. We can easily suppose that all the relevant events are strictly causally determined by prior events, and even that if we knew all the relevant events and laws, we could rationally predict Ann's giving Harry an appropriate slip. The coincidental aspect of Ann's action seems to be less objective, a matter of agent-relative, broadly psychological considerations about Ann. Psychological considerations pertinent to intentional action are not necessarily exhausted by an agent's beliefs. Conceivably, an agent can be in a certain evidential (e.g. introspective or perceptual) state indicative of a certain way of acting, while lacking a corresponding belief.[17] Note also that beliefs can be *mere* beliefs, i.e. altogether gratuitous evidentially—as in cases of mere wishful thinking. Some beliefs are evidentially grounded for an agent; others are not. An agent's evidence can include beliefs, but does not automatically include all her beliefs. Ann's evidential relation to her giving Harry an appropriate slip seems notably different from Sarah's evidential relation to her bringing her favourite game to the computer screen.

Let us try to capture the relevant evidential difference with this condition:

(4a) S A-s intentionally at t only if, at the time of S's actual involvement in A-ing at t, the process (i.e. event or series of events) indicated with significantly preponderant probability by S's on balance accessible evidence at t as being at least partly constitutive of her A-ing at t does not diverge significantly from the process that is in fact constitutive of her A-ing at t.[18]

---

[17] For discussion of the possibility of evidence without corresponding beliefs, see John Pollock (1986), *Contemporary Theory of Knowledge* (Totowa, NJ: Rowman & Littlefield), ch. 5; Paul Moser (1989), *Knowledge and Evidence* (Cambridge: Cambridge University Press), chs. 2–4, and id. (1985), op. cit., chs. 3–5. Theorists uneasy with nondoxastic evidence can construe our talk of evidence to connote suitably grounded belief-like states.

[18] We can find no reason to think that *after* S's actual involvement in A-ing, S's evidence then concerning how she A-ed can determine whether S's A-ing was intentional. Here we remain

Sarah's on balance evidence, on any plausible construal, indicates that her flipping the on/off switch at t is at least partly constitutive of her bringing her favourite game to the computer screen at t. This was, by hypothesis, Sarah's only relevant evidence. Her flipping the on/off switch was at least partly constitutive of her bringing her favourite game to the screen. Sarah's bringing her favourite game to the screen thus satisfies (4a).

Ann's giving Harry an appropriate admission slip, in contrast, runs afoul of (4a). Ann's on balance evidence, on any natural construal, significantly indicates that her giving Harry a blue slip involves her giving Harry a slip that was already blue when it left her pocket. The slip turned blue, however, only when touched by Harry. We thus have a significant divergence between what Ann's on balance evidence indicates and what actually happened in Ann's giving Harry an appropriate slip. So, (4a) enables us to deny, quite plausibly, that Ann intentionally gave Harry an appropriate admission slip.

Ann, we assume, has accessible evidence significantly indicating that her giving Harry an appropriate admission slip includes her drawing a slip from her appropriate pocket. What does such evidence involve with respect to a pocket of Ann's being 'appropriate'? It involves considerations about the pocket's contents. Minimally, it is evidence that a certain pocket contains an appropriate slip—a slip that will provide Harry with a blue admission slip. In general, Ann's possible evidence about a pocket containing an appropriate slip could indicate either (a) that the appropriate slip in her pocket is already blue, (b) that the appropriate slip in her pocket is not already blue, but turns blue shortly after leaving her pocket (say, when touched by Harry), or (c) nothing that decides between (a) and (b). Evidence significantly indicating (a) fits the original litmus-test case, and thus, given (4a), provides a case where Ann does not intentionally give Harry an appropriate admission slip. Evidence indicating (b) yields a significantly different case, a case where, for example, Ann has evidence indicating that her left pocket contains a slip of litmus paper that turns blue

---

neutral on various modes of act individuation, including disagreements about the timing of actions. If some 'overt' actions—actions essentially involving peripheral bodily movements of the agent—temporally extend beyond the cessation of the agent's pertinent bodily movements, our expression 'at the time of S's actual involvement in A-ing' refers only to portions of the intervals occupied by those movements. If, alternatively, overt actions end with the cessation of the bodily movements, our expression refers to the entire interval occupied by overt actions. (Starting at noon, Stig puts a cake in the oven, sets the oven to 350 degrees, programmes it to shut off at 12:30, and turns the oven on. By 12:30 the cake is nicely baked. *When* did Stig bake the cake? At noon? From noon to 12:30? We remain neutral. In either case, Stig's active involvement in baking the cake ends when he flips the 'on' switch.) Luck can play a role in successful action either during S's actual involvement or thereafter. This does not affect our analysis.

when touched by Harry. In such a case, Ann might very well intentionally give Harry an appropriate admission slip by giving him a slip of litmus paper.

Finally, evidence indicating (c) must still be evidence indicating that Harry gets a blue admission slip. Such evidence is simply neutral between (a) and (b). Evidence neutral in that respect is disjunctive evidence: evidence that the admission slip for Harry is either blue while in Ann's pocket or turns blue shortly after leaving her pocket. Such evidence, being disjunctive, is different both from non-disjunctive evidence indicating simply (a) and from non-disjunctive evidence indicating simply (b). If Ann has some positive evidence that significantly favours a disjunction, D, but does not significantly favour any of D's disjuncts over the others, she then has *positively disjunctive evidence* for D. Such evidence differs from *trivially disjunctive evidence* for D: evidence for D that significantly favours some proper subset of D's disjuncts over its other disjunct(s). Cases with trivially disjunctive evidence need no special treatment now, as they return us, in effect, to options (a) and (b).

Evidence significantly indicating (c), construed as *positively* disjunctive, provides a case different from the original litmus-test case. It yields a case where Ann has some positive evidence significantly favouring a disjunction, but where her evidence does not significantly favour either the disjunct that her left pocket contains a slip of paper already blue or the disjunct that her left pocket contains a slip of litmus paper that turns blue when touched by Harry. In such a case, Ann might very well intentionally give Harry an appropriate admission slip by giving him a slip of litmus paper. One of the disjuncts of what her evidence significantly supports does not diverge from, but rather coincides with, her giving Harry a slip of litmus paper. The original litmus-test case, in contrast, shows significant divergence from what Ann's accessible evidence significantly indicates. Given (4a), Ann's giving Harry an appropriate slip is thus non-intentional. Condition (4a), then, gives the proper result for the original litmus-test case.

Condition (4a) owes its effectiveness to the notion of certain on balance accessible evidence significantly indicating a process that 'diverges significantly' from the process actually constitutive of a person's performing a certain action. We doubt that the ordinary concept of intentional action allows for a precise analysis of that notion of significant divergence. The ordinary concept seems vague on this score. Our analysis, aimed at the ordinary concept, seeks to preserve this vagueness.

An example will highlight the vagueness. Jacques is an expert at his work: trick parachuting. He plans to descend by parachute from a plane, land three feet behind home plate at Wrigley Field, do one somersault, and end up on home plate. Jacques has skillfully performed this trick jump many times, and he is confidently committed to repeating it now under apparently ideal wind conditions. This time everything goes as planned except that Jacques is helped, ever so slightly, by an extremely mild, virtually undetectable wind at his back: a wind that exceeds the backwind he anticipated, on the basis of his evidence, by just .005 m.p.h. Jacques's on balance evidence indicates that he performs the trick without the aid of a backwind that strong. His on balance evidence thus diverges from the way he actually performed the trick. Did Jacques perform his trick intentionally? It is tempting to answer yes, and this answer does not obviously conflict with the ordinary notion of intentional action.

Upon altering the case by making the actual backwind exceed the anticipated backwind by 50 m.p.h., we have significant divergence from Jacques's on balance evidence. We are then inclined to say that his successfully performing the trick was not intentional, but just lucky. The possible options between .005 m.p.h. and 50 m.p.h. are numerous. It is unclear where exactly we may draw the line that distinguishes a wind that precludes Jacques's intentionally performing the trick from one that does not. The ordinary notion of intentional action fails to give a precise point of demarcation here. To that extent at least, the notion is vague, and an analysis of the ordinary notion of intentional action must accommodate vagueness. (4a) thus leaves us with some unavoidable vagueness.

The modal talk of 'accessible evidence' in (4a) also lacks exactness in ordinary use. Accessibility of evidence comes in (comparative) degrees, depending on how (comparatively) indirect access to evidence is. Some 'accessible' evidence for an agent might take a lifetime of toil for her to access—say through taxing processes of recall and introspection. Such evidence is accessible to her, strictly speaking, but not *readily* accessible.[19] *How* readily accessible must evidence be to figure in conditions for intentional action? We do not have a precise answer, or even presume that there is one. As we use 'accessible evidence', a merely physical flaw in an agent's accessing mechanism will not preclude her having accessible evidence. The ordinary concept of intentional action fails to indicate a precise degree of accessibility for suitable evidence, and our analysis follows suit. Some cases of remote accessibility might *stretch* the ordinary concept of intentional action. We find no hope, however, for a precise analysis of talk of acces-

---

[19] For discussion of the notion of 'accessible' evidence, see William Alston (1988), 'An Internalist Externalism', *Synthese* 74: 265–83; Richard Feldman (1988), 'Having Evidence', in David Austin (ed.), *Philosophical Analysis* (Dordrecht, Neth.: Kluwer), 83–104; Moser (1989), op. cit. 151–5.

sible evidence. (Hereafter our talk of evidence concerns accessible evidence.) Likewise, we do not hold out for a precise account of the talk of *significant* probability in (4a). In Section 5 we shall illustrate that probabilistic considerations pertinent to the ordinary notion of intentional action are incurably inexact. Once again, we must acknowledge vagueness in the ordinary notion of intentional action.

Consider a case that complicates matters for (4a). Ted is highly skilled at 'tube ball'. The playing equipment includes a pair of opaque, ten-foot tubes having a common two-foot-long 'mouth' and a common 'tail'; a metal ball; and an x-ray machine. Players announce whether they will try to throw the ball into the tail via tube 1 or tube 2 (the ball always gets to the tail when the playing field is unobstructed). The x-ray machine verifies the route. The best strategy for throwing a ball into a particular tube is the application of 'spin'. Balls thrown with proper clockwise spin tend to pass through tube 2. A counter-clockwise spin is the preferred strategy for tube 1. Ted has an 80 per cent success rate when attempting to go through tube 2. He is slightly less successful with tube 1.

Ted is about to have a go at tube ball, planning to try tube 2. When the x-ray machine is turned on, it indicates an obstruction in tube 2. The official tube inspector tests the tube with an official testing device—a plastic rod—and tells Ted that it is indeed blocked. The x-ray machine is then turned off to conserve energy. Ted, a daring fellow, thinks that tube 2 *probably* is blocked, but wants to have a go at that tube anyway. He throws the ball into the mouth with perfect clockwise spin, receiving sensory feedback indicating superb execution of his spinning procedure. The ball travels into the tail. As it turned out, tube 2 was unobstructed. The ball travelled through that tube into the tail. Ted thus threw the ball into the tail through tube 2. Arguably, he *intentionally* threw the ball into the tail *through tube* 2. After all, he was trying to throw it into the tail via that route, he is highly skilled at using that route, and he exercised that skill perfectly in his successful attempt. Clearly, if Ted intentionally threw the ball into the tail through tube 2, he intentionally threw the ball into the tail.

The tube-ball case raises a problem for (4a). The process significantly indicated by Ted's on balance evidence as being partly constitutive of his throwing the ball into the tail is a process encompassing his throwing the ball into tube *1*. Ted has excellent evidence that tube 2 is *blocked*. Without much difficulty, we could make that evidence even stronger, while weakening evidence that tube 2 is Ted's route. The indicated process wherein tube 1 is the route does diverge significantly from the process that was in fact partly constitutive of Ted's throwing the ball into the tail. *That* actual process involved his throwing the ball into tube 2—not tube 1.

A notable difference between Ted's intentional action and Ann's non-intentional action, in the litmus-test case, is this: Ted's behaviour is determined by skill in a way that Ann's giving Harry an appropriate admission slip is not. Ted's success thus is not coincidental in the way Ann's is. Of course, Ann is skilled at drawing admission slips from her pocket. Whether Harry's slip is blue is not, however, determined by Ann's skill. If it were, we would have a case markedly different from the original. Making sense of the litmus-test case does not, moreover, require that we imagine Ann's failing in a skill. We can easily imagine that no failure of skill is involved. The tube-ball case thus introduces the bearing of skill on intentional action in a way that the litmus-test case does not. We need to complicate (4a) to accommodate the significance of skill.

The following revision of (4a) incorporates the lesson of the tube-ball case:

(4b) S A-s intentionally at t only if (a) at the time of S's actual involvement in A-ing at t, the process indicated with significantly preponderant probability by S's on balance evidence at t as being at least partly constitutive of her A-ing at t does not diverge significantly from the process that is in fact constitutive of her A-ing at t; or (b) S's A-ing at t manifests a suitably reliable skill of S's in A-ing in the way S A-s at t.

In keeping with our comments on (4a), we neither have nor need exact conditions for the 'suitable reliability' of skill. Section 5 will confirm this. The value of (4b) does depend on a notion of *skill* that neither incorporates a notion of intentional action nor reduces skill to merely reliable reflex-like behaviour that is psychologically blind. We must avoid both conceptual circularity and a notion of skill as just mechanical reliability. We must also account for the fact that skills can come with differing degrees of reliability.

We do not need a full account of skill to appreciate (4b). We need only a notion of skill that avoids both circularity and a mechanical account. The following characterization will do: At time t, an agent, S, is skilled to some non-zero degree at A-ing in manner M if and only if S, at t, has a propensity to A in manner M, given that S has a corresponding intention in a situation suitably accommodating for S's A-ing in manner M, and that propensity exceeds any provided by mere chance given such an intention and situation. The role of intention makes the characterization suitably psychological, but does not introduce circularity. Talk of intention is not talk of *intentional action*—as Section 3 makes plain. The characterization also properly acknowledges the crucial role of an accommodating environment in the successful exercise of skill. Finally, the characterization distinguishes skill from mere statistical reliability. To have a high propensity to roll non-doubles with a pair of fair dice (simply by rolling the dice) when one has a corresponding intention is *not* to be skilled at rolling non-doubles. Such a propensity is predicted by mere chance.

In sum, (4b) captures two features to which the ordinary notion of intentional action is sensitive: suitably reliable skill and significant evidential divergence of a sort. The tube-ball and litmus cases highlight these features.

5. PREDICTIVE RELIABILITY AND LUCKY ACTION

Our troubles continue. Chuck is an experienced ticket agent at the Milwaukee Amtrak train depot. He distributes boarding passes from two piles. The pile on Chuck's left is designated for passengers travelling within 200 miles of Milwaukee. The pile on his right is designated for passengers travelling more than 200 miles from Milwaukee. Chuck has a plan for giving each passenger an appropriate boarding pass, and he is motivated to execute this plan. Tonight the 7:00 train to Chicago has attracted a large crowd of passengers. Aiming to keep departures on time, Chuck distributes boarding passes without examining them, simply by drawing from the left-hand pile for relatively local passengers and from the right for all others. During the congested rush to board, Mary requests a pass for Seattle, and Mark simultaneously requests a Chicago pass. Chuck slips up, giving Mary a pass from the left-hand pile and Mark a pass from the right-hand pile. As it happens, however, at that point the left-hand pile contained a long-distance pass, and the right-hand pile included a pass for relatively local travel. (We might imagine that Chuck also slipped up earlier in executing his plan for sorting the boarding passes.)

We can suppose that Chuck has a plan, however short-term, for giving Mary an appropriate boarding pass by drawing from the left-hand pile, and that he is motivated to execute this plan. Chuck, moreover, does give Mary an appropriate boarding pass, and he does this as a suitably direct result of his motivation to do so. We deny, however, that Chuck's giving Mary an appropriate boarding pass is an intentional action. His doing this seems too coincidental to be intentional.

Chuck's giving Mary an appropriate pass is an action. Chuck, we have supposed, followed a simple action plan: to give Mary an appropriate pass by drawing from the left-hand pile. We can imagine also that Chuck's giving Mary a boarding pass in this manner does not fit, but conflicts with, a general plan that Chuck had prior to serving Mary: viz., the plan to give appropriate passes by distributing passes from the left-hand pile to, and only to, relatively local passengers. If Chuck still had that general plan at the time of serving Mary *and* had the plan to give her an appropriate pass by drawing from the left-hand pile, then his executing the latter plan would violate the former, more general plan. Chuck's giving Mary a pass from the left-hand pile does not cohere, but conflicts, with his more general plan. It does cohere, however, with his less general plan concerning Mary.

Agents can, and sometimes do, have plans with incompatible goals. We can use the case of Chuck to illustrate this possibility. Chuck's giving Mary a pass from the left-hand pile does, coincidentally, satisfy his plan for giving Mary an appropriate boarding pass. This violates, however, Chuck's plan to give non-local passengers appropriate passes *from the right-hand pile*. The latter general plan prescribes, by implication, that Mary get a pass from the right-hand pile.

We might lean toward this simple diagnosis: Chuck does not intentionally give Mary an appropriate pass, since his giving Mary a pass from the left-hand pile conflicts with his general plan to give non-local passengers appropriate passes from the right-hand pile. This diagnosis misses the heart of the current problem. We can imagine that Chuck no longer has his general plan at the time of serving Mary, that his only relevant plan then is to give Mary an appropriate pass from the left-hand pile—while everything else in the case remains as before. On that assumption, Chuck's giving Mary an appropriate pass still does not qualify as an intentional action. His giving her an appropriate pass is too coincidental. It seems not to be relevantly different from your winning an instant lottery by luckily selecting the winning sequence of six numbers. The aforementioned simple diagnosis thus cannot serve.

Condition (4b), from Section 4, also fails to handle the case at hand. We can suppose not only that Chuck has simply the minimal plan to give Mary an appropriate pass from the left-hand pile, but also that his on balance evidence does not diverge significantly from the way he actually gives Mary an appropriate pass. We can imagine that Chuck somehow loses his earlier evidence concerning which pile of passes is for non-local passengers, but mistakenly recalls that the left-hand pile is for such passengers. To test his recollection, Chuck consults with his supervisor, who confirms it. In that case, Chuck's on balance evidence does not diverge significantly from the process whereby he gives Mary an appropriate pass. We still are disinclined to say that Chuck intentionally gave Mary an appropriate pass. We still have a case of exceedingly lucky planning and action.

The problem does not stem from the role that a false proposition plays in Chuck's evidence. We can illustrate the irrelevance of false propositions with an analogous case where Lisa selects a sequence of six numbers to win a fair Florida instant lottery. Upon punching her six numbers into the lottery computer, Lisa wins instantly. Did she intentionally win the lottery? We doubt that the ordinary notion of intentional action allows for such lucky intentional action. We thus shall capture the condition that excludes it. Lisa's evidence concerning how she wins need not diverge from the process whereby she does win the lottery. Without changing the upshot, we can easily imagine that her evidence concerning how she wins fits the process whereby she does win. Lisa can have altogether transparent evidence concerning how she punched in the six numbers to win. (4b) thus will not serve. The case of Lisa, like the case of Chuck and the boarding pass, requires a further condition.

The excessive luck in the cases of Chuck and Lisa is not a matter of divergence from such psychologically relevant factors as agents' beliefs, expectations, or evidence. In an exceptional case, Lisa need not believe, expect, or have evidence that she (probably) will not win by punching in her selected numbers. Still, her plan to punch in those numbers is exceedingly lucky—too lucky for Lisa to have *intentionally* won the lottery, under the circumstances.

The following condition takes care of the relatively objective species of luck in the cases of Chuck and Lisa:

(5a) S A-s intentionally at t only if the route to A-ing that S follows in executing her action plan, P, at t is, under S's current circumstances, a suitably predictively reliable means of S's A-ing at t. (In the limiting case of a 'basic' action, the route is non-actional, basic actions being actions not performed by way of performing another action.)

The restriction to 'the route to A-ing that S follows' handles cases where S's plan includes an existential generalization or a disjunction for A-ing. Talk of a 'suitably predictively reliable' means of acting needs explanation. Intentional action, on the intended interpretation of (5a), requires that— given just (a) S's suitably reliable non-misleading evidence concerning whether she will A at t in her present circumstances, and (b) knowledge concerning what sort of reliable skill, if any, S has with respect to A-ing at t in her present circumstances—a conceiver who understands all the relevant concepts (sufficiently to wield them in any prediction involving just those concepts) could reasonably predict that (the route followed in) S's attempted execution at t of an intention incorporating the relevant action plan P will result in her A-ing at t.[20] Our talk of 'reliable skill' got

[20] The conceiver in question could be any actual or hypothetical individual satisfying the specified conditions—including the agent S. The requirement is thus not necessarily third-

adequate explanation at the end of Section 4. *Non-misleading* evidence is devoid of false propositions.[21] So, if Chuck's actual relevant evidence includes only one false proposition (say, the proposition that non-local passes come from his left-hand pile), we simply omit this proposition to arrive at his non-misleading relevant evidence. The case of Lisa did not rely on evidence involving false propositions. We thus can assume that her relevant evidence is non-misleading.

Lisa's evidence about the lottery was supposedly typical. She has no special evidence that her six numbers will win; nor does she have any special reliable skill that enables her to win lotteries. Lisa's evidential situation with respect to state lotteries is like that of the rest of us: We do not have sufficiently reliable non-misleading evidence to make a suitably reasonable prediction that we will win. The only difference is non-evidential. Lisa luckily wins; we unluckily lose. A generally reliable friend could tell Lisa that she will win. This might seem to produce some relevant evidence, but general reliability is insufficient to produce *suitably* reliable evidence about winning a state lottery—unless the reliability extends specifically to predicting winning numbers in such a lottery. Lisa, by hypothesis, does not have access to the latter, lottery-specific reliability. She also lacks any other source providing for a suitably reliable prediction that by (executing the plan for) punching in her six numbers she will win. Condition (5a) thus enables us to say that Lisa does not intentionally win the lottery. If we suppose that Lisa does know, based on suitably reliable evidence, that her number will win, the case changes markedly. Lisa could then intentionally win the lottery. We would not then have, however, a typical Lisa playing a typical lottery.

Condition (5a) enables us to say that Chuck does not intentionally give Mary an appropriate boarding pass. Once we omit Chuck's misleading evidence, deriving from his mistaken recollection and the false advice from his supervisor, we have no basis whatever for a reasonable prediction

person. One might seek to simplify the requirement by talking just of a reliable connection, relative to certain agents and circumstances, between a certain route-type and the action-type *A*-ing. We find, however, that the notion of reasonable predictability relative to one's reliable evidence is not only conveniently familiar, but also helpful in identifying a basis for the reliable connection: one's reliable evidence. On the importance of such a basis for epistemic matters, see Moser (1989), op. cit. 194–203.

[21] Notions of nonmisleading evidence have played a notable role in attempted solutions to the Gettier problem in epistemology. For representative uses, see Keith Lehrer (1974), *Knowledge* (Oxford: Clarendon Press), 189–225; Peter Klein (1981), *Certainty* (Minneapolis: University of Minnesota Press), 148–56; Marshall Swain (1981), *Reasons and Knowledge* (Ithaca, NY: Cornell University Press), ch. 5; Moser (1989), op. cit., ch. 6. Similarities between certain Gettier-style cases and some of the cases formulated above are obvious; but we cannot pursue the Gettier problem here. On some of the history of that problem, see Robert Shope (1983), *The Analysis of Knowing* (Princeton: Princeton University Press).

that Chuck's (executing the plan for) drawing a pass from the left-hand pile will provide Mary with an appropriate, non-local boarding pass. Chuck's drawing from the left-hand pile, in the imagined circumstances, is thus not a suitably predictively reliable means of providing Mary with an appropriate pass. Nor does Chuck manifest any reliable skill that enables the suitably reliable prediction. Condition (5a), then, properly implies that Chuck does not intentionally give Mary an appropriate boarding pass.

Condition (5a) applies straightforwardly to the case of Fred and the nuclear reactor in Section 1. The route Fred followed in shutting down the reactor and preventing a nuclear explosion—a route featuring his typing the first ten digits that came into his head—lacked the requisite reliability. The condition applies also to the variant where Fred misreads the code in the safe. Again, the route he followed in shutting down the reactor and averting catastrophe lacked the required reliability. (The variant where Fred also unintentionally kills hundreds of people by unintentionally releasing a lethal chemical is handled by any one of conditions (1)–(3).)

Recall Sarah and her computer game, from Section 4. Sarah lacks evidence concerning the electronic way in which her flipping the computer's on/off switch will bring her favourite tic-tac-toe game to the screen. She none the less intentionally brings her favourite game to the screen by flipping the switch. This case poses no problem for (5a). Sarah, we can plausibly suppose, has some suitably reliable non-misleading evidence that makes justifiable for her the proposition that her flipping the switch, under her present circumstances, will bring her favourite game to the screen.[22] This evidence need not come from evidence about the electronic details of the computer. It can come rather from a certain kind of regularity of experience involving the flipping of the on/off switch and the appearance of the tic-tac-toe game on the screen. Given a familiar approach to evidence, then, (5a) is not threatened by Sarah's case. If we withhold suitably reliable non-misleading evidence from Sarah, we shall have to attribute a suitably reliable skill to her, to maintain her action's being intentional. This will make no trouble for (5a).

The notion of suitable predictive reliability and the corresponding notion of reasonable predictability are rather vague, but appropriately so. We find similar vagueness in the ordinary notion of intentional action. The following case illustrates such vagueness. B. J. enjoys basketball, and

---

[22] On the relevant notion of justifiability, in contrast with the notion of justifiedness, see Moser (1989), op. cit. 141–4. Epistemologists have given scant attention to the distinction between justifiability and justifiedness.

spends some of his leisure time trying to make baskets from the free-throw line in his college gym. He is not what we would call a 'reliable' free-throw shooter. He succeeds from the free-throw line only 50 per cent of the time. B. J. is well aware of his shortcomings as a free-throw shooter. He now sets himself to sink a shot from the free-throw line, tries to do so, and, as a direct result, succeeds.

Does B. J. intentionally sink the shot? A common conception of intentional action allows us to say that he does. Our construal of (5a) thus must not require that the relevant prediction be more reasonable than not (i.e. than its denial). We must not require that suitable reliability of prediction exceed 50 per cent. Where, then, do we draw the line? The ordinary notion of intentional action does not yield a precise line of demarcation. To illustrate, drop B. J.'s free-throw percentage to .001 per cent—while everything else in the case remains the same. The case then approaches a lottery case in certain respects, and thus can plausibly be treated in the same manner as the case of Lisa and the state lottery.[23] We can then plausibly say that B. J. does not intentionally sink the free-throw. We cannot pretend to have, in the ordinary concept of intentional action, a clear dividing line between reliability that is adequate for intentional action and reliability that is not. (Suitably modified, the case can also illustrate that the notion of significantly preponderant probability in condition (4b) resists precise demarcation.) Once again, we face vagueness that cannot be ignored. Condition (5a) properly acknowledges this vagueness.

Consider a final case. Mike, a normal person, is playing a game with a pair of fair dice. He will win $20 on his next roll if and only if he throws something other than 'boxcars' (two sixes). Mike, wanting to win, has a simple plan: He will throw a non-boxcar roll and win the money. Mike realizes that there is a slight chance that he will roll boxcars, but this does not threaten his plan. As it happens, he throws a seven. (Michael Costa suggested a case of this sort.)

Mike lacks a kind of *control* over the dice required for his intentionally throwing a non-boxcar roll. Mike has no control over which sides land face up. He thus has no control over whether, given his throwing the dice, he throws a non-boxcar role (as opposed to a boxcar roll). This consideration supports the plausible view that Mike's throwing non-boxcars is not an intentional action. To handle such cases involving *statistically reliable luck*, we need to expand on (5a) as follows:

(5b) S A-s intentionally at t only if the route to A-ing that S follows in executing her action plan, P, at t is, under S's current circumstances, a

---

[23] To be sure, B. J. has control over how his arms and hands move in attempting to sink the basket. Lisa, however, has control over her limbs too, and over which buttons she pushes.

suitably predictively reliable means of S's A-ing at t, and the predictive reliability of that means depends appropriately on S's having suitably reliable control over whether, given that she acts with A-ing as a goal, she succeeds in A-ing at t.

A full account of control is beyond this paper's scope, but a few points will help now. Other things equal, S's *skill* at t at A-ing gives S some degree of control over whether he A-s at t. Michael Jordan, for example, has more control over whether he sinks his free-throws than we do over whether we sink ours (other things equal); and we now have more control over whether we solve complex problems in modal logic than Jordan now does over whether he solves such problems. Our skill in solving problems of modal logic is largely a matter of knowledge, but knowledge can provide *control* without providing skill. Someone who knows what the winning number will be in a choose-your-own-number lottery (say, because an omniscient being told her just this time) has control over whether she wins, other things equal; but her winning is not due to any lottery-winning *skill* of hers.

6. FINAL PAYOFFS

We can now float this analysis:

Necessarily, an agent, S, *intentionally* performs an action, A, at a time, t, if and only if:
  (i) at t, S A-s and her A-ing is an action;
 (ii) at t, S suitably follows—hence, is suitably guided by—an intention-embedded plan, P, of hers in A-ing;
(iii) (a) at the time of S's actual involvement in A-ing at t, the process indicated with significantly preponderant probability by S's on balance evidence at t as being at least partly constitutive of her A-ing at t does not diverge significantly from the process that is in fact constitutive of her A-ing at t; or (b) S's A-ing at t manifests a suitably reliable skill of S's in A-ing in the way S A-s at t; and
 (iv) the route to A-ing that S follows in executing her action plan, P, at t is, under S's current circumstances, a suitably predictively reliable means of S's A-ing at t, and the predictive reliability of that means depends appropriately on S's having suitably reliable control over whether, given that she acts with A-ing as a goal, she succeeds in A-ing at t.

Condition (ii) preserves the crucial role of representational content in intentional action. It guarantees that when you intentionally perform an action of a certain type, you will have some representation of an action of that type, or at least some representation that can suitably guide the performance of an action of that type. Section 2 explained how plans can provide the needed representational content, and Section 3 explained how plans can guide actions in a suitable manner. Condition (ii) preserves the key role of representational content without entailing an excessive belief condition on intentional action. This condition also acknowledges a central role for intention and for causal factors in intentional action. Further, it avoids problems facing the so-called 'simple view' of intentional action, and steers clear of difficulties arising from two kinds of causal deviance and from so-called 'subsidiary' actions. Section 3 explained how (ii) serves these purposes.

Conditions (iii) and (iv) handle lucky actions that go beyond standard cases of causal deviance. The main difference between (iii) and (iv) is this: (iii) demands a certain sort of nondivergent evidence concerning what is constitutive of one's A-ing, if—barring a certain role for reliable skill—one does have significant evidence concerning what is constitutive of one's A-ing. In contrast, (iv) demands that one's non-misleading evidence provide for a suitably reasonable, control-sensitive prediction that one's (route followed in) executing one's action plan will result in one's A-ing. These two conditions are logically independent. Both serve, indispensably, to block cases of lucky action as characterized in Sections 4–5. Sections 4–5 showed how these conditions exclude various kinds of lucky action from the domain of intentional action.

We have shown, as well, that the ordinary concept of intentional action is vague in ways captured by conditions (ii)–(iv). The vagueness in those conditions is *intended*. We might have eliminated all such vagueness, but then we would have been capturing a notion different from the ordinary concept of intentional action.

Our analysis coheres with the popular thesis that intentional A-ing is coextensive with A-ing done *for a reason* (G.E.M. Anscombe (1958), *Intention* (Ithaca: Cornell University Press): 9; Alvin Goldman (1970), *A Theory of Human Action* (Princeton: Princeton University Press): 76; cf. Audi Ch. 4, this volume; Davidson (1980), op. cit., 6, 264). Indeed, our discussion supports that thesis against certain objections. One apparent problem comes from allegedly intentional behavioural side effects—e.g. the sniper's alerting the enemy, in a case treated in Section 3. The sniper does not alert the enemy for a reason. On our view, he does not intentionally alert the enemy either.

Luck raises other difficulties. Chuck, in Section 5, certainly had a reason to give Mary an appropriate pass. His doing so, however, was too coincidental to be intentional. So, if he gave her an appropriate pass for a reason, the thesis at hand is false. Reasons that agents *have* for *A*-ing are not, however, always reasons *for which* they *A*. We find that the action in question was too coincidental to have been done for a reason. This is not to say that Chuck did nothing at all for a reason. He *handed Mary a pass* for a reason. He intentionally handed her a pass as well. The coincidence that blocks the inference from 'Chuck intentionally handed Mary a pass and that pass was an appropriate one' to 'Chuck intentionally handed Mary an *appropriate* pass' blocks a parallel inference concerning what Chuck did for a reason.

Section 3 discussed problems that sudden, impulsive, and subsidiary intentional actions raise for the thesis that intentionally *A*-ing requires a suitable intention. Those problems bear as well on the thesis that intentionally *A*-ing is *A*-ing for a reason. Do things move too quickly for reasons to play a role in the behaviour of the person who suddenly hits her brakes to avoid striking a darting dog, or who impulsively slaps another person in anger? Do we take each of our intentional steps for a reason when routinely walking to class? Such corresponding problems merit corresponding answers. Reason-acquisition can occur at something approaching the speed of thought. Subsidiary intentional actions are, in a derivative sense, done for a reason, insofar as they are intentional actional 'parts' of 'larger' actions that are themselves done for reasons.[24]

Our analysis agrees, finally, with an assumption of common-sense psychology that the common notion of intentional action is irreducibly psychological. It rests on psychological notions of *plan, intention, evidence,* and *skill.* Agents satisfying such notions are, given common-sense psychology, markedly different from the wind-swept sand. The ordinary notion of intentional action, as just analysed, nicely coheres with this common-sense assumption. Our analysis illuminates the complex connection between thought and action.

---

[24] Intrinsically motivated actions—actions done 'for their own sakes' or as 'ends'—have also been regarded by some as problematic for the thesis at hand. For a resolution, see Mele (1992), op. cit., ch. 6.

For helpful comments, we thank Robert Audi, John Heil, Michael Zimmerman, and an anonymous referee for *Noûs*.

11

MECHANISM, PURPOSE, AND EXPLANATORY EXCLUSION

JAEGWON KIM

I want to reopen the question whether the same bit of behaviour, say an action we perform such as climbing a ladder, can be given both a 'mechanistic' explanation, in terms of physiological processes and laws, and a 'purposive' explanation, in terms of 'reasons' (e.g. goals and beliefs). In a paper published in 1968,[1] Norman Malcolm defended a negative answer. He argued that once an action has been explained by setting forth its physiological causal antecedents it is no longer open to us to explain it by citing the agent's reasons, that is, his beliefs, desires, intentions, and the like. Alvin Goldman immediately replied to Malcolm,[2] arguing that mechanistic and purposive explanations are indeed compatible, that we can in fact characterize a type of situation in which one and the same behaviour can be seen to be explainable both physiologically and rationally.

I want to reopen this debate not only because there is more to be said on this issue but also, and more importantly, because the issue has significant implications for some problems of much current interest in the philosophy of mind. A proper appreciation of the broader methodological issues and options involved will, I believe, help us to get clearer about some matters of current controversy. As we shall see, the question of explanatory com-

Jaegwon Kim, 'Mechanism, Purpose, and Explanatory Exclusion', *Philosophical Perspectives* 3 (1989), 77–108. Reprinted by permission of the Editor of *Philosophical Perspectives*.

[1] Norman Malcolm (1968), 'The Conceivability of Mechanism', *Philosophical Review* 77: 45–72, repr. in Gary Watson (1982) (ed.), *Free Will* (Oxford: Oxford University Press). Page references to this article are to the reprinted version in Watson. For an earlier defence of a position similar to Malcolm's see Alasdair C. MacIntyre (1957), 'Determinism', *Mind* 66: 28–41.

[2] Alvin Goldman (1969), 'The Compatibility of Mechanism and Purpose', *Philosophical Review* 78: 468–82; also in his (1970), *A Theory of Human Action* (Englewood Cliffs, NJ: Prentice-Hall), 157–65. For another defence of the compatibility position and a critique of MacIntyre, see Daniel C. Dennett (1981), 'Mechanism and Responsibility', in Dennett, *Brainstorms* (Montpelier, Vt.: Bradford Books). G. H. von Wright defends a 'two explanandum solution' in *Explanation and Understanding* (Ithaca, NY: Cornell University Press), 118–31.

patibility leads us to more general questions about the possibility of *multiple explanations of a single explanandum*, and the relationship between two distinct explanatory theories covering overlapping domains of phenomena. Ultimately, these issues will be seen to arise from some basic assumptions about the epistemology and the metaphysics of explanation, and, in particular, the question of 'realism' about explanations.

What Malcolm calls a 'purposive explanation' of an action is one that conforms to the familiar 'belief-desire' pattern of action explanation. Such an explanation explains an action by specifying the 'reason for which' the agent did what he did, that is, by indicating what he wanted to accomplish and what he took to be an optimal way of realizing his want. We shall refer to such explanations as 'rationalizing explanations'; these explanations provide us with the agent's considerations, explicit or implicit, that rationalize the actions to be explained. We need not think of belief-desire explanations as the only kind of rationalizing explanations ('I hit him because he insulted my wife'); nor need we think of rationalizations as the only mode of action explanation in vernacular psychology. However, belief-desire explanations seem to have a central place in our common everyday understanding of what we, and our fellow humans, do, and one could rightly claim, I think, that they constitute the basic mode of understanding actions in intentional psychology. Moreover, the question whether or not such explanations can coexist with physiological explanations of behaviour is certain to generalize to other modes of intentional explanations, and how we answer this question will have direct implications for the current debate concerning the relationship between vernacular ('folk') psychology and the systematic science of human behaviour, whether the latter is taken to be a relatively high-level 'cognitive science' or a lower-level 'neuroscience'.[3]

But this problem of the relationship between vernacular and systematic psychology can itself be further generalized: What is the relationship between two explanatory theories (especially, two successive theories) of the same phenomena? Can the same phenomena be correctly explained by two different theories? Can we accept two such theories, each purporting to provide independent explanations of the same data? Suppose we accept either the compatibility thesis, or the incompatibility thesis, regarding the two types of action explanation. Could either position be generalized? Is it *in general* the case that an event can be given more than one

---

[3] See, e.g. Paul Churchland (1979), *Scientific Realism and the Plasticity of Mind* (Cambridge: Cambridge University Press, 1979); Stephen P. Stich (1983), *From Folk Psychology to Cognitive Science* (Cambridge, Mass.: MIT Press); Terence Horgan and James Woodward (1985), 'Folk Psychology Is Here To Stay', *Philosophical Review* 94: 197–226.

explanation—or more than one type of explanation? Or is it the case that *in general* no event (perhaps, nothing) can be given more than one explanation? Are there general conditions under which explanations *exclude* each other?

I shall now place my cards on the table. On the question of the compatibility of action explanations, I think Malcolm is fundamentally right, although, as we shall see, this does not necessarily show Goldman to be wrong. I shall argue that the criticisms that have been raised against Malcolm, while they point to some interesting possibilities and need to be reckoned with, do not refute what I take to be the heart of Malcolm's arguments, and that on the special auxiliary assumptions Malcolm appears to accept, rationalizing explanations and physiological explanations do exclude each other. My central considerations will not depend on any special features of reasons and causes, or of mind and matter, but involve instead some broad reflections on the nature of explanation and causation—in particular, kinds of situation in which explanations with mutually consistent explanantia can yet compete against each other. This will lead me to formulate what I shall call 'the principle of explanatory exclusion', something that many will, I am afraid, consider absurdly strong and unacceptable. Roughly, this principle says this: No event can be given more than one *complete* and *independent* explanation. What 'complete' and 'independent' may mean in this context is obviously important, and my discussion will be sensitive to the need of making these notions clearer; I should say right now, though, that I shall not be offering general definitions of these notions, but depend rather on the discussion of specific cases to generate reasonably cohesive senses for these terms. Rather, my strategy will be this: I shall argue my case principally for *causal explanations*, advancing at the same time some general considerations that will, I hope, make the exclusion principle seem a plausible constraint on explanations in general.

1. MALCOLM'S ARGUMENT

Although the exact form of a physiological explanation of behaviour, and also exactly how we view the structure of a rationalizing explanation, are ultimately unimportant (as they should be if our results are to be of general interest), it will be useful to have some fixed points of reference. For this purpose we may simply turn to Malcolm's own view of the matter. He takes a physiological explanation of behaviour to have the familiar form of a Hempelian 'covering-law' or 'deductive-nomological' ('D-N') argument:

(N) Whenever an organism of structure S is in neurophysiological state q it will emit movement m. Organism O of structure S was in neurophysiological state q.
Therefore, O emitted m.

A rationalizing explanation for Malcolm has the following, again familiar, form:

(R) Whenever an organism has goal G and believes that behaviour B is required to bring about G, O will emit B. O had G and believed B was required for G.
Therefore, O emitted B.

Whether (R), too, is a D-N argument (Malcolm argues it is not) will play no role in the discussion to follow, although we need to assume, with Malcolm, that (R) represents the goal-belief complex as a 'cause' or 'condition' of the occurrence of the behaviour. This is important: as will become clear, the incompatibility between these explanations stands out in the starkest way when they are both construed as causal explanations—as attempts to provide causal conditions from which the action or behaviour issued.[4]

Before presenting his incompatibility argument, Malcolm tries to exclude the possibility that a rationalizing explanation of the form (R) is 'less basic than' and 'dependent on'[5] physiological explanations. I think that Malcolm's attempt is unsuccessful, for various reasons.[6] But whether or not Malcolm is successful here is less interesting for our purposes than why he makes the attempt. Recall that the provisional formulation of the explanatory exclusion principle I gave earlier prohibits only more than one *complete* and *independent* explanation for a given phenomenon. Although Malcolm does not say why he takes up the question of explanatory dependence at this point, a rationale is not far to seek: if the rationalizing explanation is *dependent* on the physiological explanation in an appropriate sense (e.g. by being *reducible* to it), then in truth there is only one

---

[4] This means that one way in which one might try to eliminate the incompatibility is to interpret rationalizing explanation as a fundamentally *noncausal* mode of understanding actions. I believe that this is an approach well worth exploring: a rationalizing explanation is to be viewed as a *normative assessment* of an action in the context of the agent's relevant intentional states. For some elaboration on this idea see my (1984) 'Self-Understanding and Rationalizing Explanations', *Philosophia Naturalis* 21: 309–20.

[5] Malcolm (1968), op. cit. 131.

[6] For one, the notion of 'dependence' used is too narrow and seems at best to characterize a special subcase; for another, his argument makes use of special assumptions needing justification and exploits what appears to be local features of the particular case on hand. For a discussion of Malcolm's argument see William L. Rowe (1971), 'Neurophysiological Laws and Purposive Principles', *Philosophical Review* 81: 502–8.

explanation here, and the question of explanatory compatibility does not arise. The two explanations could peacefully coexist, but the peace is purchased at a price: they are no longer independent explanations. The explanatory efficacy of one would have been shown to derive from the other, and ultimately the physiological explanation would have to be taken as telling a deeper and more inclusive story of how the behaviour came about.

What then is 'the exact logical relationship between neural and purposive explanations of behaviour',[7] as Malcolm puts it? He asks: 'Can explanations of both types be true of the same bit of behaviour on one and the same occasion?'[8] This is the problem of explanatory compatibility. But you will have noticed that the two explanatory schemes, (N) and (R), do not, strictly speaking, have the same explanandum; their explanatory conclusions are different, one speaking of the 'emission of (bodily movement) m' and the other of the 'emission of (behaviour) B'. Given this apparent difference in the explananda, it might appear that the question of compatibility could not arise. Malcolm is aware of this 'dual explanandum solution' (as we might call it), and responds as follows:

Take the example of the man climbing a ladder in order to retrieve his hat from the roof. This explanation relates his climbing to his intention. A neurophysiological explanation of his climbing would say nothing about his intention but would connect his movements on the ladder with chemical changes in body tissues or with the firing of neurons. Do the two accounts interfere with one another?

I believe there *would* be a collision between the two accounts if they were offered as explanations of one and the same occurrence of a man's climbing a ladder.[9]

Although exactly how this is a response to the dual explanandum problem is somewhat uncertain, Malcolm seems to think that there is some concrete event here, the man's movement up the ladder, represented by the two conclusions, which serves as the shared explanandum of the explanations. In our discussion we will assume this is the case (Goldman does not dispute this assumption); if we do not, the problem of explanatory incompatibility could be restated, though this would bring in complications.[10] We may simply note here that although the two explanandum *statements* are not equivalent or synonymous, there is an evident sense in which they 'describe' one and the same event, the same concrete happening, and that we could consider the compatibility problem stated with respect to this event

---

[7] Malcolm (1968), op. cit. 132.   [8] Ibid.   [9] Ibid. 133.

[10] I believe there is much to be said in favour of the 'two explananda' approach in the case of action explanations (see my 'Self-Understanding and Rationalizing Explanations'). I am being somewhat cavalier about this issue here because our two disputants do not raise it and my real focus is on the general question of explanatory compatibility. For an interesting recent instance of this dual explanandum approach see Fred Dretske (1988), *Explaining Behavior: Reasons in a World of Causes* (Cambridge, Mass.: MIT Press).

however described. For now it will not matter exactly what this shared explanadum is, as long as it exists.

Malcolm's argument for the claim that not both explanations can hold seems to make use of the following assumption:[11]

(I) If event C is nomologically sufficient for the occurrence of event E, then no event wholly distinct from C is necessary for E.

Using this principle, Malcolm appears to argue as follows: Suppose there is a physiological explanation of a man's ladder climbing conforming to schema (N) above. This explanation shows a certain physiological event ('neurophysiological state q') to be nomologically sufficient for the behaviour. If this physiological event is indeed *sufficient* for the climbing, the climbing should occur whether or not any *other* event (such as beliefs and desires) occurred. That is, no other event should be necessary for the occurrence of the climbing, and the physiological explanation in itself should be deemed complete and sufficient as an explanation of the behaviour. Once we know the physiological condition is present, we can be wholly confident that the ladder-climbing will occur; it isn't necessary to verify whether other events, such as beliefs and intentions, are also present.[12] That the climbing would have occurred whether or not the rationalizing belief and desire occurred surely demonstrates the causal and explanatory irrelevance of the belief and desire.[13] For an explanatory connection can hold only if a dependency relation of some sort is present; perhaps, the condition that explains why an event occurred must at least be necessary in the circumstances for the occurrence of the event. Notice, by the way, that, as thus formulated, this is a general argument entirely independent of the subject matters of the two explanations; it makes no use of the fact that one of the explanations deals in psychological states and the other in neurophysiology, or the fact that explanandum concerns human action or behaviour. This is clear from the fact that (I) is wholly general and topic-neutral.

The crucial principle (I) as stated is obviously implausible if we consider causal conditions obtaining at different times:[14] e.g. let C be nomologically sufficient for E, and E for C*, where C occurs before E, and E before C*. Then C* is nomologically necessary for E. But seemingly there is no incoherence here. Or suppose C is sufficient for C*, which occurs later, and

---

[11] As spelled out by Goldman (with minor changes of wording).

[12] This assumes, as Malcolm is aware, that beliefs and desires are not identical with physiological events—namely, that the so-called identity thesis about the mental is false. If the identity holds, we do not have two *independent* explanations. More on this later.

[13] Unless, perhaps, the behaviour is overdetermined by the neurophysiological event and the belief-desire pair. This possibility is discussed below.

[14] Goldman (1970), op. cit. 160–1.

C* in turn is necessary for E, where E is later than C*. Again, there is no evident incoherence. Following Goldman, therefore, one might revise the principle like this:

(II) If C is sufficient for a later event E, then no event occurring at the same time as C and wholly distinct from it is necessary for E.

And it is this weaker principle that Goldman tries to undermine in his discussion of Malcolm's incompatibility argument.[15]

Goldman's objection to (II) is this: Suppose that two events, C and C*, are 'simultaneous nomic equivalents'[16] in the sense that as a matter of law, C occurs (to an object) at a time if and only if C* occurs at the same time. Then if C is sufficient for E, then C*, too, is sufficient for E. If C is necessary for E then so is C*, and we may suppose C to be both necessary and sufficient for the subsequent event E. This means two distinct events, C and C*, are such that C is sufficient, and C* is necessary, for E.

There are various complex issues here involving the interrelations among necessity, sufficiency, cause, explanation, and the like. But fortunately we can largely ignore them, for what is crucial to the issue of explanatory compatibility is just this claim: if C and C* are simultaneous nomic equivalents, in the sense explained, then one constitutes an explanation for a given event if and only if the other does. If this claim is correct, the existence of physiological correlates for beliefs and desires would guarantee the possibility of both a rationalizing and a physiological explanation of an action. If all mental events have nomic equivalents in physiological states and processes (we may call this 'the psychophysical correlation thesis'), every rationalizing explanation would have a physiological counterpart with the same explanandum.

---

[15] Malcolm would be ill-advised to rest his argument on this revised principle (although the principle may be valid). For he would be powerless to show the incompatibility between a rationalizing explanation and a physiological explanation which makes use of physiological initial conditions occurring a little later or earlier than the belief and desire invoked in the rationalizing explanation. What is crucial is not that the two conditions for E occur at the same time; it's rather that they belong in distinct, independent causal chains (or chains of conditions).

[16] So we are treating C and C*, and also E, as 'event types' or 'generic events'. In fact, talk of 'necessity' and 'sufficiency' seems to make clear sense only for generic events. But our discussion can be taken to concern individual events if we take these latter to be instantiations of generic events. See for details on this conception of events my (1976) 'Events as Property Exemplifications' in Myles Brand and Douglas Walton (eds.), *Action Theory* (Dordrecht, Neth.: Reidel). However, no particular views concerning the nature of events are presupposed in the present discussion.

2. NOMIC EQUIVALENTS AND DEPENDENT EXPLANATIONS

The claim just mentioned, to the effect that if C and C* are simultaneous nomic equivalents, one is an explanation of a given event just in case the other is, holds on the Hempelian account of explanation. But this unrestricted claim is surely dubious: it could be that although the situation is as described, C* is only an 'epiphenomenon' of C, and, although C* is nomologically sufficient (and perhaps also necessary) for E, it does not explain why E occurs.[17] Thus, C could be the underlying pathological state of some disease, C* a simultaneous symptom of this state, and E a later stage of the disease. A case like this, therefore, is not one in which there are two explanations for one explanandum; for epiphenomena do not explain.

But let us not dwell on this possibility (although, as will be seen, it foreshadows others to be considered below), assuming instead something like the Hempelian nomic sufficiency account as our working model of explanation (this is what both Malcolm and Goldman do). The explanatory compatibilist may be willing to concede the possibility of epiphenomena just mentioned; for all he needs to refute Malcolm's claim is just one case in which each of two simultaneous nomic equivalents constitutes an explanans for the same event; surely, he may reason, not every case in which we have simultaneous nomic equivalents is one in which one of them is an epiphenomenon of the other. In any case, on the Hempelian model, if C and C* are nomic equivalents, the two explanations making use of them are 'nomically equivalent explanations' in a straightforward sense; also under the nomic-subsumptive account of causal relations, C and C* may be called 'nomically equivalent causes'. For it would be a matter of law that one is an explanation of a given event if and only if the other is, and that C is a cause of a given event if and only if C* is also its cause. Thus, if beliefs and desires have nomological coextensions in physiological states, for every rationalizing explanation of an action there is a nomologically equivalent physiological explanation (which we could formulate if we had sufficient knowledge of psychophysiological correlating laws). The fact that these explanations are nomically equivalent in this sense should alert us to the possibility that here we do not have two *independent* explanations of the same action. As I said, as a matter of nomological necessity, one is an explanation of the action just in case the other is.

---

[17] On epiphenomena see, e.g. David Lewis (1973), 'Causation', *Journal of Philosophy* 70: 556–67.

Thus, our interim conclusion appears to be this: In the sort of situation Goldman asks us to consider, either one of the two nomically equivalent states is an epiphenomenon of the other so that we do not have two explanations of the same event, or else we have two explanations that are not nomologically independent. But what is wrong with nomologically dependent or equivalent explanations in this sense? Aren't they sufficient to show the possibility of giving two distinct explanations of one and the same event? And if the psychophysical correlation thesis holds, aren't we assured of the general possibility of explaining behaviour both rationally and physiologically?

And there seem to be instances of just this sort in other areas of science. For example, we might explain the behaviour of some substance subjected to certain conditions by an appeal to its gross physical dispositional properties (ductility, conductivity, viscosity, etc.) on the one hand, and on the other by formulating a more theoretical account by invoking the microstructures that underlie these dispositions as their 'nomic equivalents'. Don't we in such cases have exactly the kind of example that fits Goldman's argument? Such examples seem legion: we often deepen and enrich our understanding of natural phenomena by moving away from their observable features and the rough 'phenomenological laws' that govern them, to their underlying micro-structures, and by invoking more systematic 'theoretical laws' appropriate to these states. (At least, that is the textbook account of progress in scientific theorizing.) Perhaps, rationalizing explanations are related to physiological explanations in just this way—that is, as macro- to underlying micro-explanations—via a pervasive system of correlation laws providing for each psychological state a physiological 'simultaneous nomic equivalent'.

Whether such correlation laws exist, especially for contentful intentional states ('propositional attitudes') such as belief, desire, and intention, is a controversial question on which much has been written in the past two decades. I think that a preponderance of philosophical evidence is now on the side of 'psychophysical anomalism', the thesis that there are not, and cannot be, precise laws connecting intentional states with physiological states of the brain (or any physical states).[18] If we have no confidence in the existence of such correlating laws, whether the correlations are species- or structure-specific, or uniform across all organisms and structures, the solu-

---

[18] Perhaps the most influential argument for psychophysical anomalism is one defended by Donald Davidson in 'Mental Events', repr. in his (1980) *Essays on Actions and Events* (New York: Oxford University Press). See my 'Psychophysical Laws' in Ernest LePore and Brian McLaughlin (1985) (eds.), *Actions and Events: Perspectives on the Philosophy of Donald Davidson* (Oxford: Basil Blackwell), for an exegesis and discussion of Davidson's argument and additional references.

tion in terms of 'nomic equivalents' would only be an idle possibility. But I do not want to pursue this issue of psychophysical laws here; for the general question still remains whether the existence of nomological equivalent states opens for us the possibility of having multiple explanations of a single event. That is, we want to know how things would stand if there were psychophysical correlations.

What I want to claim is this: the kind of situation Goldman describes, namely one in which two events C and C* are seen to be nomologically necessary and sufficient for each other, and in which each of them is thought to constitute an explanans for one and the same event E, is *an inherently unstable situation*. This is so especially when C and C* are each a member of a system of events (or concepts) such that the two systems to which they respectively belong show the kind of systematic nomological connections Goldman envisages for the psychological and the physiological. The instability of the situation generates a strong pressure to find an acceptable account of the relationship between C and C*, and, by extension, that between the two systems to which they belong; the instability is dissipated and a cognitive equilibrium restored when we come to see a more specific relationship between the two explanations. As we shall see, in cases of interest, the specific relationship replacing equivalence will be either identity or some asymmetric dependency relation.

Another way of putting my point would be this: a certain instability exists in a situation in which two distinct events are claimed to be nomologically *equivalent* causes or explanations of the same phenomenon; stability is restored when *equivalence is replaced by identity or some asymmetric relation of dependence*. That is, either two explanations (or causes) in effect collapse into one or, if there indeed are two distinct explanations (or causes) here, we must see one of them as dependent on, or derivative from, the other—or, what is the same, one of them as gaining explanatory or causal dominance over the other.

The tension in this situation that gives rise to the instability can be seen in various ways. First, if C and C* are each a sufficient cause of the event E, then why isn't E *overdetermined*? It is at best extremely odd to think that each and every bit of action we perform is overdetermined in virtue of having two distinct sufficient causes.[19] To be sure, this differs from the standard case of overdetermination in which the two overdetermining causes are not nomologically connected. But why does the supposed nomological relationship between C and C* void the claim that this is a

---

[19] Goldman is aware of this point but does not follow up its implications; in fact, he, like Malcolm, considers the possibility that beliefs and desires are neural states. See below for this 'identity solution'.

case of causal overdetermination? Notice the trade-off here: the closer this is to a standard case of overdetermination, the less dependent are the two explanations in relation to each other, and, correlatively, the more one stresses the point that this is not a case of standard overdetermination because of the nomic equivalence between the explanations, the less plausible is one's claim that we have here two distinct and independent explanations.

Second, if C and C* are nomic equivalents, they co-occur as a matter of law—that is, it is nomologically impossible to have one of these occur without the other. Why then do they not form a *single jointly sufficient* cause of E rather than two individually sufficient causes? How do we know that each of C and C* is not just a partial cause of E? Why, that is, should we not regard C and C* as forming a *single complete* explanation of E rather than two separately sufficient explanations of it? How do we decide one way or the other?

When we reflect on the special case of psychophysical causation, where C, let's say, is a psychological event, C* is its physiological correlate, and E is some bodily movement associated with an action, it would be highly implausible to regard C as directly acting on the body to bring about E (e.g. my belief and desire telekinetically acting on the muscles in my arm and shoulder and making them contract, thereby causing my arm to go up); it would be more credible to think that if the belief-desire pair is to cause the movement of my arm, it must 'work through' the physical causal chain starting from C*, some neural event in the brain, and culminating in a muscle contraction. If this is right, we cannot regard C and C* as constituting *independent* explanations of E. We must think of the causal efficacy of C in bringing about E as dependent on that of its physical correlate C*.[20]

I believe that these perplexities are removed only when we have an account of the relation between C and C*, the two supposed causes of a single action, and that, as I shall argue, an account that is adequate to this task will show that C and C* could not each constitute a *complete* and *independent* explanation of the action.

A case that nicely illustrates this is the identity solution: by saying that C and C* are in fact one and the same event, we can neatly resolve the situation. Malcolm is clearly aware of this (as is Goldman); for in the course of his incompatibility argument he explicitly rejects the psycho-physical identity thesis.[21] On the identity view, there is here one cause of E, not two whose mutual relationship we need to give an account of. As

---

[20] I believe this picture can be generalized; see my (1984) 'Epiphenomenal and Supervenient Causation', *Midwest Studies in Philosophy* 9: 257–70.

[21] Malcolm (1968), op. cit. 134.

for explanation, at least in an objective sense, there is one explanation here, and not two. The two explanations differ only in the linguistic apparatus used in referring to, or picking out, the conditions and events that do the explaining; they are only descriptive variants of one another. They perhaps give causal information about E in different ways, each appropriate in a particular explanatory context; but they both point to one objective causal connection, and are grounded in this single causal fact.[22]

What are other possible accounts of the relation between C and C*? The standard model of theory reduction has it that for a theory to be 'reduced to' another, the primitive theoretical predicates of the target theory must be connected via 'bridge laws' with predicates, presumably complex ones, of the base theory to which it is reduced, in such a fashion as to enable the derivation of the laws of the target theory from those of the reducer.[23] It is clear that if a bridge law of the biconditional form were available for each primitive predicate of the theory to be reduced, its reducibility is assured. For all we need to do is to rewrite the basic laws of the target theory in the vocabulary of the reducer by the use of the biconditional laws, and add these rewrites, as needed, to the axioms of the reducer. In any event, the point is that if each psychological event has a simultaneous physiological nomic equivalent, all the conditions necessary for the reduction of psychology to physiology, in the currently standard sense of reduction, are satisfied. Our intentional psychology, with all its rationalizations, would be ripe for reductive absorption into physiology and associated sciences, and rationalizing explanations would cease to be *independent* explanations of actions.[24] The relation between a rationalizing explanation and the

---

[22] An identity account in the present context would be a form of the so-called 'type identity' theory (talk of 'nomic equivalence' between C and C*, for example, implies that these represent 'generic events' or event types, not concrete events; however, the point applies to the 'token identity' theory as well. For example, Donald Davidson's causal theory of action is one example: reasons (e.g. beliefs and desires) are causes of action, but they are redescribable in physical (presumably, physiological) terms and hence are physical events; and it is under their physical descriptions that reasons and actions are subsumed under law. Thus, for Davidson, the duality of explanation vanishes (whether this is Davidson's intended result is another question, however).

[23] See Ernest Nagel (1961), *The Structure of Science* (New York: Harcourt).

[24] So, on the present construal, both Malcolm and Goldman come out right about the two types of explanation. For we are construing Malcolm to be saying that rationalizing and mechanistic explanations are not compatible as *independent* explanations; and Goldman does *not* claim that the two types of explanations are independent in our sense. In 'Mechanism and Responsibility' Daniel C. Dennett, too, addresses the compatibility issue; however, his focus is different. His main aim is to show that the behaviour of finite mechanisms, 'tropistic systems', can be explained from 'the intentional stance'. Even if Dennett's conclusion is accepted, our problem remains: What is the relationship between 'intentional-stance explanations' and 'physical-stance explanations'? Are the two types of explanations compatible when given of the same bit of behaviour?

physiological explanation to which it is reduced would indeed be like that between a macro-explanation of—to resort again to a stock example—some thermal phenomenon (the expansion of a gas upon being heated) and its underlying micro-explanation (in terms of the increasing kinetic energies of the gas molecules). Here we are not dealing with two independent stories about the phenomenon; the main difference between them is that one tells a more detailed, more revealing, and theoretically more fecund story than the other. The sort of tension that Malcolm tries to exploit when we have both a rationalizing and a physiological explanation of an action no longer exists. The reason is that the two explanations are no longer independent—one is reducible to the other.

The supposed existence of psychophysical nomic coextensions, therefore, does not show that rationalizing explanations and physiological explanations could coexist as independent explanations of actions; on the contrary, it would show that explanations of one type are reductively dependent on those of the other type. For it would place us precisely in a situation tailor-made for the physiological reduction of psychology, namely one in which rationalizing explanation will be deprived of its status as an independent mode of understanding actions, a situation that, as we saw, Malcolm wanted to exclude. If such reducibility should obtain, the claim that rationalizing explanation provides us with a distinctive mode of understanding human action would be undermined. What explanatory efficacy rationalizing explanation possesses would derive from that of the underlying physiological explanation—at least in this sense: we would be able to give a physiology-based explanation of why, and how, it is that reasons explain actions, and if we take a causal view of the situation, then precisely how, and by what mechanism, reasons cause actions.

3. CAUSAL EXPLANATIONS AND EXPLANATORY EXCLUSION

The general principle of explanatory exclusion states that two or more complete and independent explanations of the same event or phenomenon cannot coexist. The meanings of 'complete' and 'independent' are obviously crucial. I shall not be offering definitions of these terms; rather I shall focus on some specific cases falling under the intended distinctions, with the hope that, in the course of my discussion, reasonably determinate core meanings will emerge that will give the exclusion principle clear and substantial enough content. A thorough examination of explanatory exclusion will inevitably spill over into the long-standing debate over the nature of explanation, a topic on which nothing like a consensus now exists. The discussion to follow will inevitably rest on certain intuitive assumptions about how explanations, especially causal explanations, work; however, I hope that the discussion will succeed in showing that whatever model of explanation you accept, unless you take a wholly fictionalist or instrumentalist view of explanation, the principle of explanatory exclusion is a plausible general constraint.

It seems to me that the case for explanatory exclusion is most persuasively made for causal explanations of individual events. Suppose then that we have two such explanations of a single event:

Explanation A cites C as a cause of E
Explanation B cites C* as a cause of E.

What are we to think of such a situation? Various possibilities can be distinguished:

Case 1. We find that C = C*. That is, there is one cause here, not two. We saw how this works for the case of psychophysical causation under the mind–body identity theory.[25] This, when available, is the simplest and perhaps the most satisfying way of relieving the tension created by the existence of the two explanations. Such identities are often found in a reductive context where one of the explanations specifies the cause by a deeper, and more theoretical and systematic, description.

Case 2. C is distinct from C*, but is in some clear sense 'reducible' to, or 'supervenient' on, C*. This sort of situation will arise in a reductive context of the sort just considered provided that for whatever reason we stop short of *identifying* the reductively related events or states. Thus, the psychophysical case considered earlier would be an instance of this kind if we believed in the nomological reducibility of psychological states to physical states, without, however, wishing to identify psychological states with their physical correlates; or if we believed in the 'supervenience' in an appropriate sense of the psychological upon the physical, without identifying a supervenient psychological state with its physical base. In such a situation it is possible to treat causal relations involving psychological events and states as themselves supervenient upon, or reducible to, more fundamental physical causal processes. I have discussed 'supervenient causation' extensively elsewhere.[26] In any event we do not have in cases of this kind

[25] The precise formulation here would be affected somewhat by whether one takes the 'token identity' or the 'type identity' theory, and what view of the nature of events is adopted. However, the general point should apply regardless of the positions taken on these matters.

[26] In Jaegwon Kim (1979), 'Causality, Identity, and Supervenience in the Mind–Body Problem', *Midwest Studies in Philosophy* 4: 31–49; and id. (1984), 'Epiphenomenal and Supervenient Causation', *Midwest Studies in Philosophy* 9: 257–70. See also Ernest Sosa (1984), 'Mind–Body

two *independent* causal explanations of the same event. The two explanations can coexist because one of them is dependent, reductively or by supervenience, on the other.

Case 3. Neither C nor C* is in itself a 'sufficient cause' of E, though each is an indispensable component of a sufficient cause. As has often been observed, when we are called on to provide a cause or an explanation for an event we usually select a causal factour that, for various epistemological or pragmatic reasons, is believed to be the most appropriate to the situation. A stock example goes like this: we might explain why an automobile accident occurred by citing, say, the congested traffic, or the icy road, or the faulty brakes, or the driver's inexperience, etc., depending on the explanatory context, even though each of these conditions played an essential role in causing the accident. If C and C* are related in this way we do not have two *complete* explanations—in one sense of 'complete explanation', namely one in which a complete explanation specifies a sufficient set of causal conditions for the explanandum. It is clear that two incomplete explanations, in this sense, of the same event can coexist. The explanatory exclusion principle only bans more than one complete and independent explanation of the same event.

Case 3a.[27] C is a proper part of C*. If so, C as an explanation of E is neither complete in itself nor independent of C*.

Case 4. C and C* are different links in the same causal chain leading, say, from C to C* and then to E. In this case again we do not have two *independent* causal explanations; the explanans of one, C*, is causally dependent on the explanans of the other, C.

Case 5. C and C* are distinct and each a sufficient cause of E. We may think of them as belonging to two distinct and independent causal chains. This then is a case of *causal overdetermination*: E would have occurred even if either C or C* had not occurred, or had not caused it; the other would have been sufficient to bring it about. Thus, a man is shot dead by two assassins whose bullets hit him at the same time; or a building catches fire because of a short circuit in the faulty wiring and a bolt of lightning that hits the building at the same instant. It isn't obvious in cases like these just how we should formulate an explanation of why or how the overdetermined event came about; however, it is not implausible to think that failing to mention either of the overdetermining causes gives a misleading and incomplete picture of what happened, and that both causes

Interaction and Supervenient Causation', *Midwest Studies in Philosophy* 9: 271–81. For a general discussion of supervenience see my (1984), 'Concepts of Supervenience', *Philosophy and Phenomenological Research* 65: 153–76.

[27] I owe this case to Karl Pfeifer.

should figure in any *complete* explanation of the event. If this is right, the present case is not one in which two complete and independent explanations are possible for one event.

Thus I disagree with Hempel when he says that when we have a case of 'explanatory overdetermination', in which we have two or more complete D-N arguments with the same explanandum statement (e.g. 'The length of this metallic rod increased'), then either argument *singly* can be considered as 'complete' (one of them might explain it by invoking the fact that the rod was heated, and another might explain it by citing the fact that it was subjected to longitudinal stress).[28] Given Hempel's overriding concern with the inferential-predictive dimension of explanation, his position on this issue is not surprising. For as a predictive inference either D-N argument is wholly complete and sufficient. However, when it is a causal explanation of the lengthening of the rod that we are looking for, when we want to know *why* the rod's length increased, the situation seems radically altered: our understanding of why the event occurred is at best incomplete, and perhaps flawed, if we were unaware of one or the other 'explanation'.

The sense of 'completeness' of an explanation I have just invoked is different from that used in characterizing the case of 'partial cause' (Case 3 above), although this does not preclude a broader sense covering both. However, exactly how we deal with cases of causal overdetermination is not crucial to my general claims about explanatory exclusion; for it is unlikely that those who want to allow for multiple explanations of a single event would be willing to restrict them to instances of causal overdetermination. The exclusion principle would retain substantial content even if cases of overdetermination were exempted. In any event, the important point to note is this: that we have a case of causal overdetermination on hand is one way in which a satisfactory account of the relation between C and C* can go, removing the perplexities generated by the claim that each is a cause of some single event.

These considerations suggest the following simple argument for explanatory exclusion for causal explanations: Suppose that C and C* are invoked as each giving a complete explanation of E. Consider the two questions: (1) Would E have occurred if C had not occurred? and (2) Would E have occurred if C* had not occurred? If the answer is a 'Yes' to both questions, this is a classic case of overdetermination, and, as was discussed in preceding paragraphs, we can treat this case as one in which either explanation taken alone is incomplete, or else exempt all overdeterminative cases from the requirement of explanatory exclusion. If

[28] Carl G. Hempel (1965), *Aspects of Scientific Explanation* (New York: Free Press), 419.

the answer is a 'No' to at least one of the questions, say the first, that must be because if C had not occurred, C* would not have either. And this means that C and C* are not independent, and hence that the two explanations are not independent explanations of E.

The foregoing discussion of the subcases is useful as a way of making clearer what could be meant by the 'completeness' and 'independence' of explanations. When we examine the particular possibilities that seem to permit two distinct explanations of one event, we seem to be able to find—and we seem compelled to look for—reason for saying that either they are not independent or at least one of them is not complete. Two explanations of one event create a certain epistemic tension, a tension that is dissipated only when we have an account of how they, or the two causes they indicate, are related to each other. Finding out which of the cases canvassed holds for the given case is what is needed to relieve the tension.

4. REMARKS ON THE EPISTEMOLOGY AND METAPHYSICS OF EXPLANATION

When we look for an explanation of an event, we are typically in a state of puzzlement, a kind of epistemic predicament.[29] A successful explanation will get us out of this state. If our discussion is not too far off target, what it shows is that too many explanations will put us right back into a similar epistemic predicament, which can be relieved only when we have an explanation of how the explanations are related to one another.

Perhaps there is the following account of why this is so. Some writers have emphasized the unifying or simplifying role of explanation and tried to connect this with understanding.[30] It makes sense to think that multiple explanations of a single explanandum are presumptively counter-productive in regard to the goal of simplification and unification. When two distinct explanations are produced to account for a single phenomenon, we seem to be headed in a direction exactly opposite to the maxim of explanatory simplification 'Explain as much as you can with the fewest explanatory premises'. Unity is achieved through the promotion of interconnections among items of knowledge, and simplicity is enhanced when these inter-

[29] Sylvain Bromberger calls it a 'p-predicament' or 'b-predicament' in his 'An Approach to Explanation' in R. J. Butler (1965) (ed.), *Analytic Philosophy*, 2nd series (Oxford: Basil Blackwell).

[30] See, e.g. Michael Friedman (1974), 'Explanation and Scientific Understanding', *Journal of Philosophy* 71: 5–19; Philip Kitcher (1976), 'Explanation, Conjunction, and Unification', *Journal of Philosophy* 73: 207–12.

connections are seen or interpreted as dependency relations. For the main role of dependency relations in a system is that they help reduce the number of required independent assumptions or primitives. If simplicity and unity of theory is our aim when we seek explanations, multiple explanations of a single phenomenon are self-defeating—unless, that is, we are able to determine that their explanatory premises are related to one another in appropriate ways. It is clear that showing that the explanatory premises of one explanation are dependent on those of the other, in any of the senses of dependence distinguished in the preceding section in connection with causal explanations, is in effect an attempt to reduce the number of independent explanatory premises—that is, a move toward restoring the simplifying and unifying role of explanations.

These reflections, though sketchy and programmatic, provide us with a clue to a possible way of understanding the concept of dependence for explanations, a notion that we have made a rather liberal use of without a general explanation. One theme that runs through the various different cases of 'dependent explanations' we have surveyed seems to be this: if an explanation is dependent on a second, the two explanations taken together are committed to no more independent assumptions about the world than is the second explanation taken alone. This dovetails nicely with the view that explanations enhance understanding through simplification and unification. Here we would be trading in the notion of 'independent explanation' for that of 'independent assumption'; but that, I think, may well be progress.

These are general considerations not restricted to causal explanations. However, explanatory exclusion seems most obvious, and almost trivial, for causal explanations of individual events, and the reason seems to be this: we think of these explanations as directly tied to the actual causal histories of the events being explained, and their 'correctness' as explanations is determined by the accuracy with which they depict the causal connections as they exist. When two such explanations of one event are on hand, we need to know how they are situated in relation to each other on the causal map of the event; one thing that cannot be allowed to happen, if our explanations are to be coherent, is that they tell two different stories about the same region of the causal map.[31] Explanatory exclusion may seem obvious for causal explanations, but this is not to say it is trivial: the above considerations at least assume 'causal realism', the belief that there is a determinate objective fact of the matter about the causal history of any

[31] Cf. Peter Railton's notion of an 'ideal explanatory text' in (1981), 'Probability, Explanation, and Information', *Synthese* 48: 233–56; also, David Lewis (1986), 'Causal Explanation' in *Philosophical Papers II* (New York: Oxford University Press).

given event.[32] We must also assume certain metaphysical principles about causation, e.g. the principle (II) cited in Section 1 above.

I take it that *explaining* is an epistemological activity, and that an *explanation*, in the sense of the 'product' or 'theoretical content' of such an activity,[33] is something about which we can have various cognitive attitudes (e.g. accepting, doubting, having evidence for, etc.). To be in need of an explanation is to be in an epistemically incomplete and imperfect state, and to gain an explanation is to improve one's epistemic situation; it represents an epistemic gain. However, knowledge must involve the real world: to know that *p* requires the truth of *p*, and to have a causal explanation of an event requires that the event specified as its cause be, in reality, a cause of that event. Let us once again focus on causal explanations of individual events, and set aside other sorts of explanation (e.g. explanation of laws and regularities, of what a word means, of how to interpret a rule, of how a mathematical proof works, etc.) The kind of view I have just alluded to, namely that a causal explanation of E in terms of C is a 'correct explanation' only if C is in reality a cause of E, can be called an 'objectivist' or 'realist' conception of explanation. And the view that explanations must be 'real' or 'objective' in this sense can be called *explanatory realism*.

More generally, a realist conception of explanation holds that such notions as 'objective truth' or 'correctness' or 'accuracy' make sense for explanations, and do so in a more or less literal way, and that an explanation is correct or accurate *in virtue of* there obtaining 'in the real world' a certain determinate relationship between the explanandum and what is adduced as an explanation of it. Further, it maintains that an explanation represents a real addition to knowledge only if it has this property of correctness or accuracy, and that an explanation is epistemically acceptable only if we have good reason to think that the explanatory relation it purports to portray in fact holds in this objective sense. In short, it holds that explanations are appropriately evaluated on the basis of such objective criteria as accuracy and truth. Saying all this is not to slight the epistemological dimension of explanation. On the contrary: just as knowledge that something is so is cancelled if the thing is not so, an explanation of X in terms of Y is voided if either Y does not exist or an appropriate relationship between X and Y does not in reality obtain. And just as the claim to know that *p* is, and must be, withdrawn when there is reason to

---

[32] I discuss this and related topics in some detail in (1988), 'Explanatory Realism, Causal Realism, and Explanatory Exclusion', *Midwest Studies in Philosophy* 12: 225–40.

[33] For some of the basic terminological distinctions see Bromberger (1965), op. cit.; and Peter Achinstein (1983), *The Nature of Explanation* (New York and Oxford: Oxford University Press), esp. 'Introduction' and ch. 1.

believe that p does not hold, an explanation of X in terms of Y must be withdrawn, on explanatory realism, if we have reason to think that the claimed relationship does not in fact obtain between X and Y. Such things as understanding, intellectual satisfaction, making things intelligible, dispelling puzzles and apparent inconsistencies, etc. are crucial; however, we do not believe these things are *properly earned* unless an explanation is correct in some objective sense. The case for explanatory realism is best made—at least, can be made most explicitly—with respect to causal explanations, for here the notion of an 'objective correlate' of explanation has an acceptably clear sense, clear enough for explicit consideration.[34]

It is helpful to distinguish between two versions of the exclusion principle. Suppose, for some given event, you have an explanation and I have another, distinct explanation. It can be rational, from an epistemological point of view, for you to accept yours, and for me to accept mine. But can they both be 'correct' or 'true' explanations? The *metaphysical* principle of explanatory exclusion says this: they can both be correct explanations only if either at least one of the two is incomplete or one is dependent on the other.[35] There is a corresponding *epistemological* exclusion principle: *No one may accept both explanations unless one has an appropriate account of how they are related to each other.* What counts as an 'appropriate account' of the relationship, in case of causal explanations, is as illustrated in the preceding section: ideally we must know which of these cases holds, or at least be satisfied that one of these cases, though we may not know which, does.

I should add a few remarks about the individuation of explananda. Some believe that an explanandum is fixed only when a statement representing it is fixed, a view closely tied to the inferential view of explanation;[36] this is often allied with the view that it is not events as concrete occurrences but *aspects* of events (or why a given event has a certain property) that are the proper objects of explaining. Thus, we do not explain, say, the Japanese surrender to the Allied Forces or Harry's accident, but rather such things as, say, why the Japanese surrender came as late as it did or how Hirohito was able to override the objections of the powerful military leaders, or why Harry's car ran off the road in broad daylight. These disputes, however,

---

[34] Some would want to *analyse* the very notion of causation in terms of explanation, but I believe that is a mistake. See, e.g. Michael Scriven (1975), 'Causation as Explanation', *Noûs* 9: 3–16; Jaegwon Kim (1981), 'Causes as Explanations: A Critique', *Theory and Decision* 13: 293–309.

[35] It might be possible for the two explanations to be each dependent on a third, without one of them being dependent on the other. It seems that in such a situation both explanations could stand.

[36] See Hempel (1965), op. cit. 421–2.

seem largely immaterial to my present concerns: if it is aspects of events, rather than events *simpliciter*, that are explained, then explanatory exclusion would apply to these event aspects.[37] If concrete occurrences are explainable, at least in the sense of explaining *why they occurred*, then they, too, would be subject to explanatory exclusion. Matters here are somewhat complicated because there are different views about the proper construal of events in causal and explanatory contexts.[38] But trying to heed these complexities and subtleties would be a largely pointless exercise in philosophical precision for the purposes at hand.[39]

The metaphysical principle makes sense only if some form of explanatory realism is accepted—that is, only if it makes sense, literal sense, to speak of the 'correctness', 'accuracy', and 'truth' of explanations. And the acceptance of the metaphysical principle will provide a ground for abiding by the epistemological rule of exclusion. I think, though, that the epistemological principle can hold even if explanatory realism is rejected. Even if we abandon the idea that there are objective explanatory relations in the world, we may still find something cognitively and unsettling and dissonant about having to face, or accept, two or more independent explanations of the same phenomenon. The explanatory premises of one explanation need not logically contradict those of another, and there may be sufficient evidential warrant for thinking each set to be true. However, accepting the two sets of premises as constituting explanations of the same event (or any one thing), each complete in itself and independent of the other, may induce a sort of incoherence into our belief system. This may be one instance of epistemic incoherence that is not a case of logical (deductive or inductive) inconsistency or incoherence. I earlier tried to explain why this might be so on the basis of the view that the primary epistemic role of explanation is simplification and unification of our belief system. In connection with the coherence theory of justification, 'explanatory coherence' is often prominently mentioned—how explanatory relations generate mu-

[37] These seem similar to what Fred Dretske has called 'event allomorphs' in 'Referring to Events' in Peter A. French, *et al.* (1977) (eds.), *Contemporary Perspectives in the Philosophy of Language* (Minneapolis: University of Minnesota Press).

[38] For a discussion of these matters and further references see my (1973) 'Causation, Nomic Subsumption, and the Concept of Event', *Journal of Philosophy* 70: 217–36.

[39] Robert Cummins has made an interesting distinction between explanation 'by subsumption' (under a causal law) and explanation 'by analysis' (into component parts). See Robert Cummins (1983) *The Nature of Psychological Explanation* (Cambridge, Mass.: MIT Press), esp. chs. 1 and 2. Could one and the same explanandum be given explanations of these two types? According to Cummins, however, subsumptive explanation explains *changes* and analytical explanation explains *properties*, so that the explananda are different. It seems also possible to construe the two explanations as mutually complementary but each only a partial explanation of a single explanandum, under a coarse-grained individuation of explananda.

tually supportive coherence in a system of beliefs. If our speculations here have a point, it can be summarized thus: *too many explanations can be a source of incoherence rather than increased coherence.*

It is interesting to contrast this situation with *predictions* or *proofs*. As I noted briefly above, it seems that, unlike explanatory overdetermination, predictive overdetermination does not create any sort of epistemic tension, any need to look for an account of how two predictive arguments, both predicting the same phenomenon, are related. Predictive or inferential overdetermination is simply a matter of overabundance of evidence. I infer that Peggy is in, because I can hear her typing and also because her lights are on. We predict that this steel rod will get longer because we know it's being stretched, and also because we know it's being heated. There are no problems here.[40] It is when such inferences are invested with explanatory import that a need for an account of their mutual relationship arises. And this is so, it seems to me, because explanations make a claim about how things are connected in the world, a claim that is absent in mere proofs or inferences. If this is right, the fact of explanatory exclusion shows that explanations cannot be construed as mere proofs or arguments.[41]

As I said, explanatory realism seems to fit comfortably with explanatory exclusion, although it is not, I think, entailed by it. One interesting possibility is *not* to argue for explanatory exclusion on the basis of explanatory realism, but rather to go the opposite route, namely to give independent considerations favouring the epistemological version of explanatory exclusion and then advocate explanatory realism as the most natural account of it.

Before moving on to the final section I would like to deal with a possible objection: it might be said that there is no need to appeal to any special, and potentially controversial, epistemological or metaphysical views concerning explanation in order to justify something like the rule of explanatory exclusion, and that all we really need is Occam's Razor, the familiar principle of simplicity, that enjoins us to get by with the fewest possible entities, hypotheses, theoretical principles, and, of course, explanations. In reply, I would first note that the general simplicity requirement is vague

[40] Nor when we see that the same mathematical propositions can be given two different proofs. Some philosophers think, however, that certain proofs are more 'explanatory' than others, in the sense that they seem to give us an explanation of 'what makes the theorem hold'. However, one could argue, I think, that the same principle of exclusion must apply to multiple *explanatory proofs* of the same mathematical proposition.

[41] These remarks tie in with the standard discussion of 'realism' vs. 'instrumentalism' about scientific theories—especially, the common view that an instrumentalist conception of scientific theories, though viable as an account of their predictive utility, deprives them of explanatory significance.

and its application requires a more precise interpretation of the situation to which it is to be applied. In particular, we need to determine exactly at what point the entities in question begin to be multiplied 'beyond necessity'. In fact, determining where the excess baggage starts is the difficult part; the rest is trivial. The exclusion principle does the difficult work: it says that for any event more than one complete explanation is excess baggage. More, the principle helps us answer the following question: If, as is usually thought, explanations represent epistemic gains, why aren't two explanations better than one? It is not at all obvious that considerations of parsimony alone should mandate us to reject all but one explanation. We can indeed think of explanatory exclusion as a special case falling under the general simplicity requirement: it is a specific rule concerning one important way in which simplicity is to be gained in explanatory matters, and it explains why this form of simplicity is to be desired. That is, the explanatory exclusion principle provides a rationale for the application of Occam's Razor to multiple explanations of a single explanandum.

5. APPLICATIONS

In this final section I want to describe two examples from recent philosophical discussions in which the explanatory exclusion principle seems to be employed in a tacit but crucial way. The examples I shall discuss are not intended to constitute an argument for the exclusion principle; rather, they are intended to show that the principle is often accepted or presupposed, if only implicitly. Alternatively, they can be thought of as 'applications' of the explanatory exclusion principle. Evidence such as this shows that, even apart from general theoretical considerations, the principle does carry a degree of prima facie plausibility, and should not be rejected without good reason.

The account of theory reduction we earlier referred to, one that was formulated by Ernest Nagel, is a model of *conservative reduction*. For in a reduction of this kind the reduced theory survives the reduction, being conserved as a subtheory of the reducing theory. Its concepts are conserved by being tied, via the 'bridge laws', to the concepts of the reducing theory, and its laws are reincarnated as derived laws of the more fundamental theory. For a theory to be reduced in this way to another theory whose legitimacy is not in question is for it to be vindicated and legitimatized.

There is another account of reduction, due to John Kemeny and Paul Oppenheim,[42] that is thought to give us an analysis of *eliminative* or *replacement reduction*. A theory is reduced to another, on this model, just in case all the data explainable by the first theory are explainable by the second. In cases of interest, the second theory, that is, the reducer, will do a good deal better than the first, the reducee. There need be no direct conceptual or nomological connections between the theories themselves; their theoretical vocabularies may be wholly disjoint and there may be no 'bridge laws' connecting them. Nor need there be a logical incompatibility or a negative inductive or evidential relationship between them. It is just that one theory, the reducer, does its job better than (or at least as well as) the reducee, relative to their shared domain.

It is clear that any case of Nagelian reduction can be construed as a case of Kemeny–Oppenheim reduction, so that it is not strictly correct to characterize all cases of the latter as replacement or eliminative reductions. But it is also clear that any case of Kemeny–Oppenheim reduction that is not also a case of Nagel reduction is one that involves, or ought to involve, the elimination of the weaker reduced theory by the richer theory that reduces it. Thus, the phlogiston theory of combustion was reduced in the sense of Kemeny and Oppenheim to the oxidation theory, and was replaced by it. The impetus theory of motion was reduced, and eliminated, in the same sense, by modern dynamic theory of motion. And so on. A general principle like the following seems to be at work here: *If a theory is confronted by another that explains more, the only way it can survive is for it to be conservatively reduced to the latter.*

The question I want to raise is why this holds, or ought to hold. Why should we replace, and abandon, a Kemeny–Oppenheim reduced theory in favour of its reducer? Notice that the reducing theory does not in general *logically exclude* the reduced theory; there need be no logical incompatibility between them. Further, the reduced theory need not have been falsified; in fact, as far as direct evidence goes there may be good reason to think it is true. So why not keep them both? Notice the consequences of abandoning the reduced theory: its characteristic theoretical entities, properties, events, and states are no longer to be recognized as 'real'. They share the fate of the discarded theory: phlogiston had to go when the phlogiston theory was thrown out.

The reason I raise these points is that they help to give structure to the current debate concerning the future of vernacular psychology, the rich

    [42] John Kemeny and Paul Oppenheim (1956), 'On Reduction', *Philosophical Studies* 7: 6–19.

and motley collection of truisms and platitudes about our motives, desires, beliefs, hopes, actions, etc. It is in terms of such truisms that we explain, and predict at least in a limited way, the behaviour of our fellow humans and ourselves. It strikes many of us as inconceivable that we can entirely dispense with this framework of intentional psychology; it is not clear that our conception of ourselves as persons and agents could survive the loss of the vernacular psychological scheme.

However, many philosophers have raised doubts about the reality of vernacular psychology—and the reality of such states as belief, desire, and intention. The thought is that the rapidly developing and expanding 'cognitive science' will likely supersede the vernacular so that at some point in the future the rational thing to conclude is that there are no such things as beliefs and desires, and there never were. But in what sense of 'supersede'? How should vernacular psychology be related to cognitive science if it is to survive, and if the states it recognizes, such as beliefs and desires, are to continue to be recognized as real?

Those who argue for the potential, and likely, elimination of vernacular psychology, and intentional psychological states that constitute its core, often point to two considerations: first, compared with systematic cognitive science the vernacular suffers from explanatory failure, and second there is no prospect of reducing it to a systematic scientific theory. For example, Paul Churchland, a forceful proponent of this position, writes:

As examples of central and important mental phenomena that remain largely or wholly mysterious wthin the framework of FP [folk psychology], consider the nature and dynamics of mental illness, the faculty of creative imagination . . . the nature and psychological functions of sleep . . . the common ability to catch an outfield fly ball on the run . . . the internal construction of a 3-D visual image . . . the rich variety of perceptual illusions . . . the miracle of memory . . . the nature of the learning process itself . . .[43]

There are phenomena, Churchland is saying, that are adequately explained within cognitive science but untouched by the vernacular. A further implicit assumption is that cognitive science can explain everything explained by vernacular psychology. The claim then is that the vernacular is Kemeny–Oppenheim reducible to systematic cognitive science.

Churchland is also sceptical about the conservative Nagel reducibility of vernacular psychology to cognitive science. He says: 'A successful reduction cannot be ruled out, in my view, but FP's [folk psychology's] explanatory impotence and long stagnation inspire little faith that its categories

---

[43] Paul Churchland (1981), 'Eliminative Materialism and the Propositional Attitudes', *Journal of Philosophy* 78: 67–90. The quotation is from p. 73.

will find themselves neatly reflected in the framework of neuroscience.'[44] Here he is saying that a conservative reduction is unlikely because there is little reason to believe in the existence of the bridge laws connecting vernacular psychological states with neurophysiological states. Thus the structure of Churchland's argument exemplifies the pattern we discerned earlier: vernacular psychology must be eliminated because it is Kemeny–Oppenheim reducible to cognitive neuroscience without being conservatively reducible to it.[45]

Thus, we are faced with the following question: granted that neuroscience has a wider explanatory range than vernacular psychology, why can't the two coexist anyway, without vernacular psychology being nomologically reduced to neuroscience? Why should we discard the vernacular and conclude that there aren't, and never have been, such things as beliefs, hopes, regrets, and wishes?

The explanatory exclusion principle provides a simple explanation of why the two theories, even if they do not logically or evidentially exclude each other, compete against each other and why their peaceful coexistence is an illusion. For vernacular psychology and neuroscience each claim to provide explanations for the same domain of phenomena, and because of the failure of reduction in either direction, the purported explanations must be considered independent. Hence, by the exclusion principle, one of them has to go.[46]

I think similar considerations can account for an otherwise puzzling aspect of Thomas Kuhn's celebrated theory of scientific 'paradigms'.[47] According to Kuhn, successive paradigms addressing the same range of phenomena are 'incommensurable' with each other. They make use of different concepts, different methodologies, different criteria for generating problems and evaluating proposed solutions. As is well known, Kuhn

---

[44] Ibid 75.

[45] Churchland also intimates that laws of vernacular psychology have been falsified. This is a controversial point, and even if it is true, it would not force the *elimination* of vernacular psychology (at least, that of intentional psychology); all it would show is that the vernacular needs improvement. To argue for an outright elimination, some principle like explanatory exclusion seems essential; and if we have such a principle, we don't need the premiss about the falsity of vernacular psychology.

[46] The right way to save vernacular psychology, in my view, is to stop thinking of it as playing the same game that 'cognitive science' is supposed to play—that is, stop thinking of it as a 'theory' whose primary *raison d'être* is to generate law-based causal explanations and predictions. We will do better to focus on its normative role in the evaluation of actions and the formation of intentions and decisions. If vernacular psychology competes against cognitive science in the prediction game, it cannot win, and the best thing it can hope for is reductive absorption into its more systematic (and better funded) rival.

[47] Thomas Kuhn (1962), *The Structure of Scientific Revolutions* (Chicago: University of Chicago Press).

says in various places that different paradigms do not, perhaps cannot, even share the same problems; nor can they, strictly speaking, share the same data. But I am here assuming that Kuhn must allow a sense in which different successive paradigms can, and do, share an overlapping domain of subject matters. Otherwise much of his theory of paradigms makes little sense.

Now one might raise the following question about paradigms: If they are, as Kuhn says, mutually incommensurable, and hence cannot even contradict each other, why can't we accept them all? Why must we discard the old paradigm when we construct a new one? After all, no paradigm is ever literally falsified, according to Kuhn, and every paradigm serves useful explanatory and predictive purposes, making its unique scientific contributions. So why not accumulate paradigms? We could do this without fear of logical incoherence or inconsistency, for paradigms are mutually incommensurable and hence cannot contradict each other. We would have a 'cumulative theory' of scientific progress through accumulation of paradigms instead of the usual cumulative theory of scientific knowledge which Kuhn rejects.

Again, an answer is forthcoming from the explanatory exclusion principle: Kuhn takes for granted the incompatibility of successive paradigms directed at the same phenomena because he tacitly accepts the explanatory exclusion principle, and we go along with him because we, too, do not question it. I take it that, for Kuhn, each paradigm purports to provide complete and independent explanations of the data within its domain—complete and independent relative to other competing paradigms. It follows from the explanatory exclusion principle: No more than one paradigm for a single domain.

My thanks to David Benfield, John Biro, Brian McLaughlin, Joseph Mendola, and Michael Resnik for helpful comments.

12

AGENCY AND CAUSAL EXPLANATION

JENNIFER HORNSBY

1. INTRODUCTION

Some philosophical problems about agency can be put in terms of *two points of view*. From the *personal* point of view, an action is a person's doing something for a reason, and her doing it is found intelligible when we know the reason that led her to it. From the *impersonal* point of view, an action would be a link in a causal chain that could be viewed without paying any attention to people, the links being understood by reference to the world's causal workings. We might take it for granted that there are truths available to be discovered from each of these points of view. The problems about agency surface when we start to wonder whether the impersonal point of view does not threaten the personal one.

We might think that a full understanding of everything that happens when there is an action could be had without anyone's knowing who did what thing for what reasons. But then, if the whole truth about an action and its causal past and future can be given in viewing it as a manifestation of the world's causal workings, the impersonal point of view can seem to displace the personal one. Of course the personal point of view might still be adopted, even if it seemed redundant from another point of view. But two lines of thought may be used to make it seem redundant *tout court*. First, there is the thought, which Thomas Nagel has made especially vivid, that it is essential to our conceiving of our ourselves as agents that we take our actions to be completely accounted for in the terms that we use as agents; the possibility of treating actions from the impersonal point of view would then subvert our ordinary conception of ourselves.[1] Second, there is

---

[1] Or, again, free agency, if not agency itself, may be thought to be subverted: it is said that the impersonal point of view, in so far as it treats actions as happenings, and treats any happening as inevitable of occurrence, exposes freedom as an illusion.

the thought, which is familiar in contemporary philosophy of mind, that the impersonal point of view is more 'objective', or for some other reason has better credentials, than the personal one. In order for the personal point of view to be metaphysically sound, then, it would need to be sub-sumed under the other one; but the possibility of such subsumption may be doubted.[2]

Both these lines of thought introduce rivalry between the two points of view, and suggest that the impersonal one may triumph. Either the per-sonal point of view is supposed to be undermined, by being revealed to rest on an assumption that the possibility of taking an impersonal view shows to be false; or it is supposed to be refuted by the impersonal view, which is meant to be better placed for seeing the truth.

In this paper I attempt to block the idea that the two points of view are in competition. My suggestion will be that actions are not in fact accessible from the impersonal point of view.

Two fairly immediate routes to my suggestion might be taken. One starts from denying that actions are events; the other, from denying that the explanation of action is causal explanation. Each of these denials would enable one to deny, in turn, what I do deny—that actions can be located in the impersonal world of causes. But I shall not follow either route. Indeed I start by saying why I think that actions are events (Section 2), and that reason explanation is causal explanation (Section 3). This will enable me to assemble materials for an argument that makes my suggestion plausible (Section 4). I offer some further support for it (Section 5) before I treat the two problems about agency (Sections 6 and 7).

2. ACTIONS AS EVENTS

We know something about the causal past of some water's boiling if we know that the water is in the kettle that Peter switched on because he

---

My immediate concern is with the problem that Nagel discusses under the head of Autonomy (T. Nagel (1986), *The View from Nowhere* (Oxford: Clarendon Press) ch. 7, sect. 2), to which page references are given below). I agree with Nagel that 'the essential source of the problem is a view of persons and their actions as part of the order of nature, *causally determined or not*' (p. 110, my italics); but I leave it open whether there might be a separate threat to freedom such as would be suggested by the first sentence of this note. (In Nagel's own terms, the problem I discuss here is one about freedom: he distinguishes a question about agency, which he puts aside, from two problems about freedom, of which autonomy is the first.)

[2] The doubt I am thinking of here is what leads to eliminative materialism. But any philoso-pher who begins with the assumption that psychological explanation requires vindication through connection with physical science aims at such subsumption; if some such philosophers are not eliminativists that is because they do not doubt that the requirement can be met. See Section 7 below.

wanted to make a cup of tea. Something has happened because someone wanted it to. If we see the water's boiling as an event, then we may think of an action also as an event: an action is an event that causes another, where the occurrence of the other typically amounts to the agent's having something she wanted.

Someone might allow that there is causality here, but say that only a philosopher bent upon forcing causality into the event-event model would introduce 'an action'. It is Peter with whom we credit the switching on of the kettle, it may be said; and if something about him is relevant, then it is only his wanting boiling water. This response is correct in so far as it looks back to Peter and what he wanted, and recognizes that these are not events. But it ignores the fact that Peter had to do something if the water was to boil, that wanting it to boil was not enough. There is no need to invent an item to bridge the gap between Peter's states of mind and the event of his want's being satisfied: when his want was satisfied, the gap was bridged—he switched on the kettle. Or, in an alternative idiom, there was an event—his switching on the kettle.

When it is accepted that there are actions, and that they are events, questions arise about which events they are, and how many of them there are. Not every event in whose description the name of a person features is an action; there is only an action when someone does something intentionally.[3] But since a person's intentionally doing something may be the same as her doing something else (intentionally or unintentionally), there is more to be said about the individuation of actions. For my part, I accept the view that (nearly enough) if someone did one thing by doing another then her doing the one thing was the same as her doing the other: when Peter boiled the water by switching on the kettle, his boiling the water was his switching on the kettle. On this account of individuation, the various things that people do are, many of them, the bringing about of effects of various sorts. And of course a single action can bring about a series of effects: an action of Peter's was the initiation of a series that contained both the kettle's being on and the water's coming to the boil.

Even when this view of individuation is accepted, it may still be asked to what extremes we should take the idea that things people do allude to effects of their actions. Elsewhere I have argued that *causation* is implicit whenever we impute agency (see chapters 1–3 of my 1980 book[4]). Our conception of a person as an agent is a conception of something with a

---

[3] I assume the criterion of actionhood in D. Davidson (1971), 'Agency', in R. Binkley, *et al.* (eds.), *Action, Agent, and Reason* (Toronto: Toronto University Press). I take 'There is some description under which the event is intentional' to be equivalent to 'There is something the agent intentionally does'.

[4] Jennifer Hornsby (1980), *Actions* (London: Routledge & Kegan Paul).

causal power; whether we think of a person having brought about a movement of a bit of her body or a bomb's exploding in a distant field, we should see her action as her causing something—as causing the movement, or the explosion, or whatever. This view has been challenged, because it is thought that movements of bodies must be more intimately connected with actions than is suggested by calling them effects. But the view may not be incompatible with the idea that bodily movements are parts of actions—as David Lewis has pointed out in defending *piecemeal causation* (Lewis 1986: 173[5]). And bodily movements need not be denied a special status in relation to agency. For we may think that our ability to make bodily movements is constitutive of our having the power that we have as agents—to initiate series of events containing some we want. An action is the exercise of such a power, and a person's actions are the events at the start of those series she initiates.

3. REASON EXPLANATION AS CAUSAL EXPLANATION

The previous section has been concerned for the most part with the causal future of actions. But it takes something for granted also about the causal past of a person's intentionally doing something: it assumes that in finding out what Peter wanted, we learnt something about the causal history of some events. It may seem, then, that the claim which it is the purpose of the present section to defend—that action explanation is causal explanation—has already been presupposed, and that nothing is in dispute here. But the matter is not so straightforward.

What makes it complicated is that there have been thought to be two different issues about causal explanation. We are told that there are philosophers who accept that the items alluded to in giving a reason explanation play a part in the causal past of an action, but who nevertheless deny that rational explanation is itself causal explanation.[6] Supposedly these philosophers think that if you cross the road because you want to get to the other side, then there is an explanation of your crossing in terms of where you want to get to, and there is a causal connection between the fact of your wanting to be there and your crossing, but the existence of an explanation and the existence of a causal connection are separate matters. What

---

[5] D. Lewis (1986), *Philosophical Papers*, ii (New York: Oxford University Press).

[6] C. McGinn (1979), 'Action and its Explanation', in N. Bolton (ed.), *Philosophical Problems in Psychology* (London: Methuen), 26 distinguished four different theses about the explanatoriness/causal status of rational explanations. He and many others have subsequently put to work the particular (putative) distinction I am concerned with here: see below.

I mean to defend is the claim that reason explanation is causal in a sense that rules out this idea of causality and explanatoriness coming apart—the claim that reason explanation is causal-explanation (where the hyphen signals that causality and explanatoriness enter the scene together, as it were).

On the face of it, it is a strange position that these philosophers are said to occupy. For one might have thought that the best way to persuade someone that a person's having the reasons she does bears causally on what she does was to show that explanations that give people's reasons are causal-explanations. There is an argument that asks us to consider a case in which someone did something and had a reason for doing it, yet did not do it as a result of having that reason. We are asked to contrast this with the case in which we can explain her action by mentioning her reason—where she did it because she had the reason. The difference between the two cases suggests that *causation* and *explanation* are inextricable: both are introduced when we are told why someone did something—when we find the word 'because' between a statement saying what she did and a statement saying what her reason for doing it was.[7]

Why then should claims about causal connections have been thought to be separable from claims about the causal-explanatory nature of reason explanation? Presumably the answer is that we have to make allowance for those philosophers who deny that reason explanation is causal *tout court*.[8] They do not deny that reason explanation is explanation; so it might seem that in order to be able to contradict them, we have to isolate some 'purely causal' statements about mental states and actions which we, but not they, assent to. A prominent candidate for our endorsement is 'The primary reason for an action is its cause'.[9] Since someone might hold this without assuming any particular account of how the explanation of action works, there seems to arise the possibility of isolating it from any thesis about explanation, and thus of adopting the position

[7] The argument is in D. Davidson, Ch. 1 this volume, 27–41. Not that 'because' is everywhere a causal notion. Where action explanation is concerned, there may be more to say to ensure that causation has been at work when the explanatory claim can be made. But this is supported when it is seen (a) that the 'because' goes alongside other, recognizably causal idioms ('His belief *led* him to. . . .'; 'Her desire *moved* her to. . . .'; 'Her reason was *operative*'); (b) that the explanations rely on a network of empirical interdependences, recorded in counterfactuals ('If she had not wanted——, but had still believed that——, then. . . .').

[8] These are the writers to whom Davidson is responding in Ch. 1 of this volume, and whom he has cited there, p. 27, n. 1. And of course their view is still held by some today, e.g. F. Stoutland (1976), 'The Causation of Behavior', in *Essays on Wittgenstein in Honor of G. H. von Wright* (*Acta Philosophica Fennica* 28), 286–325.

[9] This was the thesis guaranteeing the availability of 'purely causal' statments that Davidson arrives at in Ch. 1. I discuss some details of Davidson's own position in the Appendix to this chapter.

that reason explanation, though it mentions causes, is not itself causal-explanation.

Well, we have seen already that support for the thesis of causal-explanatoriness may be given without assuming the availability of any 'purely causal' statements. What we should realize now is that a defence of causal-explanation need have no involvement at all with 'purely causal' statements. Indeed consideration of what goes on when action explanations are sought and found should make us very sceptical about them.

When we seek an 'action explanation', one question we usually want answered is 'Why did she do such and such thing?' We may agree that actions are events without supposing that this question is equivalent to 'Why was there an event of such-and-such kind?' Asking why a φ-d, we hope to learn something about a, the person; but if we asked why a's φ-ing occurred, a might not be a subject of concern at all. To a question about why someone did something, an expected answer usually goes: 'She thought——', or 'She wanted——'. Philosophers' official version of an answer goes: 'She thought——*and* she wanted——'. The official version is appropriate, because someone who intentionally did something had a reason for doing it, and, having a reason, she must have believed something about what would be conducive to the satisfaction of some desire she had. When a relevantly connected belief and desire are both mentioned (e.g. 'She thought she could get to the other side by crossing and she wanted to get to the other side'), the explanation is successful inasmuch as it brings us to realize that what mattered, so far as her doing what she did is concerned, is her having had the reason she did.

It may seem only a short step from this point to speaking of reasons as 'belief–desire pairs', and to saying 'The primary reason is the cause'. But if we take this step we arrive on much less firm ground. What sort of thing is the primary reason now supposed to be? It cannot be what an agent has when she has a reason; for you may have the same reason to do something as someone else, but we are surely not to suppose that your believing and desiring something causes someone else's action. If we are to make sense of it as 'the cause', then the primary reason must be an item that there is if and only if the relevant agent believes some particular thing and desires some other (related) thing. But why should we think that there is any such item as this? Why should acknowledgement that we say something about what she believed and desired in causally explaining why she did what she did lead us to accept the existence of anything that 'the cause of her action' stands for?

We are encouraged to believe in the things at issue when we are told that the agent's belief and her desire are each of them 'token states'. Then her reason (the candidate denotation of 'the cause') is meant to be the fusion, or perhaps the intersection, of two token-states. But even if we think we know what it is for a token-state to be a cause, can we be sure that we know what it would be for this sort of thing—composed somehow from two states of the same person—to be the cause?[10] And if such a fusion (or pair, or whatever) were indeed the cause of an agent's doing what she did, how would it relate to all the other causal truths about the situation? Suppose that we could explain why Jane had done something by pointing out that she didn't think that p. Is there in that case a token state of her not believing that p that was also some part of the cause?

I do not know how one should answer these questions. The point is that we do not have to answer them if we deny that the causal-explanation view relies on the idea of discrete things combining (interacting?) in the production of action. What we rely on is only a network of intelligible dependencies between the facts about what an agent thinks, what she wants, and what she does. When we know why she did something, the fact that she did it may be seen as depending crucially on the fact that she wanted some particular thing and thought some particular thing. And the dependence is of a causal sort, of course.

Accepting that *belief* and *desire* are causal-explanatory notions, we cannot but suppose that people really do think things and want things, and that whether or not someone thinks a particular thing, or wants a particular thing, may make a genuine difference to what she does and says. But if the causal reality of *belief* and *desire* is just their causal-explanatory reality, then it need make no use of a further idea—of items inside people that we latch on to when we give action explanations.[11] Once this further idea is in place, it can come to seem that the explanatory value of *belief* and *desire* is

---

[10] For serious, valiant, exhaustive, but eventually abortive, attempts to make sense of the idea of causal interaction between states of persons, see W. S. Robinson (1990), 'States and Beliefs', *Mind* 99: 33–51. Like Robinson, I think that the notion of a token-state is not unacceptable, but that it has been put to unacceptable use in philosophy of mind. My brief remarks here can only gesture towards the problems that Robinson uncovers. (Occurrences of 'state' in this paper are of two sorts: (i) those that come into descriptions of views opposed to my own, (ii) those that rely on our ordinary conception of a mental state—something a person can be in, so that a state is not a particular.)

[11] It is a good question why people should think that recognizing the dependencies we do is not enough to ensure that we have a case of the operation of causality. Hume taught that the conception we have of necessity, as a putative ingredient of our idea of causality, is a figment, since, he said, there is no impression to which our conception corresponds. Many philosophers are happy to reply to Hume that in so far as we take necessity to be inextricable from causality, we do not take it to be an isolatable, perceptible ingredient of causal transactions: searching for necessity among impressions is not the way to uncover our understanding of causation. But even when this reply has been given, the idea that our understanding of causality resides in the putative objects wherein an impression of necessity was supposed by Hume to be sought is not renounced.

quite unconnected with the value of those concepts in causal understand-ing—as if the particular contents of a particular person's beliefs and desires had nothing to do with her tendencies to do one thing rather than another. It is then that one may be led to the curious claim that 'the rational explanation of action mentions causes but is not *itself* causal explanation'.

4. ANOMALOUSNESS

The philosopher most often said to be committed to this claim is Donald Davidson. The argument that he gave for monism is the focus in the present section. So far as the alleged commitment is concerned, I shall take Davidson's part: he told us why we should think that reason explanation is causal-explanation, and he has never gone back on that.[12] Another thing I shall take over from him is the thesis of the mental's irreducibility. Nevertheless Davidson's argument runs contrary to my suggestion that actions are not accessible from the impersonal point of view. And it is by questioning it, and attempting to diagnose a widely felt dissatisfaction with it, that I hope to make my suggestion plausible.

Davidson's famous argument uses three premisses: (1) of causal depend-ence, (2) of causation's nomological character, and (3) of the mental's anomalousness (see e.g. Davidson 1980: 208[13]). Someone who wanted to demonstrate that actions (among other mental events) are present to the impersonal point of view might use only the first two premisses. Premiss (2) says that 'events related as cause and effect fall under strict determin-istic laws'; premiss (1) acknowledges (among much else[14]) that actions are related causally to other things. When the operation of strict deterministic

---

[12] Many have alleged the commitment in one or another version. P. Smith (1984), 'Anoma-lous Monism and Epiphenomenalism: A Reply to Honderich', *Analysis* 44: 83–6, is responsible for the particular formulation of the claim quoted above, at the end of Section 3. Some write as if Davidson had deliberately and explicitly committed himself to it (e.g. K. Lennon (1990), *Explaining Human Action* (London: Duckworth)); others as if it required argument to demon-strate his commitment (e.g. T. Honderich (1982), 'The Argument for Anomalous Monism', *Analysis* 42: 59–64). Some, like Smith, think that the alleged commitment does no damage; but most hold it against Davidson, and say that it shows that in his view the mental is epiphenomenal (e.g. H. Robinson (1982), *Matter and Sense* (Cambridge: Cambridge University Press)). But whatever the status or consequence of his commitment is supposed to be, an enormous volume of writing suggests that Davidson must in consistency allow that reason explanation is not causal-explanation.

[13] Donald Davidson (1980), *Essays on Actions and Events* (Oxford: Clarendon Press).

[14] It is often assumed that whereas the states and events that precede actions must be treated by an argument for monism, actions themselves can be left out. But I think that it is only a prejudice about the nature of mind that leads to the idea that *being in mental states* is problem-atic whereas *doing things intentionally* is not.

laws is thought of as something impersonally described, then the premisses combine to secure a place for actions in an impersonal account. In this argument the presence of actions to an impersonal point of view purports to be demonstrated in the same way as the physical nature of actions purported to be demonstrated by Davidson—through their location in a law-governed world.

Davidson's own argument was different. His route to monism had to be less direct: the nomological character of causality would be of no help to him in showing that mental events are physical if it were possible to see them as law-governed even while they were conceived of as belonging to mental kinds; premiss (3), of the anomalousness of the mental, is ineliminable. This premiss relies on a 'categorial difference between the mental and the physical' which ensures that mental kinds cannot themselves be nomological kinds. In Davidson, then, the application of nomological (and thus physical) vocabulary to mental particulars is shown indirectly—through the involvement of the mental with causality (premiss 1) and the involvement of causality with nomologicality (premiss 2). But the argument is like the more direct one: in finding mental items to have properties of each of two sorts, where possession of one sort (mental, personal) is the ground of an argument for possession of the other sort (physical, impersonal). In Davidson, there are the properties that mental items have in virtue of which we can treat their possessors as rational, and there are those they have in virtue of which they can be seen as situated in the nomological causal network, and which ensure they are physical.

Davidson believes that properties of both sorts—rational and nomological—can be used in explanations. And this belief is one source of the widespread supposition that Davidson ought really to deny that rational explanation is causal-explanation. There is thought to be a difficulty about a single thing's possessing two causal-explanatory properties. If there were a genuine difficulty, then a nomological story about an action's occurrence would rule out the possibility of a rational explanatory story that was also causal, so that Davidson would have to reject the causal-explanation thesis. Many have said that Davidson is in truth an epiphenomenalist: that for him, mental events are, *qua* mental, inert, since it is in virtue of their physical, nomological properties that they are causally efficacious (see n. 12). But when the matter is put like this, a reply on Davidson's behalf is easily found. He can simply deny that an item can have only one causal-explanatory property. And he has explained why we should deny this: we are often in the position of taking ourselves both to know one explanation of an event's occurrence, and to be justified in believing that there is another explanatory story about it of whose details we are actually quite ignorant. Could it not be like this where actions are concerned?[15] Perhaps the fact that there is a causal-explanatory story that we cannot tell need not interfere with the idea that we can give a rational causal-explanation.

None the less the feeling that it does interfere is widespread. If we want to understand why nomological and rational explanation, as Davidson interprets them, should be thought to conflict, then we need to remember that his conception of rational explanation was supported by considerations that are quite unaffected when the argument for monism is given. This means that the problem that so many people think they see about his retaining the causal-explanatory thesis may really be a problem about accepting the conclusion that Davidson wants us to add to the thesis. The feeling that Davidson's theses conflict may be based in a sense of conflict between the picture one gets of the operation of mental events if one accepts Davidson's version of monism on the one hand, and a picture of how we understand people. And if that is so, then the supposed difficulty for Davidson corresponds to a more general difficulty: that in attempting to view the mental impersonally, one finds that its causal efficacy is lost.

In Davidson's case, what we have to ask is why it should be accepted that there is a nomological, causal story even about the events that are actions. The Nomological Character of Causality, as it is used in Davidson's argument, says that a law lurks in any case where it is possible to rely on causal notions to make something intelligible. Can we support this even while we assume that finding people causally intelligible is a 'categorially different' matter from understanding physical causal goings on? What are the grounds for believing that rational explanations themselves mention items that can be picked out in nomological vocabulary? Well, Davidson thinks that we regularly have evidence of laws covering particular cases, and that this gives us evidence that some full-fledged causal law exists covering each and every explanation. He has said that the evidence for the operation of laws is summarized in such generalizations as 'Windows are fragile, and fragile things tend to break when struck hard enough, other conditions being right'. And he likened behavioural generalizations to generalizations like this one (see Davidson, Ch. 1 this volume, 39). So his idea must be that our ability to frame rough-and-ready generalizations about pieces of behaviour is to be taken as a symptom that they too are governed by law. But the trouble now is that the thesis of the mental's anomalousness will

---

[15] See e.g. Davidson 1980, op. cit. 219, where he speaks of generalizations which support explanations, but which are heteronomic, i.e. not stated in a form and vocabulary that points to a finished law. For more on this, see the Appendix to this chapter. See also id. (1967), 'Causal Relations', *Journal of Philosophy* 64: 691–703 (repr. in Davidson 1980, op. cit.).

seem to obstruct any full assimilation of 'behavioural generalizations' to generalizations about the breakings of windows.

The distinctive thing about rational explanations—which points to the mental's anomalousness—is that our acceptance of them relies on the 'discovery of a coherent and plausible pattern in the attitudes and actions' of a person: they are 'governed by an ideal'. In that case the special character of the mental sets answers to *Why?* questions about what people have done apart from answers to questions about why (e.g.) windows break. Davidson once said that 'our justification for accepting a singular causal statement is that we have reason to believe an appropriate causal law exists though we do not know what it is' (Davidson (1980), op. cit., 160). Well, perhaps we do take ourselves to witness the operation of physical law when we see the window break, and perhaps that is our justification for thinking that the ball's hitting it caused the window's breaking. But our justification for accepting an account of why someone did something would seem to have nothing to do with any reason we might have for believing in the world's nomological workings—not if discovery of a rational pattern is what we actually rely on, and if our aim is conformity with a rational ideal.

Even if a fully general link between 'singular causal statements' and laws could be established, it is unclear that that would help very much in an argumentative strategy for bringing mental particulars inside the scope of laws. For when an action explanation is given, it may be that there is no item said to stand to an action in the relation of 'cause' (see Section 3). If that is so, then the possibility of a single state or event's possessing two causal-explanatory properties is not something that Davidson can exploit in the present connection; if we are trying to accommodate the causal efficacy of the mental, we cannot now think of ourselves as seeking another causal-explanatory property possessed by some item already possessed of a nomological one. This point also may be seen as connected with the special explanatory character of the mental, in virtue of which it is irreducible and, in Davidson's sense, anomalous. An action explanation is not a reply to a question about why some event occurred, and, in revealing what an agent thought and what she wanted, it does not introduce any singular term for 'the cause'. Rather it shows a person's doing something to make sense by seeing her as (at least approximately) rational—as conforming (more or less) to norms of consistency and coherence in her thought and practice. Since its focus is how things were with *her*, it is no wonder that no 'purely causal' statement can be extracted from the explanation. The objective is to see a causally complex whole—a person—in a certain, intelligible light; and this fits ill with the idea of locating an item on which an event that happens to be an action may be seen to follow in the way things do, nomologically speaking.[16]

Of course Davidson himself would be the first to acknowledge that accounts of action are outside the direct reach of physical law. The present question is why physical law should be thought to reach them at all, however indirectly. In order to use the notion of a law to forge a connection between the causal-explanatory nature of a concept and the physical nature of the things it applies to, Davidson relies on a transition from the causal-explanatory to the 'purely causal'. But the connection is one that the irreducibility of the mental stands in the way of, and our inability to make the transition may be seen as a symptom of that.

My argument here can be sketchily stated by setting out the steps that Davidson needs to take:

mental → causal-explanatory → 'purely causal' → nomological → physical

Someone might start from a conception of the nomological, and look backwards, insisting that some property that the *nomological* encompasses applies to anything that has some causal-explanatory property. But then she would precisely have disregarded the special causal-explanatory character of the *mental* whose concepts have application to people; and it would be unsurprising if she seemed to reach the position that the mental is epiphenomenal. Someone else might start with a conception of the mental and try to move forwards. But the conception of the causal-explanatory she reaches at the first step provides her with no way of moving to the 'purely causal' that would take her on.

The quicker argument we considered earlier is equally affected if it aspires to bring mental states within the compass of an impersonal view. In order to see the two arguments as alike, we thought of the impersonal point of view as that from which the search for nomological explanation is appropriate. The nature of causation itself was then supposed to take us straight from a personal to an impersonal point of view.

---

[16] Consider E. LePore and B. Loewer's (1987) attempted reconciliation of (*a*) mental items' subsumability under laws, and (*b*) mental properties' being both anomalous and causally efficacious ('Mind Matters', *Journal of Philosophy* 84: 630–42). For these authors, the causal relevance of mental states consists in the truth of counterfactuals each to the effect of an item's being such that if it had lacked some property, then some event would have lacked some property. We find, then, that the claims that serve to underpin rational explanations make no essential mention of a person.

Thinking of the objective of propositional attitude explanation as I suggest, we must take it for granted that content is both explanatory and externally fixed (where content is that which is specified when it is said what people think or want or hope or . . .). I can only gesture here towards the idea that my remarks have wider application: that they are a response to what is widely perceived to be a problem about content.

personal → causal → impersonal

Again there is no way to take the necessary steps. For what constitutes the irreducibility of the mental/personal is the operation of a particular standard of causal intelligibility. But if the causal features of concepts used in action explanation are just their causal-explanatory features, then they are precisely what are missing from the impersonal point of view where a different standard of causal intelligibility is in place.

We now lack any argument for subsuming actions in the impersonal world of causes. When we start from a rational explanation, no conception of the nomological can be brought into sight. It seems that the particular character of action explanation prevents actions from being present to the impersonal point of view.

5. ACTIONS IMPERSONALLY CONCEIVED?

Before relating this conclusion to the problems about agency we began with, I want to draw attention to what I see as a sign of its correctness, and also to some habits of thought that may obscure its correctness.

Seeing something as an action requires the identification of a person and the exercise of concepts that we put to work in understanding people. This on its own does not show that an event that is an action might not also be picked out by someone operating without such concepts as *belief*, *desire*, and *intention*. But I suggest now that someone not operating with these concepts would not in fact be able to identify an action.

Consider a particular case. Bring on to the scene not only Peter's action, and the series of events which he initiated and which the action caused, but also such events as one is likely to think of as causal antecedents of an action—neuronal firings, signals going out to the nerves, muscles contracting. In the picture is a whole collection of events leading from some happening in the depth of Peter's brain all the way to an event beyond his body in which his desire's being satisfied consists. The question to ask is: 'How much of all that we have brought on to the scene does the action consist of?' About some things, we feel certain: events in the brain quite remote from the motor system are no part of the action; events in the world quite remote from Peter's body are no part of the action. But certainty about these things gives us no exact answer where to draw the lines. Looking at the picture, we have no opinion in some cases whether this or that is a part of the action.

Of course we do know exactly what the action is: it is Peter's switching on the kettle (or whatever). But having a determinate answer from the perspective from which Peter is apparent does not give us anything deter-minate to say in the terms of the picture. Nor, it seems, do we lose anything by resisting the thought that there ought to be some exact answer from this point of view, or that the answer we give from our and Peter's point of view is somehow inadequate. If we are content to accept that no answer to our question can be forced upon us, that may be because there is no answer: as the picture is drawn, we start to adopt an impersonal point of view, from which it is impossible to locate actions.

A reductionist might say that scientists would be capable of returning the answer, and that it is no surprise to find that we cannot do so without further investigation.[17] But, though it is true that a reductionist is likely to have confidence that there is a definite brain-event at the beginning of the action, when it comes to a question about the end—about the action's finishing-point, as it were—even her confidence will evaporate. For the question in this case concerns the line between an action and its effect, which has always seemed to everyone to be a philosophical question—not a question for further empirical investigation, but one about how common sense and talk operate. Yet it still does not seem that there is a definite answer to it which we have immediate intuitions about.

Thoughts about actions are much less the product of intuitions than philosophers have come by habit to suppose. Of course the thought that there are actions is, in one sense, something that no one would dream of denying. But it is not in this sense that I argued, and tried to make it seem obvious, that there are actions. What a non-philosopher means when she accepts that there are actions is that the phenomenon of action is exempli-fied: people do things (for reasons). But she does not mean (even if it can be made obvious) that there are events each one of which is a person's doing something. The word 'action' is ambiguous. Where it has a plural: in ordinary usage what it denotes, nearly always, are the things people do; in philosophical usage, what it denotes, very often, are events, each one of them some person's doing something. We may find ourselves with views which we can readily express in the language of action, and then, finding it obvious that there are actions, we (philosophers) assume that we have views which we can readily express in the language of events. Explanation of action is a case in point. We may move from knowing that we have an instance of 'action explanation' straight to thinking that we have an explanation of an action (event).[18]

---

[17] In J. Hornsby (1981), 'Which Physical Events are Mental Events?' *Aristotelian Society Proceedings* 81, sect. 3.2, I attempted to show that the reductionist would have trouble making a plausible case anyway.

[18] Where we talk e.g. about 'human action' (general, no plural), this is another use again from the two I have separated. (Presumably we find this general use in 'action explanation'. So where

Our picture may provide another case. If our opinions about *action* do not immediately yield anything definite to say about actions (events), then we should not have expected it to seem evident where the line comes between the action and its effects. Earlier I mentioned the view that movements of people's bodies must be more intimately connected to actions than is suggested when they are thought of as effects, and Lewis's claim that a movement of someone's body is both an effect and a part of her action (Section 2). It is supposed to be quite plain to common sense that a bodily movement is a part of an action.[19] But is this really something we are justified in feeling we are apt to be right about straight off? (Never mind for the moment whether we are right about it or not.) Certainly we know that no one moves her finger unless her finger moves; and we know that we can tell by observation what people do, and that we could not observe someone move her finger unless we saw her finger move. But we also know that these considerations alone could not suffice to show that her finger's moving is a part of her action—no more than similar considerations could suffice to show that Jones's death was a part of Smith's killing him. Again we know that typically when there is an action, an agent moves her body and thereby initiates a series of events, so that something she wants comes to happen. But this consideration does not circumscribe an action, beyond showing it to be where the agent is. It is not at all clear what would definitively settle the question as to which things are parts of actions. This will not seem worrying if we are aware that there need be no more plain truths about the events that are actions than there are plain truths about action (about agency, and things people do).

The events that are actions are understandably a focus of philosophical debate; but they are not ordinary objects of scrutiny. It is important to appreciate this, because the supposition on the part of philosophers that all our naïve opinions in the area of action readily come to us stated in the language of events is one source of the presumption that actions are impersonally apparent.

something is an instance of action explanation, it is actually wrong to think of it as an explanation of an action in either of the two senses of 'an action' that I have distinguished.) F. Dretske (1988), *Explaining Behavior: Reasons in a World of Causes* (Cambridge, Mass.: MIT Press) holds that actions are not events, but are complex causal processes. His argument is that a bit of behaviour is a complex causal process, and he assumes that philosophers had always meant a bit of behaviour by 'action'. Dretske is relying on the assumption that I am questioning: the assumption that the things we naturally say can readily be expressed as claims about actions.

[19] Presumably, though, it would be allowed that it takes some argument, or at least explication, to get someone to agree that bodily movements are effects of actions—as both Lewis and I think.

6. AGENCY UNDERMINED?

Thomas Nagel takes it to be evident that actions can be impersonally apparent. I turn now to the first of the two problems about agency—the one that he introduces. In his *View From Nowhere*, he assumes that we know that there is a possible picture from an 'external perspective' which includes actions in it; the 'external perspective' is supposed to provide 'an objective view of a particular person with his viewpoint [which is an internal one] included' (1986), op. cit., 3. (I hope that it will be enough for the time being to say that the external perspective of Nagel's assumption is thus an impersonal one. I leave it to the next section to relate Nagel's external/internal or objective/subjective distinction more exactly to the impersonal/personal one.)

Nagel thinks that the threat to autonomy—to the idea that 'we are authors of our actions' (1986), op. cit., 114—arises when we find that our conception of ourselves as agents is ambitious: 'our capacity to view ourselves from outside ... gives us the sense that we ought to become the absolute source of what we do' (1986), op. cit., 118. This sense 'is not just a feeling but a belief', he says, although he suspects that it may be 'no intelligible belief at all' (1986), op. cit., 114. But Nagel does not think that our inability to make the belief fully intelligible diminishes the threat to agency: we can have aspirations without knowing how they might be met.

There is no doubt that it can be disturbing to try to think about ourselves in the manner that Nagel suggests. And it may seem evasive, even unphilosophical, to insist that we turn from our thoughts to their verbal expression. Nevertheless I suggest that we have to look carefully at Nagel's words, and to ask in the first instance what he means by 'action'.

If 'actions' stands for the things we do, then, evidently enough, we do them; but they are not particulars, and we are not their authors or sources. If 'actions' stands for a class of events, on the other hand, there seems to be no better way to say how an agent relates to her action than to say that it is hers. The relation between agent and action is signalled by the genitive in phrases for actions—'*her* speaking'; '*a*'s opening the door'. We find here a sort of ownership; but it does not seem to be authorship. Perhaps the thought that we are authors, or sources, of our actions need not be taken literally at all.

I think we know what Nagel means, however. An agent is the source, or the author, of the events that she causes. Earlier I called actions the initiatings of series of events—as a way of trying to place them on the causal scene. Our sense of ourselves as authors is then the sense that we are responsible for the events in those series that we initiate; to hold ourselves responsible for an event is to take responsibility for initiating the series it belongs to. But our responsibility consists in the action's being ours, and not in its having been caused, or done, by us. Nagel makes it sound as if we might locate an agent and find her action set apart from her. But though we may separate the events she causes from the agent, we cannot separate her from the event that starts the series—which is her causing them.

When Nagel says that 'everything I do or that anyone else does is part of a larger course of events that no one "does", but that happens' (1986), op. cit., 114, he entices us into thinking that we have located actions from an external viewpoint. But what a person does is not an event, and it is therefore not a 'component of the flux of events in the world'. Nagel's ways of putting things suggest that we always have aspirations, which, in fact, we only come to seem to have when the event language is used as if it expressed things that cannot be said. Perhaps Nagel is only too right when he holds that the 'difficulty' is that 'it is impossible to give a coherent account of the internal view of action which is under threat', and that we 'cannot say what would . . . support our sense that our free actions originate with us' (1986), op. cit., 112–13, 117. Perhaps we have said everything that we need to say when we have understood what it is to be responsible for our actions' effects.

But Nagel thinks that our conception of ourselves as agents is revealed more fully when we consider the explanation of action. 'The final explanation . . . is given by the intentional explanation of my action, which is comprehensible only through my point of view. My reason for doing it is the *whole* reason why it happened, and no further explanation is necessary or possible'. And now, thinks Nagel, the trouble is that this sort of explanation, on which our sense of agency is based, is shown to be unsustainable when we take account of the possibility of an objective view; for that view 'admits only one kind of explanation of why something happened . . . ,[20] and equates its absence with the absence of any explanation at all'. Intentional explanations are shown up as inadequate, Nagel says, when we see that they 'cannot explain *why I did what I did rather than the alternative that was causally open to me*' (1986), op. cit., 116.

Intentional explanation may in fact be more powerful than Nagel allows here. At least it seems to be more powerful if we take it to be the kind of explanation in which concepts such as *belief* and *desire* are used to make sense of people and what they do and don't do—rather than as consisting in a series of once-off occasions on which 'the' reason for something

---

[20] I have extracted 'causal' at the ellipsis (1986), op. cit., 115: Nagel assumes that one who admits that action explanation is not of the 'objective' kind denies that it is causal; the assumption is not compulsory.

actually done is given. I might tell you why she refused the job, but leave you realizing that there is more you could learn to help you to see why accepting it was something she didn't do. It is true that there could come a point at which there is no more for anyone to say about why she did one thing rather than another, and I have to resort to 'Those were the reasons she saw in favour and against, and the reasons in favour weighed more heavily with her'. But it is not as if you would then suppose that you would understand better if only you could see that the event which is her action 'or a range of possibilities within which it falls, was necessitated by prior conditions and events' (1986), op. cit., 115. It seems that up to a point we can meet the demands that Nagel puts on action explanation, and that beyond that point, they are of a sort that it is simply not susceptible to.[21]

The pressure of these demands is supposed to be felt when the internal and external perspectives come together. In Nagel they are brought together through an equation of his reason for doing something with the explanation why 'it' happened. ('My reason for doing it is the whole reason why it happened.') But really Nagel's reason for doing something is not an explanation of any happening. (His reason does not explain anything, although the fact that he had it may explain why he did something.) Nor is the explanation why Nagel did something itself a reason for anything. (The explanation gives his reason.) It seems that a threat to our sense of agency has been created by an illusion that we are trying to explain an event's occurrence when in fact we are trying to make sense of a person and what she did.

I may seem to be suggesting that the barrier between the external and internal explanatory schemes is a merely terminological one. The obstacles to thinking what Nagel wants us to think are created by differences of category—between actions and things done, between reasons and explanations. But I think that these obstacles mark the presence of a genuine barrier. Accounts in terms of what a person thinks and wants are fitted to provide explanations for those who share with that person a point of view on the world. When the ideal of rationality can be brought to bear on

---

[21] Nagel appreciates this: 'the sense of an internal explanation persists—an explanation insulated from the external view which is complete in itself and renders illegitimate all further requests for explanation of my action as an event in the world' (1986), op. cit., 116. But instead of taking this to show the irrelevance of the external perspective, he takes it to be another sign of the conflict. Nagel entertains the idea that someone who insists that the external perspective be brought to bear in the domain of reasons may be using a very limited conception of what an explanation is (1986), op. cit., 117. But he says that anyone who considers herself entitled to a broader conception is under an obligation to show why the language of belief and desire doesn't introduce 'descriptions [merely] of how it seemed to the agent'. I suspect that Nagel thinks this obligation arises because he takes the internal view to be ultimately a first-personal one. See Section 7.

explaining something she has done, that can be seen as something delivered from the contents of her thoughts and wants. Those who seek and give 'action explanations' do not regard the matter impersonally or externally, any more than the agent herself does when she deliberates about what to do.

7. AGENCY REFUTED?

Nagel's problem is engendered in the first instance from within the personal view—when it seems to need to rise above itself and take on the ambitions of an impersonal view. The second problem about agency is engendered from outside—when the impersonal view seems to swamp the personal one.

The ambitions of the impersonal view are not usually seen as a problem for agency. But there must be acknowledged to be potential problems here. For there are philosophers who think that any real phenomenon, however we may actually understand it, is intelligible from an impersonal point of view. And if it could be demonstrated both that the whole truth can be told from there, and that it leaves out of account everything that is personal, then the effects would be quite devastating: at stake is the idea that anyone ever really means to do anything, or wants anything, or believes anything. These truly devastating effects are seldom contemplated, because they cannot seriously be entertained, and because those who hold the threatening metaphysical doctrine for the most part believe that it actually holds no threats—that actions and their explanation can in fact be accommodated in an impersonal view. But something slightly less devastating is more frequently contemplated, as we have seen in reactions to Davidson. His anomalous monism is thought to deprive the mental of causal efficacy: the intrusion of the impersonal view is supposed to render people's being in states of mind causally quite idle, yet somehow to leave people intelligible.

The problematic effects on our conception of ourselves would be the same whether agency was undermined, from the inside, or refuted, from without. And the idea that I am suggesting stops those effects, and ensures that there is no real threat, is the same. But different considerations show how the threat is prevented from arising in the two cases. In discussing Nagel, the strategy was to deny to the personal view the pretensions he accords to it: I tried to show its explanatory scheme as insulated from that of the impersonal view. When agency seems to face refutation, though, the ambitions of an impersonal view are called directly into question. I finish with some further explanation and defence of the idea that we may resist them.

To be satisfied with saying that actions are apparent only from what I have called the personal view, we need in the first place to be clear that this is not a view confined to a particular self. We cannot explain what someone has done, unless we know whether she has been successful in achieving what she wanted. So the point of view from which she is understood must not only be one from which she can be seen to be in states of mind representing things beyond her, but also one from which those same states of mind can be evaluated, as correct or incorrect representations. The personal point of view, then, may differ from the most 'internal' view of Nagel, of 'a particular person inside the world'.

In Nagel, it is a matter of degree to which a point of view is objective or external: 'to acquire a more objective understanding of some aspect of life or the world, we step back from our initial view of it and form a new conception which has that view and its relation to the world as object' (1986), op. cit., 5. Now the notion of an impersonal point of view as I have used it is related to Nagel's internal/external (or subjective/objective) dimension: when we step back sufficiently that we have detached from everything contingent to our human subjectivity, we have reached a point of view that is external enough to be impersonal. Two of Nagel's ideas, then, need not be in dispute. First, we can allow that one point of view may incorporate another: a state of affairs might impinge upon a point of view, but it be possible to take up a more external one from which that state of affairs and that point of view were both represented. (Perhaps this is what happens when, from my point of view, I understand another person's.) Second, we can allow that there is such a thing as an impersonal view: we have a conception of an objective world whose nature is independent of whatever conscious beings occupy it, and our own capacity to stand back entitles us to this. But to allow these things—that one view may subsume another, and that some things can be viewed quite impersonally—is not to grant that we can always step away from any phenomenon and retain a view of it.[22]

Some people are persuaded that we can step back from actions when they are told that we have 'a view of persons and their actions as part of the

---

[22] For ways to make these ideas precise, see A. Moore (1987), 'Points of View', *Philosophical Quarterly* 37: 1–20. The target at the end of Moore's paper is the 'absolute conception' of reality. Belief that such a conception ought to be attainable is surely one source of the view that actions are impersonally apparent; compare J. McDowell (1985), 'Functionalism and Anomalous Monism', in E. LePore and B. McLaughlin (eds.), *Actions and Events: Perspectives on the Philosophy of Donald Davidson* (Oxford: Basil Blackwell), 395. But aspirations more limited than aspirations to this putative conception are all that are required to generate the pressure that I am trying to counteract, or so at least my argument assumes.

order of nature'. The idea that actions are 'components of the flux of events of the world of which the agent is a part' combines with the idea that the flux of events in nature constitutes how things objectively are to make it seem that an impersonal view of actions is not only possible, but appropriate. But we need to consider carefully this thought that persons and their actions are part of nature. It seems right when we point out that nothing supernatural needed to happen for human beings to evolve, and that it is a natural fact about people that, for instance, they have the abilities they do, and thus a natural fact that there are actions. Such considerations ensure that a naturalistic view of ourselves is in order, and indeed that the personal point of view is itself a naturalistic one. But they do not help to place our actions in a world 'of nature' if a world 'of nature' is to be thought of as constituted independently of the conscious beings that occupy it. It is (as Kantians might say) an empirical question whether an event is such that it would exist whether or not we were present in the world. If the event is an action, the answer is 'No'. So where the world 'of nature' is not the naturalistic world in which we find ourselves, but the world as it might be anyway—whether there were any people, or whatever any person's states of mind might be—actions are no part of it. This is not a particularly shocking conclusion: our conception of the world independent of us is not a conception of the world including us.

The conclusion evidently fits with the Davidsonian thesis of the disparateness of two conceptual frameworks—that by which we render ourselves intelligible to one another, and that by which we understand what goes on as the operation of physical law. But the conclusion is equally evidently at odds with Davidson's monism. For it would be a very strange idea that, from the impersonal point of view, we employ conceptual resources which describe the world 'of nature' and which are not such as to identify actions, which, however, for all that, can be used to identify actions. We saw in Section 4 that we were left without any reason to believe in the identities that Davidson asserts. Without such reason, we have no inclination to use the quicker argument that we considered there for bringing the mental inside the scope of law. Arguments like that one simply assume that whatever principles govern our account of a world 'of nature' have universal application, in any area where we can use causal notions to make sense of something. And the suspicion arises that Davidson himself, in invoking the Nomological Character of Causality, has simply imported his own universalizing assumption about 'nature'.[23]

[23] There is evidence that some universalizing assumption may serve for Davidson to ground his nomological principle in the ease with which he moves from 'nomological' to 'physical': compare M. Johnston, 'Why Having a Mind Matters', in LePore and McLaughlin (eds.) (1985), op. cit., 411.

So we have to say that there are events that are not in the world 'of nature'. Perhaps this ontological doctrine is the stumbling-block. In addition to the feeling that it is a naturalistic world that we inhabit, there is the belief that the world 'of nature' is complete; and would it not be incomplete if it did not contain us and all the events we participate in? Someone who objects at this point may think that the cost of saying that we and our actions are not in the world 'of nature' is to render that a gappy world—with pieces missing where people and their actions should be. But she would be mistaken if she supposed that because people and their actions are absent from the impersonal point of view, the portions of space and time occupied by persons are missing too. We have to distinguish between an aspect of reality and a portion of reality. The claim about the completeness of what is accessible from the impersonal point of view is ruled out if it is the claim that every aspect of reality is present to it. But if it is a claim to survey the whole of space and time and deal with every portion of what it surveys, then nothing stands in its way. A correct account of an impersonal conception brings 'the whole world of nature' within its scope. Some portions of space-time are occupied by the bits of matter that people are composed from, and the account will deal with them, with flesh and blood, and nervous systems.[24]

There must, of course, be things to be said about how it can be that people are the sorts of being that we are, given that they are composed only from what can be scrutinized impersonally. It is in virtue not only of our occupying the position that we do in the world on which we act, but also of our being constructed as we are that we can have the cognitive and practical capacities that we do, and can, for instance, initiate series of events containing some of kinds we want. So there are questions about how nervous systems can subserve the phenomena of mentality and agency.[25] But these questions are not made easier by the assumption that, to everything we speak of from the personal point of view, there attaches a piece of vocabulary apt for describing things impersonally. This assumption after all is the source of the thought that actions are swallowed up from an external perspective, and of the thought that the mental is epiphenomenal. And it is not as if the assumption on its own could do anything to integrate the personal with an impersonal point of view. Davidson himself

---

[24] For the relation between the conclusion here and (a) present-day versions of physicalism, and (b) Descartes' dualism, see J. Hornsby (1985), 'Physicalism, Events, and Part-Whole Relations', in LePore and McLaughlin, 444–58, and id. (1990), 'Descartes, Rorty, and the Mind-Body Fiction', in A. Malachowski (ed.), *Reading Rorty* (Oxford: Basil Blackwell), respectively.

[25] See A. Clark (1989), *Microcognition* (Cambridge, Mass.: MIT Press) for the idea that cognitive psychology may proceed without any of the standard assumptions about connections between folk psychology and brain science.

has made this clear: in the sphere of reason-explanations, causality is 'connected with the normative demands of rationality'.[26]

There is then no new problem about integration when the assumption is abandoned, and actions are thought neither to be swallowed up nor deprived of genuinely causal explanations, but absent simply, from the impersonal point of view. When we see an action as a person's initiating a series of events, we recognize a type of event whose causal ancestry is understood from a personal, rational point of view, and whose causal successors come to be understood from an impersonal, perhaps scientific one. And we appreciate that causality is a concept that we may operate with from both points of view: people make a difference, and do so because their actions are events which make a difference.

APPENDIX

In emphasizing my real agreement with Davidson (on the causal-explanatoriness *and* irreducibility of the mental), I have ridden over some areas of disagreement. In this Appendix, I attempt to clarify these, taking in turn, (*A*) 'purely causal' statements, (*B*) the Nomological Character of Causality, (*C*) the relation between (*A*) and (*B*).

(*A*) It is assumed nowadays that we find claims such as 'Reasons are causes' or 'Beliefs and desires causally interact with one another to produce actions' to be at least as obvious as the causal-explanation thesis. Davidson's influential simultaneous defence of both the claims and the thesis (see Chapter 1 of this volume) has probably contributed as much as anything else to the prevalence of this assumption. And in Section 3 I may have let it seem to be more surprising than it really is that separate explanatory and causal elements have been supposed to be extricable from Davidson's causal-explanation thesis. I hoped to make it clear (*a*) that the claims are in fact more dubious than the thesis, and (*b*) that if we attend to Davidson's arguments, we shall give the thesis priority. The consequence is that I have ignored Davidson's own support for claims to the effect that 'purely causal' statements about actions are available.

It is worth noting that, although 'The primary reason is the cause' is one of Davidson's own formulations, it is not obvious that he endorses actual statements that would count as instances of it. All the same, Davidson certainly does believe that we are entitled to more in the way of causal

---

statements than the everyday 'because' ones. Whereas for some philosophers the purpose of making out our entitlement is served by talk of token states (and I addressed them in Section 3), for Davidson, it is served by arguing for the pervasiveness of events. Two of the things he said to this end seem to me inadequate. (1) He said that we may associate with a person's being in any mental state an event that is her coming to be in that state. But so long as we realize that an event that is the onslaught of someone's being in a state must plausibly be (identified with) a precisely datable event, there will not appear to be many of them. (2) He said that where we cannot find any candidate for the immediate cause of an action using psychological language, we are still 'sure that there was an event or sequence of events' (Ch. 1, this volume, 36). But we might accept this because we know that there is an impersonal story to be told whenever a bit of someone's body moves; in that case our acceptance again lends no support to a causal statement of the kind to which entitlement was sought—such that statements of that kind go hand in hand with truths stated when action explanations are given.

(B) In Section 4, I questioned whether our belief in laws can ground our belief in psychological causal-explanatory statements. Davidson never asserts that it can. What he does assert is that our ability to generalize—including our ability to generalize psychologically—grounds our belief in the operation of laws. (General statements linking mental and physical are said to be heteronomic (Davidson (1980), op. cit., 222), and the instantiations of heteronomic statements are said to 'give us reason to believe that there is a precise law at work' (1980), op. cit., 219.) Of course I should question this also: if explanations using 'believe' and 'desire' are credible even when they are not seen as nomologically grounded, why should these generalizations be thought to provide evidence for the operation of laws?

Evidently raising these questions does not prove the falsity of the Nomological Character of Causality. But it may make us wonder whether we could have a case for it where Davidson needs one most. I let the argument with Davidson rest here, because I think that we shall resist the motivation for the Nomological Character of Causality when we see the sort of principle that it is, in the context e.g. of the quicker argument which I contrasted with Davidson's in Section 4.

(C) In the schema in which the quicker argument was summed up (at the end of Section 4), personal, and impersonal, and causal might be taken as properties of facts (if one is prepared to talk in that way). Thus in thinking about that argument, one need not assume an account of causation with the specific ontological presuppositions of an account that is grounded in 'purely causal' statements. Though it is formulated in terms that make it comparable with Davidson's own, then, the quicker argument is an instance of a more general style of argument: namely, an argument from a conception 'of nature', which I address in Section 7. It rests on a universalizing assumption, that there are principles governing any area where we can use causal notions to make sense of something (see n. 23).

In the schema in which Davidson's own argument was summed up, nomological, causal-explanatory, and mental can be understood as second-order properties. Such an understanding may reveal the indispensability of the items (states or events) to Davidson's way of thinking: these are the particulars having the properties that have the (second-order) properties. Certainly 'purely causal' statements are needed for a monistic argument like Davidson's. For unless rational-explanatory statements are seen to be concerned with the same things as laws are concerned with—with states or events or whatever—the Nomological Principle cannot do its work. (Nor can we find heteronomic generalizations of such a form as could provide us with reason for belief in laws.)

The two schematic arguments show us then that a universalizing assumption may be held in the absence of belief in 'purely causal' statements, although a conception of the 'purely causal' is needed for Davidson's own particular universal principle to be put to work. We should also notice that belief in the ubiquity of 'purely causal' statements does not introduce any universalizing assumption all by itself: someone might think that wherever there is (as we say) an action explanation, there are statements having the form but not the import of the statements needed for an argument that actions are present from the impersonal point of view. This dialectical situation explains a certain tentativeness on my part about whether we should hold that discrete items interact in the production of action. My own opinion is that we should not hold this; but, for the purposes of the argument here, it may be enough to cast the tenet in doubt. A reader is then free to accept the principle of the Nomological Character of Causality provided that its domain is restricted so that we are outside it in the rational realm (and psychological heteronomic generalizations can then lend it no support). Alternatively she is free to carry on asserting the usual 'purely causal' statements about beliefs and desires and/or associated events, provided that she now denies that there is any principle of nomologicality having application wherever statements of a 'purely causal' kind can be asserted (and psychological heteronomic generalizations then require a different attitude from that which Davidson takes towards all heteronomic generalizations).

NOTES ON THE CONTRIBUTORS

Robert Audi is Professor of Philosophy at the University of Nebraska, Lincoln, and works in the philosophy of mind and action, epistemology, and ethical theory. His books include *Practical Reasoning* (1989) and *Action, Intention, and Reason* (1993).

Michael E. Bratman is Professor of Philosophy at Stanford University. He is the author of *Intention, Plans, and Practical Reason* (1987) and co-editor of *Introduction to Philosophy: Classical and Contemporary Readings* (1993).

Donald Davidson is Willis S. and Marion Slusser Professor of Philosophy at the University of California at Berkeley. He is the author of *Essays on Actions and Events* (1980), *Inquiries into Truth and Interpretation* (1984), and *The Structure and Content of Truth* (1990).

Wayne A. Davis is Professor of Philosophy and Department Chair at Georgetown University. He is the author of *An Introduction to Logic* (1986), *Meaning, Expression, and Thought* (forthcoming), and *Implicature* (forthcoming).

Harry G. Frankfurt is Professor of Philosophy at Princeton University. He is the author of *Demons, Dreamers and Madmen: The Defense of Reason in Descartes's Meditations* (1970) and *The Importance of What We Care About* (1988).

Carl Ginet is Professor of Philosophy at Cornell University. He is the author of *Knowledge, Perception, and Memory* (1975) and *On Action* (1990), and co-editor of *Knowledge and Mind* (1983).

Gilbert Harman is Professor of Philosophy and Head of the Program in Cognitive Studies at Princeton University. He and Judith Jarvis Thomson are the authors of *Moral Relativism and Moral Objectivity* (1995). He is also the author of *Change in View* (1986), *The Nature of Morality* (1977), and *Thought* (1973), and editor of *Conceptions of the Human Mind* (1993).

Jennifer Hornsby is Professor of Philosophy at Birkbeck College, University of London. She is the author of *Actions* (1980) and *Simple Mindedness* (1996), and co-editor of *Ethics: A Feminist Reader* (1993).

Jaegwon Kim is William Perry Faunce Professor of Philosophy at Brown University. He is the author of *Supervenience and Mind* (1993) and *Philosophy of Mind* (1996), and co-editor of *A Companion to Metaphysics* (1995).

Hugh J. McCann is Professor of Philosophy at Texas A&M University. He is the author of many papers on action theory, including 'Volition and Basic Action' (1974), 'Rationality and the Range of Intention' (1986), and 'Intrinsic Intentionality' (1986).

Alfred R. Mele is Vail Professor of Philosophy at Davidson College. He is the author of *Irrationality* (1987), *Springs of Action* (1992), and *Autonomous Agents* (1995), and co-editor of *Mental Causation* (1993).

Paul K. Moser is Professor of Philosophy at Loyola University of Chicago. He is the author of *Empirical Justification* (1985), *Knowledge and Evidence* (1989), and *Philosophy After Objectivity* (1993), and editor of *A Priori Knowledge* (1987; Oxford Reading Series), *Empirical Knowledge* (1996), and several other collections.

Brian O'Shaughnessy is Reader in Philosophy in the University of London, and teaches at King's College, London. He is the author of *The Will* (1980) and numerous articles.

FURTHER READING

1. Books

Anscombe, G. E. M. (1963), *Intention*, 2nd edn. (Ithaca, NY: Cornell University Press).

Audi, R. (1993), *Action, Intention, and Reason* (Ithaca, NY: Cornell University Press).

Aune, B. (1977), *Reason and Action* (Dordrecht, Neth.: Reidel).

Bishop, J. (1989), *Natural Agency* (Cambridge: Cambridge University Press).

Brand, M. (1984), *Intending and Acting* (Cambridge, Mass.: MIT Press).

Bratman, M. (1987), *Intention, Plans, and Practical Reason* (Cambridge, Mass.: Harvard University Press).

Castañeda, H.-N. (1975), *Thinking and Doing* (Dordrecht, Neth.: Reidel).

Danto, A. (1973), *Analytical Philosophy of Action* (Cambridge: Cambridge University Press).

Davidson, D. (1980), *Essays on Actions and Events* (Oxford: Clarendon Press).

Davis, L. (1979), *Theory of Action* (Englewood Cliffs, NJ: Prentice-Hall).

Donagan, A. (1987), *Choice* (London: Routledge).

Dretske, F. (1988), *Explaining Behavior* (Cambridge, Mass.: MIT Press).

Ginet, C. (1990), *On Action* (Cambridge: Cambridge University Press).

Goldman, A. (1970), *A Theory of Human Action* (Englewood Cliffs, NJ: Prentice-Hall).

Gustafson, D. (1986), *Intention and Agency* (Dordrecht, Neth.: Reidel).

Harman, G. (1986), *Change in View* (Cambridge, Mass.: MIT Press).

Hornsby, J. (1980), *Actions* (London: Routledge & Kegan Paul).

Kenny, A. (1963), *Action, Emotion and Will* (London: Routledge).

Mele, A. (1992), *Springs of Action* (New York: Oxford University Press).

O'Shaughnessy, B. (1980), *The Will* (Cambridge: Cambridge University Press).

Peacocke, C. (1979), *Holistic Explanation* (Oxford: Clarendon Press).

Pears, D. (1975), *Questions in the Philosophy of Mind* (New York: Barnes & Noble).

Schick, F. (1991), *Understanding Action* (Cambridge: Cambridge University Press).

Searle, J. (1983), *Intentionality* (Cambridge: Cambridge University Press).

Taylor, C. (1964), *The Explanation of Behaviour* (London: Routledge & Kegan Paul).

Taylor, R. (1966), *Action and Purpose* (Englewood Cliffs, NJ: Prentice-Hall).

Thalberg, I. (1977), *Perception, Emotion, and Action* (Oxford: Basil Blackwell).

Thomson, J. (1977), *Acts and Other Events* (Ithaca, NY: Cornell University Press).

Tuomela, R. (1977), *Human Action and its Explanation* (Dordrecht, Neth.: Reidel).

Velleman, J. D. (1989), *Practical Reflection* (Princeton: Princeton University Press).

von Wright, G. (1971), *Explanation and Understanding* (Ithaca, NY: Cornell University Press).

Wilson, G. (1989), *The Intentionality of Human Action* (Stanford: Stanford University Press).

Zimmerman, M. (1984), *An Essay on Human Action* (New York: Peter Lang).

2. Articles

Adams, F. (1986), 'Intention and Intentional Action: The Simple View', *Mind and Language* 1: 281–301.

Alston, W. (1977), 'Self-Intervention and the Structure of Motivation', in T. Mischel (ed.), *The Self: Psychological and Philosophical Issues* (Oxford: Basil Blackwell).

—— (1986), 'An Action-Plan Interpretation of Purposive Explanations of Actions', *Theory and Decision* 20: 275–99.

Armstrong, D. (1980), 'Acting and Trying', in D. Armstrong (ed.), *The Nature of Mind* (Ithaca, NY: Cornell University Press).

Audi, R. (1986), 'Intending, Intentional Action, and Desire', in J. Marks (ed.), *The Ways of Desire* (Chicago: Precedent).

Bach, K. (1984), 'Default Reasoning: Jumping to Conclusions and Knowing When to Think Twice', *Pacific Philosophical Quarterly* 65: 37–58.

Beardsley, M. (1978), 'Intending', in A. Goldman and J. Kim (eds.), *Values and Morals* (Dordrecht, Neth.: Reidel).

Brandt, R. and J. Kim (1963), 'Wants as Explanations of Actions', *Journal of Philosophy* 60: 425–35.

Bratman, M. (1992), 'Shared Cooperative Activity', *Philosophical Review* 101: 327–41.

Chisholm, R. (1964), 'The Descriptive Element in the Concept of Action', *Journal of Philosophy* 61: 613–25.

Costa, M. (1987), 'Causal Theories of Action', *Canadian Journal of Philosophy* 17: 831–54.

Farrell, D. (1989), 'Intention, Reason, and Action', *American Philosophical Quarterly* 26: 283–95.

Grice, H. (1971), 'Intention and Uncertainty', *Proceedings of the British Academy* 57: 263–79.

Harman, G. (1993), 'Desired Desires', in R. Frey and C. Morris (eds.), *Value, Welfare, and Morality* (Cambridge: Cambridge University Press).

Hart, H. (1968), 'Intention and Punishment', in H. Hart (ed.), *Punishment and Responsibility* (New York: Oxford University Press).

Kapitan, T. (1995), 'Intentions and Self-Referential Content', *Philosophical Papers* 24: 151–66.

Kavka, G. (1983), 'The Toxin Puzzle', *Analysis* 43: 33–6.

Locke, D. (1982), 'Beliefs, Desires and Reasons for Action', *American Philosophical Quarterly* 19: 241–9.

Malcolm, N. (1968), 'The Conceivability of Mechanism', *Philosophical Review* 77: 45–72.

McCann, H. (1974), 'Volition and Basic Action', *Philosophical Review* 83: 451–73.

—— (1975), 'Trying, Paralysis, and Volition', *Review of Metaphysics* 28: 423–42.

—— (1986a), 'Intrinsic Intentionality', *Theory and Decision* 20: 247–73.

—— (1986b), 'Rationality and the Range of Intention', *Midwest Studies in Philosophy* 10: 191–211.

McGinn, C. (1979), 'Action and Its Explanation', in N. Bolton (ed.), *Philosophical Problems in Psychology* (London: Methuen).

Mele, A. (1995), 'Motivation: Essentially Motivation-Constituting Attitudes', *Philosophical Review* 104: 387–423.

Pink, T. (1991), 'Purposive Intending', *Mind* 100: 343–59.

Ruben, D. (1995), 'Mental Overpopulation and the Problem of Action', *Journal of Philosophical Research* 20: 511–24.

Sellars, W. (1966), 'Thought and Action', in K. Lehrer (ed.), *Freedom and Determinism* (New York: Random House).

—— (1973), 'Action and Events', *Noûs* 7: 179–202.

—— (1976), 'Volitions Reaffirmed', in M. Brand and D. Walton (eds.), *Action Theory* (Dordrecht, Neth.: Reidel).

Smith, M. (1987), 'The Humean Theory of Motivation', *Mind* 96: 36–61.

Stoutland, F. (1985), 'Davidson on Intentional Behavior', in E. LePore and B. McLaughlin (eds.), *Actions and Events* (Oxford: Basil Blackwell).

Thalberg, I. (1984), 'Do Our Intentions Cause Our Intentional Actions?' *American Philosophical Quarterly* 21: 249–60.

—— (1985), 'Questions about Motivational Strength', in E. LePore and B. McLaughlin (eds.), *Actions and Events* (Oxford: Basil Blackwell).

Velleman, J. D. (1992), 'What Happens When Someone Acts?' *Mind* 101: 461–81.

INDEX OF NAMES